Politics and Commu in America
in America

Campaigns, Media, and Governing in the 21st Century

Robert E. Denton, Jr.
Virginia Polytechnic Institute and State University

Jim A. Kuypers
Virginia Polytechnic Institute and State University

WAVELAND
PRESS, INC.

Long Grove, Illinois

For information about this book, contact:
Waveland Press, Inc.
4180 IL Route 83, Suite 101
Long Grove, IL 60047-9580
(847) 634-0081
info@waveland.com
www.waveland.com

We dedicate this book to our families:
Rachel, Bobby, Chris, and Daisy,
who bring joy and make life worth living
and
Tammy, Rebel, and Bandit, whose love and support are constant

Contents

Preface

The foundation for this book is a volume originally published in 1985 by Robert E. Denton, Jr. and Gary Woodward, entitled *Political Communication in America*. It was among the first few books that systematically and comprehensively analyzed of the role and the function of communication in American politics. The third edition was published in 1999. Over the last twenty-five years, literally hundreds of books have been published in the area of political communication. Most of these volumes have a narrow focus, with a single topic. The area of political communication has grown as an academic focus, however, and many universities now offer a full curriculum and even degrees in this area of specialty.

Numerous colleagues reiterated the need for an undergraduate textbook that surveys the field of political communication and includes both reviews of key studies and literature as well as the more pragmatic practice and application of communication principles within the realm of politics. Though the area of political communication, as well as interest in it, has grown considerably since the last decades of the twentieth century, the basic assumptions about the nature of communication and the practice of politics have not changed dramatically. Humans are, as Aristotle says in *Politics*, "political beings" and "he who is without a polis, by reason of his own nature and not of some accident, is either a poor sort of being [a beast] or a being higher than man [a god]."[1] Since nature makes nothing in vain, a human is, according to Aristotle, "alone of the animals . . . furnished with the faculty of language."[2] Thus, it was recognized over 2,400 years ago that politics and communication go hand in hand because they are essential parts of human nature. The fields of both political science and communication claim the subject matter of other fields as part of their own content, and nearly every topic that is fit for comment by someone also contains the seeds for political and communication analysis. Of course, neither political science nor communication can claim an area of interest that is exclusively its own. For instance, the fields of sociology, mass media, journalism, and history contribute to our subdiscipline of political communication. As another example of how communication intersects with other fields and the political consequences of those intersections, consider advances in medical technology. They can be praised or blamed by how they are described, and such descriptions usually have a significant impact on the discussions of the proper role of the government in the control of new technologies. The communication analyst is always a guest (if not an intruder) on someone else's turf. Be that as it may, communication *is* fundamental to all other fields of inquiry. What we know about events is always revealed first through the communicator's art and skill.

This book concerns the roles and functions of communication in American politics. Although the frameworks for our analysis utilize conventional categories of political activity (e.g., campaigns, activity in Congress, the courts, the mass media, and the presidency) the essential points of our analysis hinge on what we consider to be pivotal communication processes. We posit that the essence of politics is *talk* or human interaction. Such interaction is formal and informal, verbal and nonverbal, public and private—but always persuasive in nature, causing us to interpret, to evaluate, and to act. Communication provides the basis of social cohesion, issue discussion, and legislative enactment. Although by no means a new perspective today, it is seldom the focus of study within the discipline of political science and is viewed as somewhat problematic within the growing social science and social psychology perspectives within the discipline of communication studies.

As perhaps befits a work on politics, this book is very inclusive of not only the work of other disciplines, but also different theoretical perspectives. Such perspectives range from the symbolic interactionist and dramatistic, to the descriptive studies within the social sciences, to the substantial body of survey research on political attitudes, as well as traditional historical, biographical, and rhetorical works that enrich our knowledge of the polity. Thus, we have utilized a variety of materials and sources from the disciplines of political science, communication, history, journalism, and sociology, as well as firsthand sources, including private memoranda, memoirs, speeches, and journalistic accounts. Although we reference classic historical works from a variety of areas, we also utilize sources from the wealth of recent publications and also employ contemporary examples.

Chapters 1 and 2 define political communication and examine the role of language and the formation of political attitudes. Chapters 3 and 4 provide a theoretical perspective on the role of communication in society, as well as identify unique functions and uses of political language, especially in developing beliefs, attitudes, and values. The vast majority of political communication is mediated. Chapters 5–7 explore the role of media and politics, the important media theories of agenda-setting and agenda-extension, and the ever increasing role and influence of the Internet in politics. The focus of the next four chapters is on political campaigns. In chapter 8 we examine campaign planning, management, and strategies; in chapters 9–11 we explore the uniqueness of presidential, congressional, and state/local campaigns. A core aspect of political campaigns is governing; political campaigns are created for selecting leaders to govern the country. Chapters 12–14 focus on governing—the functions, strategies, and tactics of political communication within the institutions of the presidency, Congress, and the courts. Chapter 15 examines the growing influence and integration of pop culture into politics. Chapter 16 identifies ethical concerns in the practice and study of politics.

This book attempts to survey the entire area of political communication. Thus, the work as a whole is more horizontal than vertical. Although the first chapter provides useful groundwork for the later ones, the reader can successfully read the chapters in or out of sequence—allowing for flexibility in meeting the diverse needs and time frames of courses, students, and instructors.

We feel that most would agree that human communication, in all its forms, is necessary for social life and that it is the quantity and quality of human communication processes that influences the structures of nations, the formation of political beliefs, attitudes, and values, as well as our behavior in relation to one another. As with all of our work, which spans nearly 30 years, this book speaks to our passion and love of political communication. The subject areas we share with you in this volume include both the theoretical and the applied. Along with our passion and our love of the subject area of political communication, it continues to be a privilege to study, participate, and share with our colleagues and students.

Notes

1 Aristotle, *The Politics of Aristotle*, trans. Ernest Barker (New York: Oxford University Press, 1970), 5.
2 Barker, 6.

Acknowledgments

Robert E. Denton, Jr., would like to thank his colleagues in the Department of Communication at Virginia Tech. For nearly twenty years, they have provided encouragement and support for now an "older" colleague with various administrative responsibilities. He also thanks Jerry Niles, Dean of the College of Liberal Arts and Human Sciences and Richard Sorensen, Dean of the Pamplin College of Business for their continued support of administrative, professional, and scholarly activities. They have understood the importance of the right "mix" of teaching, writing, and outreach activities that contribute to a gratifying career. They have supported his efforts professionally, financially, and personally. Finally, Denton wishes to thank his family, who has always supported the time allocated to the long hours in the study. Special thanks to his wife, Rachel, who deserves special praise as life partner, love, and friend. She, along with the "little dog" Daisy, provide joys in life well beyond academe.

Jim A. Kuypers would like to thank his family for their unreserved and continued support of his writing. With gratitude, he mentions Virginia Tech, which paid his salary and also funded library services such as interlibrary loan, Ebscohost, and Lexis-Nexis, all absolutely necessary to the completion of this project. The value Virginia Tech places on research allows projects such as this book to be undertaken and completed. He also wishes to thank his Department Head, R. L. Holloway, whose support during difficult times is exceptional.

Political Communication Defined

> *Within the life of the generation now in control of affairs, persuasion has become a self-conscious art and a regular organ of popular government. None of us begins to understand the consequences, but it is no daring prophecy to say that the knowledge of how to create consent will alter every political calculation and modify every political premise.*
>
> —Walter Lippmann, 1930.

Today, knowledge of how consent is created is at the heart of understanding political communication. At this writing, it appears that Osama Bin Laden is still alive but on the run. Saddam Hussein has been captured, tried, and hung by the Iraqi people. Over 130,000 American troops are in Iraq, with an additional 20,000 ordered into service. Insurgents continue to wreak havoc on American soldiers and on the Iraqi people as well, indiscriminately murdering men, women, and children. The United States is at war in the post–cold war period—a period initially marked by unprecedented peace and prosperity. Then came 9/11, which inaugurated a new era in terms of foreign policy and our "war on terror." The rules that governed American foreign policy since World War II no longer apply, making the job of politicians more difficult. Our "friends" are no longer defined by their anticommunist position, nor are our "enemies" identified by their affiliation with the Soviet Union. "In the new era," according to Anne Applebaum, "we are no longer selling democracy for its own sake, but exploring security, both for our sake and for the sake of other potential victims."[1]

On 9/11, terrorism left the domain of criminality and entered that of warfare. Just what does this change of venue mean? It means targeting not only "foot soldiers" but also the organizations and governments behind the terrorists. It means relying on the armed forces, not the police. It means securing our national borders with force, with walls, and with electronic surveillance. It

1

means conducting a vigorous defense overseas rather than on American soil and in our courtrooms. It means deploying U.S. forces on the basis of assumptions instead of an overt attack. It means using force and even preemptive strikes to deter future attacks. We are indeed experiencing a "New World Order," a new political landscape, a new era of warfare, wherein a few "thugs" can terrorize an entire nation. Small nations such as Iran, North Korea, and Venezuela can now dominate international debate and diplomacy. A few ounces of Anthrax can be more devastating to life than multiton explosives.

Domestically there appears to be a great deal of anger, frustration, and even fear. For nearly a decade, more than half of Americans routinely indicate in opinion polls that the United States is headed on the "wrong track" and that they are dissatisfied with the way things are going. Between 2004 and 2006, the Harris Alienation Index revealed that a majority of Americans believed the people running the country don't care about them, people with power try to take advantage of them, and what they think doesn't count very much any more. During this same time frame, nearly half of all Americans have negative feelings for both the Democratic and the Republican parties. In addition, about the same number think few members of Congress are honest, trustworthy, and work for the benefit of the people they represent.[2] It seems that the great polarization in the United States became vastly evident in the aftermath of the 2000 presidential election. George Bush lost the popular vote to Al Gore and, after a bitter dispute, primarily in Florida, was declared the winner by the Supreme Court. There were cries of voter fraud and corruption. Some "talking heads" and political pundits even alleged that George Bush "stole" the election. Others charged back saying that with 1.5 million uncounted absentee ballots nationwide, the popular vote was still undetermined, and that the Supreme Court ruled only on the legal issue of a recount, not on whether George Bush should be president.

It was political analyst Michael Barone of the *National Journal* who in 2001 labeled the United States as the "49 percent nation."[3] In fact, at the time, George W. Bush was the third consecutive winner of the presidency with less than 50 percent of the vote. We had become the "red" versus the "blue" nation. The red/blue distinction began with the publication of an electoral map in the *New York Times* showing the states where Bush received a plurality of votes in red and those of Gore in blue.[4] The distinctions were geographically striking. The terms "red" and "blue" became code words, not just politically, but culturally as well. "Red" America is comprised of small-town, religious folks, and "blue" America is much more secular, urban, and diverse.[5]

In 2004, Americans, once again, chose "red" over "blue" by a slightly larger margin. As James Ceaser and Andrew Busch viewed it, Americans "made this choice not crushingly or overwhelmingly, but clearly and decisively. No one could call the 2004 election a landslide, but Republicans emerged from the election ascendant as the nation's majority party."[6] Although some academics do question the red/blue dichotomy of the United States, Larry Sabato thinks the differences are real and "were stark in 2004, a great gulf separating the average audience one would encounter in the

Northeast or California from those of the South or Midwestern breadbasket states."[7] The 2004 presidential contest was one of the closest electoral margins in American history (the sixth closest after 1800, 1824, 1876, 1916, and, of course, 2000). It is also significant to note that Bush's popular vote margin was the slimmest ever for a reelected president.[8]

Another indication of the polarization of politics in the United States is revealed in media usage. Evidence suggests that Americans tend to select their source of news based on perceptions of philosophical and ideological leanings within the news broadcasts. Some pundits argue that Fox News is for conservatives and viewed primarily by Republicans; CNN is for liberals and viewed by Democrats. The same is said for newspapers, with the *Wall Street Journal* favored by conservatives and the *New York Times* by liberals. Liberals tend to watch the mainstream network news; conservatives listen to talk radio. Technology allows for even more selective and personal media choices, especially with the increasing role and impact of the Internet and the rise of the "blogosphere." You will read more about the media and bias in chapter 6, and more about the Internet and politics in chapter 7.

Although it appears that partisan politics and rivalries have suddenly dominated our social and cultural landscape, this has always been the case. We recognize that one cannot escape "politics." Politics, broadly defined, is the "currency" of social life. From the sublime to the ridiculous, politics influences our lives on a daily basis. Just consider the wide range of activities determined by politics:

- Who serves in office and how long
- Where we send troops
- The laws that are passed
- When we can vote, drive, enter contracts, or drink a beer.
- The rate of taxes and the level of public services
- What is taught in public schools
- Whether a road is built or a bridge is safe
- How often one's household garbage is collected

And consider the range of *feelings* that flow out of political discourse:

- Frustration that "our" group has been neglected by the state legislature
- Elation with a Supreme Court ruling that confirms our beliefs
- Annoyance with the president for backing away from a campaign pledge
- Pride in press reports that "our" senator has decided to fight for a favored federal program
- Anger at the offhand remarks of a congressional leader in the House
- Inspiration from a feature film in which the leading character demonstrates political courage

However one defines politics, it simply cannot be avoided.

The focus on the communication aspect of politics has a long history. Aristotle recognized the natural kinship of politics and communication in his writings *Politics* and *The Rhetoric*. In the former, he established that humans are "political beings [who] alone of the animals [are] furnished with the faculty of language." Speech "serves to indicate what is useful and what is harmful, and so also what is just and what is unjust. For the real difference between man and other animals is that humans alone have perception of good and evil, just and unjust, etc."[9] In the latter, he began his systematic analysis of discourse by proclaiming "rhetorical study, in its strict sense, is concerned with the modes of persuasion."[10] Thus, it was recognized over 2,300 years ago that politics and communication go hand in hand because they are essential parts of human nature.

For G. R. Boynton, "politics is conversation, talk, argument and persuasion, and communication."[11] More specifically, he defines politics as "conversations flowing through institutionalized channels punctuated by the vote." In fact, politicians spend almost all of their time, whether in hearings, in briefings, at public meetings, making public announcements, or campaigning, "engaged in talk, in argument and persuasion, and in conversation."[12] The "vote" is the way they or we, depending upon the context, "register" the current state of the talk before returning to the ongoing conversation.[13] The "institutionalized channels" are all the "sites" in which conversations take place. It tends to be primarily through the mass media, but it could be on the campaign trail, through press releases, letters, and the like. As Boynton concludes, "there are many conversations and many channels and great interaction between public and officials."[14]

Human communication is the vehicle for political thought, debate, and action. David Easton, from a "system perspective" of politics and human behavior, demonstrates the role of communication in "politics."[15] Our political system processes a multitude of inputs from our social environment that become outputs of political structures, values, and actions. Communication channels the inputs, structures the outputs, and provides feedback from political system to the environment. The vast multitude of interactions literally constructs our political, economic, and social institutions. According to Dan Nimmo and David Swanson:

> In its political dimensions, communication is a force for both conflict and consensus; political campaigns in . . . democracies are about both change and stability; strong empirical evidence can be adduced for, and valuable insights derived from, conceiving political communication as both empowerment and marginalization, produced and consumed by citizens who are more or less autonomous, cognitive, intentional, and creative actors as well as shaped by powerful historical, social, and other structures.[16]

In short, we do not advance a notion of politics that exists apart from how it is communicated; rather, we believe that a political communication focus asks one to view politics—in all its varied forms—as taking place through communication. This takes on special importance when one considers that "every citizen who deliberates and creates messages about civic affairs—estimating ends and means, selecting arguments and evidence, weighing factors of advantage, justice, and virtue—engages in political rhetoric." [17]

General Characteristics of Political Communication

Although the types of political messages and the forms they take are nearly limitless, there are commonalities among them. We recognize that many features of messages we discuss in this book are not exclusive to the political world; they are, however, more than casual companions to it and deserve consideration by those wishing to better understand the general nature of political discourse. The most general characteristics of political communication include these four elements: (1) has a short-term orientation, (2) is based on specific objectives, (3) is primarily mediated, and above all, (4) is audience centered.

Short-Term Orientation

Among the most common realities governing political life is a general preoccupation with transitory issues and limited time frames. Messages are typically planned, prepared, and delivered with an eye to *immediate* outcomes. For example, should land be rezoned from rural to commercial to allow for a new strip mall? Should the state raise its sales tax to make up for a budget shortfall? Should federal housing assistance be extended an additional year for victims of Hurricane Katrina? These examples represent common political messages that must enter the continuous flow of public discussion within a period of time that is both beneficial to the communicator and timely for the mass media and their audiences.

The limited and specific time frames for political campaigns are rather obvious—after votes are cast, the campaign is over. But the public discussion and consideration of issues are comprised of many rather distinct "campaigns" and specific initiatives. Issues are discussed in a variety of ways, over numerous time periods. Before any legislation is passed to deal with an aspect of a larger social issue, very specific and planned communication takes place within a specific time frame and with a specific outcome in mind. According to Lloyd Bitzer, most "political messages occur in specific historical situations and are essentially responsive to them. Political speakers find themselves in situations that present problems, crises, obstacles, or other kinds of exigencies which they seek to modify by addressing messages to mediating audiences— that is, to audiences which have sufficient power to modify the exigencies." [18]

This process, of course, is even more complex and difficult in the current 24/7 news cycle with so many channels, avenues of expression, and polarizing issue advocates. Even so, when an issue or problem is identified, appropriately articulated, and disseminated through a targeted "campaign" until it reaches a critical mass of the public call for resolution, then some action occurs. The action could be a new law, a court ruling, a national or state referendum, or a single designated "investigation." The public attention soon moves on, perhaps returning to the issue or problem once again at a later date. In all of this, there are two important points to remember: (1) for every concern, there appears to be a cycle of interaction, negotiation, and completion; and (2) the cycle and time frame seem to be getting shorter.

As an example of this, consider how the 1973 Supreme Court ruling of *Roe v. Wade* did not end controversy over abortion, but rather exacerbated it. Across the nation, for more than thirty-four years, political discussion, debate, and legislation has centered on various questions: When may abortions be performed? What constitutes "legal" versus "illegal" abortions? Who should perform abortions, technicians or physicians? Should states regulate, define, and provide guidelines for abortions? Should there be some provisions for parental notification, informed consent? Should procedures such as partial birth abortion be allowed to continue? Each question leads to discussion, debate, and perhaps to referendums and legislation. Policy discussions on abortion, like most political communication, benefit from a window of opportunity that can pass as quickly as it appears. Every election, for instance, generates calls for even more campaign finance reform, limits on negative advertising, and banning announcements of vote returns before the polls close across the nation. However, specific action in these areas is woefully lacking, and continues to be elusive.

The point here is that political communication seeks practical and immediate results. Its effectiveness usually hinges on its adaptation to the transient nature of public opinion and the fleeting attention of the mass media. It is often criticized for its "rudderless" and "hypocritical" messages. Yet, taken on its own terms, political communication can only be understood when there is a willingness to reconstruct the immediate political context—the relevant climate of public opinion—that a public figure feels duty-bound to honor. Although it may be the case that novels, inspirational speeches, movies, and other forms of communication are valued for their capacity to be measured against timeless standards, serious attempts to shape opinion rarely profit from comparisons against similar invariant critical yardsticks. In a sense, whereas the judgments about great works of literature are tied to timeless values and the expressive elements of the author, political communication draws upon time-bound context and expression linked to the political expediencies. Hoyt Hopewell Hudson provides us with a fuller understanding of this distinction. Although Lincoln's Gettysburg address is now viewed as a poetic work that transcends the tendrils of time, it was at the time of utterance viewed as a political speech:

> Lincoln's Gettysburg speech is sometimes described as if it were a poetical discourse by a man who had brooded much in solitude, and who disregarded or "rose above" the occasion in order to express universal truths and emotions. Without denying the element of universality in this

speech, we must say that what Lincoln did was to seize the occasion, with its already deep emotional associations, and to utilize all the elements of it in the performance of his task of persuading the members of his audience to help carry on the war. From our point of view, now that the occasion for such persuasion is past, we can fit the speech into its historical and biographical setting and read it very much as we read a speech in a drama, and with a similar delight. But at the time it was a piece of persuasive discourse with a very specific end view.[19]

We remember Lincoln's speech today because it has become associated with timeless values embraced by Americans. Given that the overwhelming majority of political speeches are time-bound, not timeless, it makes sense that we recall so few. Political communication is put together to be consumed, not savored.

Communication Based on Objectives

The lion's share of political behavior is directed to some specific end, even when it takes on the appearance of predictable ritual. What is overlooked in the common complaint that political *talk* is a meaningless substitute for political *action* is the important fact that political talk is often intended to increase the prospects of the talker, who is the agent for certain political ideas. Every political campaign tries to fulfill this objective, giving credibility to a campaigner by making him or her the vehicle for reasonable proposals and familiar values. Perceptions of a candidate's intellectual honesty and authenticity typically rank high among these values.

Much of the political talk of campaigns, of legislation, and of public discourse is carefully molded, crafted, and even sometimes tested to insure an intended effect. Sound bites are created, answers to anticipated questions are rehearsed, and messages are targeted to very specific audiences who are, in actuality, essential constituents. According to Brian McNair, political communication is "purposeful communication about politics."[20] This includes all forms of communication by political actors for achieving specific objectives, communication addressed to political actors by nonpolitical actors, and communication about political actors and their activities. Political actors, according to McNair, are "those individuals who aspire, through organizational and institutional means, to influence the decision-making process."[21] Thus, purposeful communication is *directive*, in that it is intentional; *persuasive* communication designed to alter a belief, attitude, value, or lead to some individual or collective action.

Importance of the Mass Media

Because political communication is largely mediated communication, the mass media are basic to the study of politics. No claim about the conduct of modern political life seems more self-evident. Speeches, press conferences, pleas for support, justifications of controversial decisions all imply the presence of constituencies—audiences for those acts. Most of those audiences are reached only by the extended coverage provided by the mass media. There are two assumptions about this process that we should consider.

First, the role of political reporting is dedicated—in philosophy, if not always in practice—to a watchdog role over those public officials who are clearly within their own sphere of influence. In the familiar terms of this philosophy, the free press performs an adversarial function that provides a check, a "fourth branch of government," to keep a wary eye on the other three. "The only security of all," Thomas Jefferson said, "is in a free press." This is an obvious and largely undisputed objective of the political press in the United States. Although we take it for granted, the norm of a constitutionally protected independent press is perhaps the greatest single contribution the United States had made to the lore of democracy.

Second, the mass media function in a way that reverses the familiar reporter–subject relationship. In forms that are detailed more fully in chapter 6, the political press controls the interpretation of the news as well as reports the news. Especially in this century, journalists have sometimes been able to *lead* rather than just *follow* the course of an unfolding political story. Critics claim that too many politicians lead by reacting to the whims of public opinion polls rather than by creating public opinion through argument, information, and public debate. Too often, the practice of U.S. politics requires the ability to follow an agenda of issues and events largely fabricated or generated in America's newsrooms. The political newsmaker still initiates the raw materials for many stories, but the control and management of political information is now largely in the hands of privately controlled news and entertainment enterprises.

When Theodore Roosevelt denounced the muckraking press just after the turn of the twentieth century, he was not paying a compliment to the new investigative muscle of the William Randolph Hearst or Ida Tarbells. He was making what has since become a familiar complaint based on the realization that the public media place their own commercial demands on those engaged in political discourse. Like nearly all politicians of his time and later, Roosevelt savored the attentions of the press, but not their insatiable thirst for stories intended to capture the public imagination, thereby selling more papers and bringing in additional advertising revenue. The drive for readership created a narrative thread of political news that usually carries within it popular images of good and evil; heroes and villains; and national idealistic notions of justice and injustice.

As we will discuss, the media compete with politicians to set public agendas, define issues, and frame public debate. For the public, the mass media, including the increasing role of the Internet, become the primary source of political information, knowledge, and opinion on issues and campaigns of concern.

Audience-Centered Politics

All practical communication is audience centered. However, political discourse is especially audience centered or audience sensitive. Political actors are motivated by the desire to gain the support of specific constituencies. Political messages are not neutral; they are created with a targeted audience in mind. Such an audience-centered approach properly forces the analyst to think in terms of the processes that govern the search for a consensus, or to its unmaking. The arts of compromise, emphasis, de-emphasis, and simplification are all very much a part of this process. Rather than lamenting the avenues for blatant manipulation that are implicit in such a point of view, *we prefer to think of an audience-centered activity as wholly natural and nominally democratic.* In a large sense, the business of political communication involves communication to the public. On this point John Dewey wrote:

> Human acts have consequences upon others, that some of these consequences are perceived, and that their perception leads to subsequent effort to control action so as to secure some consequences and avoid others. Following this clue, we are led to remark that the consequences are of kinds, those which affect the persons directly engaged in a transaction, and those which affect others beyond those immediately concerned. In this distinction we find the germ of the distinction between the private and the public. When indirect consequences of an action are confined, or are thought to be confined, mainly to the persons directly engaged in it, the transaction is a private one.[22]

There can be no doubt that politics offer the potential for pandering to the lowest of human impulses. The price we pay for an open political system is the risk that there will be excesses. We believe, though, that the greater danger lies not in the manipulation of audience allegiances to political ideas, but in the society that minimizes opportunities for the articulation of such ideas. At their best, democratic societies are strengthened by exchanges between those in a position of authority and by citizens with countervailing rights to revoke it. The opposite, totalitarian nations, seek to control, diminish, or eliminate such interaction. However, for this model of democracy to be successful, the citizens must be well informed and educated. Otherwise citizens are mere sheep to be herded.

Political Communication Defined

There is something inescapably seductive about describing political communication so that it is nearly synonymous with obfuscation. Analysts are frequently tempted to characterize it in terms of the abuse it gives to some set notion of "The Truth." In short, political communication is frequently defined to accentuate its negative characteristics. This tendency is based in part on what we think is the mistaken assumption that political address is primarily about discovering *the right* solution to a problem, or concealing *the wrong* one. If an observer believes that one side in a debate has the correct answer, the only possible way to explain the other side is in terms of the obfuscation of ideas. George Orwell's widely admired description of political address is a case in point:

In our time, political speech and writing are largely the defense of the indefensible. Things like the continuance of British rule in India, the Russian purges and deportations, the dropping of the atom bombs on Japan, can indeed, be defended, but only by arguments which are too brutal for most people to face, and which do not square with the professed aims of political parties. Thus political language has to consist largely of euphemism, question-begging and sheer cloudy vagueness.[23]

Although writing in 1949, Orwell's statement applies equally well today. For instance, simply substitute British rule in India with continued Chinese occupation of Tibet, or Russian purges and deportations with Taliban purges and punishments, and the idea expressed by Orwell sees the light in the political language used today.

Paul Corcoran provides a similar expression of disillusionment that functions implicitly as a kind of operational definition of political communication:

Contemporary political language . . . has assumed a peculiar and in some sense an inverted social function as a technique of linguistic expression. This is borne out in the uses to which political language is often put: not to convey information, but to conceal or distort it; not to draw public attention, but to divert or suppress it. In short, contemporary political language may play precisely the reverse role from that classically conceived for political rhetoric. Instead of a rhetorical "method" to inform, persuade and enlighten, contemporary political language aims at an etiolated monologue which has no content, which placates, and which bears no relationship to the organization, coherency and clarification of information and ideas.[24]

These descriptions are superficially likable; criticizing the rhetoric of U.S. political leaders is something of a national sport. They actually tell us very little because *they render political communication deficient by definition*. By this, we mean that the only task that remains for the analyst of political communication as described above is to point out its inherent irrationality. Not surprisingly, it is much easier to do that than to explain how it works: how audiences are affected by it, how converts are made, and how groups and institutions adjust to its more fluent advocates. To better understand how this works, let's look at a negative definition for another subject—architecture. A negative focus might be to label it as the "design and building of what are largely inadequate and deficient structures by people intent on profiting at the expense of others." Without doubt, architects do build ungainly, inhospitable, and aesthetically unappealing structures. The essence of architecture, like the essence of political communication, involves more, however. The problem, of course, is that negative definitions masquerade *judgments* as *descriptions*, indicting general processes by inviting consideration of negative examples to stand in for the whole. This synecdochic process means that if one dislikes a policy, the easiest way to attack it is to dismiss the general category of communication used to defend it.

This debate over the nature of practical persuasion is far from new. Aristotle's seminal discussion of public advocacy in *The Rhetoric* over 2,300 years ago was partly a rejection of the low priority to which Plato had relegated it. Plato craved certainty and exactitude from human institutions; he distrusted practical persuasion since it could be used to allow the weaker case to seem the stronger or evil to triumph over good. Aristotle noted that the art of rhetoric was like many other arts in that it can be used for evil or beneficial purposes: "A man can confer the greatest benefits by a right use of these, and inflict the greatest of injuries by using them wrongly."[25] This argument about the nature of political discourse lives on even today; one often hears politicians decrying their opponent's use of "mere rhetoric," while they themselves work for "action."

A more positive consideration of political communication endorses the view that it is unrealistic to base an understanding of political debate on the hope that there can be a kind of *universal* standard from which to measure its validity. On most political questions (i.e., questions involving choices with competing advantages to different constituencies) the truth is not easily located. This is because politics is not primarily about truth telling, but consensus seeking; in short, it is audience centered. Political conflict typically concerns itself with decisions implying the values or preferences of an audience rather than determinations of fact, even though there may indeed be relevant facts that should inform political debate. The bulk of most practical discourse is centered on the mobilization or reinforcement of public opinion: a process that certainly involves rationality and fact-finding, but frequently denies a superior point of view.

We endorse what seems to be an enlightened distinction made by Chaim Perelman and L. Olbrechts-Tyteca between arguments of all forms that *demonstrate* and those that *argue*.[26] The former tend to be analytic, arbitrary, and *a priori*: as in the synthetic formulas of physics and mathematics where the same conclusions are generated by a wide diversity of individuals. A true demonstration provides no reasonable basis for dissent. On the other hand, arguments—the ever-present products of what may be legitimate differences of opinion—exist in the realm of preferences. Political conflict is legitimate when it originates in pluralist thought about values and priorities. A position put forward in a dispute is necessarily a combination of the individual's intellectual and social history as well as the history of the group that he or she seeks to influence. Enlarging this distinction further, consider Kenneth Burke's distinction between semantic and moral-poetic meaning. One way to understand moral-poetics is by contrasting it to what Burke called semantic meaning. Semantic meaning embraces "detached operationalizations," "tested assertions," and is linked with logical positivism.[27] Its ideal is "*to evolve a vocabulary that gives the name and address of everything in the universe*"; thus, to name, and to name only—in other words, a vulgar materialism.[28] It strongly asserts *a correct meaning*. Moral-poetics also seek to name, but does so with the realization of being laden with emotional values and attitudes. So, moral-poetics name, but also "suggest exhortations for the promotion of *better* names."[29] Moral-poetics therefore contain the seeds for both descriptive and normative growth. Burke believed these different ways of meaning to be not antithetical, but rather elements of a graded series of meanings: a range say, from sheer exhortation to mathematics.

Consider, for example, the ongoing politics involved in the federal government's management of national forests. To what extent should the National Forest Service permit the harvesting of timber on federal lands by private companies? Furthermore, should such sales of public timber be at market price or lower? Policy for land use may be set by unelected officials in the Forest Service or its parent agency, the Department of Agriculture; however, debate may also flare up on this question in Congress and within the president's own staff. Facts will help various interested parties determine a position on this continually renewed debate, but the answer finally depends on how we rank the service's obligations to conservationists, to lumber industries and their employees, and to the aesthetics of harvesting woodlands. There are clearly moral, logical, and evidentiary bases for arbitrating questions such as those above; however, to start from the premise that political address is a form of obfuscation because it fails to tally with some *a priori* standard is to force it into alien territory. Such a perspective may well carry a reassuring certainty, but it fails to provide the tools that are necessary to discover the processes and varied perspectives that mediate political decisions.

Political Communication as a Distinct Area of Study

In 1981, Dan Nimmo and Keith Sanders proclaimed that political communication was an emerging field of study.[30] Although its origin, as already noted, dates back millennium, a "self-consciously cross-disciplinary" focus began only in the late 1950s. Thousand of books and articles later, colleges and universities offer a variety of graduate and undergraduate coursework in the area in such diverse departments as communication, mass communication, journalism, political science, and sociology. In Nimmo and Sanders's early assessment, the "key areas of inquiry" included rhetorical analysis, propaganda analysis, attitude change studies, voting studies, government and the news media, functional and systems analyses, technological changes, media technologies, campaign techniques, and research techniques.[31] In a survey of the field in 1984, the same authors and Lynda Kaid found additional, more specific areas of concern such as the presidency, political polls, public opinion, debates, and advertising.[32] Since the first study, they also noted a shift away from the rather strict behavioral (social scientific) approach.

Nearly a decade later in 1990, Dan Nimmo and David Swanson announced "political communication has developed some identity as a more or less distinct domain of scholarly work."[33] They noted that the scope and concerns of the area further expanded to include critical theories and cultural studies. Anne Johnston's review of the field identified four major categories of scholarship: election communication, political communication and news, political rhetoric, and political attitude formation and dynamics.[34] The primary domain at that time comprised the role, processes, and effects of communication within the context of politics broadly defined.

Now nearly two decades later, political communication is offered as area of specialty at both the undergraduate and graduate levels. All the major professional organizations in the disciplines of communication and political science offer interest groups or divisions dedicated to the scholarship of political communication. There is even growing interest in the subfields of political sociology and political psychology. In addition, the field has supported several dedicated scholarly books.

In the most recent review of the field, Yang Lin identifies five scholarly traditions that inform the study of political communication.[35] The first is the rhetorical analyses of public discourse. This approach traditionally is more historical and qualitative (humanities based). The second is the post–World War II research focusing on the nature of persuasion and propaganda. For instance, the role of the mass media in impacting public opinion was at the core of Lasswell's studies. The third line of research informing the study of political communication is the tradition of voting studies. Unlike the others identified thus far, this tradition utilized both qualitative and quantitative (social scientific) measures of analysis. The forth tradition is media effects. This is arguably the second oldest tradition of scholarship. Attitude change is the focus of this line of research using primarily quantitative methods of investigation. The last tradition is what Lin refers to as the institutional study of the press and government related to public opinion and can be traced back to 1922 and Walter Lippmann's classic study, *Public Opinion*. This tradition forecasts the beginning of the agenda-setting research.[36]

For Bruce Gronbeck, the idea of political communication, in sum, is an extension of a centuries-long effort to understand the relationships between *rhetoric* and *politics*.[37] He argues:

> the coming of "political communication" as an architectonic term has fostered a dual recognition: that "politics" and "politicalization" encompass both institutional and public-symbolic processes productive of collective policy, visions of polity, and even self-identities; and that humane studies of such processes always must include definitional, analytical, interpretive, and evaluative moments if the social world is to be productive of life, liberty, and the pursuit of happiness.[38]

Toward a Definition of Political Communication

Democratic politics is concerned with the power to decide. Everyday political acts function to influence decisions or to defend them. Certainly since the time of ancient Greece, rhetoric is the lifeblood of democracy. Public discourse and persuasion are modes of information, knowledge, and political power. The public communication that accompanies most forms of political activity serves to alter, justify, or clarify the range of choices that are in dispute in the public arena. The more open the society and the more active the political press, the better the chances that rhetorical disputes will be productive vehicles for governance.

Thus, any definition of political communication addresses issues of content, intentions, and structure of such interactions. Craig Allen Smith defines political communication as "the process of negotiating a community orientation through the interpretation and characterization of interests, of power relationships, and of the community's role in the world."[39] By examining the major concerns of those who study political communication, Nimmo and Swanson define it as "the strategic uses of communication to influence public knowledge, beliefs, and action on political matters."[40] Bob Franklin in 1995 viewed political communication as the "interactions between media and political systems locally, nationally, and internationally."[41] This definition covers the content of media, political and media actors, and the effects on the audiences and political processes.

Richard Perloff defines political communication as "the process by which a nation's leadership, media, and citizenry exchange and confer meaning upon messages that relate to the conduct of public policy."[42] This definition recognizes it is a process that does not happen automatically or instantaneously. He identifies three critical players: the leaders, the media, and the public. Furthermore, the definition acknowledges the interaction's ultimate impact or influence on public policy. Perloff also recognizes several contextual factors: political communication is influenced by our economic system (media owned by private interests); is influenced by historical factors; and plays an important role in our democracy. "In an ideal world," Perloff states, "elites would use the communications media to inform and influence people, helping improve their lot in life, and to also put aside their personal interests to work for the common good."[43]

More recently, Bruce Gronbeck argues that, from a theoretical perspective, the definition of political communication has moved "away from *politics* as titular term to *politicalization* as central to political activity and from political outcomes understood as policy (legislative-judicial politics) expanded to include those we now conceptualize as polity matters (identity politics)."[44] For Gronbeck, the key to understanding the Aristotelian conception of rhetoric and politics "is to conceive of politics as grounded in citizens' needs and mores and of rhetoric as a tool for symbolically turning citizens' needs and mores into the bases of public policy."[45]

Brian McNair suggests another way to investigate political communication is to focus on the relationships of various elements.[46] He identifies three elements: political organizations, media, and citizens. Political organizations are broad social collectivities that include political parties, public interest groups, social movement groups, or government. Media is the generic term to include all modes, means, and levels of mediated communication. McNair also views citizens as individuals or social groups with common purpose. What is relevant about this perspective is that the forms of communication define the relationships among the elements. Citizens write letters, make speeches, or form groups to better impact the political environment. Media also have a wide range of activities that include writing stories, editorials, or commentary as well as provide analysis, take polls, or simply provide platforms for citizens and political actors, to name just a few. Finally, political organizations orchestrate events, make news, contact citizens, media, and so on. For McNair, the patterns and channels of communication provide the most insight in considering the scope of political communication activities.

The Four Concerns of Political Communication

We think the above definitions of political communication are valuable. Political communication *is* a process, *is* strategic, and *is* unique in terms of form and content. We have taken our time to arrive at this section in order to better flesh out our definition of political communication. Although we agree with a simple definition that political communication is politics viewed through a communication perspective, we also wish to provide a nuanced and extended definition that reflects the complexity and richness of the topic. We view political communication from a more broad and encompassing perspective: *as public discussion about the allocation of public resources (revenues), official authority (who is given control; i.e., the power to make legal, legislative and executive decisions), official sanctions (what the state rewards or punishes), and social meaning (what does it mean to be an American and the role of citizen, implications of social policy, and so forth.).* The public discussion of the above content areas is comprehensive, utilizing intrapersonal, interpersonal, small group, and mass communication processes. At best, the language of political communication is a valuable mediating agent that replaces sheer violent conflict, and makes orderly change possible. It serves to prepare the way for eventual compromise and acceptance by making arguments, facts, and opinions a part of the public record on an issue. It is also the language of the faction, of the friend and of the foe. It may sharpen differences beyond the point of repair, or it may dull them. It can be a vehicle to mask what should be highlighted, or it may actually repair what has been deeply divisive. One can express optimism for its ability to transform the society for the better; but one can also despair over its widespread abuse. The rhetoric of politics can be many things: therapeutic, divisive, alienating, inspiring, or informational. The strategies and tactics of political communication are limitless but tend to be linked to the context, such as political campaigns, debates, political advertising, and so forth. We turn now to each of these for major concerns of political communication.

Revenue. The much-vaunted cliché that politics is about the exercise and control of power finds it best examples in discourse involving the power to spend. Protracted negotiations over the allocation of scarce resources are common to every society. Potential alterations in the way public money is spent inevitably produce organized advocacy and opposition. Whether to build local baseball fields or patch potholes, whether to permit federal funding of abortions or the leasing of federal lands to oil speculators, all only hint at the broad range of resource-based debates that reach Americans daily. Not all political issues involve conflict over the use of public funds, but the exceptions are rare. Especially in the legislative arena, real commitments to legislative action are revealed more in amendments specifying how a given piece of legislation will be funded than in general endorsements of the legislation. Every city mayor and agency executive who are guided by these actions know that the intent of most legislation inevitably exceeds what scarce available revenues will actually permit.

Control.   The question of who decides is the focus of the political campaign. In all levels of government elected public officials are given the power to act as trustees of the public interest. They may be municipal judges, school board officials, legislators, governors, or presidents. The heart of American faith in republican democracy resides in the assignment of power based on the "consent of the governed." Unlike any other political event, the political campaign galvanizes the public by giving ephemeral political ideals a universal reference point in the features of a specific personality. Appealing to the electorate's shared vision of its future, the candidate uses real and invented traits of character to enact one part in an ongoing drama of contested leadership. Arguably, the power of the ballot may be overestimated in this age when so many complex bureaucracies and civil service systems have replaced the citizen-politician. Although decreasing numbers of employees in the public sector are accountable through the electoral process, the chain of responsibility ends most dramatically with the elected leader. He or she is at least nominally accountable for the massive professional government that can never be voted in or out of office; that is, for the enormous number of nonelected bureaucrats responsible for the day-to-day running of our local, state, and federal governments.

Sanctions.   A class of political discussion arises from official statements that accompany administrative decisions, court rulings, and the consideration of legislation. Political sanctions typically are initiated as governmental actions—either legislated or enforced—that require the compliance of certain segments within the population. Laws defining criminal conduct are the most obvious forms of sanctions, but sanctions may include a presidential decision to deploy new weapons systems in a foreign locale, or an attempt by some members of the Congress to forbid it. They are represented by the decision of a big city mayor to give tax incentives to a commercial developer, or the federal judge's award of precious water rights to a state bordering on a river. Because sanctions are governmental and are judicial responses to problems that have usually created social conflict, they often set in motion a cycle of public discussion that pit political officials against a range of opposing factions. With the exception of judges, disputes frequently surface between the sanctioning agents of government and a wide variety of traditional opponents, including journalists, corporate leaders, opposing political leaders, academics, and even television personalities. Any of these advocates may play for the attention of the larger public by focusing interest on the wisdom or failures of a public policy. In doing so, they frequently initiate public discussion on the wisdom of a sanction's advocates and detractors as well. The current federal and state debate concerning homosexual marriage is a prime example. Some of this discussion creates high political drama, because deep public divisions about where the state should impose its official and moral weight involve the highest of stakes, including finely-tuned feelings of status and well-being.

Meaning. The process of political communication does more than enact legislation, and elect officials. Political discourse defines issues and candidates as well as the roles as citizens and government, our beliefs and values as Americans, and our sense of place and of history. Through it, we provide a rationale and context for our collective actions. As Americans, we struggle with historical views of the purpose of the War Between the States, our role in Vietnam, or our role in Iraq. We debate whether the act of abortion is a *medical procedure* or *merely murder*. We question whether federal subsidies are *corporate welfare* or *engines of economic growth*. Does affirmative action *perpetuate discrimination* or *ensure equal opportunity*? The issues and questions are countless. Through political communication, we come to understand our values, issues, and culture.

Summary

For many political pundits and observers, the United States is a divided nation—divided politically, geographically, culturally, and philosophically. However, from a historical perspective, partisan politics and rivalries have always dominated our social and cultural landscape. Especially in a democracy, one simply cannot escape politics. For us, politics is conversation, discussion, and argument; human communication is the vehicle for political thought, debate, and action. It is a practical, process-centered, decision-oriented activity. Because it is dependent on the approval of specific audiences, its utility is strongly restricted by time and by the willingness of the political media to make its messages accessible. We have necessarily cast our net quite broadly. Political communication includes speeches and addresses, whether heard firsthand or reported in highly edited segments. It also includes many other forms of public discussion: reports, public letters, defenses of administrative action or inaction, hearings, mediated accounts of events from the press, and even ostensibly nonpolitical messages such as films and prime-time television. Ultimately, a crucial factor that makes communication political is not the source of a message, but its content and purpose.

We identify the general characteristics of political communication as: short-term orientation, based on specific objectives, primarily mediated, and audience centered. Political communication has become a distinct area of academic investigation and specialty. It is also a practical art of campaigning, governing, and public persuasion. Political communication is a process, is strategic, and is unique in terms of form and content. We provide a broad definition of political communication as the "public discussion about the allocation of public resources, official authority, official sanctions, and social meaning." We will explore this definition as well as the various forms, activities, and contexts of political communication in the forthcoming chapters.

Notes

[1] Anne Applebaum, "The New World Order," in *Our Brave New World*, ed. Wladyslaw Pleszczynski (Stanford, CA: Stanford University Press, 2002), 19.

[2] PollingReport.com/right.html, retrieved 3/30/06.

[3] As cited in James Ceaser and Andrew Busch, *Red Over Blue: 2004 Elections and American Politics* (Lanham, MD: Rowman & Littlefield, 2005), 33.

[4] Ibid., 1. The color choice by the *New York Times* is not lost on political observers. Traditionally the color red in politics often denoted left-leaning tendencies and also communism. That the *Times*, itself a paper charge with liberal bias by many Republicans, would describe Republican leaning states as "red," is a noticeable irony.

[5] Ibid., 18.

[6] Ibid., 2.

[7] Larry Sabato, *Divided States of America* (New York: Longman, 2006), x.

[8] Ibid., 53, 54.

[9] Aristotle, *The Politics of Aristotle*, trans. Ernest Barker (New York: Oxford University Press, 1970), 5.

[10] Aristotle, *Rhetoric*, trans. W. Rhys Roberts (New York: Modern Library, 1954), 22.

[11] G. R. Boynton, "Our Conversations about Governing," in *Political Communication Research: Approaches, Studies and Assessments*, ed. D. Paletz (Norwood, NJ: Ablex, 1996), 102.

[12] Ibid., 109.

[13] Ibid., 109.

[14] Ibid., 110.

[15] As cited in Dan Nimmo and David Swanson, "The Field of Political Communication: Beyond the Voter Persuasion Paradigm," in *New Directions in Political Communication: A Resource Book*, ed. David Swanson and Dan Nimmo (Newbury Park, CA: Sage, 1990), 33.

[16] Ibid., 22.

[17] Lloyd F. Bitzer, "Political Rhetoric," in *Handbook of Political Communication*, ed. Dan Nimmo and Keith Sanders (Beverly Hills, CA: Sage, 1981), 228.

[18] Ibid., 239.

[19] Hoyt Hopewell Hudson, "Rhetoric and Poetry," *Quarterly Journal of Speech Education* 10, no. 2 (1924): 145. H. L. Mencken would later make this same distinction, but with remarkably different conclusions: "The Gettysburg speech was at once the shortest and the most famous oration in American history. Put beside it, all the whoopings of the Websters, Sumners and Everetts seem gaudy and silly. It is eloquence brought to a pellucid and almost gem-like perfection, the highest emotion reduced to a few poetical phrases. Lincoln himself never even remotely approached it. It is genuinely stupendous. But let us not forget that it is poetry, not logic; beauty, not sense. Think of the argument in it. Put it into the cold words of everyday. The doctrine is simply this: that the Union soldiers who died at Gettysburg sacrificed their lives to the cause of self determination that government of the people, by the people, for the people, should not perish from the earth. It is difficult to imagine anything more untrue. The Union soldiers in the battle actually fought against self-determination; it was the Confederates who fought for the right of their people to govern themselves. H. L. Mencken, *A Mencken Chrestomathy* (New York: Vintage Books, 1949) 222–223.

[20] Brian McNair, *An Introduction to Political Communication* (London: Routledge, 1995), 4.

[21] Ibid., 5.

[22] John Dewey, *The Public and Its Problems* (New York: Henry Holt, 1927), 12.

[23] George Orwell, "Politics and the English Language" in *The Orwell Reader* (New York: Harcourt, Brace, 1949), 363.

[24] Paul Corcoran, *Political Language and Rhetoric* (Austin: University of Texas Press, 1979), xv.

[25] Aristotle, *Rhetoric*, 23.

[26] Chaim Perelman and L. Olbrechts-Tyteca, *The New Rhetoric*, trans. John Wilkinson and Purcell Weaver (Notre Dame, IN: University of Notre Dame Press, 1969), 509–514.

[27] Kenneth Burke, *The Philosophy of Literary Form*, 2nd ed. (Baton Rouge: Louisiana State University Press, 1967), 141. Another way of viewing this conceptual struggle is commensurate with the discussion of philosophical pairs by Perelman and Olbrechts-Tyteca. See Chaim Perelman and L. Olbrechts-Tyteca, *The New Rhetoric: A Treatise on Argumentation* (Notre Dame, London: University of Notre Dame Press, 1971): 411–459.

[28] Burke, *The Philosophy of Literary Form*, 141.

[29] Ibid., 146.

[30] Dan Nimmo and Keith Sanders, "Introduction: The Emergence of Political Communication as a Field," in *Handbook of Political Communication*, ed. Dan Nimmo and Keith Sanders (Beverly Hills, CA: Sage, 1981), 11–36.

[31] Ibid., 17–27.

[32] Keith Sanders, Lynda Kaid, and Dan Nimmo, "Survey of Political Communication Theory and Research," in *Political Communication Yearbook: 1984*, ed. Keith Sanders, Lynda Kaid, and Dan Nimmo (Carbondale: Southern Illinois University Press, 1985), 283–308.

[33] Dan Nimmo and David Swanson, "The Field of Political Communication: Beyond the Voter Persuasion Paradigm" in *New Directions in Political Communication*, ed. David Swanson and Dan Nimmo (Beverly Hills, CA: Sage, 1990), 8.

[34] Anne Johnston, "Selective Bibliography of Political Communication Research, 1982–1988" in *New Directions in Political Communication*, ed. David Swanson and Dan Nimmo (Beverly Hills, CA: Sage, 1990), 363–390.

[35] Yang Lin, "Fragmentation of the Structure of Political Communication Research: Diversification or Isolation?" in *Handbook of Political Communication Research*, ed. Lynda Kaid (Mahwah, NJ: Lawrence Erlbaum, 2004), 70–71.

[36] Ibid., 70–71.

[37] Bruce Gronbeck, "Rhetoric and Politics," in *Handbook of Political Communication Research*, ed. Lynda Kaid (Mahwah, NJ: Lawrence Erlbaum, 2004), 151.

[38] Ibid., 151.

[39] Craig Allen Smith, *Political Communication* (San Diego, CA: Harcourt Brace Jovanovich, 1990), vii.

[40] Nimmo and Swanson, "The Field of Political Communication," 9.

[41] As cited in Christina Holtz-Bacha, "Political Communication Research Abroad: Europe," in *Handbook of Political Communication Research*, ed. Lynda Kaid (Mahwah, NJ: Lawrence Erlbaum, 2004), 464.

[42] Richard Perloff, *Political Communication* (Mahwah, NJ: Lawrence Erlbaum, 1998), 8.

[43] Ibid., 10–11.

[44] Gronbeck, "Rhetoric and Politics," 138.

[45] Ibid., 138.

[46] Brian McNair, *An Introduction to Political Communication* (London: Routledge, 1995), 5.

Language and Politics

> *And however important to us is the tiny sliver of reality each of us has experienced firsthand, the whole overall "picture" is but a construct of our symbol systems.*
>
> —Kenneth Burke

In chapter 1 we offered a very broad definition of politics and argued for the centrality of human communication as the vehicle for political thought, debate, and action. In this chapter, we further clarify our definition of political communication by providing a theoretical perspective of the role of communication in society and by identifying unique functions and uses of political language.[1]

Communication, Society, and Social Order

At the heart of our perspective of government and politics is the notion of interaction. Interaction is not so much a concept as it is an orientation for viewing human behavior and, ultimately, society. Through interaction, people are continually changing and, consequently, so is society; interaction is a process involving acting, perceiving, interpreting, and acting again. This interaction among individuals gives rise to a reality that is largely symbolic. Thus, it is through symbolic interaction with others that meaning is given to the world and creates the reality toward which individuals act.

Interaction, as a concept, is not limited to spoken and written language; objects also exist in physical forms that are given meaning through social interaction. Depending on our social groups and frames of reference, specific objects may "communicate" success, status, and acceptance. The cars we drive, the watches we wear, and even the pens we use are more than means of transportation, instruments for telling time, and tools of communication. Compare a Mercedes to a Chevy, a Rolex to a Timex, or a Mont

Blanc to a Bic. These and all objects should be viewed as *social* objects; that is, as objects that carry social meaning beyond their pragmatic function. For the peasant, a rake is a gardening tool as well as a weapon of revolution; the transformation from one to the other results from social interaction. Objects take on meaning for individuals as they interact with others. Interaction is the very fabric of society. Societies, therefore, consist of individuals in a constant and steady state of interaction. When we interact, we influence the behavior of each other. Behavior, then, is created by interaction rather than simply being a result of interaction.

Individuals, of course, interact within larger networks of other individuals and groups. Although many of society's networks are far removed from individuals, the impact of such networks may be considerable. For example, not every member of our society is a member of a church or subscribes to a specific religious denomination, but congregations and evangelicals played a major role in the presidential elections of 2000 and 2004. Such social networks—formal or informal, social or political—provide a framework within which social action takes place. The networks, therefore, are not determinants of action. This is to say, they do not *cause* an individual to act in a particular way, rather, they help shape or guide the action of individuals within the networks. We can even view the structural aspects of society, such as social roles or class, as setting conditions for behavior and interaction rather than as causing specific behavior or interaction.

Edward Sapir argued that the structure of a culture's language determines the behavior and habits of thinking in the culture:

> Human beings do not live in the objective world alone, nor alone in the world of social activity as ordinarily understood, but are very much at the mercy of the particular language which has become the medium of expression for their society. . . . The fact of the matter is that the "real world" is to a large extent unconsciously built up on the language habits of the group.[2]

Similarly, Jacob Mey, believes language always reflects the "conditions of the community at large":

> Among these conditions are institutions that society, that is, the social humans, have created for themselves: the legislative, the executive, the judiciary, and other organs of the state; the various religious bodies such as faiths and churches; human social institutions such as marriage, the family, the market and so on. In all such institutions and bodies, certain human agreements and customs have become legalized, and this legalization has found its symbolic representation in language.[3]

Even if one were to minimize the impact of language that Sapir and Mey suggest, there is no doubt but that human interaction is at the core of human existence. It gives meaning to the self, to symbols and languages, to social networks and societies, to worldviews, and to social objects.

Symbols

It is impossible to talk of human interaction without addressing the symbolic nature of human beings. We carry on distinctively human behavior and interaction through the medium of symbols and their attached meanings. What distinguishes humans from lower animals is our ability to function in a symbolic environment. Humans alone can create, manipulate, and use symbols to control their own behavior as well as the behavior of others. Yes, all animals communicate; however, humans are uniquely symbolic.

George Herbert Mead defined symbols in terms of meaning. A system of symbols provides the "means whereby individuals can indicate to one another what their responses to objects will be and hence what the meaning of objects are."[4] The human, as a cognitive creature, functions in a context of shared meanings communicated through language (which is itself a group of shared meanings or symbols). Symbols, however, are more than a part of a language system. Joel Charon defines a symbol as "any object, mode of conduct, or word toward which we act as if it were something else. Whatever the symbol stands for constitutes its meanings."[5] This definition has important implications for individual action as well as for the nature of society. Consider the flag of the United States, for example. We use the word—flag—to describe it; the word "flag" itself is a symbol for the actual object. Yet the flag is itself—the actual object—a symbol that imparts numerous meanings: patriotism, freedom, and so forth.

We believe that nearly all human interaction is symbolic. Human action in all its forms represents something more than what we immediately perceive about that action. Actions have a deeper meaning since symbols form the very basis of our overt behavior. Human action is the by-product of the stimulus of symbols. Before we formulate a response to any situation, that situation must be defined and interpreted in order to ensure that our response is appropriate. Meanings for symbols derive from interaction in specific social contexts. New interaction experiences may result in new symbols or new meanings for old symbols that may, consequently, change one's understanding or perception of the world. Our view of the world changes as our symbol system is modified through interaction; this process suggests that our reality consists of symbolic systems.

Social Reality

Simply stated, our understanding of reality becomes a social product arising from interaction or communication. Reality for each of us, therefore, is limited, specific, and circumscribed. Of course, we sometimes use communication to extend or limit "realities." That is, through communication we often seek to share our perception of the world with others. However, to discover our own reality or that of someone else, we must first learn the symbol system and then learn the shared meanings of the symbols. We arrive at mutual understanding and subsequent action through communication or interaction. This construction of reality is an active process; it involves recognition, definition, interpretation, action, and validation through interaction. Communication becomes the vehicle for the creation of society, culture, rules, regulations, behavior, and so on. From such a chain of actions grows a complex and constantly changing matrix of individual and societal expectations.

The capacity to learn culture (or the process of socialization) enables us to understand one another and at the same time creates behavioral expectations. Consequently, we are in a continual state of orienting our behavior to that of others.

Society

The symbolic perspective recognizes the dynamic, changing nature of society. Individuals are constantly interacting, developing, and shaping society. One way to view society is as individuals in interaction, individuals acting in relation to each other, individuals engaging in cooperative action, and individuals communicating with self and others. We exist in action, and consequently we must be viewed in terms of action.

This *interactivist* orientation rejects the notion that human society is simply an expression of preestablished rules of individual or group interaction. New situations are constantly arising, requiring modification or reinforcement of existing rules of society. Previously determined joint actions were the products of the backgrounds and experiences of participants who bring unique "worlds of objects," "'sets of meanings," and "schemes of interpretation." In this way, all joint action is "new," although it may result from interaction influenced by a familiar pattern of action. For Kenneth Burke, language is *action*, and our language choices shape our views of the world and thus our response to social phenomena in coordination with others:

> "Action" by all means. But in a complex world, there are many kinds of action. Action requires programs—programs require vocabulary. To act wisely, in concert, we must use many words. If we use the wrong words, words that divide up the field inadequately, we obey false cues. We must name the friendly or unfriendly functions and relationships in such a way that we are able to do something about them. . . . the names embody attitudes; and implicit in the attitudes there are the cues of behavior.[6]

Simply put, the way in which we describe our world—how we use words to name people, actions, events, and so on—provides cues for ourselves and others for appropriate behavior. For example, we call the flag of the United States *sacred*, and some argue for a constitutional amendment to formally protect it from *desecration*.

Bound up with this notion of words as action is the idea that self-control (how we use our free will) is inseparable from social control. The interrelationship between social control and self-control is the result of commitment to various groups that produce a self-fulfillment, self-expression, and self-identity. Social control is not, therefore, a matter of formal government agencies, laws, rules, and regulations. Rather, it is a direct result of citizens identifying and internalizing the values of a group so that the values become essential to their own self-esteem, which in turn motivates them to act to support the social order. Adherence to the rules of society becomes a fair price to pay for membership in the society.

In some sense, then, we grow into and agree to use a common system of symbols that define who we are individually and as a society. For Don Faules and Dennis Alexander, regulation is the "symbolic processes that induce change or maintain stability in self and others."[7] Of course, language provides the major framework dictating ways of thinking and seeing society. Language and symbols regulate behavior in numerous ways, for example by creating expectations, producing negative bias, or by allowing a norm or value to supersede other symbols. Symbols also create social sanctions (e.g., war as God's will) and function as master symbols (e.g., to die for freedom).

Generating Political Support

The sections above present an abstract view of how we communicate, both as individuals and as a society. When considering politics in this abstract view, it becomes necessary to link the functions and characteristics of government to the symbol using nature of society. Mass support for any individual, institution, or system of government is not automatic; instead it is a long, continual, and active process. The greatest task confronting any government is to generate enough support for governmental authority and action to meet the needs of all segments of society. Richard Rose identifies three criteria that gauge the impact of governmental actions on the fabric of society.[8] The first criterion is the scope of a government activity: how many individuals of the population are affected by the action? The second criterion is the intensity of the impact of the government's action: how much importance does the general public attach to the action? The third criterion is the frequency of impact of governmental decisions: how often or how long are individuals affected by governmental policy or action? These criteria gauge the magnitude of influence of government over society.

In order to act for us, the government must possess a certain level of legitimacy. David Easton defines political legitimacy as "the conviction on the part of [a citizen] that is right and proper for him to accept and obey the authorities and to abide by the requirements of the regime."[9] Legitimacy, according to Easton, is a two-way proposition. It is desirable for citizens because it sustains political order and stability and consequently minimizes stressful changes and surprises. On the other hand, a sense of legitimacy is advantageous for authorities because it becomes the most significant device for regulating the flow of diffuse support.

According to David Green:

> Language is the most powerful of human weapons. Armed force may keep
> people in a state of unwilling subjection for years, even for generations.
> Only through language, however, can human understanding itself be
> manipulated and people brought to cooperate in their own subjugation.[10]

Another way of considering this is to think about how humans voluntarily
allow themselves to be controlled by the ideas at the center of their government. The public both *authorizes* and *allows* its government to exercise
power on its behalf. Of this process of authorization, Lloyd Bitzer writes:

> A public is a community of persons who share conceptions, principles,
> interests, and values, and who are significantly interdependent. This com-
> munity may be characterized further by institutions such as offices, schools,
> laws, tribunals; by a duration sufficient to the development of these institu-
> tions; by a commitment to the well-being of members; and by a power of
> authorization through which some truths and values are accredited.[11]

In this sense, then, public knowledge, "may be regarded as a fund of truths,
principles, and values which could only characterize a public," and the public
who holds this knowledge in common "is made competent to accredit new
truth and value and to authorize decision and action."[12]

Political Settings

From Green's perspective, the history of language is also the history of
politics: "Politics is a process of conflict resolution, conflict creation, and conflict management; and political language at once reflects and contributes to
these processes."[13] Naturally, language and policy are closely related as well.
Of course, it is through the use of language that all of this comes about—specifically, language used in political settings. A political setting, as defined by
Murray Edelman, is "whatever is background and remains over a period of
time, limiting perception and responses."[14] For him, "it is more than land,
buildings, and physical props. It includes any assumptions about basic causation or motivation that are generally accepted."[15] The setting, then, creates
the perspective from which mass audiences will analyze a situation, define
their response, and establish the emotional context of the act that enfolds.
Political actors must carefully assess the situation, calculate the appropriate
action, and identify the proper roles to assume. Settings, therefore, condition
political acts. Take the flag desecration example mentioned above. Since the
late 1980s there have been recurrent calls for an amendment to the Constitution to ban flag desecration, such as burning of the flag as a form of political
protest. The political setting, as of this writing, involves the United States
actively engaged in a War on Terror. Thus any calls for passing or not passing
an amendment prohibiting flag desecration must be seen within this setting.

Implicit in the discussion is the need for governments to create appropriate political settings that legitimize a set of values. The assumption is that

control over the behavior of others is primarily achieved by influencing the definition of the situation. In a democracy, the secret is to act in such a way that an image of the actor or the scene is created that stimulates others to act as desired. Thus, political actors, by having us voluntarily agreeing that one set of values is better than another and that their definition of the situation (setting) is correct will have us behave in a certain way. For instance, does our society condone order or anarchy as a value? Applied to traffic control, we see a definition of the situation drawing upon the shared value of order—stop on red; go on green; pass on the left; and so on. The overwhelming majority agree with this definition, thus shaping behavior—we act (drive) in a certain way.

Getting others to share one's reality is the first step toward getting others to act in a prescribed manner, and this task is best achieved by creating or defining reality for others. Furthermore, the use of potent symbols, rituals, and myths is useful in creating commonalities in the midst of national diversity. Dan Nimmo succinctly describes the interrelationship of these:

> By inducing people to respond in certain ways, to play specific roles toward government, and to change their thoughts, feelings, and expectations, significant political symbols facilitate the formation of public opinion. As significant symbols of political talk, the words, pictures, and acts of political communicators are tip-offs to people that they can expect fellow citizens to respond to symbols in certain anticipated ways.[16]

The entire process, however, yields more than desired behavior. Soon, the process becomes a commitment and total belief in the institutions and system of government. However, as Green recognizes, "because politics is an ongoing struggle for power, the competition to define political terms is constantly being renewed."[17] In short, according to Peter Hall, "power, the control of others, is accomplished by getting others to accept your view and perspective. This is achieved by controlling, influencing, and sustaining *your* definition of the situation since, if you can get others to share your reality, you can get them to act in the manner you prescribe."[18]

Political Symbols

We have already argued that humans live in a symbolic environment. Our "significant symbols" arise through the process of social interaction. A significant symbol, defined by Mead, is one that leads to the same response in another person that it calls forth in the thinker.[19] Thus, significant symbols are those with a shared, common meaning. Consequently, a political vocabulary of significant symbols that provides common understandings among individuals may evolve; these symbols are socially constructed, and become common references that facilitate interaction among people so they can solve the problems of the group life. In short, political communication is, at its best, the manipulation and understanding of political symbols. We now turn to discuss several distinct groupings of those symbols.

There are three ways an individual can respond or relate to a significant symbol. First, there is a content or informational dimension. The content dimension is rather easy to pinpoint and define. Facts are rather readily recognizable but are susceptible to manipulation. Second, there is an affective or emotional dimension to a symbol. Such responses are less predictable and result from years of cultural socialization. Politically, the trick is to use symbols where the affective responses are rather predictable. Third, there is an evaluative dimension reflecting the importance of the symbol. Each of these dimensions is defined through interaction and hence becomes a rather potent motivator for action.

There are a large number of significant political symbols in society. In the discussion that follows, we wish to emphasize the dynamic, evolving, and emerging nature of political symbols. Not all political symbols resonate with equal weight, however, and researchers in this area have put forth several ways of assigning value to different groupings of symbols. For instance, Roger Cobb and Charles Elder provide a hierarchical typology of political symbols that is most useful.[20] They identify four types of stimulus objects as the universe of political symbols. At the top of the hierarchy are *symbols of the political community* comprising its core values: "Old Glory," democracy, equality, liberty, and justice fall within this category. Next are *symbols of the political regime,* or those relating to political norms of the society. These include such concepts such as due process, equal opportunity, or free enterprise. Third in the typology are *symbols associated with formal political roles and institutions* such as the President, Congress, or FBI. The last type, *situational symbols,* is comprised of three components. These components include: governmental authorities (President, Vice President, mayors, etc.), nongovernmental authorities (Brian Williams, Jesse Jackson, Heritage Foundation, etc.), and the political issues (deficit, health care, drilling in ANWR, etc.). Those symbols high in the typology are the most abstract and general, whereas those in the lower divisions are more specific in nature. Abstract political symbols are more encompassing, applicable, salient, and less temporally specific.

The point of the above is that all politicians use abstract symbols, especially during campaigns. Although we can certainly pigeonhole the different symbols, audience response to the symbols is not as clear-cut; there is no stimulus-response as in a science. From this perspective, those hearing them used in a speech or reading them in a newspaper often interpret the meaning of political symbols. Thus, classification of a symbol without the appreciation of the social construction and interaction aspects of symbol making is limited in utility. On the informational level, the same information may be gleaned from the more specific symbols but is certainly debatable for those higher in the typology. The affective nature of all the symbol types depends upon the rather unique experiences, culture, and socialization of an individual or group. The same is true for the evaluative level.

How do political symbols work? It is through their abstract semantic hollowness that symbols become so powerful. Although political symbols function as objects of common identification, they simultaneously allow for idiosyncratic meanings to be attached. Two individuals may disfavor abortion but do so based upon differing—religious or constitutional—arguments. The same individuals may disagree about abortion for rape victims but clearly support congressional or presidential action disavowing the practice of abortion. Political symbols are powerful, not because of the broad commonalities of shared meaning, but because of the intense sentiments created and attached to them resulting in the perception that the symbols are vital to the system. As elements of the political culture, political symbols serve as stimuli for political action. They serve as a link between mass political behavior and individual political behavior.

There are aspects unique to symbols that endow them with power whether political or not. Myth, ritual, and ideology are three such symbolic forms. They are especially valuable in arousing public action.

Myth. Joseph Campbell provides an insightful way thinking of myths: "myths are public dreams, dreams are private myths." Myths bridge the old and the new; they are composed of images from the past that help us cope with and understand the present. Myths function to reduce the complexity of the world, identifying causes that are simple and remedies that are apparent. "In place of a complicated empirical world," Edelman observes, "men hold to relatively few, simple, archetypal myths, of which the conspiratorial enemy and omnicompetent hero-savior are the central ones."[21] Think of Thesseus slaying the Minotaur; or of Luke Skywalker's struggle with Darth Vader. Janice Hocker Rushing and Tom Frentz write:

> All myths are narratives, but not all narratives are myths. If you say to me, "today I got up at 6:30, brushed my teeth, took a shower, ate breakfast, read the paper, and came to school," that's a brief narration of your first few hours. But that's not a myth. See, myths are long-enduring stories, often anonymously created, that dramatize a culture's deepest beliefs and dilemmas. They tell of origins and destinies, are filled with heroes and villains, and educate the young into the society's values.[22]

We take the time to discuss myth because virtually all of our political behavior lies within the realm of myth. For example, James Barber argues that myth is the essence of human politics:

> The pulse of politics is a mythic pulse. Political life shares in the national mythology, grows in the wider culture, draws its strength from the human passion for discovering, in our short span of life on this peripheral planet, the drama of human significance. Ours is a story-making civilization; we are a race of incorrigible narrators. The hunger to transform experience into meaning through story spurs the political imagination.[23]

Politics, then, draws upon a multitude of images that are constructed over time and comprised of various values, prejudices, facts, and fiction—in short, upon myths.

Nimmo and Combs provide four views of or orientations to social myths.[24] Each view shares insight into the social construction of myths. The *common sense* view of myths perceives them as simple distorted beliefs based more on emotion than fact. They are dangerous, therefore, because of their falsification of truth. The *timeless truth* view of myths, in contrast, argues that what is important is the fact that people believe the myths. Thus, the issue of accuracy is not important. Myths must be dealt with as true because they are believed to be true by the general public. The *hidden meanings* view of myths is a compromise of the other two. Here, all myths are believed to contain some element of truth or of moral principle. Consequently, all myths are grounded in truth. Finally, the *symbolic* view of myths defines myths as "collective representations" of society's beliefs, values, ideologies, cultures, and doctrines. Myths symbolize codes of approved beliefs, values, and behavior and thus function to legitimize authority. Each of these approaches to myths emphasizes the dynamic and utility aspects of myths. They are constructed through social interpretations of the past and become predictions of the future.

We prefer the definition of myths given by Nimmo and Combs for discussing political communication. This definition views myths as credible, dramatic, socially constructed representations of perceived realities that individuals accept as permanent, fixed knowledge of reality while forgetting (if they were even aware of it) their tentative, imaginative, created, and perhaps fictional qualities.[25] This definition acknowledges the dramatic nature of myths.

There are several different types of political myths.[26] *Master myths* are national in scope and encompass the collective consciousness of a society. These are usually utopian in nature. One such prevailing myth in the United States is the myth of the American dream. We believe that if we work hard, there is no limit to our capacity for success. Such a myth serves to motivate individuals and reinforce societal values.

Another prevalent form of political myth in the United States is myths of *us and them*. These myths focus on social structures or collectivities. Specific groups, movements, and governmental institutions encourage this type of myth development in order to generate credibility, to enlist support, and to sustain existence. *American democracy* and *free enterprise* are examples of myths that reduce the complexity of our systems of government and economy to rather abstract notions. We all know that our government is a form of democracy and our economy is a variation of free enterprise. Nevertheless, the myths serve to legitimize the governmental institutions.

Myths are *definitional* as well. In addition to defining what is preferred, good, and proper, myths can also define what is bad, unjust, and evil. The notions of communism and socialism are fraught with criticism in the United States, even though most of Europe has been more socialist than democratic for many years. In their defining role, myths sanction and reinforce societal values. For example, consider how President Bush linked the War on Terrorism to our myths about totalitarianism in World War II: the president stated that like "the ideology of communism, Islamic radicalism is elitist, led by a self-appointed vanguard that presumes to speak for the Muslim masses." Drawing from American public knowledge about the cold war, the president continued with the comparisons: "Like the ideology of communism, our new enemy pursues totalitarian aims."[27]

We achieve the uplifting of the individual through *heroic myths*. Humans need heroes for motivation and emulation. To state that George Washington, our founding father, never told a lie not only adds esteem for the individual but also espouses the virtue of honesty for the citizenry. Benjamin Franklin's ideals of prudence and imagination filter down to us as ideals ripe for emulation. For many Americans, particularly Southerners, Robert E. Lee and Stonewall Jackson fulfill this function, as do many other famous—mythic—Americans.

Finally, an ever-increasing category of political myths are *pseudo-myths*. They are myths in the making. Most politicians, especially during elections, are attempting to be perceived as the "heroic underdog," the "common man," or the "new maverick." The messages created and disseminated by the candidate are designed to reinforce desired images. The mass media, discussed in chapters to follow, plays an important role in the development of pseudo-myths. Consider, for instance, the 2000 presidential campaign of George W. Bush who spoke of "compassionate conservatism," a "brand" of conservatism that is more accommodating, less judgmental while still maintaining core principles.

Within the realm of politics, myths serve several useful purposes. First, and perhaps the most obvious, myths increase public comprehension and understanding of rather complex notions, theories, or structures. Second, myths unite a society and create common bonds among the populace. Myths can reinforce and articulate common elements within a diversity of social mores. The careful construction of political myths can prescribe proper and legitimate public beliefs, attitudes, values, and behavior. Third, political myths offer unique identities for the citizens; they provide the link between the individual and the polity. Although broad in nature, myths become personalized and the views or morals expressed become internalized. Finally, myths are persuasive. Myths can legitimize, stimulate, and motivate behavior; they can sustain commitments to a specific polity.

Political myths are, in summary, socially conceived, created, permeated, and structured entities. Because they are real, political myths are credible and pragmatic; because they are socially constructed, political myths are dramatic, involving a story, actors, and morals.

Ritual.   In many ways, ritual functions in the same manner as myth. Edelman defines ritual as "a motor activity that involves its participants symbolically in a common enterprise, calling their attention to their relatedness and joint interests in a compelling way."[28] Ritual is the bridge between the individual and society. It functions as a leveler, providing instant commonality. By allowing one to become a part of a larger entity, ritual promotes conformity in a rather satisfying way. Just as myths unite people, so do rituals for they act to evoke and reinforce a certain value, belief, attitude, or desired behavior.

Bruce Gronbeck views presidential inaugurals as rituals and "moments of cultural transmission."[29] Inaugurals link past and present in the symbolic acts of remembrance, legitimization, and celebration. Ronald Reagan's first inaugural especially followed this pattern. Although 1981 was not a time for great celebration, Reagan held out hope for future prosperity. He recognized Jimmy Carter's help in transition of power, a direct appeal to legitimization. He talked of being confirmed by the people and asked for God's help. In terms of remembrance, Reagan went from the difficulties of the recent past to the heroes of the more distant past, invoking the names of Washington, Jefferson, Lincoln, and Kennedy. According to Lawrence Rosenfield, these types of epideictic (ceremonial) speeches recognize "virtue, goodness, [and] the quality inherent in object or deed."[30] Thus, when someone give a speech praising a courageous deed, that speech does not necessarily praise the person who acted courageously but instead praises the *quality* of courage that "makes a claim on men's respect for all time."[31] Michael Carter writes that epideictic rhetoric functions as ritual.[32] He argues that when used properly, epideictic "ritual achieves meaning and function that is beyond the potential or ordinary, pragmatic behavior and language."[33] Thus, these types of epideictic speeches serve to maintain and carry on our cultural identity. Carter, for example, argues that epideictic rhetoric "does not attempt to change beliefs but to strengthen the beliefs that already form a bond among the participants."[34] In this manner, epideictic rhetoric can "bring order and meaning to an otherwise chaotic and meaningless series of events."[35]

Ideology.   The original Greek meaning was "the science of ideas." Craig Smith defines ideology as "a set of socially shared preferences about the nature of life, built on shared values and priorities, shared authorities, and/ or shared derivations. Whatever a community collectively believes or imagines is its ideology."[36] From this perspective, ideology is more than a set of political norms. Rather, it is linked to an individual's perception of political reality. Ideologies are socially constructed and are in a continual process of definition and interpretation. Ideology is a symbolic belief system that functions to turn listeners into believers and believers into actors. For the individual, internalizing an ideology requires a continual assessment of political acts based upon norms or values that become a permanent motivation for political action.

Bernard Brock and colleagues posit that "ideology provides the structures of understanding that unite disparate citizens in effective political action."[37] In fact, they argue that political ideology is inherent in the very definition of democracy: "Any theory of democratic governance consistent with the definition that stresses the rule of the people will include an appeal to the consistency of beliefs, values, and assumptions that constitute the political culture. This consistency emerges with a stable ideology."[38]

Ideology possesses several useful functions in democratic action.[39] First, it provides a consensus in the definition of a situation. Within a couple of days after the events of 9/11, our leaders portrayed the assault as a "sneak attack" on our nation by terrorists. Second, ideology provides legitimacy. It endorses the proper response, in this case, the "War on Terrorism." It also provides the moralization of action—not just an appropriate response, but a just and moral response. An ideology helps citizens identify with a national project and with the leaders. Finally, it situates events appropriately in our history.

The United States, however, is generally characterized as being less ideological than most nations. Our political system focuses on specific issues and personalities rather than on political parties and abstract ideologies. Brock and his colleagues lament that the terms *liberal* and *conservative* actually mean very little. As used today,

> they are devoid of historical content and offer little to predict how one group or the other will respond to changing circumstances. This lack of coherence, context, and predictability has a debilitating effect on political decision-making. It produces a political discourse that distances citizens from engaging with one another, and it prevents the vibrant debates and discussions essential for a democratic process.[40]

Historically, political parties were formed to create clusters of individuals who shared a specific perspective on the fundamental issues of governance. Today, Brock and his colleagues argue, few candidates, especially those running below the presidency, regularly associate with a political label as the primary means of presenting their candidacy. Politicians target voting groups— the retired, soccer moms, hunters—with promises and sound bites rather than offer an ideology of the role of government in our collective lives.

Ideology, whether from the right or left, is seldom complicated. To accept an ideology, however, implies a commitment toward a specific social reality. On a larger scale, the commitment toward an ideology links one to a community of believers who largely share the same interpretation of the world. Thus, such a commonality of viewing reality provides a strong rationale for specific societal behavior or action.

Michael Calvin McGee uses the concept of *ideographs* to help us understand how the abstract nature of ideology is brought down to the concrete level of our daily lives. Following the work of Richard Weaver, McGee argues that ideographs are the link between the political rhetoric we use daily and our larger ideology. According to McGee, ideographs are:

> one-term sums of an orientation, the species of "God" or "Ultimate" term that will be used to symbolize the line of argument the meanest sort of individual *would* pursue . . . as a defense of a personal stake in and commitment to the society. The important fact about ideographs is that

they exist in real discourse, functioning clearly and evidently as agents of political consciousness. They come to be as a part of the real lives of the people whose motives they articulate.[41]

Examples of ideographs found in political discourse are: "equality," "freedom," "freedom of speech," "law and order," "liberty," "national security," "privacy," "private property," and "rule of law."

McGee identifies several important characteristics of ideographs, and we discuss three of them below.

 ● *"An ideograph is an ordinary language term found in political discourse."*[42] According to Ronald Lee:

> ideographs are not technical terms, words used by experts or privileged insiders; they are terms that appear regularly in ordinary public talk. These are words that you will encounter on the news, hear on talk radio programs, find in the texts of political speeches, encounter in grade school classrooms, and use in everyday conversation.[43]

● *"It is a high-order abstraction representing collective commitment to a particular but equivocal and ill-defined normative goal."*[44]   This means that ideographs are ambiguous in exact meaning but do carry an enormous psychological impact. As Lee states:

> For instance, the words "liberty," "freedom," and "equality" are emotionally evocative, but they have little cognitive meaning unless tied to specific situations. They are general enough in their meaning that they may be used in a wide variety of contexts. The ideograph "liberty" might be employed by either side in the abortion debate or it might be evoked by either side in the controversy over the meaning of separation of church and state.[45]

● *"It warrants the use of power, excuses behavior and belief which might otherwise be perceived as eccentric or antisocial, and guides behavior and belief into channels easily recognized as acceptable and laudable. Ideographs such as 'slavery' and 'tyranny,' however, may guide behavior and belief negatively by branding unacceptable behavior."*[46]   Following McGee, Lee states that the

> essential function of an ideograph is to warrant the exercise of power. Taking or not taking action is justified in the name of ideographs. Some ideographs are positive ("liberty," "freedom," "equality") and behaviors that can be justified by positive ideographs are regarded as socially acceptable. Some ideographs are negative ("tyranny," "socialism," "censorship") and behaviors that further these values are branded as unacceptable.[47]

It is important also to note that ideographs do not always carry an ideological meaning, for instance "free" or "freedom," as in the sentence, "I'm free tonight, so let's go see a movie." Ideographs are especially important for understanding the relationship between leaders and citizens. They are the storehouse of words and phrases from which leaders select appeals to warrant exercises of power. These are the terms that are used when leaders claim to be acting in the name of "the people." For example, consider these words of President Bush, with ideographs in quotations:

> America's commitment to "individual freedom" and "democracy" provides the foundation for our society. As a Nation, we cherish the values of "free speech," "equal justice," and "religious tolerance," and we steadfastly oppose the forces of "cruelty," "injustice," and "tyranny." Since the founding of our country, the Bill of Rights has served to guide our people and our Government to ensure basic "human rights" and "liberties." The United States is a country where all citizens have the opportunity to voice their opinions, practice their "faith" and enjoy the blessings of "freedom."[48]

Myth, ritual, and ideology represent aspects of the unique nature of political symbols. First, political reality is socially constructed and created through the use of political symbols. There is a participant dimension to political discourse. Second, political symbols are pragmatic in nature. No matter how abstract the idea or concept, the evoking of political symbols affects behavior. Political discourse is persuasive and pervasive and influences beliefs, attitudes, and values. Finally, political discourse is dramatic. This means that nearly all political discourse seeks to construct a certain reality. Of course, there is usually a great deal of competition in constructing realities.

Political Language

Sharon Jarvis makes four assumptions about the nature of politics and political language or discourse.[49] First, as we have already noted, citizens come to know politics through discourse or interaction. Second, citizen discourse about politics is led, but not fully determined by, the discourse of the "elite" (certain politicians, pundits, religious or social leaders). Such discourse contains clues for understanding and behaving. Third, labels function as powerful shortcuts in modern life and have important psychological effects on citizens. Finally, the meanings of political terms indeed will shift from time to time and may become broader, narrower, or change entirely.

Socialization depends on language and is key to the process of creating legitimacy. Language, as the means of passing cultural and political values within or between generations of people, provides a group or individual a means of identification with a specific culture, values, or political entity. As people assess their environment, language is created, and it can structure, transform, or destroy the environment. Words are the molds for concepts and thoughts and become symbols reflecting beliefs and values. Thus, the creation of language, or symbol systems, is required before societies and political cultures can develop. Language serves so many invaluable functions: as the agent of social integration; as the means of cultural socialization; as the vehicle for social interaction; as the channel for the transmission of values and ideology; and as the glue that bonds people, ideas, and society together.

Language, therefore, is a very active and creative process that does not reflect an objective reality but creates a reality by organizing meaningful perceptions abstracted from a complex world. Language becomes a mediating force that actively shapes one's interpretation of the environment. According to Claus Mueller:

> Metaphorically, language and the words embedded in it are posed between the individual and his environment and serve as an invisible filter. The individual attains a certain degree of understanding through the classification made possible by concepts that screen and structure perception.[50]

We feel it is obvious, then, that political consciousness is dependent upon language, for language can determine the way in which people relate to their environment. At the very least, language should be viewed as the medium for the generation and perpetuation of politically significant symbols, the very symbols discussed earlier. Thus, political consciousness results from a largely symbolic interpretation of sociopolitical experience. To control, manipulate, or structure the interpretation is a primary goal of politics in general. A successful politician will use, intentionally or not, rather specific linguistic devices that reinforce popular beliefs, attitudes, and values. Politically manipulated language can promote and reinforce the existing political regime or order.

By way of summary, it is clear that what makes language political is not its particular vocabulary or linguistic form, but the substance of the information the language conveys, the setting in which the interaction occurs, and the explicit or implicit functions the language performs. As Doris Graber observes, "When political actors, in and out of government communicate about political matters, for political purposes, they are using political language."[51] Political language, then, is about power, social relationships, morals and ethics, identity, to name only a few items. But, as Paul Corcoran warns, "while language shapes and empowers its users, the unhappy consequence is that language reproduces and reinforces exploitation, inequality, and other traditions of power."[52] Leaders win and lose; the public is empowered or enslaved, informed or misled by the *strategic* use of language. In fact, Corcoran argues:

> *All* language is political because every speech setting, however private and intimate, involves power relations, social roles, privileges, and contested meanings. It is not simply *difficult* to separate out the intermingling of politics and language. Rather, one *cannot* distinguish between politics and language because they do not occupy separate spheres of existence that merely "overlap." In a much stronger sense, language articulates and confirms all the things that we call political: the weak and strong, the valued and the rejected, the desired and the undesirable, "us" and "them."[53]

Just consider the policy implications of whether you consider "abortion" a "medical procedure" or "murder"; whether "affirmative action" is a program ensuring "equal opportunity" or "governmental discrimination"; or whether the terrorist acts on 9/11 should be viewed as criminal acts or acts of war. As Edelman reminds us:

> The potency of political language does not stem from its descriptions of a "real" world but rather from its reconstructions of the past and its evocation of unobservables in the present and of potentialities in the future, language usage is strategic.[54]

It is also important to understand that politics as talk does not imply politics is all talk and no action. Politics as talk *is* action, in very important, although sometimes very subtle, ways. To win the public debate in defining abortion as murder is the first step toward legislative action. Moreover, the very way we discuss these issues also suggests how we understand our political world. In 1962, Richard Weaver argued that analysis of language is key to understanding political ideology. Interestingly, through his analysis, Weaver found that conservatives tend to argue from definition and liberals from circumstances.[55] Weaver believed that the types of arguments a person uses can be used to make a connection between the person and his or her worldview. This is true because how a person argues is in part determined by how that person classifies reality. In short, Weaver argued that when a person uses a particular argument, that person is actually *asking listeners to agree with a particular view of reality.*

Weaver identified four main arguments; he ranked the first three in descending order according to their ethical worth. We will examine these arguments, using a national conversation on the subject of illegal immigration and what to do about it. In the examples below, we look at how various opponents and supporters of illegal immigration have argued:

1. Definition. *"One way to interpret a subject is to define its nature—to describe the fixed features of its being. Definition is an attempt to capture essence. When we speak of the nature of a thing, we speak of something we expect to persist. Definitions accordingly deal with fundamental and unchanging properties."*[56] For Weaver, this is the most ethical form of argument. People using this line of argument embrace idealism; they are committed to the idea that things have a nature. Knowledge is held at level of universals. U.S. Representative Roscoe Bartlett uses this form of argument in the comments that follow: "Illegal means illegal. We cannot reward illegal behavior and preserve respect for the Rule of Law in our country," said Bartlett. "Illegal aliens are criminals. That is why I oppose amnesty for illegal immigrants."[57]

2. Similitude. *"We say that it is like something which we know in fuller detail, or that it is unlike that thing in important respects. From such a comparison conclusions regarding the subject itself can be drawn. This is a very common form of argument, by which probabilities can be established."*[58] Next in line for ethical worth, using this line of argument suggests a person slightly less confident about his or her ability to fully know the truth about something. It implics an inability to reveal a thing's core essence. For instance, U.S. Senator John Cornyn stated:

> If I show up at a convenience store and buy something, I can present my debit card or Visa or Master Card. In a matter of seconds, the clerk can swipe the card and it can authorize that purchase using modern technology. Why can we not use something similar—maybe with a few more bells and whistles—to allow employers to determine whether a person they want to hire is in fact eligible to work?[59]

3. Cause and effect.   Interpretation of experience in causal relationships. *"The process of interpretation is then to affirm it as the cause of some effect or as the effect of some cause. And the attitudes of those who are listening will be affected according to whether or not they agree with our cause-and-effect analysis."*[60] Argument from circumstance is a type of cause-and-effect argument. Third in the ethical hierarchy, cause and effect reasoning—often called argument from circumstances—focuses on the realm of becoming. That is to say, things are in flux to those using this form of argument. Often pragmatic, this line of reasoning asks audiences to accept a lower order of reality. When dealing with circumstances, using this line of argument suggests a surrender of the power of reason, that in the present circumstance, reason is powerless. This is the "Devil made me do it" line of argument. Consider the words of Philadelphia Police Commissioner Sylvester Johnson as an example of cause and effect reasoning:

> The primary reason to refrain from making local enforcement of immigration law mandatory is that it undermines the basic function of local police. As officers, we must engender trust within the communities we serve. A significant portion of that population includes both documented and undocumented persons. Crime does not discriminate. Requiring immigration enforcement by local Departments will create distrust among persons from foreign lands living in the United States.[61]

4. Authority and testimony.   Evidence is accepted not directly, but *"on the credit of testimony or authority. If we are not in position to see or examine, but can procure the deposition of someone who is, then deposition may become the substance of our argument."*[62] U.S. Senator Jon Kyl uses argument from authority when he relies on a study originating from the University of Arizona:

> Aside from uncompensated health-care costs, communities are also required to bear the costs of arresting, prosecuting, and jailing illegal immigrants who commit other crimes. According to a study by the University of Arizona, those costs amounted to as much as $125 million per year—and that was just in the 28 southwestern border counties in Arizona, California, New Mexico, and Texas.[63]

Arguments by authority must be judged differently than the first three since it is only as good as the credibility of the original source.

Summary

We have certainly drawn a rather large circle. We began with a consideration of symbols and human language. Through language we construct the reality that influences our beliefs, attitudes, and values leading to behavior. Through interaction with others, we come to know who we are and how we fit in and our social roles. Language structures our world. Indeed, our understanding of social reality is a product arising from a constant and steady state of interaction—with self, with others, and in groups. In political settings, we use symbols to evoke feelings, create a sense of community and shared values as well as serve as stimuli for political action. Cultural myths, rituals, and ideology are powerful symbolic forms in arousing public action. Language that is "political" is the means for passing along cultural and political values to future generations and provides identification with a specific culture or political entity. We learn that talk is political action and argument is getting others to agree with a particular view of reality.

Notes

[1] Some material for this chapter appears in "The Advocate and the Management of Symbols" in *Persuasion and Influence in American Life, Fifth Edition* by Gary C. Woodward and Robert E. Denton, Jr. (Long Grove, IL: Waveland Press, 2004), 51–82.

[2] In Sharon Jarvis, *The Talk of the Party* (Lanham, MD: Rowman and Littlefield, 2005), 21.

[3] J. Mey, *Pragmatics: An Introduction* (Oxford: Blackwell, 2001), 115–116.

[4] George H. Mead, *Mind, Self, and Society* (Chicago: University of Chicago Press, 1972), 122.

[5] Joel Charon, *Symbolic Interactionism* (Englewood Cliffs, NJ: Prentice-Hall, 1979), 40.

[6] In Bernard Brock et al. *Making Sense of Political Ideology* (Latham, MD: Rowman & Littlefield, 2005), 46.

[7] Don F. Faules and Dennis C. Alexander, *Communication and Social Behavior* (Boston: Addison-Wesley, 1979), 130.

[8] Richard Rose, *People in Politics* (New York: Basic Books, 1970), 196–197.

[9] David Easton, *A Systems Analysis of Political Life* (New York: John Wiley and Sons, 1965), 279.

[10] David Green, *Shaping Political Consciousness* (Ithaca, NY: Cornell University Press, 1987), ix.

[11] Lloyd F. Bitzer, "Rhetoric and Public Knowledge," *Rhetoric, Philosophy, and Literature: An Exploration*, ed. Don M. Burks (West Lafayette, IN: Purdue University Press, 1978), 68.

[12] Ibid., 68.

[13] Green, *Shaping Political Consciousness*, 7.

[14] Murray Edelman, *The Symbolic Uses of Politics* (Urbana: University of Illinois Press, 1964), 102–103.

[15] Ibid., 103.

[16] Dan Nimmo, *Political Communication and Public Opinion in America* (Palo Alto, CA: Goodyear, 1978), 69.

[17] Green, *Shaping Political Consciousness*, 3.

[18] Ibid., 15.

[19] Mead, 122.

[20] Roger Cobb and Charles Elder, "Individual Orientations in the Study of Political Symbolism," *Social Science Quarterly* 53: 82–86.

[21] Edelman, *The Symbolic Use of* Politics, 16.

[22] Janice Hocker Rushing and Thomas S. Frentz, "The Mythic Perspective," in *The Art of Rhetorical Criticism*, ed. Jim A. Kuypers (Boston: Pearson, Allyn & Bacon, 2005).

[23] James David Barber, *The Pulse of Politics* (New York: Norton, 1980), 20.

[24] Dan Nimmo and James Combs, *Subliminal Politics* (Englewood Cliffs, NJ: Spectrum Books, 1980), 9–13.

[25] Ibid., 16.

[26] Ibid., 26–27.

[27] George W. Bush, "President Commemorates Veterans Day, Discusses War on Terror" (Office of the Press Secretary, November 11, 2005). Retrieved 11 September 2007 from http://www.whitehouse.gov/news/releases/2005/11/20051111-1.html

[28] Edelman, *The Symbolic Use of Politics*, 16.

[29] Bruce Gronbeck, "Ronald Reagan's Enactment of the Presidency in His 1981 Inaugural Address," in *Form, Genre and the Study of Political Discourse*, ed. Herbert Simons and Aron Aghazarion (Columbia, SC: University of South Carolina Press, 1986), 226–245.

[30] Lawrence W. Rosenfield, "The Practical Celebration of Epideictic," *Rhetoric in Transitio.* Ed. Eugene E. White. (University Park: Penn State University Press, 1980) 135.

[31] Ibid., 135.

[32] Michael F. Carter, "The Ritual Functions of Epideictic Rhetoric: The Case of Socrates' Funeral Oration." *Rhetorica* 9.3 (1991): 209–232.

[33] Ibid., 212.

[34] Ibid., 226.

[35] Ibid., 223.

[36] Craig Allen Smith, *Political Communication* (San Diego: Harcourt Brace Jovanovich, 1990), 29.

[37] Brock et al., *Making Sense of Political Ideology*, 37.

[38] Ibid., 51.

[39] Ibid., 60–63.

[40] Ibid., 2.

[41] Michael Calvin McGee, "The 'Ideograph': A Link between Rhetoric and Ideology," *Quarterly Journal of Speech* 66 (1980): 7. Here McGee makes reference to the work of Richard M. Weaver and his work on Ultimate Terms and their relationship with the Tyrannizing Image of a culture. See, Richard M. Weaver, *The Ethics of Rhetoric* (Chicago: Henry Regnery Company, 1953).

[42] McGee, "The Ideograph," 15.

[43] Ronald Lee, "Ideographic Criticism," in Jim A. Kuypers, ed., *The Art of Rhetorical Criticism*, (Boston, MA: Allyn & Bacon, 2005), 317.

[44] McGee, "The Ideograph," 15.

[45] Lee, "Ideographic Criticism," 317.

[46] McGee, "The Ideograph," 15.

[47] Lee, "Ideographic Criticism," 317. Angle brackets in original changed to quotation marks.

[48] George W. Bush, "Human Rights Day, Bill of Rights Day, and Human Rights Week, 2002" (Office of the Press Secretary, December 9, 2002). Retrieved 9 September 2007 from http://www.whitehouse.gov/news/releases/2002/12/20021209-10.html

[49] Jarvis, *The Talk of the Party*, 42.

[50] Claus Mueller, *The Politics of Communication* (New York: Oxford University Press, 1973), 16.

[51] Doris Graber, "Political languages" in *Handbook of Political Communication*, ed. Dan Nimmo and Keith Sanders (Beverly Hills, CA: Sage, 1981), 196.

[52] Paul Corcoran, "Language and Politics" in *New Directions in Political Communication*, ed. David Swanson and Dan Nimmo (Newbury Park, CA: Sage, 1990), 53.

[53] Ibid., 53.

[54] Murray Edelman, *Constructing the Political Spectacle* (Chicago: University of Chicago Press, 1988), 108.

[55] Brock et al., *Making Sense of Political Ideology*, vii.

[56] Richard M. Weaver, "Language Is Sermonic," in *Dimensions of Rhetorical Scholarship*, ed. Roger E. Nebergall (Norman: Department of Speech, University of Oklahoma, 1963), 53.

[57] Roscoe Bartlett, "Congressman Roscoe Bartlett Announces That He Will Oppose Any Immigration Bill That Includes Amnesty for Illegal Aliens" (May 26, 2006). Retrieved 11 September 2007 from http://bartlett.house.gov/News/DocumentSingle.aspx?DocumentID=44408

[58] Weaver, "Language Is Sermonic," 53.

[59] John Cornyn, "The Comprehensive Enforcement And Immigration Reform Act Of 2005" (July 26, 2005). http://www.cornyn.senate.gov/index.asp?f=record&rid=236985&gid=5

[60] Weaver, "Language Is Sermonic," 53.

[61] United States Senate Committee on the Judiciary, "Testimony of Philadelphia Police Commissioner Sylvester M. Johnson United States Senate Judiciary Committee" (July 5, 2006). Retrieved 11 September 2007 from http://judiciary.senate.gov/testimony.cfm?id=1983&wit_id=5494

[62] Weaver, "Language Is Sermonic," 54.

[63] John Kyl, "Border & Immigration Issues." Retrieved 11 September 2007 from http://kyl.senate.gov/legis_center/border.cfm

Functions, Styles, and Strategy
The Uses of Political Language

> *Political language—and with variations this is true of all political parties, from Conservatives to Anarchists—is designed to make lies sound truthful and murder respectable, and to give an appearance of solidity to pure wind.*
> —George Orwell, "Politics and the English Language"

In chapter 2, we discussed very specific characteristics of political language. That theoretical overview was necessary to better understand and appreciate the intricate nature of political communication. To further enhance one's understanding of the nature of political language, one should also be familiar with the functions and uses of political language, which is the subject of this chapter. Specifically, we discuss the functions of political and governmental language, the styles of governmental language, and the strategic uses of political language.

Functions of Political Language

In 1981, Doris Graber identified five pragmatic functions of political language: (1) information dissemination, (2) agenda setting, (3) interpretation and linkage, (4) reflecting on the past and projecting the future, and (5) action stimulation.[1] Although our understanding of each function has changed during the intervening years, the basic functions have remained the same. It is useful here briefly to discuss each of these functions, although they will be discussed in greater detail in other chapters.

Information Dissemination

The most obvious way political information reaches the public is through the sharing of explicit information about the state of the polity,

43

which is vital to the public's understanding and support of the political system. This type of information sharing occurs especially in democratic nations where the public expects open access to the instruments and decision making of government officials. The public, if sensitized to uses of language, also can obtain information by what is not stated, how something is stated, or when something is stated. Oftentimes, especially in messages between nations, the public must read between the lines of official statements to ascertain proper meanings and significance. Such inferences are useful in gauging security, flexibility, and sincerity. Sometimes the connotations communicate more truth than the words themselves. Are our relations with Communist China, for instance, "open," "guarded," or "friendly?" There are times, especially in tragedy, that the very act of speaking by an official can communicate support, sympathy, or strength. Thus, the act of speaking rather than the words spoken conveys the meaning of the rhetorical event.

Agenda Setting

The agenda-setting function of political language primarily occurs in two ways. First, before "something" can become an issue, some prominent politician must articulate a problem and hence bring the issue to public attention. The issue can be rather obvious (terrorism), in need of highlighting (status of American public education), or created (the Mexican border fence). A major way political language establishes the national agenda is through its control of information disseminated to the public. Within this realm, there is always a great deal of competition, and there are only a limited number of issues that can maintain public attention. Although certain self-serving topics are favored by a person, party, faction, or group, the same topics may be perceived as meaningless or even harmful by others. Presidential "State of the Union" addresses are very direct attempts by presidents not only to portray their assessment of the social and economic health of the nation but also to set the legislative goals and agendas for the impending legislative session.

While President Nixon attempted to put limits on discussions and public attention with regard to the Watergate break-ins and tapes, rival groups wanted public debates and revelations to continue. During the Carter administration, rival politicians maintained pressure on the president to resolve the Iranian hostage situation. His failure to end the ordeal led to his sound defeat in 1980. During Ronald Reagan's final years in office, the Democratic Congress attempted to discredit his administration by probing into the "Iran-Contra scandal." Investigations and public hearings of the charges of exchanging arms for hostages dominated public attention and restricted Reagan's domestic and foreign policy initiatives for over a year. George Bush Sr. was successful in justifying the Gulf War, not on the basis of economic interests, but as a need to teach the "Hitler-like" dictator, Saddam Hussein, a lesson and to help our allies in Saudi Arabia. However, he lost the pending election because of his failure to convince Americans of his domestic policy concerns. Early in his first administration, Bill Clinton wanted to reform our health-care system but failed in his attempt to persuade Americans that the system was in a state of "crisis." George W. Bush enjoyed widespread bipartisan support in his handling of 9/11 and the initial stages of the war in Iraq. By his second term, however, Bush's popularity reached historic lows. Opposition voices charged the United States entered the Iraq conflict under false pretenses, and from the most radical elements there were even calls for both the immediate withdrawal of American forces and Bush's impeachment.

Interpretation and Linkage

The very act of calling the public's attention to a certain issue defines, interprets, and manipulates the public's perception of that issue. Links are established between particular beliefs and candidates or between original goals and specific outcomes. Control over the definitions of a situation is essential in creating and preserving political realities. Participants in election primaries, for example, all proclaim victory regardless of the number of votes received. The person receiving the most votes becomes the "front runner." The second-place winner becomes "the underdog" candidate in an "uphill battle." The third-place candidate becomes a "credible" candidate, an alternative for those "frustrated" or "dissatisfied" with the "same old party favorites." Political language defines and interprets reality, creating a rationale for future collective action.

Past and Future

A great deal of political rhetoric and language deals with reflecting on the past and predicting the future. Candidates evoke past memories and associations to stimulate a sense of security, better times, and romantic longings. They present an idealized future under their leadership and predict great success if their policies are followed. Some predictions and projections achieve formal status in the form of party platforms or major addresses at inaugurals or state of the unions. Nearly all such statements involve promises—promises of a brighter future if followed or Armageddon if rejected.

No president since Dwight Eisenhower was more successful in projecting a positive future and glorious past than was Ronald Reagan. The positive themes of the Reagan presidency were heroism, faith, and patriotism. He welcomed heroes, espoused faith in God and country, and surrounded himself with icons of American myth and culture. In the reelection of 1984, his ad spots proclaimed, "It's morning again in America," showing a wedding, a family moving into a new home, fertile fields, and employed construction workers. His rhetoric provided a sense of momentum, tradition, and historical significance. The characters of his stories were both historical and symbolic, reflecting the values of family, freedom, nationalism, and faith, to name only a few. An important function of political language, therefore, is to link us to past glories and reveal the future in order to reduce uncertainty in a world of ever-increasing complexity and doubt.

Interestingly, in the 1996 presidential campaign, Clinton spoke of the future by using the notion of "a bridge to the twenty-first century" in contrast to Dole's portrayal of an America from the past. In his nomination acceptance speech, Dole wanted to be the "bridge to a time of tranquility, faith, and confidence in action." Clinton, in contrast, said he did not want to be a bridge to the past, but "a bridge to the twenty-first century."[2] This single contrast highlighted the difference between the two candidates, in terms of vision, youth, and outlook. When Dole talked about why he was running, he used words like "duty," "honor," "integrity," "trust," "God and country." Though powerful, these are the words of previous generations, certainly not of the current generation of adults who never faced the challenges of a world war or the Great Depression and who want to hear about opportunities for having access to material goods, economic security, health care, and day care. In another example, in 2000, after Bill Clinton lied about his indiscretions, George W. Bush promised to restore dignity and integrity to the White House. Four years later, Bush's more positive view of the future and his strength and commitment to traditional core American values prevailed in contrast to John Kerry's more pessimistic visions.

Action Stimulation

Finally, and perhaps most importantly, political language mobilizes society and stimulates social action. Language serves as the stimulus, means, or rationale for social action. Words can evoke, persuade, implore, command, label, praise, and condemn. Political language stimulates public discussion and behavior about the allocation of public resources, authority, and sanctions. In virtually every major presidential address, there is some call to action: to support a piece of legislation, to call your congressional representative about an issue, or to volunteer for some form of public service.

Functions and Styles of Governmental Language

We now turn to a fuller discussion of the uses of political language. In particular we will review two major aspects involved in understanding how political language functions, primarily from the perspective of those representing the government.

The Functions of Governmental Language

Craig A. Smith identifies five functions of governmental language that are both pragmatic and programmatic: to unify, to legitimize, to orient, to resolve conflicts, and to implement policies.[3] The power and effect of this language flows from the established, citizen-accepted authority of the governing body. Thus, whether at the federal, state, county, or local level, the functions of governmental language remain constant.

From a governmental perspective, language generates a sense of inclusion and participation among citizens. Language also legitimizes and confirms in the minds of the public the authority, role, and justification of governmental actions. Related to the agenda-setting function identified above, governmental language explains our national goals, policies, hopes, and desires as well as articulates our needs, problems, and shortcomings. Social conflicts are resolved by issue discussion, explanation, debate, and negotiation. Finally, government implements policy through the creation of legislation and regulatory interpretation. From this perspective, the language of government encompasses elected officials, government agencies, and government employees.

Styles of Governmental Language

Murray Edelman identifies four distinctive governmental language styles used to maintain the political order.[4] They include: hortatory, legal, administrative, and bargaining styles. Hortatory language is the style most directed toward the mass public. It is employed by individuals and contains the most overt appeals for candidate and policy support. Because of this, the most sacred of national symbols and values are evoked in an attempt to reach the public. The more sacred the symbol or value drawn upon, the greater the likelihood the public will react to its usage. Consider the burning of the flag of the United States as a form of political protest. Although this issue surfaced during the Vietnam era, many today think of the discussion beginning with the Supreme Court case *Texas v. Johnson* (1989). In that 5–4 ruling, the Court upheld Johnson's right to burn the flag as a form of political speech. At first, the "decision touched off an intense and massive uproar across the United States,"[5] and shortly after the movement to add an anti–flag-desecration amendment to the Constitution was begun, with the latest attempt failing by a single vote in the U.S. Senate.

Legal language encompasses laws, constitutions, treaties, statutes, contracts, and so on. It is the specialized language of lawyers, courts, and legislatures. It attempts to be precise but is often ambiguous to the general public. Legal language compels argument and interpretation, oftentimes flowing from the official language of the court to the public language of politics. For instance, consider the 2006 Supreme Court ruling in *Hamdan v. Rumsfeld, et al.* Salim Ahmed Hamdan, a Yemeni national and Osama bin Laden's former chauffeur, had been captured by Afghani forces in 2001 and turned over to the U.S. military, which transported him to Guantanamo Bay. He was scheduled for trial by a military tribunal as an enemy combatant. In June 2006, the Court narrowly ruled that President Bush had not been granted authority by Congress to order trials before a military tribunal for Guantanamo Bay detainees. This *legal* ruling set in motion a flurry of *public* discussions about the decision's meaning and also about what to do in its wake. For example, U.S. Senators Lindsey Graham (R-SC) and Jon Kyl (R-AZ) issued a joint statement regarding the ruling:

> We are disappointed with the Supreme Court's decision. However, we believe the problems cited by the Court can and should be fixed.
>
> It is inappropriate to try terrorists in civilian courts. It threatens our national security and places the safety of jurors in danger. For those reasons and others, we believe terrorists should be tried before military commissions.
>
> In his opinion, Justice Breyer set forth the path to a solution of this problem. He wrote, "Nothing prevents the president from returning to Congress to seek the authority he believes necessary."
>
> We intend to pursue legislation in the Senate granting the Executive Branch the authority to ensure that terrorists can be tried by competent military commissions. Working together, Congress and the administration can draft a fair, suitable, and constitutionally permissible tribunal statute.[6]

Administrative language is certainly related to legal language; it is the language of bureaucrats, of the rules and implementation of laws, and of interpretation of regulations. The style usually encourages public suspicion and ridicule. Interestingly, administrative language, in its attempts to be clear and concise, is often as confusing to the public as legal language is. For example, consider the public discussions concerning the government's use of eminent domain, an act whereby the federal, state, or local government can force property owners to sell their property for public or private use supported by the government. In *Kelo et al. v. City of New London*, the Supreme Court in 2005 seemed to expand the government's authority in this area, setting off a flurry of political, legal, social, and importantly, administrative activity. Take, for instance President Bush's June 2006 "Executive Order: Protecting the Property Rights of the American People." In it the president used *administrative* language to spell out the government's response to the *legal* language of the Supreme Court:

> By the authority vested in me as President by the Constitution and the laws of the United States of America, and to strengthen the rights of the American people against the taking of their private property, it is hereby ordered as follows:
>
> *Section 1. Policy.* It is the policy of the United States to protect the rights of Americans to their private property, including by limiting the taking of private property by the Federal Government to situations in which the taking is for public use, with just compensation, and for the purpose of benefiting the general public and not merely for the purpose of advancing the economic interest of private parties to be given ownership or use of the property taken.[7]

Bargaining language style "offers a deal, not an appeal," and is acknowledged as the real catalyst of policy formation. Yet, public reaction or response politically is avoided. Once a bargain is created, the rationalization of the bargain often assumes the hortatory language style. It attempts to describe or define a "win-win" situation, avoiding the notion of compromise.

It is important to note that these language styles are content-free and are not limited to certain individuals or government agencies. For example, a president must utilize the linguistic devices in the bargaining style to win congressional approval of legislation, in the legal style to draft special legislation, in the administrative style to enforce or provide the mechanics for operationalizing the legislation, and in the hortatory style to gain public support for a measure. Each style responds to and creates a different communication situation and subsequent behavior. In addition, crisis, confidence, patriotism, and action may all be created to achieve the final goal. The basic assumption, as Edelman notes, is that the public "responds to currently conspicuous political symbols; not to 'facts,' and not to moral codes embedded in the character of soul, but to the gestures and speeches that make up the drama of the states."[8] In short, the public finds it easier to look to the talk of political actors, and this talk "pushes" certain political symbols over others. The true facts and moral implications are often overshadowed by the power of the political symbols used.

Strategic Uses of Political Language

We have drawn a rather large circle. We began chapter 2 by discussing the inherent symbolic nature of humans and continued by discussing the role and importance of communication in society. Recall that political symbols are the direct link between individuals and the social order. As elements of a political culture, they function as a stimulus for behavior. The use of appropriate symbols results in getting people to accept certain policies, to support various causes, and to adhere to governmental authority. Political symbols are the means to social ends and are not the ends themselves.

The creation, definition, and acceptance of political symbols is, however, a long process. As emphasized in this chapter, successful leadership and control depend on the successful creation and manipulation of political language and symbols. We perpetuate political symbols in order to preserve the prevailing culture, political beliefs, and values. Political language creates, alters, and maintains the "social state."

It is important to remember that the *context* and the *content* of the interaction are what make the use of language political. The context can range from a local candidate talking at a reception, to speeches in the halls of Congress, to the rally of citizens outside a courthouse, to the president giving a live, nationally televised speech. As for content, recall that in chapter 1 we identified the broad content areas of political communication as dealing with resources, control (authority and power), sanctions (rules and regulations), and social meaning. Context and content do not, however, *determine* what a political actor says. Within any given situation a person has a wide variety of options from which to choose: Which context to emphasize? Which content to include or to exclude?[9] Additionally, an individual has a large choice of strategies from which to choose. Below are among the most common strategic uses of political language:

- **Argumentation and persuasion**. Political language is used to discuss, debate, and negotiate issues and legislation. As already mentioned, political rhetoric is not neutral; it is persuasive, whether altering attitudes, beliefs, and values or reinforcing them. Political language is about advocacy, creating a "symbolic reality" from a particular perspective, for a specific purpose.

- **Identification**. Political language creates commonality, understanding, and unity. Language is a way to relate to others, to build bridges of understanding. Politicians, both verbally and nonverbally, attempt to demonstrate they understand their constituents and share their beliefs, attitudes, and values. According to Kenneth Burke, "you persuade a person only insofar as you can talk the person's language by speech, gesture, tonality, order, image, attitude, identifying your ways with this person's."[10] The importance of language as it relates to nationalism can be viewed in light of the debate over English as our "standard" language. A "homogeneous linguistic community" is argued in terms of shared values. Tapping social identity is another important use of political language. Language links us as a social class or ethnicity or cultural heritage and appeals to an audience based on socialization and common experiences. In this sense, then, language can provides a rallying point for issues and commonality of efforts.

- **Reinforcement**. The process of persuasion (the altering of beliefs, attitudes, and values) is a very difficult process. Most political communication is designed to reinforce existing beliefs and attitudes—to reinforce public preferences. Politicians target key constituent groups by reflecting or mirroring their beliefs, attitudes, and values. They "reinforce" group convictions and hence loyalty or support. Much of presidential discourse is about reinforcing our national goals and values. Although political discourse can be used to change public attitudes the dominant strategic use of political language is reinforcement.

- **Inoculation**. This is a message strategy that promotes resistance to attitude change. By strengthening existing attitudes, individuals become less susceptible to subsequent persuasive attempts. In its simplest sense, an inoculation occurs when a political actor introduces the audience to a weakened form of the opposition's argument and then refutes that argument in its weakened form. What is intriguing about this strategy is that when persuaders acknowledge counterarguments or introduce negative information related to their own position, audiences are not only more likely to believe the rhetor, but also will be less likely to process or believe counterarguments or alternate information in the future. This is most useful in political campaigns, especially in generating resistance to the influence of political attacks by opponents. For this reason, many political pundits opined that it would have been better for then presidential candidate George W. Bush to have acknowledged earlier in the campaign his previous drinking problems, especially the "Driving Under the Influence" conviction that was revealed just days before the 2000 election. Some suggest that the "DUI" revelation not only cost a majority of the vote but nearly cost him the election as well. Note that inoculation is not about altering attitudes but is about reinforcing (or tolerating) existing attitudes.

- **Polarization**. Political language can create likenesses and commonalities as well as distinguish or separate people, issues, and ideas. Interestingly, sometimes the best way to define an issue or position is by detailing what it is not—in short, by contrasting the concept with its opposite. Ronald Reagan, for example, was good at articulating American values of freedom and free enterprise by comparing the United States with Russia. Of course, a more direct mode of polarization is simply labeling the opposition, issue, ideology, and so forth, as "bad." Although polarization may divide, it also unites in the sense that it helps clarify positions, actions, and even aspects of ideology. As noted in the chapter 1, some argue that today the United States is the most polarized in its history. For some political observers, the harshness of political campaigns, the "we versus they" perspective on most issues, and the "all or none" strategy of winning at all costs have all contributed to a polarized nation.

- **Defining**. As mentioned earlier, campaigns are often contests to determine the winning definitions of social reality. As Chaim Perelman states, every "time an idea can be defined in more than one way, 'to define' comes to mean to make a choice, which could be admissible without discussion only if its consequences were negligible for the processes of reasoning."[11] Is the economy strong or weak? Is the crime rate high or low? Are our values strong or slipping? Is the opponent liberal or conservative? In essence, whose view of reality are voters going to believe? Edward Schiappa argues that all definitions are political because "definitions always serve particular interests" and "the only definitions of consequence are those that have been empowered through persuasion or coercion."[12] Naturally, not all definitions are equally important. Some may involve matters of life and death while others are more trivial. He also thinks all language is persuasive. "Just as definitions are persuasive in the sense that they encourage people to use word X in a particular way and understand what X is, so, too, do all descriptions prescribe a view of the way some part of reality is."[13] Naming and describing, from his perspective, are "acts of entitlement."

Through such linguistic practices, we give our experiences meaning and make sense of reality. By entitling a given phenomenon, we locate that phenomenon in a set of beliefs about the world that includes beliefs about existence-status (what things are real or not) and essence-status (what qualities we may reliably predicate about the phenomenon). Because the range of possible entitlements is theoretically infinite, any given act of entitling should be seen as a persuasive act that encourages language users to understand that-which-is-entitled in particular ways rather than others.[14]

Successfully defining issues or policies so that they resonate with the voting public (i.e., reinforce existing beliefs) is the goal of this strategy.

- **Labeling.** Similar to the strategic use of defining, labeling is effective because it renders judgment by making positive or negative associations. For example, how we act toward and perceive an individual differs greatly if we are told the person is inquisitive or nosey, cool or frigid, reflective or moody, thorough or picky, forgetful or senile. Labels tell us what is important about an object and what to expect; socialization prescribes how we should act or interact with the object defined. Labeling also forces us to make judgments and evaluations, which causes the potential for abuse. During World War II, for instance, it was easier to justify killing a "gook" or a "jap" than a person. Are our soldiers in Iraq shooting at "terrorists" or "insurgents"? Upon reviewing survey and experimental research, Sharon Jarvis identifies four aspects of how political labels help citizens make sense of politics.[15] First, because labels are broadly understood, most citizens can provide some definition or characteristics associated with labels, such as "liberal or conservative." Second, labels enhance citizen decision making. Party labels, for example, provide the sole rationale for candidate selection for many regardless of the political race. Third, labels impact citizen impressions and views of individuals. Once again, the labels "liberal" or "conservative" stimulate rather clear sets of perceptions of attitudes and behaviors of the candidates so labeled. Finally and somewhat related, labels are distinct and citizens identify specific set of views, positions, and actions that separate opposite labels such as democrat/republican or liberal/conservative.

- **Expression**. This represents more than the instrumental functions of political language. Virtually all political symbols, rituals, and language are expressive in nature. Political language allows for the expression of frustration as well as specific policy ideas, of hopes as well as fears, and of successes as well as failures. As the functions of political language identified above illustrate, much of political language is expressive rather than programmatic. It is also important to recognize the expressive function of political language as entertainment in American popular culture. Novels, films, television, and popular journalism all contain messages about issues, politics, and society. Chapter 16 explores this growing area of interest and importance.

- **Preserve or gain power.** Postmodern social science literature views political communication in terms of power, domination, or control; that is, some group or elite exploits, controls or distorts language in order to preserve or gain power. However, as we argued in chapter 1, we view political language as the attempt to get others to share the same worldview about what is good or bad, right or wrong, just or unjust. Kenneth Hacker identifies three dimensions of power.[16] The first dimension of power is conflict over concrete political interests revealed in policy preferences. In this case, language is objective and descriptive. The second dimension of power is control over how issues are defined, debated, and acted upon. Language is critical in framing issues, defining concepts, and so forth. The final dimension of power is control over agendas and decision making. Language here is more utilitarian once again. Power in language is exhibited in many ways: arguments grounded in language that legitimizes rule of those who govern, appeals to moral authority, or narratives of preferred behavior, to name a few. It is also important to recognize that *how* something is said gives language power as much as *what* is said.

- **Create drama**. Most political events are dramatic. For some scholars, politics is living drama and worthy of study. For Hugh Duncan, "failure to understand the power of dramatic form in communication means failure in seizing and controlling power over men."[17] It is important to remember that social dramas are not only symbolic screens or metaphors but also social reality derived from social interaction and integration. For example, to focus on dramas of authority one should ask: Under what condition is the act being presented? What kind of act is it? What roles are the actors assuming? What forms of authority are being communicated? What means of communication are used? What symbols of authority are evoked? How are social functions staged? How are social functions communicated? How are the messages received? What are the responses to authority messages? The drama can involve one person or many, a symbolic (rhetorical) event or physical act, one moment or a specific period of time.

All of these elements demonstrate the strategic uses of language in politics. Our position is that public views on issues must be mobilized. Issues are identified and then presented to the public in symbols that appeal to past allegiances or to future goals. Neither issues nor specific positions on issues exist in a vacuum. Connecting policies to the attitudes and values of the public insures that they will receive full consideration. Political office and legislation are the result of using appropriate symbols to create political followings and mass support.

For Kenneth Burke, politics is a study of drama composed of many acts.[18] He suggests that we view political action as a drama on a stage. *Act* is the pivotal concept. We can investigate *scenes* that encompass and surround the act, for the scene provides the context for an act. Next, we should consider the *agents* involved in an act—the actors who mold, shape, create, and sustain movements. Likewise, consideration of the *agency* (the channels of communication in an act) helps reveal the impact of rhetorical activities. In short, how was the act performed? Finally, consideration of *purpose* of an act aids in discovering meaning of the act.

Drama is part of the communication process whenever public issues and views are created, shared, and given life. Ernest and Nancy Bormann used the concept of "group fantasy themes" to analyze this process.[19] A relatively small number of people may attach significance to some term or concept such as the notions of justice, freedom, or the American dream. These "fantasies" are shared and passed on to others, and are often contained in messages that channel through the mass media to the general public. When the theme of the fantasy (called "fantasy theme") has "chained through the general public," there emerges a "rhetorical vision," which is a "symbolic reality created by a number of fantasy types and it provides a coherent view of some public problem or issue."[20] Slogans or labels that address a cluster of meanings, motives, or emotional responses usually indicate the emergence of a rhetorical vision. There are several useful implications to the notion of fantasy themes. As a result of creating and sharing fantasies, there is a greater sense of community, cohesiveness, and shared culture. There are, then, common beliefs, attitudes, and values upon which to live and act, and communication is the foundation of it all.

Today, many scholars note that political campaigns are presented as dramas complete with winners, losers, good-guys and villains. The medium of television, in particular tends to reduce abstract or ideological principles to human, personal components. Television is a very "personalistic" medium. With television, the presenter dominates. It is a medium for actors and animate objects. Entertainment values encourage "tabloid journalism," which has become the mainstay of news today.

> The tabloid reporting style is designed to heighten readers and viewers' sensory experience with the news. The details of stories are presented in graphic form. Tabloid news is written in dramatic, engaging, and readable prose presented in short paragraphs and set off with attention-grabbling headlines and visual accompaniments. TV tabloids feature quick cuts between plots and subplots, highlighting conflict and crisis.[21]

As former anchor and journalist for ABC News, David Brinkley acknowledges, "the one function that TV news performs very well is that when there is no news we give it to you with the same emphasis as if there were news."[22] Personalized mediums link political issues and actions are to individuals. We are essentially presented choices between political actors rather than choices about policies. Victims, villains, and heroes are easier to identify and address than complex issues, causes, or ideas.

Summary

In this chapter, we covered the functions and styles of governmental language, followed by an overview of the strategic uses of political language. We have come to understand how language can be used to control us, confuse us, and hide information from us and to unite us. To communicate effectively and to understand the communication of others we must analyze the words they've chosen, the context and content of their presentation, the symbolism used in constructing the message. Language is powerful; almost all communication is political and influences our worldviews and political attitudes.

Notes

[1] Doris Graber, "Political Languages," in *Handbook of Political Communication*, ed. Dan Nimmo and Keith Sanders (Beverly Hills, CA: Sage, 1981), 195–224.

[2] Marion Just, "Candidate Strategies and the Media Campaign," in *The Election of 1996*, ed. Gerald Pomper (Chatham, NJ: Chatham House, 1996), 87.

[3] Craig Allen Smith, *Political Communication* (San Diego: Harcourt Brace Jovanovich, 1990), 61–62.

[4] Murray Edelman, *The Symbolic Uses of Politics* (Urbana: University of Illinois Press, 1964), 133–48. Robert Hariman also identifies four main styles of political discourse used to maintain power: the realist style, the courtly style, the republican style, and the bureaucratic style. See Robert Hariman, *Political Style: The Artistry of Power* (Chicago: University of Chicago Press, 1995).

[5] Robert Justin Goldstein, "Speech: Flag-burning; An Overview," First Amendment Center (June 28, 2006). Retrieved 11 September 2007 from http://www.firstamendmentcenter.org/Speech/flagburning/overview.aspx

[6] "Senators Graham, Kyl Statement on Hamdan Ruling," Senator Graham Press Release (June 29, 2006). Retrieved 11 September 2007 from http://lgraham.senate.gov/index.cfm?mode=presspage&id=258047

[7] George W. Bush, "Executive Order: Protecting the Property Rights of the American People" (Office of the Press Secretary, June 23, 2006). Retrieved 11 September 2007 from http://www.whitehouse.gov/news/releases/2006/06/20060623-10.html

[8] Edelman, *The Symbolic Uses of Politics*, 172.

[9] Richard E. Vatz discusses this in "The Myth of the Rhetorical Situation," *Philosophy and Rhetoric* 6 (1973): 154–161.

[10] Kenneth Burke, *A Rhetoric of Motives* (Berkeley: University of California Press, 1969), 55.

[11] Chaim Perelman, *The Realm of Rhetoric* (Notre Dame: University of Notre Dame Press, 1982), 62.

[12] Edward Schiappa, *Defining Reality* (Carbondale: Southern Illinois University Press, 2003), 69.

[13] Ibid., 113.

[14] Ibid., 116.

[15] Sharon Jarvis, *The Talk of the Party* (Lanham, MD: Rowman and Littlefield, 2005), 50–52.

[16] Kenneth Hacker, "Political Linguistic Discourse Analysis," in *The Theory and Practice of Political Communication Research*, ed. Mary Stuckey (Albany: State University of New York Press, 1996), 29.

[17] Hugh Duncan, *Symbols in Society* (New York: Oxford University Press, 1968), 25.

[18] Kenneth Burke, *A Grammar of Motives* (Berkeley, CA: University of California Press, 1967).

[19] Ernest Bormann and Nancy Bormann, *Speech Communication: A Comprehensive Approach* (New York: Harper & Row, 1977), 306–317.

[20] Ibid., 311.

[21] Richard Davis and Diana Owen, *New Media and American Politics* (New York: Oxford University Press, 1998), 96.

[22] Ibid., 260.

Political Socialization and the Formation of Political Attitudes

The meaning of presidential communication is embodied in us, in the roles, values, and purposes through which we attach meaning to the activity.
—David Michael Fyfe

Are you a Democrat or a Republican? Are you a conservative or a liberal? Do you support or oppose the death penalty? Do you support or oppose abortion on demand? Do you support or oppose additional forms of gun control and registration? We suspect by this time in your life, you are able to answer these and numerous related questions rather quickly. But can you express *why* you are a Democrat or a Republican, a conservative or a liberal, a supporter or a nonsupporter of the policies mentioned above? This chapter focuses on the sources and process of how we form our political beliefs, attitudes, and values. We also investigate how we make political decisions, such as whether or not to vote; if so, for whom; and do we even think our vote or participation makes a difference.

We reported in chapter 1 that over the last decade or so, more than half of all Americans have expressed concerns that our nation is heading in the wrong direction, that those holding state and national public office are not genuinely concerned about the average citizen, and that most politicians are neither honest nor trustworthy. We continue to experience declines in citizen voting and a rise in public cynicism. Why? Although there is no simple answer, there are clues in our social and political environment and also seeds planted years ago through our political socialization process.

The Political Socialization Process

The process of learning about politics and our political system is generally referred to as "political socialization." Although specific definitions differ, Roberta Sigel defines it as "the process by which people learn to adopt the norms, values, attitudes, and behaviors accepted and practiced by the ongoing system."[1] Similarly, James Gimpel, Celeste Lay, and Jason Schuknecht define political socialization as "the process by which new generations are induced into political culture, learning the knowledge, values, and attitudes that contribute to support of the political system."[2] The content of what is transmitted is important if the goal of *perpetuation of values consistent with the governance of the nation* is to be met. Successful transmission of values will lead to practices and actions that, if successful, will enhance political participation, knowledge and support for our democratic processes. The bulk of this transmission occurs early in life; as research demonstrates, what is learned during childhood correlates with adult political behavior and opinions.

Jarol Manheim's definition of political socialization is somewhat more dynamic, viewing it as a lifelong process that gives rise to individual attitudes that impact political and electoral behavior:

> It is through the process of political socialization that an individual acquires the values and beliefs of the political culture (as well as other politically relevant values and beliefs), that he continually learns to interpret or to reinterpret his personal encounters with political reality, and, in fact, that he even learns to define what constitutes political reality to begin with.[3]

So political socialization is a lifelong process of learning and developing social and political attitudes. In addition to the learning and developing dimensions, there is a third important dimension to the concept: our interaction with others. According to Michael Carpini, viewed in this light,

> Political socialization is a continuing process influenced by ongoing interactions with family and friends, the workplace, and significant personal and societal events, as well as through life cycle changes that affect one's contact with and relationship to the political and social world.[4]

Thus, the general goal of political socialization is citizen education resulting in support of the political system or regime. This is accomplished through social interaction.

The process starts early. Initial research from the 1950s and 1960s showed a very linear and hierarchical process of the transmission of political values and behavior to youths in the United States. Kindergarten students are generally able to identify key political figures such as current and past presidents and may well identify with a specific political party. David Easton and Jack Dennis identified four psychological processes or stages of children's development of political attitudes and beliefs. The first stage is "politicization" where children become aware of authority figures and institutions beyond their parents, relatives, or teachers. They recognize power as reflected in laws and government. The second stage, personalization, is when children begin to link "political authority" to specific individuals rather than in terms of governmental institutions. They distinguish among the various representatives of government such as police officer, governor, congressman, and president. With the linkage to individuals, children gain respect for these figures, liking and admiring specific leaders such as George Washington, Robert E. Lee, or Martin Luther King, Jr. The third stage is idealization, when children view those with political authority as benevolent, trustworthy, helpful, and kind. Finally, the process of institutionalization occurs when children are able to differentiate between local and federal government. They can distinguish between such institutions as Congress and City Hall, the City Police and the Highway Patrol.[5]

Outcomes of Political Socialization

The various definitions of political socialization reveal several important outcomes of the process. *The first is general political knowledge.* We know that learning is an active process. "Individuals actively collect, store, modify, interpret, and incorporate new information with what they already know about the world. This activity proceeds according to their goals, motives, and needs."[6] Essential to every definition of democracy is the need for an informed and knowledgeable citizenry. Information is critical for citizens to make informed judgments and evaluations of elected officials. Incomplete or inaccurate information can lead to bad public decisions. By political knowledge, researchers mean "the capacity of citizens to recall facts about what government is and does." This includes our history, political structures, identities, and roles of officeholders, for example.[7]

Jarol Manheim identifies four models or theories that describe the ways of political learning or the acquisition of our general political knowledge.[8] Each attempts to explain a different way of learning. In reality, of course, our learning is a result of a mixture of all four.

Accumulation theory argues that political learning is an incremental process with the addition of very discrete units of knowledge, information, and beliefs. Our political attitudes are the sum of inputs at any given time. Political attitudes are useful and serve "to summarize an individual's political experience, as well as the lessons drawn from that experience."[9] Thus, when confronted with a choice, whether it is supporting a candidate or an issue position, political attitudes and predispositions guide our evaluation and choice. Political attitudes are anchored in our political experience and guide our choices for years. For example, those who experienced the Great Depression and the New Deal influenced a generation of Americans to have very positive attitudes toward the Democratic Party, and the party reaped decades of support. As citizens, we do not view our political experiences as a whole. Rather, the accumulation of various discussions, events, and experiences happens over time and "constitutes a virtually endless series of discrete encounters between individuals and the associates with whom they share a social space."[10] With accumulation theory there is no set sequence or pattern to the learning of politics, nor is there any systematic connection of the various elements of learning. This theory recognizes the various bits of knowledge that contribute to the cognitive component of political attitudes.

Interpersonal transfer explains the affective judgments and relationships with political figures. Our storehouse of experiences in interpersonal relationships is transferred over to political situations. As an example, when a child comes to recognize the president as an authority figure, the child will make an association between the father as authority figure for the family and the president as the authority figure for the nation. The understanding of the role of father is directly transferred to that of president. The understanding of the presidency comes from the extension of understanding an earlier, nonpolitical role of father.

The *identification model* is similar to the interpersonal transfer, but the learning is more direct. When an individual identifies with someone held in high esteem, he or she then proceeds to imitate that person's attitudes and behaviors as well as to reflect the values of the person. Here, the learning is the direct "transmission" of values from the source to the recipient. In short, it is the ritual of imitation rather than reasoning (or perhaps even understanding) that results in the learning. An obvious example is when a student adopts the beliefs, attitudes, and values of an admired teacher.

According to the *cognitive developmental theory*, we are all limited in our ability to understand political phenomena. The more developed our mental capabilities in dealing with abstractions, the better we are able to understand the subtleties of abstract political concepts such as political ideologies or philosophies. This model highlights the need for critical thinking and evaluation of candidates and social issues. As citizens, we need a set of critical-thinking skills in order to make reasonable judgments and political choices.

Evidence shows a continual decline in the level of political knowledge across the United States, and we know that those who posses the least political knowledge are the least likely to participate in political activities.[11] Sadly, current trends also reveal that even those with satisfactory levels of political knowledge are becoming less likely to influence others in terms of voting working on a campaign or attending political meetings.[12]

A second outcome of political socialization is political efficacy. There are two types of political efficacy. *Internal efficacy* refers to the perception and belief that one has the resources and knowledge to impact or participate in the political process. It is, as Gimpel and colleagues define it, "one's self-confidence regarding involvement in politics."[13] *External efficacy* refers to the perception that government is responsive to citizens' attempts to be heard. Am I heard; can my efforts make a difference? Today, as already noted, we see declines in voting and rising feelings of cynicism. Clearly, the external efficacy seems to be in jeopardy.

A third outcome of successful political socialization is frequency of political discussion. It follows that those who know more about politics are more likely to discuss politics and political issues. Discussion is a way to gain information, clarify points, and influence the thoughts of others. A free marketplace of ideas is vital to the concept of democracy. Diversity of thought and respect for dissent are hallmarks of the values of freedom and justice. When multiple viewpoints are heard and expressed, the "common good" prevails over "private interest." Another value of democracy is a process referred to as collective deliberation on disputes about issues and fundamental values. It is national and public debate that determines the collective wisdom and will of the people. Thus, at the very heart of democracy is public communication. The quality of that public communication directly impacts the quality of our democracy and society at large.

A fourth outcome of successful political socialization involves positive attitudes and support of the system of government. It is important for citizens to respect public officials and trust that justice and fairness will be the hallmarks of the judicial system. Expressions of support for the political system means not only voluntarily obeying laws and supporting policy decisions but also voting and participating in other political activities. In the United States, respect for the political process supersedes winning or losing a particular campaign or vote. We respect the outcome and expect to lobby, campaign, or vote again; we do not turn to lobbing bombs or lopping heads to get our way.

Agents of Political Socialization

An agent of political socialization is "any person, institution, event, or other source from which we take cues as to how we should think or behave with regard to politics."[14] There are four generally agreed upon agents: families, schools, social/peer networks, and media. Without question, the *family* has the greatest amount of influence in the political socialization process, and the most long-lasting influence of the family on children is party affiliation. This allegiance occurs early and tends to remain throughout one's life, short of some significant life event. As important as religion is to Americans, religion as a source of political and social views is considered more of a family characteristic than a separate source of political influence. It is not so much our religious affiliation as the basic principles of faith that guide our behaviors. As already mentioned, at an early age children develop political beliefs about authority, property, and political symbols. By age five and continuing through adolescence, children form and hold specific "orientations" regarding the president and other political leaders, political parties, political institutions, social issues, and ideology.[15] More recent research shows that the transmission of political values to children is strongest in families where the parents are active politically. There is also a correlation between the family's socioeconomic status and religious values as factors influencing children's academic achievements as well as possession of positive political values. Scholars are noting the importance of family structure in the political socialization process, especially in terms of self-efficacy and self-esteem. Children raised in single-parent homes consistently have lower feelings of efficacy than those raised in two-parent households. Children from single-parent homes also develop less confidence in their ability to influence the political system.[16]

Another source of lifelong family influence is one's spouse. Studies tend to show that the longer a couple is together, the more they tend to share common political attitudes, beliefs, and voting patterns. This may not mean that one is influencing, forcing, or even persuading the other, but rather that spouses share common life experiences that shape their political attitudes collectively in the same direction. In fact, the highest levels of couple commonality are found for party identification, vote choice, and religiosity.[17] Thus,

> spouses tend toward like-mindedness because of the selection processes that bring them together in the first place. After marriage, mutual socialization also works to produce commonalities in political outlook over time. Because of this process, in both a relative and an absolute sense, husbands and wives really do begin to look more alike as the marriage ages.[18]

After families, the second greatest amount of influence is through the *schools*. They provide general civic education and rituals such as stating the Pledge of Allegiance that help shape students' attitudes toward government. Of course, individual teachers can exert a great amount of influence, to the chagrin of some parents. Overall, schools are most effective in teaching obedience to authority, the mechanics of our system of government, and the broad responsibilities of citizenship.[19] However, there are differences in political socializations based on the economic and social backgrounds of the students. Those from homes with college-educated parents and from upper socioeconomic backgrounds are more interested in politics, pay more attention to news, perform better on tests of civic knowledge, and have higher levels of electoral participation.[20] In sum, according to Barbara Bardes and Robert Oldendick, "it appears that while the school system may be successful at instilling loyalty and patriotism in children as well as obedience to the law, it has much less impact on the formation of attitudes toward political institutions and processes in this country. The impact of family and the community in which the child is raised may be reinforced by the civics curriculum for children from upper socioeconomic levels, but may have little impact on the political opinions and outlook of children from other backgrounds."[21] Interestingly, most studies find little influence of civic courses on students' political awareness, knowledge, or participation. Where it is successful, students tend to be more successful academically and believe teachers and administrators to be fair and just.[22]

Next in influence are our *social networks* or peer group pressure. Social network members exert a strong influence on key political decisions such as candidate choice, partisan support, and issue opinions. As a result, there is a significant amount of influence outside of the family circle.[23] The role and influence of friends, neighbors, and close associates tends to be one of rein-forcement. We tend to associate with those of similar political beliefs, atti-tudes, values, and socioeconomic and class backgrounds. Thus, our peer and social networks provide information and support of preexisting beliefs and attitudes. Some of our peers take on leadership roles; since the mid-1950s there has been a focus on how social or public leaders act as both filters of mediated content and as sources of interpersonal influence. One explanation, the "two-step flow" process, argues that an individual may play the role of opinion leader—serving as a conduit of information and analysis obtained through the mass media and then sharing an interpretation or opinion with others who accept the judgment and call for action. Historically, studies have revealed the existence of opinion leaders in all social groups and economic levels. They still reflect the same basic values and demographic characteristics of the group but are perceived by group members to have some expertise.[24]

Another major agent of political socialization is the *media*. The medi-ated socialization process also starts early in life, providing the "raw mate-rial" that makes up our political beliefs, attitudes, and values. Much of what is taught to children through interpersonal interactions with family, peers, and teachers originates from the media.[25] It is important to note that both entertainment and public affairs programming continue to shape one's per-ceptions on all types of social issues. The general consensus is that exposure to mass media content impacts three broad aspects of a young person's polit-ical socialization: the cognitive (awareness, knowledge, images of politics), the affective (interest, attitudes toward political leaders and issues, and attachment to the political system), and the behavioral (interpersonal dis-cussion, political participation).[26] In short, the mass media impact *what we think* about politics, *how we feel* about politics, and *what we do* politically. After reviewing studies of the role of the media as part of the socialization process, Carpini concludes:

> The media influence the norms, values, beliefs, attitudes, opinions, and actions that constitute democratic engagement. This impact begins early in life and continues throughout the life cycle; it is mitigated or enhanced by a number of factors, from the type and amount of media attended to, to the content of media messages, to characteristics of view-ers, listeners, and readers. The effects of media are both direct and indi-rect and operate through both affective and rational pathways.[27]

Within the last decade, the notion of the "third person effect," as explained by George Comstock and Erica Scharrer, has emerged as the predominant paradigm for explaining the relationships among the media, individuals, and public opinion. Phillips Davidson introduced the concept in 1983. The "third person effect" refers to the tendency for individuals to claim that while the media don't influence them, the media certainly do influence others. This effect is true whether you are talking about voting, purchasing products, or forming an opinion on a social issue. Regardless of the element or variable under investigation, generally people think others are much more influenced by media than themselves.[28]

Families, schools, social/peer networks, and media are the four agents of political socialization. Except for media, all other agents of political socialization are products of the local social and political environments that most often reinforce the political values of the community. Through interaction, as noted in chapter 2, citizens gain information and seek advice; both activities may well lead to persuasion and shared political experiences and viewpoints. Political influence does develop through patterns of communication among citizens. In terms of interpersonal interaction, with whom and how we discuss politics are influenced by the social characteristics of our community, neighborhood, and larger social networks. Of course, we tend to surround ourselves with those of similar beliefs, attitudes, and values. For instance, Huckfeldt and colleagues found strong evidence of clustering of political preferences generated within communication networks in the 2000 presidential campaign. Over 70 percent of those surveyed and identified as "strong Republican" reported that not a single discussant within their social network supported Al Gore; likewise, nearly 70 percent of those self-identified as "strong Democrat" had no discussant within their social network supporting George W. Bush.[29] Contextual elements such as race, class, income, age, to name a few, also influence our discussion groups. For example, the element of community diversity may well influence the degree of tolerance for others. Party competition may be another element of influence in the political environment. People who are raised in an area or state dominated by a single party may be less motivated to participate and vote, especially if they and their parents favor the minority party. Also, feelings of trust and efficacy for the system may be less when minority voices are not represented in government. Thus, there are numerous elements in our social and political environments that may influence our beliefs and values.

Levels of Interaction

Silvo Lenart investigated three levels of interpersonal political processes: person-to-person, group-to-person, and opinion climate-to-person.[30] The person-to-person level comes from the classic "two-step flow" model of political influence. As mentioned above, opinion leaders are very similar to the individuals they influence in terms of attitudes, beliefs, and values. They tend to belong to the same primary groups such as family, friends, or coworkers. Most of the communication is *homophilic*—based on shared values, similar education and religious background, as well as the same social status. Most studies show this to be the most powerful mode of influence. The role of the media becomes more secondary in terms of influence.[31]

Studies investigating group influence on individuals come primarily from "network analysis" and "social context" research. This perspective views individuals as highly interdependent with others in homogeneous groups where members conform to group goals and identity through peer pressure. The interpersonal relationships provide networks of communication and anchor points for individual beliefs, attitudes, and values. The more cohesive the group is, the higher the level of individual satisfaction and the greater the tendency to influence and to be influenced by others.[32] Through social interaction with group members, individuals learn which attitudes are in agreement and thus have the potential for positive reinforcement and social approval. Once again, the more homogeneous the group is, the greater the effect on individual behavior.

> At the level of referent group influence, the attribute of homogeneity is an important factor that determines the influence direction of referent group discussion on candidate preferences. For very cohesive referent groups such as the family, the direction of the effect should be characterized by reinforcement of prior attitudes; whereas less cohesive referent groups should present influences that to some extent compete with, or at the very least question and thus weaken, prior attitudes.[33]

The mass media are viewed by many to function as an opinion climate. In terms of media, Lenart finds that media and individual discussants are "inherently information source competitors." That is to say, both act as preeminent sources of political information. For example, if one's political conversation with one's family overlaps with media political content, then that conversation will tend to reinforce media effects. Moreover, the more cohesive and homogeneous the group, the more the interactions tend to amplify media influences.[34]

Influential work started to emerge in the 1950s showing the power of opinion climates. Soloman Asche, for example, demonstrates how many people may end up agreeing with what they perceive to be the majority point of view. Through numerous experiments, Asche and colleagues asked individuals to determine which of three lines matched a fourth line in length. The answer was obvious, and all participants but one of those who took part in each multiround test were collaborating with Asche. The collaborators would all agree on the obviously correct line during the first two rounds, but after that would agree that an incorrect line was the correct match. When it came time for the noncollaborator to say which line was the correct match, Asche found that only 2 of 10 would provide the answer they truly thought to be correct. Two of 10 would agree with the majority 2 or 3 times and then revert back to their original thoughts. However, 6 in 10 would continue to agree with the majority, even though the majority was clearly giving the wrong answer.[35]

Along these lines, a powerful explanation of how we relate to the political and social environment is the concept of "the spiral of silence." Prominent German pollster Elisabeth Noelle-Neumann introduced the concept in 1974.[36] It provides insight into why people think the media have such strong influence when, empirically, studies find very minimal direct effects. She posits that we are constantly surveying our social environment for cues about what is popular and what is in disfavor. On issues of political or social importance, we assess and form an impression among various viewpoints that have the most public support. We make such evaluations, according to Noelle-Neumann, because we do not want to be perceived as ill-informed and risk being isolated by others. As a result, if our opinions or viewpoints are not those of the majority view, then we will suppress the expression of our opinion. Rather than confront those of opposing views, we simply tend to keep quiet. Thus,

> the spiral of silence holds that (a) those in the minority will curb the expression of their views, with (b) the result that the impression of public opinion resulting from the tripartite of personal experience—others, events, and media—will be distorted toward an overestimate of support for the majority and an underestimate of support for the minority.[37]

As a way of summary, Comstock and Scharrer reviewed the body of scholarship on political socialization. They provide three propositions:

- Although the mass media are often central in the dissemination of news about what has transpired, their influence on the judgments and opinions of individuals is small.

- Political dispositions are largely rooted in personal experience where socialization by parents, the resulting allegiances to one or another political party and ideological outlook, and the social influence of those with whom one associates play major roles.

- There is a strong tendency to conform to the expectations of others.[38]

Issues of Political Socialization

One issue of particular interest for researchers is the stability of childhood political socialization. Changes occur resulting from "life cycle effects" and "generational effects."[39] The tendency for older citizens to classify themselves as more conservative than younger citizens is an example of "life cycle effects." As we age, we tend to become more socially conscience, less comfortable with change, and more interested in our families' overall well-being. Younger citizens, in contrast, are more focused on their personal well-being, pursuing a career, starting a family, and establishing friendships.[40]

In addition, those born during a certain era tend to demonstrate similar political views and share the same ideology. Those of the depression era tended to be strong Democratic voters. Americans prior to 1930 were more likely to reflect Republican leanings. Baby Boomers, those born in the 1950s are equally split between Democratic, Republican, and Independent affiliations. Interestingly, those who came of age in the turbulent 1960s tend to demonstrate less attachment to political parties primarily as a result of their disagreement with the political system of their youth.[41] Those coming of age during the Reagan era tend to identify more with the Republican Party. Partisanship, once fixed by childhood socialization or a generational event, tends to stay fixed for the rest of our lives.

Compared to most other nations, however, Americans do not think about politics from a strict ideological perspective. In fact, most research on the topic finds that "the proportion of the citizens who exhibit consistent, well-integrated attitudes across a range of policy issues is rather small."[42] Interestingly, since 1972, those who identify themselves at the extreme of the liberal–conservative continuum have remained very stable. Only 2 percent of Americans identify themselves as "extremely liberal" and between 3 and 4 percent identify themselves as "extremely conservative." However, over this same period of time, although the number of self-identified liberals has remained rather constant at around 20 percent, self-identified moderates have decreased from near 40 percent to 30 percent, and self-identified conservatives have increased from upper 30 percent to 45 percent.[43]

nrty identification has seen more nuanced change. There has been a decline in Democratic affiliation, especially since 1966 when nearly half of Americans called themselves Democrats. By the mid 1970s, several changes in the voting behavior of individuals were noted. Party loyalty was increasingly volatile from election to election, and voters were more likely to split their vote between candidates of both major parties. Party labels and loyalties became less dominant as individual candidates became the attraction. As a result, the second phenomena of change was the rise of independents—voters who did not identify with either party. Finally, there were several significant shifts in voting patterns during the last half of the twentieth century. There were realignments among groups moving from one party to another. Perhaps the most notable, according to Comstock and Scharrer, was the South moving from solidly Democratic to virtually Republican. Ronald Reagan receives much credit for this evolution.[44]

As of this writing, about a third of Americans identify with the Democratic Party; Republican Party affiliation has increased from 25 percent in the early 1980s to 33 percent. The big difference, as noted above, is in the increase in the number of people who claim they are independent of either party. Historically, independents stood at about 20 percent. However, over the last decade that percentage has increased to about one-third, equal to that of the other two parties.[45] Here are some other party differences: Democrats have high levels of support from black Americans and Americans of Jewish ancestry and a slight advantage with women; the lower a person's income and education level, the greater the support as well. Conversely, those of higher income and with a college education tend to support Republicans in greater numbers.

Although party affiliation is more volatile now then in decades past, it is still the best predictor of voting behavior. A review of the literature reveals four propositions related to party affiliation and voting:

- The vast majority of voters make up their minds long before a presidential campaign starts in earnest.
- There is a high degree of party loyalty with individuals casting votes for the candidates of the same party repeatedly.
- About 20 percent of voters who profess to deviate from past voting return and vote for the party of historical choice.
- Because of the process of selective perception, most voters only attend to messages favorable to, or supportive of, issue position or candidate. Thus, the role of the media becomes one of reinforcement of existing attitudes and values.[46]

In addition to party affiliation, there are four other major influences on voting behavior revealed in the literature on the psychology of voting.[47] The first are the *pragmatic material interests* of the voter reflected in demographic characteristics such as race, religion, class, age, or sex. This group of theories was developed in the field of economics and is known as the "rational choice" theory of decision making. What is in the best interest of the individual as a consequence of being white or black, evangelical or secular, white collar or blue collar, mid-career or retired, or male or female? Consequences and outcomes of candidate preference are assessed in terms of relative merit and self-interest. Some refer to this as "pocketbook voting."

The second group of explanations of how we decide to vote is based on *personal sympathies or resentments* and focuses on which groups may benefit from or be damaged by the social policies of the candidate. This dimension deals with what tends to be the hot-button issues of the day such as affirmative action, welfare, social security benefits, prescription drug programs, homosexual marriage, and so on. Self-identity impacts development of social and political attitudes. Affiliations with social, religious, cultural, national, or political groups influence attitudes on issues and thus guide political action.

Another influence on one's vote is the basic *political ideology or principles* identified by the candidates and parties. Here the vote is based on strongly held beliefs and values about the role of government in our lives. Voting on principle, for many, is voting based on political ideology and philosophy. One could support immigration and understand the great desire of people who wish to become part of the American Dream but think they should follow established law to do so. Thus, these voters may favor tougher illegal immigration laws and practices as a matter of principle of law.

Finally, *selective exposure* is another powerful motivational force in processing political information. We only attend to information and elements that support our view and provide our rationale or confirm our decision.

These influences vary for any individual, with numerous combinations and strengths possible. Complicating all of this is the very real consideration that we take shortcuts in making most political decisions. We develop mechanisms that assist us and speed up the decision-making process. We tend to broadly categorize or group issues or candidates. In short, we both stereotype and generalize. We label a candidate liberal or conservative, an issue solution as involving too much federal government or the need for even more federal government intervention. Our categories prejudice or influence our decisions. We edit some decisions by ignoring or eliminating certain aspects of the decision. For example, we may simplify our choice of candidates by only voting for familiar candidates or those for whom we have voted in the past. We may follow the "endorsements" or recommendations of trusted friends, respected publications, or special interest groups to make our decision. Even the notion of "electoral viability" or voting for the person we think will win may become our value of judgment.

In terms of political decision making, Comstock and Scharrer conclude,

> socialization, allegiance, and the influence of those with whom one associates would create the framework of values and loyalties, dispositions and preferences, and evaluations and judgments by which pragmatic interests, symbolic gestures, and the adoption of a particular political philosophy translate into specific opinions and votes.[48]

Summary

There are so many variables that we do not really know for certain why a person votes for a particular candidate over another. We do know what influences a voter's behavior, and this begins with political socialization, the life-long process of obtaining political knowledge and developing political beliefs, attitudes, and values. Ultimately, our support of and participation in our system of government are critical outcomes. We also know that parents, peers, schools, life events, and the media are key agents of the socialization process.

Because the demographic composition of our nation has changed so much over the last two decades, Gimpel and colleagues question the validity of the political socialization research of the 1960s and 1970s: "The relationships between the new generation of youth and the primary agents of socialization—parents, schools, media, and peers—have been altered in many important ways."[49] They think the specific social context or the environment in which children are raised greatly influences the political attitudes and values they develop. For them, the social context structures the quantity and flow of information as well as social interaction patterns. The contextual environment impacts how children learn, what opinions they form and how they will express themselves politically. Put another way, the "direct impact of structural environmental factors is mediated through family and school relationships, which are more immediate sources of casual influence on an individual's sense of efficacy, political knowledge, nationalistic sentiment, tolerance of diversity, and other dispositions germane to the political socialization process."[50]

The work of Gimpel, Lay, and Schuknecht find that among the children at most risk for poor socialization and nonparticipation are "blacks, Latinos, the poor and those living in a single-parent household, the children of the foreign-born, women, those with low educational aspirations, those living in noncompetitive or low-turnout political environments, the nonreligious, those who are not attentive to news media, students who avoid or simply are not exposed to discussions of politics, and those who dislike their government-related courses and otherwise doubt that school authorities treat them fairly. For the respondents who possess more than a few of these risk factors, the likelihood of nonparticipation as an adult is exceedingly high."[51]

The current generation will begin to replace the "baby boom" generation in the electorate by about 2010. Gimpel and colleagues predict that the younger generations are likely to carry very different beliefs, attitudes, and values into the electorate, especially on the issues of social security, payroll taxes, and health-care benefits. They found high levels of cynicism present in today's schools, but pessimism about what government can do may also reflect a sign of self-reliance—a spirit that government can't solve all the problems and that individuals must act.[52] This may be a good thing.

Notes

[1] As cited in Barbara Bardes and Robert Oldendick, *Public Opinion: Measuring the American Mind* (Belmont, CA: Wadsworth, 2000), 72.
[2] James Gimpel, Celeste Lay, and Jason Schuknecht, *Cultivating Democracy* (Washington, DC: Brookings Institution Press, 2003), 13.
[3] Jarol Manheim, *The Politics Within* (New York: Longman, 1982), 70.
[4] Michael Carpini, "Mediating Democratic Engagement," in *Handbook of Political Communication Research*, ed. Lynda Lee Kaid (Mahwah, NJ: Lawrence Erlbaum, 2004), 410.
[5] Bardes and Oldendick, *Public Opinion*, 73–74.
[6] Mira Sotirovic and Jack McLeod, "Knowledge as Understanding: The Information Processing Approach to Political Learning," in *Handbook of Political Communication Research*, ed. Lynda Lee Kaid (Mahwah, NJ: Lawrence Erlbaum, 2004), 258.
[7] Gimpel, et al., *Cultivating Democracy*, 14.
[8] Manheim, *The Politics Within*, 71–74.
[9] Robert Huckfeldt, Paul Johnson, and John Sprague, "Individuals, Dyads and Networks," in *The Social Logic of Politics*, ed. Alan Zuckerman (Philadelphia: Temple University Press, 2005), 27.
[10] Ibid, 30.
[11] Gimpel, et al., *Cultivating Democracy*, 14.
[12] Sotirovic and McLeod, "Knowledge as Understanding," 368.
[13] Gimpel, et al., *Cultivating Democracy*, 25.
[14] Manheim, *The Politics Within*, 74.
[15] Carpini, "Mediating Democratic Engagement," 408.
[16] Gimpel, et al., *Cultivating Democracy*, 37.
[17] Huckfeldt, et al., "Individuals, Dyads, and Networks," 66.
[18] Ibid, 70.
[19] Bardes and Oldendick, *Public Opinion*, 80.
[20] Ibid, 77–80.
[21] Ibid, 80.
[22] Gimpel, et al., *Cultivating Democracy*, 37–38.

[23] Huckfeldt, et al., "Individuals, Dyads, and Networks," 132.

[24] George Comstock and Erica Scharrer, *The Psychology of Media and Politics* (Boston: Elsevier Academic Press, 2005), 29.

[25] Carpini, "Mediating Democratic Engagement," 408.

[26] Sotirovic and McLeod, "Knowledge as Understanding," 359.

[27] Carpini, "Mediating Democratic Engagement," 421.

[28] Comstock and Scharrer, *The Psychology of Media and Politics*, 3.

[29] Huckfeldt, et al., "Individuals, Dyads, and Networks," 24.

[30] See Silvo Lenart, *Shaping Political Attitudes* (Thousand Oaks, CA: Sage, 1994).

[31] Ibid, 18–20.

[32] Ibid, 20–22.

[33] Ibid, 23.

[34] Ibid, 108.

[35] Soloman E. Asche, "Effects of Group Pressure upon the Modification and distortion of Judgments," in *Groups, Leadership, and Men* ed. H. Guetzkow (Pittsburgh: Carnegie, 1951).

[36] See Elisabeth Noelle-Neumann, *The Spiral of Silence, Second Edition* (Chicago: University of Chicago Press, 1993).

[37] Comstock and Scharrer, *The Psychology of Media and Politics*, 13.

[38] Ibid, 33.

[39] Bardes and Oldendick, *Public Opinion*, 76.

[40] Ibid, 90–91.

[41] Ibid, 90–91.

[42] Ibid, 100.

[43] Ibid, 101.

[44] Comstock and Scharrer, *The Psychology of Media and Politics*, 32.

[45] Ibid, 105.

[46] Ibid, 28.

[47] See Comstock and Scharrer, *The Psychology of Media and Politics*, 30–32; Richard Lau, "Models of Decision-Making," in *Oxford Handbook on Political Psychology*, ed. David Sears, Leonie Huddy and Robert Jervis (New York: Oxford University Press, 2003), 23–45; and Charles Taber, "Information Processing and Public Opinion," in *Oxford Handbook on Political Psychology*, ed. David Sears, Leonie Huddy and Robert Jervis (New York: Oxford University Press, 2003), 446–451.

[48] Comstock and Scharrer, *The Psychology of Media and Politics*, 31.

[49] Gimpel et al., *Cultivating Democracy*, 7.

[50] Ibid, 9.

[51] Ibid, 201.

[52] Ibid, 206–08.

The Media and Politics[1]

News media use by American politicians did not begin with the age of television but has been going on since before the Revolution of 1776. Early Patriots were fond of handing out banned pamphlets; newspapers advocated political positions; books presented erudite positions on a particular political philosophy. The War Between the States saw a partisan press as well, as did the days before World War I. In terms of electronic media, radio stands out as a benchmark of sorts. In the early 1920s, President Harding used radio to speak directly to the American public, and on December 6, 1923, President Coolidge gave the first broadcasted State of the Union address. Campaigns stopped dead in their tracks when Herbert Hoover made eight nationally broadcast radio speeches the focal point of his 1928 presidential campaign. Radio was the dominant media for politics until 1952.

In 1952, what was to be just a small footnote to campaign history became a milestone in the use of political media. Democrat Adlai Stevenson and Republican Dwight Eisenhower had begun their presidential campaigns, but it was Eisenhower's running mate, an aggressive young senator from California named Richard Nixon, who created much of the news. Many vice presidential contenders pass in and out of public attention with a minimum of national interest. Nixon was different. Early in the campaign it became evident that he was a lightning rod for attention and in deep trouble. The eventual outcome was one of those moments in history when a public figure's redemption hangs by the thread of a single event. In this case, Nixon was able to preserve his political career in a single 30-minute nationwide television speech. The address was a master political move and an early glimpse of the role the media would increasingly play in defining our national political life.

The episode began with the charge that Nixon had used campaign funds to establish a private "slush" fund of $16,000.[2] The suggestion that he was skimming money from his fund-raising efforts was severely aggravated by the fact that Eisenhower was slow to come to Nixon's defense, fueling press speculation that the scrappy senator was in deep political trouble. Days passed until it became evident to Nixon that he would have to engineer his own political salvation. Speaking to the nation from a living room set in an empty Hollywood theater, he justified the necessity to seek outside financial support to run for the Senate. In the process, he saved his place on the ticket and probably rescued his future.

The address was a masterful apologia, dramatically recounting his financial means to an audience of perhaps 60 million people.[3] In a perfect adaptation to the strengths of television, the speech translated the personal into the political. With his wife at his side, he reviewed his own modest finances to vindicate the implication that he was making a fortune in politics: the paid-off loan on his Oldsmobile, his mortgage on a modest home, a $4,000 life insurance policy. "It isn't very much," he noted, "but Pat and I have the satisfaction that every dime that we have got is honestly ours." And then the man known for his ability to play congressional hardball seamlessly extended himself into the unfamiliar vernacular of television to find the perfect homey touch. He regretted that Pat did not have a mink coat. "But she does have a respectable Republican cloth coat, and I always tell her that she would look good in anything." There was the gift of a dog named Checkers that the kids had grown to love. "I just want to say this, right now, that regardless of what they say about it, we are going to keep it."[4]

On television, the virtues of domesticity could have their own political benefits. Nixon's indignation over "smears" and "innuendo" was wrapped in the rhetoric of middle-class honor. The alleged use of a political fund had been transformed into something altogether more personal and visceral. Nixon asked viewers to decide his fate by writing to the Republican National Committee, but he need not have worried. The appeal yielded thousands of telegrams of support and forced Eisenhower out of his indifference. Arguably, 30 minutes of political rhetoric has never had a greater effect on the course of American history.

The speech was an omen of a new age in American political life where personal attributes would take on more vividness than policy decisions, where peripheral matters of conduct would begin to compete for attention with the substance of political ideas. The speech signaled a new reality brought on by the entry of television into the political world. This medium—which is more about attitude than information, more about style than substance—has changed the nature of political discourse and challenged journalists and politicians to use it as effectively as they used the older discursive medium of the printed page. If the press could generate doubts and television could amplify them, politicians could use the same popular medium to create effective defenses.

To be sure, the news environment comprises more than television, and all of the news media have changed to deal with the staggering growth and expansion of the electronic media in recent U.S. history. Radio emerged in the 1920s and television in the 1950s. It is the availability of cable, which began in the 1980s, and the Web, starting in the 1990s, that provides continually expanding forums, bringing together political agents and the news industry in an uneasy relationship. Those in public life seek power by having their messages heard and accepted. Their counterparts in the media have a commercial need to find interesting stories and pictures and a professional need to demonstrate their independence.

This chapter explores the tensions built into the relationship between political figures and events and the news media. Although almost every topic in this book touches on the news media, our goal in this chapter is to review some essential features and problems common to traditional notions of the political news media; we specifically discuss the impact of the Internet on politics in chapter 7. After beginning with four clarifications about what it means to talk about "political media," we explore basic frameworks for assessing how news and our nation's civil life interact, including the essential concept of media gatekeeping. We discuss these at length because public attitudes about politics are heavily shaped by the storytelling preferences of news organizations. We also examine the distinguishing features of "free" and "paid" media, as well as the "attack" and "news management" models of the press. The chapter closes with an estimation of the effectiveness of mediated political messages.

Media and Politics: Traps and Clarifications

Politics in the Larger Media Universe

By the term "media," we mean the news and entertainment industries—large and small—who sell their wares to the general public on a routine basis. We include newspapers, broadcast news programs, political advertising, Internet sites, and purchased media, which was the vehicle for Nixon's television address described above. Our focus here is specifically on the news and public relations aspects of political media. The role of politics in other forms of entertainment is considered in chapter 16.

The mix of media available to Americans is enormous, including nearly 14,000 radio stations, 2,218 television stations, 12,000 periodicals, and about 1,450 daily newspapers.[5] Over 65 million households subscribe to one of the nation's 7,926 cable systems.[6] About one household in two subscribes to a newspaper. No nation comes close to the United States in producing the sheer volume of mass media content. Moreover, our consumption of it is equally voracious. The average American family has a television on for more than eight hours a day.[7] According to the Pew Research Center, 40 percent of Americans read a daily newspaper, 36 percent listen to radio news, 54 percent watch local television news, and 28 percent watch the nightly network news.[8]

Establishing the enormous size of the American media environment is the easy part. It becomes more difficult to define the portion that deals—broadly speaking—with political content. It is obvious that most media content is not news, at least in the traditional journalistic sense, and most news is not about politics. The dominant components of the most heavily consumed media include mixtures of information and entertainment, much of it centered on film and sports celebrities. Even the traditional center of "serious" television news—the three broadcast networks' prestigious half-hour early evening news programs—represents only a brief interruption of a schedule dominated by entertainment. Moreover, their share of viewers has fallen to below half of all of those watching television at the time,[9] with a steady decline of households watching, dropping from 60 percent in 1993 to just 28 percent in 2006.[10] At the same time, "hard news" is also in competition with other features and information in U.S. newspapers. Even the most prestigious examples of the daily press such as *The New York Times* have been criticized for ethical lapses and the softening of their journalistic rigor in favor of entertaining features.[11]

Even if the bulk of American media is about entertainment rather than information, there is still no shortage of political news for those who wish to seek it. Policy and political discussion abounds in newspapers such as *The Wall Street Journal, Washington Post, The Washington Times*, and *Los Angeles Times*. It exists in abundance in periodicals such as *The Nation, The Weekly Standard, The New Republic, National Review, Slate* (online), and *Washington Monthly*. One finds it also on television's PBS stations, C-SPAN, CNN, FOX News, MSNBC, and scores of related Internet sites. Pockets of thoughtful discussion also inhabit the airwaves, notably on public radio. Although output and audience for all of these sources of political content is small relative to the entire universe of American media, it is still easily available to those who are interested, and those who are interested tend to be politically active.

Media and the Limits of What We Know about Politics

By their very nature, the events and the participants of political culture are rarely witnessed firsthand. Instead, they are reconstructed for us by intermediaries. Like any arena where the discussion of human motivations carries significant weight, politics invites narration, interpretation, and summation. Debates in a state assembly, hearings on Capitol Hill, or thick reports issued by an executive agency research staff often seem incomprehensible in their original form, and it takes a press report to make sense of them. As the great journalist Walter Lippmann noted, "The world that we have to deal with politically is out of reach, out of sight, out of mind. It has to be explored, reported, and imagined." Through the mass media an individual learns "to smell, hear, or remember. Gradually he makes for himself a trustworthy picture inside his head of the world beyond his reach."[12] In short, news offers a mediated reality.

In an important sense, news is also less a comprehensive mirror of events than an interpretation of what events mean; it is less about hard information than about the stories of key actors in our national dramas. News provides a window on the "defining moments" of the present, an imperfect but frequently vivid narrative of pivotal events in our public life. According to the Associated Press survey of U.S. editors, the top six stories for 2005 were (1) Hurricane Katrina, (2) the Papal transition, (3) Iraq, (4) the Supreme Court, (5) oil prices, and (6) the London terrorist bombings. The extensive and extended coverage given to each story not only defined important features of the news culture of that year, but it also determined our national consciousness—the private and public discourse of American life in a particular period. Although the stories that editors and publishers decide to focus on do provide Americans with greater news coverage of an issue or event, those stories may not be what Americans find of greatest interest. According to The Pew Research Center U.S. News Interest Index, the six most closely watched news stories of 2005 were (1) Katrina and Rita, (2) high gasoline prices, (3) Indian Ocean Tsunami, (4) London bombings, (5) situation in Iraq, and (6) President Bush's Social Security plan.[13]

The Shared Rhetorical Nature of Politics and News Media Reporting

Members of the news media and those in political life are—in many ways—working at the same enterprise. Both must attribute motives to actions. Both must explain the intangible principles that form the rationales for political action. Both must please audiences with reconstructions of attitudes and events that are inexact and diffuse. If a politician chooses to talk about the plight of "the poor in America," the reporter assigned to cover the story must exercise similar *rhetorical* options to relay the tone and nature of the event to the reader or listener. But what is the rhetoric? In the sense we use the term, rhetoric is "the strategic use of communication, oral or written, to achieve specifiable goals."[14] Rhetorical communication is strategic in that it is intentional. There is some planning ahead about what to say, if communicators want their messages understood in a particular manner. This is the case with both members of the news media and politicians.

As mentioned above, both the news media and politicians want certain motives explained, principles expounded, and audiences pleased. These goals, although sounding similar, do differ to some extent. Politicians want your vote; the news media want you as an audience member. Politicians want your political support on various issues; the news media want you to think about certain issues. Both, then, seek to please their respective audiences. As Michael Novak notes, the political impulse to please a constituency is usually every bit as strong in the journalist as it is in the politician, and may be even more so—as well as corrupting.

> The tradition of American journalism demands "news," an "angle." Something "different." Something "fresh." . . . The world isn't made that

way—"There's nothing new under the sun," men believed for thousands of years—and good politics is seldom a matter of novelty. But journalism has a voracious appetite for novelty.

Commentators, I think, fail to see how corrupting the practices of journalism truly are: the cult of celebrity, the cult of "news," the manipulative skills of "riding the wire," supplying two new daily "leads," grabbing headlines," manufacturing "events" and "statements." Journalists speak as if money were the great corrupter of our times; but the corruption of intelligence and imagination by the demand for "news" is deadly.[15]

In a word, journalism—like politics—is a rhetorical endeavor. It uses communication to give order to a disordered world.

Media and Pluralism

It is important to remember that the term *media* is a plural concept and, as such, carries limitations. As a name representing what we know to be a major force in our lives, the idea of the media is irresistible. However, the trend toward thinking of media in the "singular" is common in everyday discussion (e.g., "the media *has* ruined the Senator's chances for reelection.") and implies a more unified enterprise than is sometimes justified. Consider that media outlets can have starkly different owners, objectives, audiences, and ways of constructing and delivering their messages. A local television newscast in Atlanta, for example, shares little more than a few headlines with *The Atlanta Journal-Constitution, The Atlanta Jewish Times, The Atlanta Nation,* and other media from the same region.

In the most simplistic characterization, one could consider all information or entertainment directed to large collections of individuals as part of "the mass media." According to Joseph R. Dominick, mass media are

> the channels used for mass communication. Not only the mechanical devices that transmit and sometimes store the messages (TV cameras, radio microphones, printing presses), but also the institutions that use these machines to transmit messages. When we talk about the mass media of television, radio, newspapers, magazines, sound recording, and film, we will be referring to the people, the policies, the organizations, and the technology that go into producing and distributing mass communication.[16]

When we use the term *media* in this book, however, we refer specifically to the *news media*. Often described as "the press," the "news media" refers specifically to those individuals who report the "news," be it through writing or oral reporting. According to Jennifer Akin:

> The distinction between news and entertainment can at times be fuzzy, but news is technically facts and interpretation of facts, including editorial opinions, expressed by journalism professionals. Which facts are included, how they are reported, how much interpretation is given, and how much space or time is devoted to a news event is determined by journalists and management and will depend on a variety of factors

ranging from the editorial judgment of the reporters and editors, to other news events competing for the same time or space, to corporate policies that reflect management's biases.[17]

The inherent variety alluded to in the paragraphs above often produces a conceptual muddle when we overreach for phrases that are sometimes too broad to be meaningful. The complaint that some elections are won by "media campaigns," or that the Clinton and Bush presidencies were "media driven," means less when we assume that a unique species of political life has been defined. Virtually every political event, at virtually every level, is known through what is written or reported about it, from reports about school board actions in local papers and citizen's newsletters, to the latest dispatch from the White House carried by CNN or FOX News. In this sense, all of politics is *mediated*, and always has been. Even in the life of George Washington one finds public relations problems thought to have been invented in the age of radio and television: press fascination with his personality, a chain of publicity-based "pseudo events" leading up to his appointment as president, "news management" in the publication of his Farewell Address, and the kind of elevation to celebrity status that would have made *People* magazine proud.[18] Thomas Jefferson describes a similar experience with the press of his day:

> During the course of [my] administration, and in order to disturb it, the artillery of the press has been leveled against us, charged with whatsoever its licentiousness could devise or dare. These abuses of an institution so important to freedom and science are deeply to be regretted, inasmuch as they tend to lessen its usefulness and to sap its safety.[19]

We highlight the historical nature of press–politician interaction to show that politics has always been influenced by, and an influencer of, the mass media. In describing the function of media sources that influence Americans, therefore, it is important to specify contexts, messages, and audiences. Each moment in public life is unique, fostering different realities created by different media. The media are plural.

Media and the Tendency to Overattribute Causation

Since World War II, researchers in the social sciences have been exploring the complex relationships that exist between news sources and public attitudes. The impulse for this research is enormous, because we tend to assume that the collective impression of the culture is a product of what the media delivers to us. This belief that our attitudes are direct products of media consumption has been called media determinism: the intuitive belief that media messages directly determine attitudes and behaviors. To say—as many did— that John Kerry lost the 2004 presidential election to George Bush because he looked aloof and elite on television, or that Bush had better one-liners for the 6:00 PM news, is to posit a relationship between media exposure and what we think and do as citizens. Although wholesale acceptance of this position is suspect, there is considerable research suggesting that media do have great influence. George Comstock and Erica Scharrer write:

> The increasing prominences of the media in interpreting events and the reduced exposure to the words of the politicians covered, the emphasis on the negative and unfavorable that may undermine political support and loyalty . . . the heightening of public involvement by the parade of constant personalities and intermittent crises, the increased attention to what the public is thinking about politicians and political campaigns that leaves individuals with few doubts about majority opinion and the popular acceptance or rejection of candidates—these are all developments in journalism that increase the likelihood that the information disseminated by the mass media will influence public opinion.[20]

Even so, attributions of causation assigned to various forms of the media are extremely difficult to establish. Extensive research over the last 60 years has yet to resolve a number of questions. For example, how accurate are media usage studies? Are correlations between public attitudes and intense media coverage causally related, or are they simply two arbitrary points in a process that involves other hidden forces? Additionally, are the media so collectively powerful that they function like "magic bullets," piercing the thought processes of everyone in their path?

Generally speaking, survey research reflecting public attitudes, and monitoring studies summarizing media content, are conceptually more solid than studies that seek to link exposure to media content with changes in attitudes. To put it simply, it is easier to ask people what they think, or to summarize the news stories to which they are exposed, than to determine how specific news content affects their judgment about a reported event. For example, we have a clear understanding of how people use their time processing the news and what that news contains.[21] However, it is a far more difficult task to determine how specific individuals react to certain media and its content. This latter approach involves the use of elaborate attempts to manipulate message- and source-related variables and to assess how they have affected people who volunteered to be experimental subjects.

One notable study undertaken by Shanto Iyengar and Donald Kinder subtly altered the order of news stories in pretaped television news broadcasts to test the idea that prior stories could alter people's reactions to later ones. Most interestingly, by changing the sequence of stories, they could induce subjects to change their judgments of the effectiveness of the president. They found that early stories on topics such as the rate of economic inflation "primed" viewers to assess the chief executive in terms of how he dealt with such issues.[22] A more recent study by Robert K. Goidel, Craig M. Freeman, and Steven T. Procopic examined the relationship between television news and crime reality show viewing and an individual's perception of juvenile crime rates. These researchers found that "television viewing is associated with misperceptions that juvenile (and adult) crime is increasing when, in fact, it is decreasing. For juvenile crime, television news—and not reality-based programming—is associated with misperceptions regarding crime rates." Although the authors caution readers that "the associations between attitudes and media exposure are generally quite modest," they also found that the evidence "is highly suggestive of a more general conclusion: Greater television viewing is associated with greater misunderstanding of juvenile crime."[23]

Experimental design is, however, prone to a host of problems. Experiments occur in artificial environments; their duration is usually short-term, even though the most important media effects are those that last. It is also difficult to isolate subjects from other outside influences. Additionally, few experimental groups represent the diversity of the population.[24] As Kathleen McGraw and Milton Lodge note, it is tempting to make judgments about the effects of "a neatly packaged information environment" such as a speech. But even "in controlled laboratory studies, we do not yet have a firm grasp of how much of what kinds of information gets attention and is used."[25] Additionally, and perhaps most importantly, these studies can fall short because they study human beings, and by our very nature as human, we are psychologically too complex and variable to be adequate subjects for study by social scientific methods. Science seeks out invariable rules that govern the physical world; humans simply cannot be counted upon to act the same way for the same cues. For all of these reasons, then, measuring the effects of media exposure is a relatively limited form of political research. The more common approach is to infer possible or likely effects based on evidence of wide and pervasive exposure to certain media and frequently repeated messages.

Even within the limits of current research and analysis, a number of important conclusions are clear about how news shapes our political attitudes. Among the most important are the following:

- No single mass media source commands total loyalty and certain credibility. There is little reflexive acceptance of persuasive or informative messages, including those of the most prestigious mass media.

- Individuals are generally selective about what they hear, making the actual effects of any political communication difficult to predict. Conclusions other than those intended by the sender are sometimes reached. Messages may be considered, momentarily accepted, and then later rejected.

- There is a great deal of elasticity in the attitudes of individuals. Attitudes may be stretched and momentarily altered by the appeals contained in a news story or an editorial or political broadcast. However, individuals with preexisting beliefs are likely to retain those beliefs.

- Because opinions and attitudes are the products of many experiences, the messages of the mass media must be treated as only a few among many causes. To imply that the media alone are prime causes in attitude formation is to overlook other sources of attitudes, especially those gained from interpersonal contact. Attitudes are produced interactively rather than unilaterally.

In short, although the news media play an enormous role in our day-to-day political reality, they are not the only, or the most important, source of attitude formation. Individuals have their perceptions shaped by many forces, and many factors other than the consumption of news media products play a part in their political behaviors.

Six Major Trends in the News Media

We take the position that politics and the news media go hand-in-hand. With that in mind, the nature of the news industry can directly impact the manner in which those engaged in politics, whether citizen or professional politician, communicate and receive various messages. In 2006, the Project for Excellence in Journalism released its annual report on the state of the news media. This report identified six major trends.

1. "The new paradox of journalism is more outlets covering fewer stories."[26] This means that there are increasing sources for news, and as this occurs, the slice of the audience pie each source receives shrinks, as does the total number of employees for each organization. Additionally, as the size of the national organizations shrink, "we tend to see more accounts of the same handful of stories each day. And when big stories break, they are often covered in a similar fashion by general-assignment reporters working with a limited list of sources and a tight time-frame."[27]

2. "The species of newspaper that may be most threatened is the big-city metro paper that came to dominate in the latter part of the 20th century."[28] Although the nation's top three national papers and also smaller newspapers managed to hang on to their circulation in 2005, large city papers saw large circulation drops. They are being supplanted by both Internet use and the rise of small audience "niche publications." The problem with this is that "the big metros are the news organizations most likely to have the resources and aspirations to act as watchdogs over state, regional, and urban institutions, to identify trends, and to define the larger community public square. It is unlikely that small suburban dailies or weeklies will take up that challenge."[29]

3. "At many old-media companies, though not all, the decades-long battle at the top between idealists and accountants is now over."[30] The large media companies no longer see themselves as protectors of the public trust, but rather companies in the business of making money. "The most cogent explanation for why journalism in the public interest has lost leverage was probably offered by Polk Laffoon IV, the corporate spokesman of Knight Ridder. 'I wish there were an identi-

fiable and strong correlation between quality journalism . . . and newspaper sales,' he said. 'It isn't . . . that simple.'"[31]

4. "That said, traditional media do appear to be moving toward technological innovation—finally."[32] In the years following the rise of the Internet, news outlets essentially treated the Web as a place to republish what came out in print; there was little in the way of innovative use of the new communication technologies made available. Change is finally underway, and as explained by Pew, a "big reason was that much of the revenue growth in these companies is now coming from online (and from niche products such as youth newspapers). In network television, for instance, viewers of ABC News can now watch an evening newscast from that network online three and a half hours before one is broadcast on television."[33]

5. "The new challengers to the old media, the aggregators, are also playing with limited time."[34] News aggregators, such as Google.com, Yahoo.com, and the Drudgereport.com are in the business of taking the published reports of news organizations and bundling them together for audience consumption. Thus, consumers stop paying for news from traditional sources, paying instead other sites that use the traditional sources. Although beneficial for those searching for a one-stop location for all their news needs, the difficulty arises in that the "more they succeed, the faster they erode the product they are selling, unless the economic model is radically changed."[35]

6. "The central economic question in journalism continues to be how long it will take online journalism to become a major economic engine, and if it will ever be as big as print or television."[36] One of the main difficulties in making online content pay is that so much information is available free of charge. Whereas a print newspaper brings in subscription revenue as well as advertising dollars, consumers expect online content to remain free to them, thus bringing in only advertising dollars. "All this only adds to the likelihood that the next battleground will be producers of old media challenging Internet providers and Internet aggregators to begin compensating them for content, the model that exists in cable."[37]

Basic Frameworks for Assessing Political Media

In this section, we wish to share three of the key ideas that can be used to productively assess how politics is reconstructed for public consumption. They include the pivotal concept of media gatekeeping, the crucial distinctions between the use of paid and free media, and the relationships between politicians and reporters. Each of these is considered in turn below.

Gatekeeping and the Political Landscape

The term *gatekeeping* was first used in social scientific literature in 1947 by Kurt Lewin. Initially it was used to describe how a mother or wife was the one who decided what ended up on the table for dinner.[38] Simply put, the gatekeeper is the one who decides what passes through the gate. Three years later in 1950, David Manning White introduced us to the eponymous Mr. Gates, an imaginary newswire editor operating in gatekeeping fashion.[39] In media studies, gatekeeping theory is about story selection; who decides what stories shall pass through the media gate. According to Pamela J. Shoemaker and colleagues, gatekeeping is the "process by which the vast array of potential news messages are winnowed, shaped, and prodded into those few that are actually transmitted by the news media."[40] The rules of gatekeeping vary by media type. Local television news is heavy on crime reporting, for example, and limited in foreign or political news. Many observers consider the news output of most stations as little better than what supermarket tabloids offer their readers.[41] The so-called "prestige press" of major newspapers generally reverses these priorities, though even the best metropolitan papers are seeking ways to retain readers, whose numbers are declining.[42] Comstock and Scharrer believe that the news media canvass events to determine which merit placement among the reported news stories of the day. The audience receives a distillation of the news filtered by the media.[43] The bases of story selection—and for the emergence of a leader or issue into public awareness—are diverse. The filtering process is an interesting and vital area for exploration of the business of news. The issue of what is reported is especially important in the political realm, because politics is generally less visual and entertaining than are other kinds of news stories, such as those dealing with rural disasters.

Some analysts, such as Herbert Gans, have emphasized the traditional journalistic rules for story suitability. Something has news value if it involves public officials, affects the nation, has an impact on large numbers of people, or says something about where we are going.[44] Additionally, an event may be deemed worthy of coverage if it contains a degree of novelty, an element of action, actual or potential conflict, and so on.[45] Although Gans was writing in 1980, these remain familiar journalistic standards today—based in part on pleasing the largest possible audience and in part on traditional journalistic criteria for assessing what is important for news consumers to know.[46] Others have approached the study of news and information content by exploring topic and story selection from a consensual perspective. In this view "news" is what our priorities, fantasies, and national history tell us it is. It is a group product—a matter of agreement based on shared attitudes and routines.[47]

One pioneering account of this consensus model of news focuses on the 1972 presidential campaign. In his study, Timothy Crouse firmly planted the concept of "pack journalism" into the lexicon of political analysis. Crouse provided evidence that reporters traveling with a presidential candidate frequently let the work of their colleagues govern their own perspectives toward specific campaign events. Living and traveling together for days at a time, some members of the press became collaborators in developing their stories, reaching agreement on particular "angles" or "leads."[48]

Twenty years later, Republican consultant Mary Matalin noted that little had changed since Crouse's study. Waging the 1992 Bush campaign against Bill Clinton, she was particularly annoyed at what she saw as the tendency of major news organizations to "all bounce off each other and write stories to fit into a common contextual analysis." She particularly noted the power of whatever the major wire services were reporting:

> First the wires file their stories. They service most newspapers and file continuously, and they keep updating their pieces as the day or event unfolds. The other political writers from the dailies file. If these writers vary significantly from what the wires ran as their lead, their editors will go back to them and say, "This is not what's running on the wires. Reconstruct your story."[49] Pack journalism, then, sets in out of fear of failing to cover what will become the next big story and therefore appearing noncompetitive to the audience.[50]

Not much has changed today, except perhaps reporters are aware of the public distaste for pack journalism. On this point Frank Russell writes:

> Journalists have begun to recognize that public disaffection demands that they give an account of themselves when they appear to be "going too far" in their pursuit of news. [P]rint reporters are specifically addressing themselves to concerns about their insensitivity or lack of compassion, either by acknowledging the obtrusiveness of, and implicitly distancing themselves from, "the pack" or by suggesting that television news-workers, with their cameras and cables and microphones, are the real problem.[51]

Most of the journalistic values that govern the gatekeeping process have to do with what makes an interesting story. Presidents and congressional leaders, for example, are more interesting to editors than are institutions. Personal details are usually better copy than policy ideas. Scores of observers have assessed the gatekeeping tendencies built into the story format.[52]

Although their conclusions vary, certain themes tend to reappear, including the following:

1. *Political action is framed within the conventions of melodrama.* No point of reference has proved more durable in popular reports of political behavior than the terms and concepts associated with drama. Political reporting rarely ignores the elements of theater. Roles, scenes, acts, and audiences are endemic to descriptions of political events.[53] Television news in particular, notes Paul Weaver, is governed by melodramatic bias.[54] It is characterized by intensified peril, simplified values, and exaggerated intensity. Characterizations of melodramatic images of foolishness, villainy, and heroes are com-

mon. They are used in themes that are equally familiar: the triumph of the individual over adversity, justice winning over evil, redemption of the individual through reform, and the rewarding of valor or heroism. Stories may not always have happy endings, but the reader or viewer is usually left with the impression of what the ending should be. As Dan Nimmo and James Combs note, news reporting is "a literary act, a continuous search for story lines."[55] Reflecting the logic that has long dominated the writing style of the news weeklies such as *Time* and *Newsweek,* former NBC News Chief Reuven Frank vividly made the same dramatistic point in what has since become a widely reprinted memo to his staff:

> Every news story should, without any sacrifice of probity or responsibility, display the attributes of fiction, or drama. It should have structure and conflict, problem and denouement, rising action and falling action, a middle, and an end. These are not only the essentials of drama; they are the essentials of narrative.[56]

Elisabeth Anker writes that melodrama employs emotionality to provide an unambiguous distinction between good and evil. It clearly designates who is a victim, hero, or villain. It "structures the presentation of political discourse."[57]

2. *Personalization is preferred over policy.* News frequently encourages us to look at cases and examples rather than at pure ideas. Melodramatic structure depends on vivid characterization, including the sketches of a person's public persona and private self. In contemporary news, we often understand issues by seeing how they play out in the lives of the famous and the ordinary. These subjects may be agents for change, victims of inaction or social neglect, or villains responsible for creating social unrest. To be sure, it has always been the case that the character of the public figure has been a subject of public interest. The politics of ancient Greece enshrined the role of *ethos* and its central idea that personal qualities are important to strong leadership.[58] Theatre and storytelling in general encourage explorations of linkages that connect specific personal qualities to public behaviors.

From the 1930s on, the widespread acceptance of psychoanalysis, film, the novel, and gossip columns have all contributed to interest in the details of the individual life; television, of course, has intensified this pattern. In Richard Sennett's phrase, television especially is "compulsively personalistic."[59] It easily serves as an instrument that invites the careful measurement of intention and motive. We frequently cannot conceive of the principles governing foreign policy until we see graphic portrayals of the residents who would be affected. We cannot tolerate extensive discussion of tax law revisions without seeing depictions of affluence or poverty. Television frequently reduces policy debates to their material and personal dimensions.

In a relatively typical week in 2006, for example, most of the time the three major television network news shows were consumed with stories about the actions of particular persons. Between August 6 and 12, top stories included Israel's Prime Minister Ehud Olmert and the leader of the terrorist organization Hizbullah, Hassan Nasrallah; British Prime Minister Tony Blair, who remained on vacation during the aftermath of the failed al-Qaeda plot to blow up nine jetliners; Representative Cynthia McKinney's (D-Ga.) failed primary runoff against Hank Johnson; and speculations on the health of Fidel Castro. During this and many other weeks, policy discussion without an anchor in someone's personal story was uncommon.

The case of McKinney is especially interesting, given that her public life has been dogged with questions about her character and behavior (e.g., allegedly striking a Capitol guard in 2005). Given her limited congressional impact (64 bills introduced in nine years with only one passing), her prominence in the news must be explained from a different perspective than her political power or her policy initiatives.[60] As Sennett implies in *The Fall of Public Man,* her media recognition might be tied to a shift in the landscape of American politics:

> A political leader running for office is spoken of as "credible" or "legitimate" in terms of what kind of man he is, rather than in terms of the actions or programs he espouses. The obsession with persons at the expense of more impersonal social relations is like a filter which discolors our rational understanding of society.[61]

Americans sometimes wonder why our news media have become so fascinated with the private lives of our national leaders. Sennett's answer is that we have forgotten the art of formal public communication, where roles are clearly defined and the decision to enter into public discourse carries the responsibility to put the needs of institutions before private considerations.

3. *"Official" voices are the prime interpreters of events.* Routine versions of news usually give an enormous amount of credibility to presidents, leaders of Congress, heads of corporations or federal agencies, and other leaders. A "top-down" model for reporting events gives leaders a special place in the story because of their formal/structural role and because stories are easier to tell when focusing on one rather than many. This is not a new phenomenon. For example, summing a 20-year period, Leon V. Sigal found in 1973 that *The Washington Post* and *The New York Times* used government officials for approximately three-fourths of their news sources. Additionally, 60 percent of the news covered was derived from official sources such as news releases, government proceedings, and press conferences.[62] Other researchers since have found this to hold true.[63] Kathleen A. Hansen sums up well the potential impact of such concentration of sources: "When

news content is heavily ladened [sic] with official government statements, comments and interviews and government statistics and documents, the perspectives and views of other affiliated sources (e.g.,
labor, education, business, public interest groups) are slighted. Unaf-
filiated sources (average citizens) have even less access for their viewpoints and concerns."[64]

Consider the coverage of the Watergate break-in and cover-up, a pivotal event in recent American history, which was largely told through
official sources. David Paletz and Robert Entman conclude that most
of the coverage was at least initially careful not to undermine the
legitimacy of official White House explanations.[65] For a very long
time President Nixon's participation in the cover-up was neglected in
favor of reports about the possible involvement of other officials.
Paletz and Entman note that, even while they are lauded as watchdogs, the news media effectively protect "the powerful," giving them
legitimacy as the primary interpreters of events.[66] In another example, consider television coverage of the Persian Gulf War. Janet E.
Steele found:

> Expert sources are selected and used according to how well their
> specialized knowledge conforms with what can be termed televi-
> sion's "operational bias" in favor of predictions, players, and poli-
> cies. Experts are asked to make short-term predictions, to analyze
> the motives and makeup of the major players, and to provide com-
> mentary and analysis on a limited range of issues. These processes,
> moreover, have the effect of undermining the very goal of objectiv-
> ity that encourages journalists to seek out experts in the first place.
> [A] small group of former public officials, retired military person-
> nel, and analysts from think tanks dominated television news cover-
> age of the Persian Gulf War; these experts framed the conflict in a
> narrowly technical and logistical interpretive context.[67]

This pattern of coverage can be seen in major event coverage even
today—the second Gulf War and Hurricane Katrina are just two
examples from recent memory.

4. *Political reporting has drifted toward an emphasis on "personality" and
"interpretation" rather than ideology.* Perhaps reflecting the pace of
television, or the natural interest it places on human motives, political
reporting is somewhat different from what it was several generations
ago. The reader of a newspaper earlier in the twentieth century was
more likely to find news reports of political activity dominated by
long excerpts of speeches and remarks. For a number of years in the
1920s and 1930s even radio was content to carry political addresses
with a minimum of commentary. By contrast, the gatekeeping objective of much contemporary political reporting focuses on personalities and strategies, not on the content of political utterances. Faced

with the choice of recounting to reader or viewers what a particular figure said or analyzing the motives behind remarks addressed to a specific audience, more and more journalism seems to emphasize the latter. Moreover, studies since the 1980s have shown an ever-shrinking amount of time devoted to sound bites from politicians and an ever-increasing amount of time devoted to the commentary of journalists. Thomas Patterson defines a sound bite as a "block of uninterrupted speech by a candidate [or politician] on television news."[68] Hallin demonstrated the shrinking nature of the sound bite, finding that from 1968 to 1988 sound bites from presidential candidates on the evening news of the major networks fell from 43.1 seconds to 8.9 seconds.[69] The extent of the time switch becomes more obvious when one considers that by the 1992 elections, "reporters and anchors spoke for 6 minutes for every minute that the candidates spoke for themselves in the form of a sound bite."[70] Even in print the amount of reportorial interpretation is on the rise, with the "average length of a continuous quote from a candidate in the front-page *New York Times* stories in 1960 at 14 lines compared to 6 lines in 1992."[71] The Center for Media and Public Affairs found that during the 2000 election

> reporters took three quarters (74 percent) of spoken air time while the candidates had a mere 11 percent, and other sources had 15 percent since Labor Day. The three networks [ABC, CBS, and NBC] were almost identical in their allotment of air time among candidates, journalists, and other sources."[72]

This pattern is represented well by the familiar sight of a network correspondent delivering a "stand up" summary against the backdrop of a voiceless politician talking in the background. The option to let the politician's words speak for themselves is increasingly ignored. The reporter feels the need to act as narrator and interpreter, not simply telling the viewer what has just been said but assessing the "real" motivations behind the event. Consider Leslie Stahl's opening narration for a CBS report on the 1980 presidential campaign: "President Carter chose the heart of George Wallace country for today's traditional campaign kickoff; he chose Alabama because he was concerned that the Wallace vote among Southerners and blue collar workers may be slipping to Ronald Reagan."[73] Or consider this opening narration by NBC's Brian Williams, reporting on President Bush's 2005 Veterans Day Address:

> Across the country, Veteran's Day is very often about aging soldiers in dwindling numbers who perhaps put on a uniform that doesn't quite fit the way it used to and march in the parade where they live. Today, President Bush used the occasion to come out hard against criticism of the Iraq war. He said it hurts the troops and helps the enemy. The Democrats shot back, as you'll soon hear, and this Vet-

eran's Day quickly became a fight over those who are fighting and
dying overseas right now.[74]

Joseph Cappella and Kathleen Hall Jamieson call this the "strategy structure" pattern of journalism, which presumes that politics is about winning, not
about solving problems. In the strategy structure, policy positions are interpreted as a means of gaining a voter block to advance the candidacy or retain a
position in the polls. Candidates' words and actions are seen as outward signs
of strategic intent and as maneuvers rather than forms of self-expression.[75]
They argue that this structure comes at a big price for national discourse,
because it inherently casts politics as a cynical and manipulative enterprise.

Gatekeeping is thus the process of editing content to fit into the limited
space available for news. Giving officials preference, using the strategy structure, focusing on people rather than ideas, and emphasizing the melodramatic are only the most familiar of many processes for shaping the political
realities we come to know.

Paid and Free Media

There is no greater threshold in the world of politics than that which
separates paid messages and those that reach the public via "free" channels.
The former include advertisements and tracts, campaign ads, or direct mail
appeals sent out to mobilize supporters of an interest group or politician.
The latter includes information that reaches the reader, viewer, or listener in
the context of news. Such journalistic coverage of a politician or group is
obviously "free," though not necessarily positive.

Paid media.   It is easiest to see the distinction between free and paid
media in the political campaign. Campaigners running for major elective
offices purchase stunningly expensive blocks of television time to present
messages wholly controlled by them. According to Comstock and Scharrer,
these political ads, "constructed with visual and political expertise by professional production teams and members of the campaign staff and carefully
placed in particular media markets to address specifically targeted audiences, are very pricey. This creates a situation in which only those with
access to large amounts of money can run for major office."[76] In 2004, the
Federal Election Commission found,

> Congressional campaigns raised a total of $798.7 million in the 18
> months of the 2003–2004 election cycle ending June 30, an increase of
> 32% from the comparable period in the 2001–2002 campaign. . . . The
> Commission found that 1,908 Senate and House candidates spent $487.1
> million from January 1, 2003, through June 30, 2004 (up 36% from
> 2002), and reported cash on hand of $482 million (up 29%) at the end of
> the second quarter of 2004.[77]

For the 2004 presidential elections, George W. Bush raised over $367 million
and John Kerry raised over $326 million. Each spent approximately 95 percent

of the amount raised.[78] During the 2003–2004 fund-raising cycle, the Democratic Party raised in excess of $679 million and the Republican Party in excess of $782 million.[79] To raise these huge sums, candidates must set aside large blocks of time to woo contributors and to convince them that media access is essential to the campaign. To a large extent, fund-raising to pay for media efforts to reach voters has become the second occupation of incumbents.

For their part, candidates note that the modern campaign requires enormous cash to buy media access. With the exception of the smallest local media outlets, the price for a one-time message carried by a newspaper or local television station can run up to several thousand dollars. Presidential candidates contend with national media such as television, which may require an enormous outlay of money for one 30-second commercial during prime time; the cost is in part determined by the popularity of the show. In 2005–2006, for example, FOX might charge as much as $705,000 for a 30-second spot during an episode of *American Idol*, whereas NBC might charge a smaller sum, $350,000 for spot during *The Apprentice*.[80] These figures are merely the beginning. The only chance to have a sustained impact on voters is if media time and space purchases are duplicated many times over.

The place of advertising in the political process has divided many observers. By the 1970s, some, including broadcast historian Erik Barnouw, were noting that its effect on our civic life "has been devastating."[81] The literature of political communication, for instance, overflows with case histories of national and regional campaigns that relied on misleading or fraudulent ads, especially those that "go negative."[82] Guido H. Stempel suggests that a reason for low voter turnout

> is negative advertising. . . . Conventional wisdom has it that negative advertisements win votes, but there are plenty of examples to the contrary. And negative advertisements convince some voters that there is no reason to vote. If Candidate A's ads tells you that Candidate B is a bum, and Candidate B's ads tells you that Candidate A is a scoundrel, why vote?[83]

Others, such as Gary Mauser, have defended the idea that campaigns should more closely resemble the marketing processes used by commercial interests. Marketing theory, he argues, has a legitimate place in the electoral process.[84] Marketing does not necessarily mean lack of informative content. In their content analyses of campaign communication, Thomas Patterson and Robert McClure reached the surprising conclusion that television ads for candidates were often richer in significant content than network campaign news. Although commercials are surely full of their own nonsense, blatant exaggerations, and superficial symbolism, presidential candidates do make heavy use of hard issue information in their advertising appeals. In fact, during the short period of the general election campaign, presidential ads contained substantially more issue content than network newscasts. This information is particularly valuable to people who pay little attention to the newspaper. Advertising serves to make these poorly informed people substantially more knowledgeable.[85] William L. Benoit and colleagues, in their study of the 2000 presidential election, found that television spots do influence voters. "Those who were exposed to presidential campaign ads were better educated (enjoyed greater issue knowledge) and more likely to offer issues as a reason for preferring a candidate *(higher* issue salience)" than those who were not exposed to those same campaign ads.[86] In this sense, political commercials are associated with increased knowledge about the candidates and issues in a campaign. Comstock and Scharrer "conclude that political commercials can be informative, especially when truly attended to rather than peripherally experienced."[87]

The journalistic urgency for creating drama in campaign stories, for allowing reporters to have greater billing than their subjects, and for focusing on the "strategy structure," all point to the inadequacies that make campaign advertising something of a necessity. Seasoned political journalists may criticize advertising's "sterile" and "contrived" nature. However, there is little evidence that those who cover the political beat are doing much to increase the public's competence to master the substance of important political issues.

Again, we stress that this situation is long-standing. In her detailed study of the 1974 California gubernatorial campaign, Mary Ellen Leary details this problem. The race produced significant press attention, and yet none of the six television stations Leary monitored allowed the candidates to speak in any sustained way to the public. The eventual winner, Jerry Brown, accumulated only 57 minutes of speaking time on all the newscasts over the course of the entire campaign. "With such abbreviated news exposure," she concluded, "advertising time became the critical avenue for getting a message across to television viewers."[88] Michael Robinson and Margaret Sheehan found a similar pattern in CBS's coverage of the 1980 presidential election. The network covered a good deal of personal information about Jimmy Carter and Ronald Reagan, along with their motivations and campaign plans. Less time was given to what they actually said.[89] Television is not, however, the only medium available. Radio and direct mail also play important roles as forms of paid media. Radio spots are easy to prepare. They are also relatively inexpensive and easy to target to particular regions and audiences. Voters in states such as Delaware, New Hampshire, and New Jersey are more efficiently reached via local radio than via television, which crosses more political boundaries.

Direct mail also has the virtue of being easy to target to particular audiences. As an advertising medium, it ranks with newspapers and television in total revenues. Adopting the techniques used by bulk-mail marketing strategists, politicians and public interest groups now frequently use direct mail appeals distributed to thousands of preselected addresses. A number of firms specialize in the collection and sale of mailing lists tailored to meet particular target audiences. The goal is usually to find receptive supporters who will contribute money or time to a candidate or cause, often with great success. For example, in his effective 1996 win of a seat in the Senate, New

Jersey's Robert Torricelli invested heavily in direct mail fund-raising, spending a total of $122,677 in fees to a firm specializing in solicitations. The effort yielded handsome returns, producing $17 in donations for every dollar spent "prospecting" for them.[90] Direct mail may also be used to target potential voters in an attempt to persuade them to vote for a particular candidate. EMILY's List[91] is particularly effective at using direct mail.

> In May of 2006, Ohio WOMEN VOTE! sent 14 different mail pieces contrasting Betty Sutton's honest leadership with her opponents' questionable ethical standards in a district [eight-way Democratic primary for a U.S. House seat in Ohio's 13th congressional district] where voters had grown weary of political corruption. By surveying voters, EMILY's List was able to identify key messages, test the effectiveness of mail pieces, and modify the persuasion strategy accordingly. Ohio WOMEN VOTE! helped Betty Sutton go from four percent in the polls to leading her well-funded, well-connected opponents by sending 468,336 pieces of mail.[92]

What seems increasingly evident in assessing the use of paid media in campaigns and other settings is that the technology and cost continue to advance at a much faster rate than our knowledge of its effectiveness. Presidential campaigns now make extensive use of satellites to reach supporters and quickly capture opposition ads as they are broadcast. Phone banks are activated to mobilize preselected constituents who may contribute to a campaign or write a letter to a member of Congress. Sites on the Web reach communities of like-minded voters and activists delivering reports on pending congressional votes and recent political activity.

Free media. Much has already been said about "free" media in our earlier discussions of agenda setting and gatekeeping. From the perspective of the political agent, media are "free" if they give publicity to your cause in the context of a news story. Finding ways to court journalists is a necessity at all levels of American political life, because there is never enough money to purchase all the paid media a politician will desire. The process of winning favorable coverage involves a kind of courtship based on the principle of reciprocity. In return for the coverage news gatherers give to a press conference or speech, publicity seekers make attempts to have these events conform to standard definitions of news. Their goal is to produce the "good press" that results when a story leaves a generally favorable impression with the reading and viewing public. The relationship is inherently loaded with tension, much like a troubled marriage. Politicians generally want favorable interpretations of their actions. They need to be heard and understood. The press, on the other hand, does not want to be "taken in" and "used." Elsewhere in this text we have more specifically detailed the nature of press relations in political campaigns (chapter 8), the White House (chapter 12), and Congress (chapter 13).

This constant courtship and tension is evident on nearly every page of Katharine Graham's exhaustive 1997 *Personal History.* In her memoir she documents in fascinating detail the many channels and back channels of communication between *The Washington Post* and the power structure of official Washington. Graham assumed leadership of the newspaper after her husband's suicide, and she inherited an institution that had alternately befriended and alienated every modern presidential administration. The brilliant but erratic Phil Graham led the paper before his death in 1963. At the same time he had become an intimate friend of John Kennedy and many key officials in his administration. As she describes it, the paper seemed close to functioning as an administration mouthpiece in the early 1960s. The following terms of Lyndon Johnson and Richard Nixon were far more varied, with the paper alternately supporting and challenging their most visible and controversial actions. Katharine Graham was a frequent guest of Lyndon Johnson in the White House and at his home in Texas. Though press coverage of the Vietnam War strained their "intimate" and "friendly" relations, it was not until Richard Nixon's presidency that the proprietors of the *Post* broke dramatically with an administration. Watergate vividly enacted the "adversarial" model of journalism, attracting many more into its ranks as a result but also making administrations much more wary of the impact of the national media. In its aftermath, neither the Grahams of *The Washington Post* nor the American public would be as unconditionally supportive of an American president as they had once been.

We can also see this relationship from the White House's point of view. For example, Ari Fleischer, in *Taking Heat: The President, the Press, and My Years in the White House*, details his experiences during his tenure as press secretary from 2001 to 2003.[93] In it he provides examples of the many ways the press attempted to have him say something he did not mean and also how the press would often look for a "conflict" about which to report. Fleischer also spends a good deal of time asking why the press reported similar behaviors of President Clinton and President Bush, differently.

Politicians and Reporters: Two Models of Their Uneasy Relationship

One useful way to assess the nature of free media is to consider two popular but contrasting models of the relationships that can exist between news makers and news reporters. We call one model, which gives power to the former, the *news management model*. The other model, which gives more power to the press, we call the *attack press model*. The news management model emphasizes the power of key leaders and officials to control information that is released through the pipeline of the press. The power to dictate story lines, "the message of the day," and show attractive pictures that leave a positive impression rests with those who can manage and manipulate information for their own advantage. Reporters covering the presidency often assume this model is dominant.[94] Many feel like they are hostages to an advance script prepared by the campaign to win favorable press coverage.

There is no shortage of "rules" for securing "good press." Even today these rules are usually similar to those identified by Mark Hertsgaard as part of the Reagan White House.[95]

- Plan ahead
- Stay on the offensive
- Control the flow of information
- Limit reporters' access to the president
- Talk about the issues you want to talk about
- Speak in one voice
- Repeat the same message many times

A specific case that can be documented from the White House files of Lyndon Johnson is especially revealing of news management practices today; thus we provide an overview here. Johnson was long aware of his inadequacies as a television spokesman for his own administration. Television captured all too well his turgid defenses of administration policies. At best, he was a slow and stiff public speaker, a style that concealed what others who knew the private Johnson recognized as a more animated and likable man. He sought help from Robert Kintner by making the former president of NBC television his special assistant. Although Kintner's duties varied, and his tenure was comparatively short, he worked to improve the sagging Johnson image.

A sampling of some of the confidential memos Kintner sent to the president just before and after the 1967 State of the Union address points to the broadcaster's ability to tap the support of former colleagues for political gain. They demonstrate the tendency common in all forms of politics to build bridges between what are supposedly separate power blocks: politicians and the press. In one case, Kintner sought to put Johnson's speech in a favorable context by using key White House figures to brief (that is, to provide talking points to) reporters from *The New York Times, The Washington Post, Time* magazine, and the networks:

> I had a meeting with [Johnson advisors] Harry McPherson, Doug Cater, Joe Califano and Walt Rostow, particularly in relation to the meaning of the Civil Rights portion of your State of the Union address, but also in relation to the principal points of the talk. We divided up various key [journalism] people in town to background including, [Max] Frankel, [James] Kilpatrick, [Joseph] Kraft, [Tom] Wicker, [Hedley] Donavan, [Charles] Bartlett, Joe Alsop, etc. . . . In addition, I will try to do some work with the news chiefs of ABC, NBC and CBS.[96]

In the news management model, then, key leaders have the power to shape coverage that is in their own interests. We may well see this same trend operating with the Bush White House's appointment of former FOX news reporter Tony Snow to the position of press secretary in 2006.

The "attack press" model takes a different view, making the institution of journalism more powerful. In this form "the fourth branch of government" is a powerful check on the other three, a force to be reckoned with because its power to narrate events is also the power to judge. As James Fallows notes:

> Everyone knows that big-time journalists have become powerful and prominent. We see them shouting at presidents during White House press conferences. We hear them offering instant Thumbs up/Thumbs Down verdicts a few seconds after a politician completes a speech. We know that they swarm from one hot news event to the next—from a press conference by Gennifer Flowers, to a riot site in Los Angeles, to congressional hearings on a Supreme Court nominee.[97]

One can easily substitute Cindy Sheehan for Flowers, or a spontaneous celebration by Cuban expatriates over Castro's diminishing health for the LA riots, or the 9/11 Commission for the Supreme Court to see the long-lasting nature of Fallows's comments.

Larry Sabato has similarly described what he sees as excessive press interest in stories that play on public suspicions that politicians are corrupt.[98] We now expect the news media to seek out "wounded" politicians "like sharks in a feeding frenzy." Watergate, the Iran-Contra affair, the Monica Lewinsky affair, and other assorted lapses in judgment have primed the press's appetite for stories that suggest investigative rigor. The wounds may have been self-inflicted, and the politician may richly deserve his or her fate, but journalists now take center stage in the process, creating the news as much as reporting it, changing both the shape of election-year politics and the contours of government.[99] As Comstock and Scharrer note, the "frenzy occurs when multiple press outlets pursue a scandalous revelation or an unfortunate gaffe. There is a surfeit, an arguable excess, because the topic remains on the news agenda at the expense of other, often more significant, stories."[100]

The reporting that came out of the Watergate affair, for example, probably contributed to a feeling of romance and vindication for a probing and even hostile form of journalism. Unfortunately, recent years have shown no sign of public fatigue in what many see as an excessive news media interest in sensationalistic reporting that offers little more than the appearance of investigative work. As one reporter noted after leaving a newsweekly in 1996, "I felt at *Newsweek* we were less interested in covering the essence of the Republican revolution than in the divorce rates of the freshman class."[101] Ten years later, this trend continues still.

Aside from the goal of investigating wrongdoing, attack journalism has also taken another form that could be called the *journalism of attitude*. It seems increasingly easy to find reporters and columnists who communicate more attitude than information: writers who use the sparest of facts or information as springboards into extended put-downs of political figures and their actions. Fed by television's fascination for punchy debate about political topics (e.g., CNN's *Crossfire*, MSNBC's *Hardball*, and others), some journalists now make their reputations on their abilities to offer caustic one-liners at the expense of public officials. For instance, *New York Times* political columnist Maureen Dowd on occasion writes with cutting wit about the imperfect physical appearance of a leader. At other times she invents a soliloquy, offering what she *thinks* may be going on in a politician's head. In one such piece in 2003, she portrayed President Bush, who had just arrived on the *U.S.S. Lincoln*, as a character out of the movie *Top Gun*:

> out bounded the cocky, rule-breaking, daredevil flyboy, a man navigating the Highway to the Danger Zone, out along the edges where he was born to be, the further on the edge, the hotter the intensity. He flashed that famous all-American grin as he swaggered around the deck.... Compared to Karl Rove's ... mythmaking cinematic style, Jerry Bruckheimer's movies look like *Lizzie McGuire*. This time Maverick [President Bush] didn't just nail a few bogeys ... this time the Top Gun [President Bush] wasted a couple of nasty regimes.... He swaggered across the deck to high-five his old gang.[102]

Putting words in the president's mouth, she has him utter: "That's right ... I am dangerous."[103]

To be sure, politics has always had its satirists and cartoonists, ranging from Will Rogers to Jules Fieffer; or to today's Web sites, such as whitehouse.org or thepeoplescube.com. Anyone going into public life needs a sturdy sense of humor. But many journalists have grown increasingly uneasy with the journalism of attitude that has edged into more traditional reporting. Its effect over time seems to be to pull reporting away from ideas and toward feelings that merely pander to the latent hostilities of the public. As one journalist who left daily reporting noted, "It's a business that grinds people up."[104]

Message Saliency: Basic Considerations

Jimmy Carter once appeared on a game show just four years before he became president, and no one then knew who he was. The object of the show was to guess a person's line of work. In 1973, though, the Georgia governor was a complete unknown, nationally.[105] That he could go from obscurity to prominence in such a short period of time demonstrates the potency of mass media exposure. U.S. Senator Barack Obama also went from obscurity to recognition. A nationally unknown Illinois state senator, while running for the U.S. Senate in 2004 he was allowed to give the keynote address at the Democrat National Convention. The media feeding frenzy that surrounded this event catapulted Obama, like Carter, from obscurity to prominence. Just two years a U.S. Senator, Obama is now seeking the Democratic nomination for president.

By far the most vexing problem facing political advocates is attempting to predict the impact that individual messages or entire campaigns will have on mass media audiences. Our predicament at the beginning of the twenty-first century is still much like that of tobacco magnate George Washington Hill at the beginning of the twentieth. He believed that half of the money that his company spent on advertising was wasted. The unsolved problem, Hill said, was to find out which half.[106] We tend to remember the spectacular successes—the effective speech or series of commercials that dramatically transformed a troubled situation into a victorious one. Richard Nixon's "Checkers" address cited at the outset of this chapter, Bill Clinton's masterful run for the presidency in 1992, the tide of negative publicity about the pharmaceutical industry are but a few of the hundreds of catalytic events where attitudes changed in response to an effective marriage of media and message. Like television advertisers who can sometimes dramatically increase the market share for a given product, every public figure with access to the mass media audience is conscious of the benefits they can bring.

Our knowledge of what makes successful appeals remains incomplete, however. "Some kinds of communication on some kinds of issues, brought to the attention of some kinds of people under some kinds of conditions, have some kinds of effects." That was Bernard Berelson's 1948 summation of the state of mass media research.[107] It still seems valid to us today. It is extremely difficult to accurately link media exposure to attitude change, and the matter is further complicated by increasing suspicions in the general public that the news media are often "unfair, inaccurate and pushy."[108] Moreover, the public finds that the press also "hurt democracy" (33 percent), "are politically biased" (60 percent), and "favor one side in politics" (72 percent).[109]

Probably the most compelling evidence of rapid impact comes in campaigns, where private tracking polls register the impact of heavy media advertising. These small sample polls are taken frequently—often every day—as the campaign moves into high gear. Shifts in public interest in an issue, in approval for one political approach over another, and in candidate responses to attacks are all closely monitored and frequently lead to adjustments in daily tactics. Pollsters point out that they discover a great deal in tracking polls about what is working and what is not.[110] Moreover, reporters are quick to identify the "geniuses" running campaigns: Dick Morris for Bill Clinton or Karl Rove for George Bush. Be that as it may, even in "textbook" cases of alleged advertising effectiveness—such Richard Nixon's victory in 1968—it is possible to overestimate media power. As one member of that campaign has since conceded, the effect of the entire paid media blitz was "not large compared with the real determinants of the election's outcome," including an increasing dislike of Lyndon Johnson.[111]

Consider as well some of the broad obstacles that need to be addressed in assessing media impact in less volatile periods. One of the certainties regarding human attitude formation, for example, is that attitudes are highly resistant to short-term appeals. Opinions, beliefs, and attitudes tend to be elastic when pressed against the hard surface of an opposing point of view.

They may momentarily give some ground to a persuasive appeal. They are likely, however, to assume their old shape when the stimulus for change is withdrawn.[112] Individual speeches, occasional exposure to advertisements, and similar short-term encounters are unlikely to have much effect on what we think and are even less likely to produce durable changes in attitudes and behaviors. When we concede, as we must, that attitudes are shaped by long-term factors, *we are also forced to recognize that simple experimental or survey research on attitude formation becomes extremely difficult to devise, given the pluralism of influences that exist in ordinary life.* A corporation introducing a new product on the market may indeed be able to trace the effectiveness of advertising and other marketing strategies, because public knowledge of the new items will have started from a "zero" base. No similar information vacuum exists for most presidential candidates, national issues, or pending legislative questions. All usually have some public history and level of interest that has already been established.

It is also important to note that political attitudes or related behaviors, such as voting, signing a petition, or speaking on behalf of a position are more likely to be intensified rather than changed. This is because the process of changing our attitudes is much more difficult than the process of forming them. The first involves discarding an inconsistent or conflicting attitude in favor of a new one, a process that is very slow and usually incremental. The latter is psychologically easier; something is simply added or intensified rather than replaced. This explains why most changes that occur in individuals subject to political appeals are defined in terms of the *activation* or *crystallization* of attitudes. If individuals have an interest in an event, they are more easily drawn to new information that confirms their interest, a factor that plays a big part in determining whether a news story is important or not. Thus, for better or worse—Americans have generally low levels of interest in political campaigns and policy debates (see table 5.1).

Over the past twenty years, the Pew Center for the People and the Press has tracked the extent to which random samples of Americans have followed over 550 news stories. In descending order, the list below is a sample of stories ranging from those often followed "very closely" to those rarely followed. Out of the total of over 550 stories, none of the top 20 dealt with political processes, although several focused on war actions, and the aftermath of 9/11.

If media effects are inexact, then what conclusions can we draw? We offer three. (1) *Consumers of all forms of political discourse are selective rather than reflexive.* That is to say, we are most likely to give our attention to the information that is most readily available to us, and that comports with our preexisting beliefs. (2) *For most consumers there is an enormous gap between time spent with any mass medium and what one would normally expect in the way of effects.* For all the rhetorical skills utilized by a side in a political conflict, recall and attitude-change levels can be surprisingly low.[113] As a form of protection against the constant buffetings created by new information, the

Table 5.1   Public Attentiveness to News Stories: A Selected Sample

Date	Event	Percent who followed these stories "very closely"
July 1986	Challenger disaster	80%
October 2001	Terrorist attacks on the U.S. (general)	78%
September 2001	Terrorist attacks on World Trade Center and Pentagon	74%
October 2005	Impact of Hurricanes Katrina and Rita	73%
November 1989	San Francisco earthquake	73%
September 2005	High gas prices	71%
May 1992	Rodney King case/verdict and riots	70%
October 1987	Little girl in well, Texas	69%
April 1999	High school shooting in Littleton, CO	68%
August 1990	Iraq's invasion of Kuwait	66%
October 2002	Sniper shootings near Washington, DC	65%
July 1986	U.S. air strike on Libya	58%
September 1990	Increase in price of gas	56%
January 2003	Debate on war with Iraq	55%
December 1996	Outcome of the Presidential election	55%
July 1999	Death of JFK Jr. and 2 others	54%
September 1997	Death of Princess Diana	54%
May 1993	Waco, Texas, Branch Davidian incident	50%
June 1994	O.J. Simpson case	48%
October 1991	Break-up of the Soviet Union	47%
May 1993	Rodney King trial and verdict in LA	47%
July 1986	Chernobyl accident	46%
September 2002	Anniversary of 9/11 attacks	39%
August 1998	Clinton–Lewinsky investigation	33%
February 2002	Abduction of WSJ reporter Daniel Pearl	24%
September 1996	Possible life on Mars	8%
July 2003	Publication of Hillary Clinton's book	8%
April 1990	Tom Cruise's split from wife	2%

typical consumer apparently shuts much of it out. (3) *Political communication needs to be envisioned as occurring in tiers of influence, where the mass media function as both the carrier as well as shaper of messages.* Our constant focus on the media as a means of mass persuasion mistakenly gives them sole possession of the power to persuade, yet such a simplification distorts what is a far more complex reality.

In addition to being initiators of their own forms of influence, the mass media are acted on by many external forces. They are both the targets and agents of control. As noted above, their content can be subject to news management by some elites such as the president, a powerful institution like NASA, or their own corporate hierarchy.

What we have described is a diffuse system of communication. None of the many contributors to the political process—the press, the advertising industry, campaign consultants, power blocks, and powerful individuals—have a complete franchise on the political process. At various times all are able to influence the news agenda, while at other times conceding its formation to others.

Summary

The relationships between the news media and various types of political blocks are subtle and variable. As the opening sections of this chapter suggest, even the best crystal ball for exploring this process is bound to remain partly cloudy. The term *media* is itself a problematic concept, as are attributions of media power in shaping political attitudes. Even so, there are several basic frameworks for assessing how political agents interact with those in the media and information business. They include the core concept of gatekeeping, which explains the essential processes by which content is selected and shaped. As we noted here, the rules of media gatekeeping are especially important in understanding how political events reach the public. Among other things, those rules give preference to officials over dissidents and to events that conform to the conventions of narration and melodrama.

Other basic frameworks for assessing the media's role in the political process hinge on distinctions between "free" and "paid," and on vary different models of the power relationship between members of the news media and the groups they cover. The "attack press" model assumes that journalism is its own power center, able to shape and influence public perceptions about those who participate in America's civil life. The "news management" model reverses the arrows and assigns greater control to news makers and their skillful public relations specialists. Both models can be useful in different settings, although there are limitations in our abilities to estimate the effectiveness of specific messages on specific channels.

A recurring theme throughout this section is that the media and the political world represent two blocks in an unsteady relationship. As we have described it, the press and the political world need each other and frequently develop alliances of convenience. However, each also remains capable of sustaining goals that are at odds with the other, frequently to the benefit of the American public. The "system" seems to work best when these elements are truly semiautonomous, when friction between them provides a larger window to the political landscape. We sometimes view this friction as a sign of our national disintegration. In some ways, though, events such as the Watergate or Whitewater scandals—with their conflicting White House, congressional, and national press objectives—demonstrated the vibrancy of American pluralism. We should expect no less from a society so well-endowed with the technical means for creating a truly enlightened democracy.

Notes

[1] Gary Woodward contributed to portions of this chapter, originally found in Robert E. Denton, Jr., and Gary Woodward, *Political Communication in America*, 3rd Edition (Westport, CT: Praeger, 1998), 63–92.

[2] This amount in 2005 dollars would be a little under $120,000 when linked to the Consumer Price Index.

[3] Richard Nixon, *Six Crises* (New York: Pyramid, 1968).

[4] Ibid., 122.

[5] United States, *The World Factbook* https://www.cia.gov/library/publications/the-world-factbook/print/us.html

[6] "History of Cable Television," *National Cable and Telecommunications Association*. Retrieved 11 September 2007 from http://www.ncta.com/ContentView.aspx?contentId=54

[7] Peter Feuilherade, "TVs and PCs 'take over US homes,'" *BBC News* (October 7, 2005). Retrieved 11 September 2007 from http://news.bbc.co.uk/2/hi/technology/4318318.stm

[8] "Online Papers Modestly Boost Newspaper Readership," The Pew Research Center for the People and the Press (July 30, 2006). Retrieved 11 September 2007 from http://people-press.org/reports/display.php3?ReportID=282

[9] Andie Tucher, "You News," *Columbia Journalism Review* (May/June, 1997): 26, 29.

[10] "Online Papers Modestly Boost Newspaper Readership."

[11] Joellen Perry, "Sign of the Times," *U.S. News and World Reports* (May 18, 2003). Retrieved 11 September 2007 from http://www.usnews.com/usnews/culture/articles/030526/26times.htm. See also Edwin Diamond, *Behind the Times* (Chicago: University of Chicago Press, 1995), 381–386.

[12] Walter Lippmann, *Public Opinion.* (New York: Macmillan, 1930) 29.

[13] "Top Ten Stories of 2005," *World Press.org* (February 3, 2006). Retrieved 11 September 2007 from http://www.worldpress.org/2256.cfm

[14] Jim A. Kuypers and Andrew King, "What is Rhetoric?" in Jim A. Kuypers, ed. *The Art of Rhetorical Criticism* (Boston: Pearson, Allyn & Bacon, 2005) 4–5. Italics omitted.

[15] Michael Novak, *Choosing Our King* (New York: Macmillan, 1974), 174.

[16] Joseph R. Dominick, *The Dynamics of Mass Communications: Media in the Digital Age*, 8th ed. (Boston: McGraw Hill, 2005), 14–15.

[17] Jennifer Akin, "Mass Media," *Beyond Intractability: A Free Knowledge Base on More Constructive Approaches to Destructive Conflict* (March 2005). Retrieved 11 September 2007 from http://www.beyondintractability.org/essay/mass_communication/

[18] Forrest McDonald, *The Presidency of George Washington* (New York: Norton, 1975), 24–26.

[19] Thomas Jefferson, "2nd Inaugural Address, 1805," in *The Writings of Thomas Jefferson* Memorial Edition, ed. Andrew Lipscomb and Albert Bergh (Washington, DC: Thomas Jefferson Memorial Foundation, 1903–04) 3:380.

[20] George Comstock and Erica Scharrer, *The Psychology of Media and Politics* (Burlington, MA: Elsevier Academic Press, 2005), 60.

[21] Along with others, *Tyndall Weekly* keeps track of how much time the networks are spending on major news stories. See http://www.tyndallreport.com/. See Doris A. Graber, *Mass Media and American Politics,* 7th ed. (Washington, DC: Congressional Quarterly, 2005).

[22] Shanto Iyengar and Donald R. Kinder, *News That Matters* (Chicago: University of Chicago Press, 1987),112–133.

[23] Robert K. Goidel, Craig M. Freeman, and Steven T. Procopic, "The Impact of Television Viewing on Perceptions of Juvenile Crime," *Journal of Broadcasting and Electronic Media* 50.1 (2006): 134–135. Although this study focuses on a rather narrow sample of the population in Louisiana, we feel it is a good example of the type of effects research presently being conducted.

[24] Iyengar and Kinder address many of these issues in their own research, pp. 6–15. See also Neal Riemer, Douglas W. Simon, and Joseph Romance, *The Challenge of Politics: An Introduction to Political Science*, 2nd Ed. (CQ Press, 2006), esp. Chapter 4—"The Scientific Enterprise."

[25] McGraw and Milton Lodge, "Political Information Processing: A Review Essay." *Political Communication* 13 (1996): 133.

[26] Project for Excellence in Journalism, "Executive Summary," *2006 Annual Report on the State of the News Media*. Retrieved 11 September 2007 from http://www.stateofthenewsmedia.org/2006/index.asp

[27] Project for Excellence.

[28] Project for Excellence.

[29] Project for Excellence.

[30] Project for Excellence.

[31] Project for Excellence.

[32] Project for Excellence.

[33] Project for Excellence.

[34] Project for Excellence.

[35] Project for Excellence.

[36] Project for Excellence.

[37] Project for Excellence.

[38] Kurt Lewin, "Frontiers in Group Dynamics," *Human Relations*, 1, no. 2 (1947): 145.

[39] David Manning White, "The 'Gatekeeper': A Case Study in the Selection of News," *Journalism Quarterly* 27 (1950): 419–427.

[40] Pamela J. Shoemaker, Martin Eichholz, Eunyi Kim, and Brenda Wriley, "Individual and Routine Forces in Gatekeeping," *Journalism and Mass Communication Quarterly* 78 (2001): 233.

[41] Max Frankel, "Live at 11: Death." *New York Times Magazine*, (June 15, 1997): 20.

[42] A trend that has been steady for some time, see "Newspapers: Audience," *State of the News Media, 2007: An Annual Report on American Journalism*. Retrieved 11 September 2007 from http://www.stateofthenewsmedia.org. Also see Elizabeth Gleick, "Read All about It." *Time* (October 21, 1996): 66–69.

[43] Comstock and Scharrer, *The Psychology of Media and Politics*, 171.

[44] Herbert Gans, *Deciding What's News* (New York: Vintage, 1980) 146–152.

[45] Ibid., 167–171.

[46] These categories and concerns go back further than Gans's 1980 study. See also Galtung, J. & Ruge, M. Holmboe (1965): *The Structure of Foreign News. The Presentation of the Congo, Cuba and Cyprus Crises in Four Norwegian Newspapers*, Journal of Peace Research, vol. 2, pp. 64–91.

[47] For instance, see Michael Schudson, *The Power of News* (Cambridge, MA: Harvard University Press, 1995), 12–14.

[48] Timothy Crouse, *The Boys on the Bus* (New York: Ballantine, 1972), 22–23.

[49] Matalin and James Carvill, *All's Fair* (New York: Random House/Touchstone, 1994) 126–127.

[50] Comstock and Scharrer, *The Psychology of Media and Politics*, 88.

[51] Frank Russell, "'These Crowded Circumstances': When *Pack Journalists* Bash *Pack Journalists*," *Journalism* 4.4 (2003): 455.

[52] For instance, see Susan Dente Ross, "*Pack Journalism*: May Occur When Journalists Join Together in Covering Events," in Margaret A. Blanchard, ed., *History of the Mass Media in*

the United States, An Encyclopedia. Chicago: Fitzroy Dearborn, 1998) 489–490; Dan Nimmo and James Combs, *Mediated Political Realities,* 2d ed. (New York: Longman, 1990); Lance W. Bennett, *News: The Politics of Illusion,* 2nd ed. (New York: Longman, 1988); Gans, cited above; Edward Epstein, *News From Nowhere* (New York: Vintage, 1974); Robert MacNeil, *The People Machine* (New York: Harper and Row, 1968).

53 James Combs, *Dimensions of Political Drama.* (Santa Monica, CA: Goodyear, 1980), 1–17.

54 Paul Weaver, "Captives of Melodrama," *New York Times Magazine*, (29 August 1976): 48–57.

55 Dan Nimmo and James Combs, *Mediated Political Realities,* 2d ed. (New York: Longman, 1990), 28.

56 As cited in Epstein, *News from Nowhere*, 4–5.

57 Elisabeth Anker, "Villains, Victims and Heroes: Melodrama, Media, and September 11," *Journal of Communication* 55.1 (2005), 23.

58 Craig R. Smith, following Aristotle, defines *ethos* as "the persuasive force of the credibility of the speaker." See Craig R. Smith, *Rhetoric and Human Consciousness: A History,* 2nd ed. (Long Grove, IL: Waveland Press, Inc., 2003), 73. For a full discussion of *ethos* see, George A. Kennedy, *Aristotle on Rhetoric: A Theory of Civic Discourse* (New York: Oxford University Press, 1991).

59 Richard Sennett, *The Fall of Public Man.* (New York: Vintage, 1978), 284.

60 Count as of July 2006. See Ernie Suggs and Sonji Jacobs, "McKinney, Johnson Clash Over Finances, Donors," *The Atlanta Journal-Constitution* (August 1, 2006). Retrieved 16 August 2006 from http://www.ajc.com/news/content/metro/dekalb/stories/0731metdebate.html

61 Sennett, *The Fall of Public Man*, 4.

62 Leon V. Sigal, *Reporters and Officials: The Organization and Politics of Newsmaking* (Lexington, MA: D.C. Heath and Co., 1973).

63 Here are a few examples of this: Kathleen A. Hansen and Jean Ward, "Local Breaking News: Sources, Technology and News Routines," *Journalism & Mass Communication Quarterly* 71 (Autumn 1994): 561–572; Kathleen A. Hansen, "Source Diversity and Newspaper Journalism," *Journalism Quarterly* 68 (Fall 1991): 474–482; Jane Delano Brown, Carl R. Bybee, Stanley Wearden and Dulcie M. Straughan, "Invisible Power: Newspaper News Sources and the Limits of Diversity," *Journalism & Mass Communication Quarterly* 64 (Spring 1987): 45–54; Dan Berkowitz, "TV News Sources and News Channels: A Study in Agenda-Building," *Journalism & Mass Communication Quarterly* 64 (Summer-Autumn 1987): 508–513; Guido H. Stempel and Hugh M. Culbertson, "The Prominence and Dominance of News Sources in Newspaper Coverage," *Journalism Quarterly* 61 (Autumn 1984): 671–676.

64 Hansen, "Source Diversity," 475. Evidence suggests, however, that local papers rely less on governmental sources. See, for instance, Debbie Owens, "An Analysis of News Sources in Two Miami Newspapers' Coverage of the Overtown and Liberty City Riots of 1989," *Howard Journal of Communication* 3 (1991): 149–154; Michael W. Salen, "News of Hurricane Andrew: The Agenda of Sources and the Sources' Agendas," *Journalism & Mass Communication Quarterly* 72 (Winter 1995): 826–840.

65 David Paletz and Robert Entman, *Media Power Politics* (New York: Free Press, 1981), 158.

66 Ibid., 157.

67 Janet E. Steele, "*Experts* and the operational bias of television *news*: The Case of the Persian Gulf War," *Journalism & Mass Communication Quarterly* 72, no. 4 (1995): 809.

68 Thomas E. Patterson, *Out of Order* (New York City, NY: Random House, 1993), 74.

69 Daniel C. Hallin, "Sound Bite News: Television Coverage of Elections, 1968–1988," *Journal of Communication* 42, no. 2 (1992): 5–24.

70 Comstock and Scharrer, *The Psychology of Media and Politics*, 105.

71 Ibid., 105.

72 Center for Media and Public Affairs, "Journalists Monopolize TV Election News: Study Finds Less Air Time, Shorter Sound Bites For Candidates" (October 3, 2000). Retrieved 11 September 2007 from http://www.cmpa.com/election2004/JournalistsMonopolize.htm

73 Robinson and Margaret Sheehan, *Over the Wire and on TV: CBS and UPI in Campaign '80* (New York: Russell Sage, 1983) 214–215.

[74] "Republicans and Democrats Resume Dispute Over Iraq War," *NBC Nightly News* NBC News Transcripts, 11 November 2005. Obtained online using Lexis-Nexus on 13 August 2006.

[75] Joseph N. Cappella and Kathleen Hall Jamieson, *Spiral of Cynicism: The Press and the Public Good* (New York: Oxford University Press, 1997) 34.

[76] Comstock and Scharrer, *The Psychology of Media and Politics*, 114–115.

[77] "Congressional Fundraising Continues to Grow" (Federal Election commission, August 18, 2004). Retrieved 11 September 2007 from http://www.fec.gov/press/press2004/20040818canstat/20040818canstat.html

[78] Information obtained at http:www.opensecrets.org

[79] Ibid.

[80] Steve McClellan, "Fox Breaks Prime-Time Pricing Record," *Adweek* (September 12, 2005). Retrieved 11 September 2007 from http://www.adweek.com/aw/search/article_display.jsp?vnu_content_id=1001096022

[81] Erik Barnouw, *The Sponsor: Notes on a Modern Potentate* (New York: Oxford University Press, 1978), 96.

[82] Michael Pfau and Henry Kenski, *Attack Politics: Strategy and Defense* (Westport, CT: Greenwood, 1990).

[83] Guido H. Stempel III, *Media and Politics in America* (Santa Barbara, Ca: ABC Clio, 2003), 34–35. Similar results are discussed by Thomas Patterson. *The Vanishing Voter: Public Involvement in an Age of Uncertainty* (New York City, NY: Knopf, 2003).

[84] Gary Mauser, *to Campaign Political Marketing: An Approach Strategy.* (New York: Praeger, 1983), 19.

[85] Patterson and Robert McClure, *The Unseeing Eye: The Myth of Television Power in National Politics* (New York: G. P. Putnam's, 1976), 22– 23.

[86] William L. Benoit, Glenn. J. Hansen, and R. Lance Holbert, "Presidential Campaigns and Democracy," *Mass Communication and Society* 7, no. 2 (2004).

[87] Comstock and Scharrer, *The Psychology of Media and Politics*, 159.

[88] Mary Ellen Leary, *Phantom Politics: Campaigning in California* (Washington, DC: Public Affairs, 1977), 90–91.

[89] Michael Robinson and Margaret Sheehan, *Over the Wire and on TV: CBS and UPI in Campaign '80* (New York: Russell Sage, 1983), 59.

[90] Dwight Morris, "Weeds in the Garden State." *PoliticsNow* (8 October 1996): 3.

[91] EMILY's List is self-described as "the nation's largest grassroots political network." Retrieved 11 September 2007 from http://www.emilyslist.org/about/

[92] "WOMEN VOTE! Activities." Retrieved 11 September 2007 from http://www.emilyslist.org/do/women-vote/doing_now.html

[93] Ari Fleischer, *Taking Heat: The President, the Press, and My Years in the White House* (New York City, NY: William Morrow & Company, 2005).

[94] Peter Stoler, *The War Against the Press.* (New York: Dodd and Mead, 1986), 165–180).

[95] Mark Hertsgaard, *On Bended Knee: The Press and the Reagan Presidency* (New York: Shocken, 1989) 34–35.

[96] Robert Kintner, Memo of January 11, 1967, White House Central File. Austin, TX: LBJ Library.

[97] James Fallows, *Breaking the News* (New York City, NY: Pantheon, 1996), 6.

[98] Sabato himself capitalized on this in 2006 when he accused then U.S. Senator George Allen of using racial slurs during his college days. See, "New 'N Word' Woe for George Allen" (September 26, 2006). Retrieved 11 September 2007 from http://www.cbsnews.com/stories/2006/09/26/politics/main2039589.shtml

[99] Larry Sabato, *The Rise of Political Consultants.* (New York: Basic Books, 1981) 1.

[100] Comstock and Scharrer, *The Psychology of Media and Politics*, 102.

[101] Howard Kurtz, "The New Reform School," *Washington Post*, (12 May 1997), B1.

[102] Maureen Dowd, "The Iceman Cometh," *The New York Times* (4 May 2003), D13.

[103] Maureen Dowd, "The Iceman Cometh," *The New York Times* (4 May 2003), D13.

[104] Kurtz, "The New Reform School," B1.

[105] Betty Glad, *Jimmy Carter: In Search of the Great White House.* (New York: W. W. Norton, 1980), 218.

[106] Andrew Hacker, "Poets and the Packaging of Desire," *New York Times Book Review,* (24 June 1984): 31.

[107] As cited in Cliff Zukin, "Mass Communication and Public Opinion," in *Handbook of Political Communication,* ed. Dan Nimmo and Keith Sanders, (Beverly Hills, CA: Sage, 1981), 359–390.

[108] "Press Unfair, Inaccurate and Pushy," The Pew Center for the People and the Press, (May 22, 1997): 1–3.

[109] "Public More Critical of Press, But Goodwill Persists: Online Newspaper Readership Countering Print Losses," The Pew Research Center for the People and the Press (June 26, 2005). Retrieved 11 September 2007 from http://people-press.org/reports/display.php3?ReportID=248

[110] Sabato, *The Rise of Political Consultants*, 76–77.

[111] Leonard Garment, *Crazy Rhythm.* New York: Times Books, 1997), 136.

[112] Graber, *Mass Media and American Politics*.

[113] For instance, see Robert M. Entman, *Democracy without Citizens* (New York: Oxford University Press, 1989), 32–36.

Agenda Setting, Agenda Extension, and the Political Landscape

> *Freedom of the press is essential to the preservation of a democracy; but there is a difference between freedom and license. Editorialists who tell downright lies in order to advance their own agendas do more to discredit the press than all the censors in the world.*
>
> —Franklin D. Roosevelt

In the last chapter we saw that gatekeeping theory explores the bases used for determining how much space or time certain events will receive in a given media outlet. In this chapter we will see how the agenda-setting function assigns the role of focusing attention on certain topics and away from others. It is both obvious and important to note that the media collectively exert a considerable influence in determining the agenda of topics that will surface in the public consciousness. "The press," Walter Lippmann noted, "is like a beam of a searchlight that moves restlessly about, bringing one episode then another out of darkness into vision."[1] As the pioneering studies by Maxwell McCombs and Donald L. Shaw have suggested, our knowledge about and interest in various news topics are largely governed by what the mass media decide to call news.[2] After a discussion of agenda setting, the remainder of this chapter will explore the concept of agenda extension, which involves the potential shaping of our knowledge of the news.

Agenda Setting

The agenda-setting power of the media is their ability to focus their light on what would otherwise be a dark corner of our national life. As Bernard C.

Cohen explains, the press "may not be very successful in telling its readers what to think, but it is stunningly successful in telling its readers what to think about."[3] Of particular interest to us, is that this agenda-setting function of the press helps explain how press reports interact with political discourse and the public perceptions of that discourse. In so many words, the press offers us a good indication of the issues and events that informed voters will be talking about. Studies of the agenda-setting function of the media suggest that it does "have a great deal of influence" on political decision making; in particular, the media are especially influential in telling the general population what issues and events to think about.[4]

For example, in their seminal study, McCombs and Shaw argue that voters learn about an issue "in direct proportion" to the attention given that issue by the press; moreover, voters tend to consider important those issues and events defined as important by the media.[5] Further, these researchers assert that the news media provide voters with the "major primary sources of national political information."[6] Other studies have found that the news media have the potential to set our government's agenda, even at the highest levels.[7] McCombs and Shaw explain:

> The press is an independent force whose dialogue with other elements of society produces the agenda of issues considered by political elites and voters. Witness the major role of the elite press as a source of information among major decision makers. Through its winnowing of the day's happenings to find the major events, concerns, and issues, the press inadvertently plays an agenda-setting influence role.[8]

However, this influence is not uniformly unidirectional. Summing up research in this area, Guido H. Stempel states that one must look at the interaction among members of the media, news sources, and consumers of the news: "Agenda setting raises the question of which of the three sets the agenda—the media, the politicians, or the public. Research has established that each does so in certain circumstances."[9] We believe the strongest effect occurs from the news media to the public, and this is where we focus the remainder of this chapter.

Often, the longer an issue remains in news focus, the more the public perceives it as a crisis. Stressing the importance of this consideration, Michael B. Salwen writes that many politicians "will address issues only when these issues are perceived as crises by the public."[10] Agenda-setting studies do strongly suggest, then, that the news media shape not only what the public "perceives" as "political reality" but also how political elites understand what voters and opinion leaders are thinking about.[11] George Comstock and Erica Scharrer found that individuals "look to the news media to determine the topics and events they should be concerned about, inferring that only important matters find their way to newspapers, newsmagazines, and newscasts and setting their own stated priorities of issues accordingly."[12]

Although we believe that the press is in a unique position to set the agenda of discussion for the public, one specific exception concerns statements made by the president. Because he is the major source of news at the national level, the president is in a "strategic position to influence the agenda" of the press.[13] McCombs and colleagues found evidence of "presidential influence on subsequent press coverage."[14] Although the president is occasionally able to influence coverage of issues, other politicians and social leaders are not in the same position of authority.

Given the degree to which the public relies on the press for information, we can see how the "news media exercise a near monopoly as sources of information and orientation."[15] On this point Doris A. Graber writes:

> We look at the front page of the newspaper and expect to find the most important stories there. We may watch the opening minutes of a telecast eagerly and then allow our attention to slacken. As a result, agenda setting by the media leads to uniformities in exposure as well as in significance ratings of new items. When the media make events seem important, average people as well as politicians discuss them and form opinions. This enhances the perceived importance of these events and ensures even more public attention and, possibly, political action.[16]

This effect is most noticeable with new events or issues that have not been previously discussed or that are beyond one's personal experience.[17]

Arguably the most significant political news story in recent U.S. history was the product of dogged reporting that eventually forced other media to follow suit. The 1972 break-in of burglars at the Watergate complex in Washington was initially a local crime story of little interest to anyone beyond a few reporters and editors at *The Washington Post.* It became much more, as links were established between the burglars discovered in the offices of the Democratic Party and members of President Nixon's reelection committee. Other media were slow to see the significance of the break-in that resulted in the cover-up that would in turn lead to the resignation of the president on the eve of an impeachment trial. However, through continual coverage, attention became fixed, and other news outlets followed.[18] More recently, after CBS's *60 Minutes II* broke the Abu Ghraib prisoner abuse story on April 28, 2004, the news media accorded it months of intense coverage.[19] *The New York Times* alone ran 32 days of front-page coverage on this issue between May 1 and June 1, 2004. *The Los Angeles Times* ran 26 days of front-page coverage. The extreme focus by the *Times* and other news sources led this to be one of the most talked about events of 2004. Ultimately, the attention given to this issue by the press led to the U.S. Senate voting on October 5, 2005, "to set new limits on interrogating detainees in Iraq and elsewhere, underscoring Congress's growing concerns about reports of abuse of suspected terrorists and others in military custody."[20] In terms of agenda setting, consider that as *The Los Angeles Times* ran so many front- page stories on this one story, the story of the beheading of Nicholas Berg received one mention on page 16.[21] Those who set the agenda make the decisions about how much coverage an issue or event receives.

Largely speaking, the actual news agendas of the most circulated U.S. newspapers seem to have changed little over the past 20 years; there has been, however, a shift in the kinds of stories favored by the network news organizations The table below shows the percentage of all stories filed by reporters (in rounded numbers), appearing on the nightly news programs of the major television networks between for 1977–2003, according to story topic.

ABC, CBS, NBC Nightly News Topics Over Time: Percentage of All Stories

	1977	1987	1997	June 2001	Oct. 2001	2002	2003
Government	37%	32%	18%	5%	7%	5%	16%
Foreign/Military	21	19	15	17	10	21	25
Defense	1	1	3	6	29	16	3
Domestic	8	7	5	18	34	12	16
Crime	8	7	13	12	4	12	6
Business	6	11	7	14	5	11	12
Celebrity/Enter.	2	3	8	5	0	2	2
Lifestyle	4	11	14	13	1	17	6
Science	4	5	6	4	11	2	2
Accidents/Disasters	9	5	10	4	0	3	10
Other	N.A.	N.A.	N.A.	3	0	N.A.	2

Another way to look at this is to consider that each nightly news broadcast consists of about 30 minutes of news. If you were to watch each weeknight for a month, roughly 10 hours of news, this is what you would have seen in 2003.[22]

   97 minutes on foreign affairs

   74 minutes on government matters

   22 minutes on accidents and disasters

   16 minutes on crime

   7 minutes on education

   4 minutes on the environment

   1 minute on culture and the arts

   1 minute on family and parenting

The reasons for these changes over time are difficult to track. Some suggest that television news is more responsive to the commercial need to follow audience tastes, generally with greater attention to news they "want" to know rather than "need" to know.[23] Others point out that the most highlighted stories on the network news are not necessarily the ones to which the public pays the most attention.[24]

During the mid 1990s, agenda-setting researchers began to investigate second-level agenda-setting effects.[25] Agenda setting describes the role of the news media in focusing the public's attention on a particular object or issue in preference to another object or issue. Second-level agenda setting explores how the media focus audience attention on particular attributes within a particular object or issue. As Comstock and Scharrer write,

> News reports often focus on particular properties of candidates, events, and issues, especially in the medium of television in which constraints on time and an emphasis on simplicity largely eliminate the possibility of presenting multiple aspects within a single story.[26]

In terms of politics, the literature suggests that those exposed to the news will use the highlighted aspects to make their decisions about candidates; that is to say, whatever characteristics of a candidate are highlighted by the news will be the same characteristics used by those exposed to the news to judge that candidate.

Agenda Extension

Whereas agenda setting serves to focus public attention on an issue, and second-level effects point to the highlighting of some aspects of a particular event or person over others, agenda extension occurs when the media move beyond a neutral reporting of issues, persons, and events. In short, researchers in this area have discovered that the reportorial practices of the news media still tell us *what* to think about; however, such practices also tell us *how* to think about it.

A limitation of agenda-setting research is that it is not designed for assessing the potential impact of *how* attributes are presented to the public. For example, in the 2004 elections, were George Bush's campaign themes positively or negatively framed (we discuss framing in detail below) when compared to the themes expressed by John Kerry? Russell Dalton and colleagues provide a good example of using agenda setting to determine coverage of candidates' issues.[27] Looking at the 1992 presidential election and the national press coverage of the candidates, the researchers found that candidates' "messages are well represented in press coverage of the campaign."[28] Of note is that these researchers found no bias in the coverage provided by the papers simply because the papers covered the issues brought up by the candidates. Using an agenda-extension perspective, one moves beyond frequency of reporting on an issue, event, or attribute to examine the manner in which the specific issue, event, or attribute is presented—thus one may look for ways that news reporters and editors slip in—consciously or not—their evaluations of the subject matter, thus inviting readers and viewers to think about an issue in a particular way.

This evaluative component to news was first highlighted in the 1980s by researchers exploring the agenda-setting functions of the press. Their studies reveal two considerations that move beyond agenda setting and relate to the public evaluation of political leaders; these aspects are called priming and framing. One way of understanding priming and framing is by looking at the contextual cues of journalists, which provide audiences a means "by which to evaluate the subject matter" under consideration.[29]

Priming

In its simplest form, priming is "the effects of the content of the media on people's later behavior or judgments related to that content."[30] According to many priming researchers, priming "occurs when this increased attention increases the prominence of these issues in the judgments people form about public officials."[31] Priming works because "by calling attention to some aspects of national life while ignoring others, network news programs determine the standards by which presidents [and political leaders] are judged."[32] Iyengar and Kinder explain that this occurs because public attention is highly selective and that the public relies mainly on information that is easily accessible. The public's judgments about political matters are due in part to what standards come to individuals' minds; they are also due to those "considerations that are, for whatever reason and however briefly, accessible."[33] Mainstream news outlets are easy and accessible sources for news.

In general, the findings of priming studies suggest that news coverage that implies a politician's responsibility for a situation at the national level encourages viewers to attach more importance to that politician's performance on that particular situation when evaluating overall performance. This "effect appears to be stronger for problems that are relative newcomers to the American political agenda, problems for which the public's understanding is still in formation."[34] However, when issues are ongoing—abortion, affirmative action, etc.—the effects of priming may not be as strong.[35] Priming has its effect as a product

> of a change in what items are more easily accessed in memory due to recent and/or frequent activation induced by consumption of media messages. Media outlets, by focusing on certain topics, tend to make knowledge about those topics more likely to be culled forth in working memory, and thus more likely to be used in generating opinions about political actors and events.[36]

Anne Johnston, in a review of media scholarship, discovered this priming effect is well documented.[37] Much of this research focuses on the president. For example, the American public becomes primed to evaluate the president by how well he handles the issue covered by the press. Thus, the greater the press coverage, the more the public will evaluate the president's success or failure in relation to the content of that press coverage. A survey of the work in this area suggests that, "problems prominently positioned in television [news] broadcasts loom large in evaluations of presidential performance."[38] In this light, news stories provide their audiences with more than the important subjects to think about; the coverage also provides "contextual cues or frames in which to evaluate those subjects."[39]

Shanto Iyengar and Adam Simon, studying the effects of network news coverage during the first Gulf War, define priming as the "ability of news programs to affect the criteria by which political leaders are judged."[40] For these researchers, priming involves the correlation among patterns of news coverage and how the public evaluates the performance of politicians. They found that effects on evaluation are strongest in the area of performance and weakest in the area of personality. In analyzing the news coverage of the Gulf War, Iyengar and Simon found that newscasts focused primarily on foreign policy concerns over other potential concerns that could have occupied the time of the first president Bush. Correspondingly, in terms of the role that priming played, foreign policy "performance assessments tended to override economic assessments in their impact on . . . ratings of George Bush during the Gulf crisis."[41]

Thus, it appears that the more the news media cover an issue, the more the public's evaluation of success or failure will be made *in relation to the content of media coverage* as opposed to the actual actions of a particular political actor. In addition, this "effect appears to be stronger for problems that are relative newcomers to the American political agenda, problems for which the public's understanding is still in formation."[42] Thus, when announcing new public policy initiatives, when public knowledge is in flux and new knowledge is constantly being injected into the public's evaluative consciousness, the effects of priming could be considerable. However, when issues are ongoing—abortion, affirmative action, etc.—the effects of priming may not be as strong.[43]

Recent work on priming has extended priming studies to nonnews media. For example, R. Lance Holbert and colleagues found that viewers of *The West Wing* retained more positive images of Bush and Clinton after watching the television program. Viewing *The West Wing* seems to

> prime more positive images of the U.S presidency that subsequently influence individual-level perceptions of those individuals most directly associated with this office. [The] positive images of the U.S. presidency offered on *The West Wing* result in more positive viewer perceptions of those who hold or have held the office.[44]

Another study focused on the priming effects of late-night comedy shows and found that there "was a main effect of watching late-night comedy on evaluations of candidates."[45] This same study found that "viewers were more likely than nonviewers to base their evaluations of George W. Bush on character traits after he appeared on the *Late Show with David Letterman*."[46] This finding is of particular interest given that previous priming research focusing on the news media found that priming effects are linked with policy and not with personality.

Framing

Framing moves beyond priming because it involves the relationship between qualitative aspects of news coverage—contextual cues—and how the public interacts with and interprets the news. William A. Gamson asserts that a "frame is a central organizing idea for making sense of relevant events and suggesting what is at issue."[47] Facts are neutral until framed, so how the press frames the facts surrounding an issue or an event will affect public understanding of that issue or event. In this way, facts "take on their meaning by being embedded in a frame or story line that organizes them and gives them coherence, selecting certain ones to emphasize while ignoring others."[48] We define framing as *the process whereby communicators act to construct a particular point of view that encourages the facts of a given situation to be viewed in a particular manner, with some facts made more noticeable than others*. When speaking of political and social issues, news media frames actually attempt to define our understanding of any given issue. On this point, Jim A. Kuypers writes:

> Frames operate in four key ways: they define problems, diagnose causes, make moral judgments, and suggest remedies. They reside in the communicator, the receiver of the message, and the culture at large. Frames are often found within a narrative account of an issue or event, and are generally the central organizing idea. Frames are all around us, and are a normal part of the communication process; we need ways to negotiate the massive amounts of information that comes to us everyday, and frames provide the interpretive cues for otherwise neutral facts. Large and complex ideas and events need framing since they have so many elements upon which we could focus our attention. Framing analysis can help us to see how we construct interpretations of our environment.[49]

As emphasized by Michael Ryan, framing is an important process, for *news media frames*

> help individuals create *personal frames* as they provide pertinent bits of information, or news. They often create or stress the central ideas that assign meaning to events and they help determine which events are salient, thus "making a piece of information more noticeable, meaningful, or memorable to audiences. An increase in salience enhances the probability that receivers will perceive the information, discern meaning and thus process it, and store it in memory."[50]

For Robert M. Entman, "frames reside in the specific properties of the news narrative that encourage those perceiving and thinking about events to develop particular understandings of them."[51] Certain key words, metaphors, concepts, symbols, and visual images found within a narrative account (a news story) help one to discover what frame is there. Understood in this manner, frames are manufactured by particular words and phrases that consistently appear within a narrative and "convey thematically consonant meanings across . . . time."[52] Framing thus elevates the salience of some ideas over others while making some ideas virtually invisible to an audience.

The majority of researchers consider the framing process to begin with the interaction of sources and journalists. Moreover, most

> researchers believe that political elites... or the press... have the upper hand in framing that occurs during political campaigns. The behaviors and thoughts of audiences, who are potential voters, are typically viewed as impacted by frames constructed via interactions between political elites and the press.[53]

Once established, the frame guides audience and journalist thinking. Entman called this initial interaction "event-specific schema." Once in place, event-specific schema encourages journalists to "perceive, process, and report all further information about the event in ways supporting the basic interpretation encoded in the schema."[54] As an example of this process, consider this study that examines the press coverage of the Watergate break-in. Gladys Engel Lang and Kurt Lang found that the framing process begins after media gatekeepers decide to publish a particular story, and the decision is made concerning how much attention to give to the story.[55] At the point when an issue emerges, its media frame becomes crucially important; then, by continually focusing on an issue, the media thrust it into the forefront of national thought. For example, the Watergate break-in coverage was first put into the framework of the 1972 election campaign between Richard Nixon and George McGovern, but the public thought of it as the usual run-of-the-mill partisan politics. However, the news media persistently published stories, eventually switching the frame through which to view the break-in. As soon as the news media switched frames, moving from the framework of the presidential campaign to a framework of continual Washington corruption, the nation became obsessed. We agree with Graber that this type of "manipulative journalism raises philosophical, ethical, and news policy questions."[56]

Certainly providing contextual cues for interpretation are a necessary part of news media responsibility. The difficulty arises when the news media place their partisan context over that which is naturally suggested by the issue or event being covered.[57] We do know that frames can influence public opinion on certain issues; that is, the frames chosen for an issue influence our judgments regarding that issue. As an example of this, consider the following study by Paul M. Sniderman and colleagues, which uses mandatory testing for HIV (human immunodeficiency virus) as its controlled frame. These researchers found that the effect

> of framing is to prime values differentially, establishing the salience of the one or the other. [A] majority of the public supports the rights of persons with AIDS [acquired immunodeficiency syndrome] when the issue is framed to accentuate civil liberties considerations—and supports... mandatory testing when the issue is framed to accentuate public health considerations.[58]

Thomas Nelson and colleagues provide another example of the potential power of news frames. These researchers used a local news story about a Ku Klux Klan march as their study's controlled frame and presented their research audiences with either one of two stories:

> One framed the rally as a free speech issue, and the other framed it as a disruption of public order. Participants who viewed the free speech story expressed more tolerance for the Klan than those participants who watched the public order story.[59]

The results of these studies are striking and point to the need for further studies determining the effects of framing on the formation of political attitudes.

Zhongdang Pan and Gerald M. Kosicki suggest another way of using frame analysis to understand news stories. These researchers suggest that each news story will have a theme that "functions as the central organizing idea" of the story and that these themes provide readers with cues that prompt them to understand and interpret a news story in a specific manner.[60] The cues within themes are various word choices used as tools that news reporters and editors use to construct news discourse and thus influence how the audience processes the news. Viewed in this manner, themes function as frames and the cues within themes may be likened to framing devices. In this way, the framing of news stories is reduced to word choices made by the journalists—words in a vocabulary. The words chosen by news reporters and editors may reveal the way they categorize that which they report. One way of understanding frames, then, is to consider how word choice often "signifies the presence of a particular frame."[61]

For example, look to descriptions of Yugoslavian President Slobodan Milosevic used by American reporters during the U.S.–NATO bombardment of Serbia. President Milosevic was described, for example, as an "evil dictator," "a cruel and determined enemy," and "a brutal dictator." Comparisons with Hitler were frequently made: "Adolf Hitler had a 'final solution.' Slobodan Milosevic has 'ethnic cleansing.' Each leader's term gives a brilliant, if not positive, spin to his massacres."[62] Consider, however, alternate ways one might describe Milosevic: the "Yugoslavian leader," "Yugoslavian president," or the "Yugoslavian commander-in-chief." With these labels, thoughts about Milosevic's legitimacy are different than those associated with the more pejorative labels.[63] From a framing perspective, the specific word choices made by editors and reporters help to frame the news story so that it facilitates a dominant reading of that story. Pan and Kosicki pointed out that framing analysis allows researchers to provide information about how an issue is discussed in the news and "how the ways of talking about the issue [are] related to the evolution of the issue in political debates."[64]

Other researchers point to the power of already established frames to guide reportorial practices on an issue or event. For example, Jim A. Kuypers and Stephen Cooper compared news reports made by embedded reporters and behind-the-lines reporters during the second Gulf War.[65] They argued that

> when journalists frame, they construct a particular point of view that encourages the facts of a given situation to be interpreted in a specific way. Thus journalists can, knowingly or unknowingly, guide the interpretation of readers toward a particular point of view.[66]

The authors matched stories run by embedded reporters and behind-the-lines reporters by date of publication and discovered that the reporting varied greatly between the two groups of reporters. Those journalists who were embedded with combat troops "often described the war in terms of the weakness of Iraqi army resistance; the frequency with which regular Iraqi forces deserted or surrendered; and the joy of Iraqi civilians at the demise of the Hussein regime."[67] In contradistinction, those stories filed by

> behind-the-lines journalists described the war in terms of the potential of Iraqi forces to mount significant unconventional counterattacks; the ferocity of the Iraqi irregular forces; the inadequacy of Allied war planning; and the vulnerability of the Allies' long supply lines.[68]

Kuypers and Cooper attribute these differences in framing to the inability of behind-the-lines reporters to "divorce themselves from the editorial positions of their respective papers, and the general climate of press opposition concerning military action."[69] Drawing attention to the power of established frames, the authors state,

> The power of the behind-the-lines reporters' established frames greatly influenced how they reported the war; whereas embedded reporters, observing direct contradictions of their previously established frames, were in a better position to report on what they actually witnessed.[70]

At present, framing research seems somewhat disjointed. Although some researchers suggest that this is a difficulty to be overcome,[71] others suggest it is healthy, and that the variety of framing studies leads to a better understanding of media and politics. Paul D'Angelo, for example, writes that framing studies actually constitute a multiparadigmatic area of endeavor. He suggests that three interacting paradigms represent framing research to date: the *constructionist*, the *critical*, and the *cognitive*. The constructionist paradigm assumes that "journalists are information processors who create 'interpretive packages' of the position of politically invested . . . sources . . . in order to both reflect and add to the 'issue culture' of the topic."[72] From this perspective, researchers are looking for ways in which frames are used as a tool–kit "from which citizens *ought to* draw in order to form their opinions about issues."[73]

In contrast, those operating under the critical paradigm suggest that "news organizations select some information and intentionally omit other information such that different frames of a topic will either not exist or will still foster a single viewpoint supportive of the status quo."[74] Those operating from this perspective feel that news frames are actually the "outcome of newsgathering routines by which journalists convey information about issues and events from the perspective of values held by political and economic elites" and that these frames in turn "dominate news coverage." Some researchers have even found that the press inserts its own political perspective into its framing process.[75] Ultimately, though, those operating from within this paradigm look for how news frames act to affect the political consciousness of news audiences.

The cognitive paradigm begins with the assumption that humans are prone to use the most accessible information in order to make decisions. Researchers here are interested in discovering how a person's exposure to a news frame will alter that individual's train of thought. In order to have this effect, news frames must be accessible for a person. "Cognitivists are interested in how an individual's encounter with a news frame becomes an interpretation that is stored in memory and activated in future encounters with similar frames."[76]

Many studies combine these paradigms, which complicates analysis. In addition, many studies are not designed to discover paradigmatic nuances; rather, the goal is to explore content; to discover what frames lurk in the news. Because of this, determining the paradigm to which they belong becomes an inferential process. The important point is that frames influence news consumers in ways yet to be fully understood. We know they exist, but research has only just begun to suggest ways that they influence our thinking and political behaviors.

To sum our discussion of frames, keep in mind six important considerations.

1. Frames are a central organizing principle found within news stories.

2. Frames encourage us to view an issue, or even view it in a particular way, by highlighting certain facts and downplaying others.

3. Once frames are established, opinions and facts running counter to the frame fall by the wayside.

4. Frames are made up of key words, metaphors, symbols, visual images, and concepts.

5. There may be a dominate frame in a news story, or several frames competing for attention.

6. Frames persist over time, so one should find the same frame operating over time in the news coverage of a particular issue or event.

Types and Sources of Bias in the News Media

Since the late 1960s, academics, media professionals, and partisan pundits have proclaimed allegations of news media bias. It is, of course, in the arena of politics that we see both the most public allegations and the most academic studies of news media bias. In particular, conservative politicians, pundits, and talk show celebrities have openly complained about the liberal bias of the mainstream news media and most cable news organizations.[77] One such critic, Brent Bozell, founded the Media Research Center in 1987 to "bring balance and responsibility to the news media" and to systematically document "the extent of media bias."[78] By 2002, with hundreds of studies, the Center claimed it "proved the leftist influence dominating the American media."[79] The controversy is far from over; the "left" has recently challenged such assumptions with several trade publications alleging no bias, or even a conservative bias.[80]

Although sparring among pundits continues, the attitude of the general public reveals less contention. Several polling and survey organizations continue to track negative attitudes of the general public for the press. Recently, perceptions of political bias have risen, and a growing number of Americans even question the news media's patriotism. In 2006 the Gallup polling organization found that 44 percent of Americans thought the media were "too liberal" while 19 percent found the media "too conservative."[81] In 2005 the Gallup poll indicated 35 percent of Americans thought network anchors were "too liberal" while 13 percent thought they were "too conservative."[82] Since 2000, Gallup finds that over 60 percent of Americans think that news organizations' stories and reports are often inaccurate. A national study conducted by the Pew Research Center for the People & the Press (2005) reveals increasing politicization of attitudes toward the news media. Self–identified Republicans are the most critical.[83] In 2007, Zogby found that only 11 percent of Americans believed mainstream news refrained from taking political sides. Sixty-four percent of Americans "said the media lean left, while slightly more than a quarter of respondents (28 percent) said they see a conservative bias on their TV sets and in their column inches."[84] Not entirely unexpected, this division to some extent reflects political party identification:

> While 97% of Republicans surveyed said the media are liberal, two-thirds of political independents feel the same, but fewer than one in four independents (23%) said they saw a conservative bias. Democrats, while much more likely to perceive a conservative bias than other groups, were not nearly as sure the media were against them as were the Republicans. While Republicans were unified in their perception of a left-wing media, just two-thirds of Democrats were certain the media skewed right—and 17% said the bias favored the left.[85]

Thus, there are clear perceptions of bias among the general public.

Academics have attempted to identify and measure news media bias utilizing a variety of methods and from many different perspectives. A review of the literature reveals mixed results and conclusions leaving the issue of bias largely unresolved. However, one can identify several sources or types of potential bias. Looking at nearly 100 scholarly articles and contemporary texts focusing on some aspect of media bias, we have isolated the various "types" or sources of potential media bias. In the pages that follow we present these types of bias and then conclude by reviewing several studies that attempt to explain the public perceptions of unfairness and news media bias. The various studies and discussions of news media bias generally group into six broad categories: ideological and partisanship bias; coverage bias; process bias; conservative bias; "no bias"; and perceptual or "hostile media effect" bias. Within each area there are several sources of potential bias.

Ideological and Partisanship Bias

Today the most frequent allegation of media bias stems from the liberal ideology and democratic partisanship of contemporary journalists. For example, in 1981, Robert Lichter published survey data generated from media self-descriptions:

> [at] least 81% of the news media had voted for the liberal Democrat for President in every election going back to 1964. He found that 90% favored abortion; 83% found nothing wrong with homosexuality; only 47% believed adultery to be wrong; 50% had no religious affiliation; and 85% seldom or never attended church or synagogue.[86]

Elaine S. Povich, in 1996, published similar results, although they were limited to Washington journalists: Sixty-two percent agreed or somewhat agreed that their job was to suggest potential solutions to social problems. Concerning political orientation, 22 percent said they were liberal, 39 percent liberal to moderate, 30 percent moderate, 7 percent moderate to conservative, and 2 percent conservative. Party affiliation was 50 percent Democrat, 37 percent independent, 4 percent Republican, and 9 percent other parties.[87] Contrast this with the rest of the United States: 18 percent said they were liberal, 40 percent moderate, and 39 percent conservative.[88] Party affiliation was 31 percent Democrat, 39 percent independent, and 30 percent Republican.[89] On the issues mentioned above, 42 percent of Americans would favor a law that would restrict all abortion except to save the life of the mother.[90] When asked about how they feel, 74 percent of Americans consider homosexual behavior unacceptable.[91] Seventy-nine percent feel adultery is always wrong (up to 90 percent if "almost always wrong").[92] Eighty-three percent consider themselves Protestant or Catholic (2 percent Jewish), and 61 percent attend church or synagogue at least once a month.[93]

Following the Lichter study, a *Times Mirror* survey found that 56 percent of the press considered themselves to be very to somewhat liberal, with only 18 percent very to somewhat conservative.[94] However, after charges of liberal bias went mainstream in the mid-1990s, press self-reporting suddenly shifted: now only 22 percent of the national press considered themselves liberal, 5 percent conservative, and almost two-thirds, 64 percent, considered themselves moderate.[95] The Kaiser Family Foundation survey in 2001 found that members of the news media were four times as likely to identify themselves as "liberal" than as "conservative." The survey also revealed that members of the media were more than seven times more likely to identify themselves as "Democrat" than as "Republican."[96]

These demographics represent long-standing trends. Between 1988 and 1996, over 60 percent of newspaper journalists identified themselves as "Democrat," "liberal," or "lean to Democrat or liberal."[97] In 2004, 68 percent of journalists voted for John Kerry and 25 percent for George W. Bush.[98] Only 7 percent professed conservative leanings compared to nearly one-third identifying themselves as liberal.[99] Without question, journalists tend to be more liberal and identify with the Democratic Party more than the general public does.

Of course, the key question is whether or not such tendencies influence the coverage and reporting of news. We have found some evidence that it does. For instance, some studies find an ideological and democratic partisan bias in the reporting of facts,[100] or the general treatment of individuals reveals the partisan bias, especially when covering campaigns.[101] In *Press Bias and Politics: How the Media Frame Controversial Issues*, Kuypers employed a comparative framing analysis in his study of press bias.[102] He compared six speeches given by five politicians to the coverage of those speeches found in 116 mainstream U.S. papers. His findings suggest that the mainstream press in the United States operates within a narrow range of liberal beliefs. Kuypers argues that this hurts the democratic process in general by ignoring or even dismissing nonmainstream left positions and vilifying many moderate and the vast majority of right-leaning positions. Because of this, only a narrow brand of liberal thought is supported by the press; all other positions are denigrated. Those with more conservative views will certainly feel the brunt of the press's bias. However, those who embrace moderate political beliefs, regardless of party affiliation, will be hurt when they step to the right of the press position. The press will actively help certain politicians and social leaders on the left who espouse the same view of the country that the press has adopted. However, those who step beyond this narrow brand of liberal reporting, moving even further to the left, will be ignored or denigrated. In short, if a political leader, regardless of party, spoke within the press-supported range of acceptable discourse, he or she would receive positive press coverage. If a politician, again regardless of party, were to speak *outside* of this range, he or she would receive negative press or be ignored. In this manner, then, the American press acts to shut out the full range of political voices in the country. Kuypers also found that the liberal points of view expressed in editorial and opinion pages were found in hard news coverage of the same issues.

In 2005 Tim Groseclose and Jeff Milyo published a study that used think tank quotes in order to position mainstream news outlets in the political spectrum.[103] The key idea in the study was to discover which think tanks were quoted by news outlets and then to match those quotes with the political position of members of the U.S. Congress who quote them in a nonnegative way. These researchers based their research

> on a standard gauge of a lawmaker's support for liberal causes. Americans for Democratic Action (ADA) tracks the percentage of times that each lawmaker votes on the liberal side of an issue. Based on these votes, the ADA assigns a numerical score to each lawmaker, where "100" is the most liberal and "0" is the most conservative. [T]he average ADA score in Congress (50.1) was assumed to represent the political position of the average U.S. voter.[104]

Looking through mainstream news coverage over a 10-year period, the researchers tallied the number of times each media outlet referred to think tanks and policy groups, such as the left-leaning NAACP or the right-leaning Heritage Foundation. Next, they did the same exercise with speeches of U.S. lawmakers. If a media outlet displayed a citation pattern similar to that of a lawmaker, then Groseclose and Milyo's method assigned both a similar ADA score.[105]

Of note is that

[of] the 20 major media outlets studied, 18 scored left of center, with CBS' *Evening News*, *The New York Times* and the *Los Angeles Times* ranking second, third, and fourth most liberal behind the news pages of *The Wall Street Journal*. Only Fox News' *Special Report with Brit Hume* and *The Washington Times* scored right of the average U.S. voter.[106]

Coverage Bias

Somewhat related, some studies find bias relating to the reporter's role as gatekeeper. Not only are reporters much more likely than the average population to have liberal social views and favor Democrats, they also tend to select stories that support liberal causes, positions, or candidates. Thus, especially among network and national reporters, news stories tend to reflect liberal beliefs, attitudes, and values of reporters.[107] There is a body of literature that finds various types and forms of coverage bias where one candidate, perspective, or view gets more frequency and length of coverage either in number of stories or in column inches.[108] Some studies focus on statement bias where members of the media insert their own opinions into reporting. The bias is coded as favorable or unfavorable based on the tone of the journalists' reports.[109] For example, The Center for Media and Public Affairs (CMPA) found that John Kerry received 58 percent positive evaluations compared to 64 percent negative evaluations for Bush in a content analysis of news stories on ABC, CBS and NBC evening news from Labor Day through Election Day 2004. Kerry received the most favorable news coverage of any presidential candidate since 1980 when the Center began such analyses. The only exception to the Democratic candidate receiving more favorable evaluations was in 1988 when George H. Bush received slightly better press reports than Dukakis.[110] The same trend holds beyond election coverage. George W. Bush received 71 percent negative evaluations during his first 100 days in office and 67 percent negative during the first 100 days of his second term.[111]

However, some scholars argue that the coverage bias may not be ideological or partisan. The amount, tone, and subject matter of coverage are based on a candidate's standing in public opinion polls.[112] As a result, the more favorable one stands in the polls, the more favorable and positive the press coverage. Shah and his colleagues, after examining the presidential campaigns from 1984 through 1996, found that the winning candidate tends to have generally more favorable than unfavorable coverage.[113] Watts and his colleagues went one step further and argued that the rise in public opinion and perceptions of a "liberal media bias" actually results from increasing news reports on the subject itself.[114] Thus, such media discussion of the potential of a liberal bias shapes the attitudes of primarily conservatives and partisan Republicans.

Civic Journalism or Theoretical Bias?

The basic function, role, or model of the press has evolved throughout American history. As news journalism was establishing itself as a profession, the dominant view was that the news media served as a conduit for information and as a mirror reflecting the events of the world. By the mid-twentieth century, objectivity was the norm. With the emergence of the "watchdog" function of the media, an adversarial relationship developed between the press, government, and business—especially in the post-Watergate era. The principal role of the press was to discover "truth" and serve as a check on government. However, more recently, the media have moved from informing to advocacy, primarily under the guise of civic journalism. Beyond investigating claims and statements made by the government, the media have now expanded the definition of "social responsibility" to also provide analysis and interpretation of events. They must educate the public on social issues, problems, and concerns. The goal is to reduce issues to concrete choices and to stimulate public action. This new role of the media clearly goes beyond the norms of objectivity or fairness. It provides news from a perspective, or point of view, complete with judgment and a call for social action. From this perspective, the practice of contemporary journalism is, by definition, bias.

There is also a rather inherent individual bias as part of the news gathering and reporting process. As individuals, reporters select stories, decide how to use sources, and construct narratives. Indeed, by definition, the very concept of framing implies a specific way to view, interpret, or understand a certain event or issue. As Robert Entman observes, by selecting some aspects while ignoring others, framing promotes "a particular problem definition, causal interpretation, moral evaluation, and/or treatment recommendation."[115]

Of course, as human beings, our very knowledge of the world is subjectively constructed and modified through social interaction with others. We are a product of our beliefs, attitudes, values, and experiences. Therefore, it should not be surprising that "liberals" would view the world, issues, or problems differently than "conservatives." Additionally, if the vast majority of journalists are indeed "liberal," then why not expect a "liberal" bias in reporting, especially given the contemporary view of civic journalism?

Conservative Bias

Interestingly, in contrast to the general sentiment of a liberal bias, there are some scholars who find a distinct conservative bias in the media. Some suggest there exists a conservative ideological/party bias.[116] For others, the argument is based on viewing the media as primarily businesses. Although reporters and editors may be liberal, media owners and corporation leaders are conservative and are always concerned about the bottom line—profit— thus providing some moderation of viewpoints and perspectives.[117] Business is, by itself, a conservative enterprise and, as such, must work to maintain the status quo.[118] Others argue that all big business owners must be conservative and influence in some way the day-to-day reporting practices of the rank- and-file reporters. Although some media owners are conservative (Rupert Murdoch, Sumner Redstone), there are also a number of high-profile liberal media owners as well (Ted Turner, Michael Eisner, George Soros, Leslie Moonves).

No Bias

Of course, to complicate the issue even more, there are a number of studies that simply find no bias of any type across all media and contexts.[119]

Perceptual Bias

Given the mixed findings, several scholars have attempted to explain the obvious increase in public charges of media bias. A group of studies dealing with audience perceptions of bias have found that certain psychographics such as political affiliation or ideology will influence individual judgments of bias. Many of these studies center around the notion of "selective perception." Based on an individual's ideology or party preference, opposing messages will be perceived as biased or unfair.[120]

Several studies found that individuals with very strong political or ideological beliefs are much more likely to perceive media reports as "hostile" to their own views.[121] Robert Vallone, Lee Ross, and Mark Lepper were the first to coin the phrase "hostile media phenomenon" to explain how characteristics of ideology and partisanship contribute to perceptions of unfair news reporting.[122] They found that individuals exposed to the identical stimulus would perceive different images and attributions of bias. Albert Gunther further provided evidence of the "hostile media phenomenon," finding that Democrats generally view newspapers and television news as too favorable to Republicans, while Republicans think both newspapers and television are too favorable to Democrats.[123] Kathleen Schmitt, Albert Gunther, and Janice Liebhart found that opposing partisans assign different valences to the same message or media content. For them, "selective categorization" best explains the "hostile media effect."[124] Likewise, Vallone, Ross, and Lepper found that even neutral reports are perceived as partisan by those who think the media are biased, referring to the effect as "biased perception of media bias."[125] This finding has been replicated in several studies.[126]

Additional and related studies find that other characteristics beyond issue involvement or partisanship may affect views of news source bias. There is some evidence that those of a skeptical disposition towards politics and public affairs are predisposed toward distrust of media in general. In fact, according to Lee, the best predictor of a media bias perception is political cynicism.[127] The more distrusting and cynical people are at a personal and a political level, the more likely they are to perceive a media bias, although political cynicism is a stronger predictor than personal cynicism. Finally, Watts and his colleagues found that the mere coverage of people proclaiming media bias increased the likelihood that the public in general will label the media as biased regardless of actual content.[128]

Summary

We reviewed the concepts of agenda setting, agenda extension, and types of news media bias. Agenda-setting theory explains how the news media exert influence on political decision making. In particular, it describes how the news media decide what issues and events will receive the most coverage. Second-level agenda-setting theory looks at how reporting focuses our attention on particular aspects of an event or a person to the exclusion of other aspects. Agenda extension is useful for revealing when the media move beyond neutral reporting of issues, persons, and events. Researchers in this area have discovered that the reportorial practices of the news media still tell us *what* to think about (agenda setting) and also *how* to think about it (agenda extension). Researchers looking at these aspects focus on how the media prime their audiences to judge the items in news stories. They also look at how the media frame an issue or event. Research in agenda extension looks specifically for *how* attributes are presented to the public.

Certainly since the 2000 presidential race, the United States has been characterized as a 50/50 nation. Politics today is as polarized as any time in our nation's history. The intensity of political discourse has spilled into the practice of journalism. Allegations of a liberal and Democratic Party bias were first mentioned during the Nixon Administration. However, the rise of talk radio and the start of FOX News fed the public perception of a liberal, anti-Republican bias in the media.

Surprisingly, as Graber observes, "the extent to which biased reporting based on party preferences is a problem in U.S. media is not fully known, because scholars have rarely investigated media bias outside the election context."[129] Although there are conflicting studies of media bias, there is no doubt that the vast majority of journalists as individuals, and coming from a social science or humanities educational background, are more liberal than the general population. In addition, according to numerous surveys, they tend to be supporters of the Democratic Party. It is also true that the very news gathering and reporting process are inherently individual and subjective. Finally, the changing role and function of journalism has greatly contributed to the public's perception of bias. In the end, it is not a question of *if* there is media bias, but one of identifying the various types and sources of bias *in* media.

Notes

[1] Walter Lippmann, *Public Opinion* (New York: Macmillan, 1930), 364.
[2] Maxwell E. McCombs and Donald L. Shaw, "The Agenda-Setting Function of Mass Media," *Public Opinion Quarterly* 36 (1972): 176–187.
[3] Bernard C. Cohen, *The Press and Foreign Policy* (Princeton: Princeton University Press, 1963), 13.
[4] Judith S. Trent and Robert V. Friedenberg, *Political Campaign Communication: Principles and Practices*, 5th ed. (Lanham, MD: Rowman & Littlefield, 2004), 134.
[5] McCombs and Shaw, "The Agenda-Setting Function of Mass Media," 177.
[6] Ibid., 185.
[7] Sheldon Gilberg et al., "The State of the Union Address and the Press Agenda," *Journalism Quarterly* 57 (1980): 584–588.
[8] Maxwell E. McCombs and Donald L. Shaw, "Agenda-Setting and the Political Process," in *The Emergence of American Political Issues: The Agenda-Setting Function of the Press*, ed. Donald L. Shaw and Maxwell E. McCombs (St. Paul, MN: West, 1977), 151.
[9] Guido H. Stempel III, *Media and Politics in America* (Santa Barbara, CA: ABC Clio, 2003), 55.
[10] Michael B. Salwen, "News Media and Public Opinion: Benign Agenda-Setters? Opinion Molders? Or Simply Irrelevant?" *Florida Communication Journal* 18, no. 2 (1990): 17.
[11] There are a multitude of studies confirming the enormous agenda-setting influence of the media. See, for example, Maxwell E. McCombs, *Setting the Agenda: The Mass Media and Public Opinion* (Cambridge, UK: Polity Press, 2004).
[12] George Comstock and Erica Scharrer, *The Psychology of Media and Politics* (Burlington, MA: Elsevier Academic Press, 2005), 172.
[13] Gilberg et al., "The State of the Union Address and the Press Agenda," 585.
[14] Reported in Maxwell E. McCombs and Sheldon Gilberg, "News Influence on Our Pictures of the World," *Perspectives on Media Effects*, ed. Jennings Bryant and Dolf Zillmann (Hillsdale, NJ: Erlbaum, 1986), 14.
[15] Ibid., 11.
[16] Doris A. Graber, *Mass Media and American Politics*, 7th ed. (Washington, DC: CQ Press, 2006), 194.
[17] Ibid., 194–195.
[18] Bob Woodward and Carl Bernstein, *All the President's Men* (New York: Simon & Schuster, 1974).
[19] "Abuse of Iraqi POWs by GIs Probed: *60 Minutes II* Has Exclusive Report on Alleged Mistreatment" (April 28, 2004). Retrieved 11 September 2007 from http://www.cbsnews.com/stories/2004/04/27/60II/main614063.shtml
[20] Charles Babington and Shailagh Murray, "Senate Supports Interrogation Limits: 90–9 Vote on the Treatment of Detainees Is a Bipartisan Rebuff of the White House," *The Washington Post* (October 6, 2005), A1.
[21] Sherry Ricchiardi, "Missed Signals," *American Journalism Review* (August/September 2004). Retrieved 11 September 2007 from http://www.ajr.org/Article.asp?id=3716
[22] Adapted from: "Network TV," *State of the News Media 2004: An Annual Report on American Journalism*. Retrieved 11 September 2007 from http://www.stateofthemedia.com/narrative_networktv_contentanalysis.asp?cat=2&media=4
[23] Gary Woodward, *Perspectives on American Political Media* (Boston, MA: Allyn & Bacon, 1997) 74–87.
[24] "What Was—and Wasn't—on the Public's Mind . . . And How Opinions Changed During 2005," The Pew Research Center for the People & the Press (December 27, 2005). Retrieved 11 September 2007 from http://people-press.org/commentary/display.php3?AnalysisID=125
[25] For examples of studies exploring agenda-setting second-level effects see, Maxwell McCombs, "The Future Agenda for Agenda Setting Research," *Journal of Mass Communication Studies* 45 (1994): 171–181; Maxwell McCombs, Donald L. Shaw, and David Weaver, *Communication and Democracy: Exploring the Intellectual Frontiers in Agenda-Setting Theory* (Mahwah, NJ: Erlbaum, 1997); Spiro Kiousis, Philemon Bantimaroudis, and Hyun Ban, "Candidate Image

Attributes: Experiments on the Substantive Dimension of Second-Level Agenda Setting," *Communication Research* 26, no. 4 (1999): 414–428; Sei-Hill Kim, Dietram Scheufele, and James Shanahan, "Think About It This Way: Attribute Agenda-Setting Function of the Press and the Public's Evaluation of A Local Issue," *Journalism & Mass Communication Quarterly* 79 (2002): 7–25; Spiro Kiousis, "Compelling Arguments and Attitude Strength: Exploring the Impact of Second-Level Agenda Setting on Public Opinion of Presidential Candidate Images," *Harvard International Journal of Press/Politics* 10, no. 2 (2005): 3–27.

[26] Comstock and Scharrer, *The Psychology of Media and Politics*, 175.

[27] Russell J. Dalton, Paul Allen Beck, Robert Huckfeldt, and William Koetzle, "A Test of Media-Centered Agenda Setting: Newspaper Content and Public Interests in a Presidential Election," *Political Communication* 15 (1998): 463–481.

[28] Ibid., 463.

[29] Trent and Friedenberg, *Political Campaign* Communication, 135.

[30] David R. Roskos-Ewoldson, B. Roskos-Ewoldson, and F. R. D. Carpentier, "Media Priming: A Synthesis," in *Media Effects: Advances in Theory and Research*, 2nd ed., ed. Jennings Bryant and Dolf Zillmann (Mahwah, NJ: Erlbaum, 2002), 97.

[31] R. Andrew Holbrook and Timothy G. Hill, "Agenda-Setting and Priming in Prime Time Television: Crime Dramas as Political Cues," *Political Communication* 22 (2005): 278. These authors follow the lead of Shanto Iyengar and Donald Kinder, *News that Matters* (Chicago: University of Chicago Press, 1987).

[32] Shanto Iyengar and Donald R. Kinder, "More than Meets the Eye: TV News, Priming, and Public Evaluations of the President," in *Public Communication Behavior*, Vol. 1, ed. George Comstock (Orlando, FL: Academic Press, 1986), 136.

[33] Ibid., 139.

[34] Ibid., 162.

[35] Zhongdang Pan and Gerald M. Kosicki, "Priming and Media Impact on the Evaluation of the President's Performance," *Communication Research* 24, no. 1 (1997): 3–30.

[36] Holbrook and Hill, "Agenda-Setting and Priming in Prime Time Television," p. 279. See also Vincent Price and David Tewksbury, "News Values and Public Opinion: A Theoretical Account of Media Priming and Framing," in *Progress in Communication Sciences: Advances in Persuasion*, Vol. 13, ed. George A. Barnett and Franklin J. Boster (Cambridge, MA: MIT Press, 1997), 173–213.

[37] Johnston, "Trends in Political Communication: A Selective Review of Research in the 1980s," in *New Directions in Political Communication: A Resource Book*, ed. David L. Swanson and Dan Nimmo (Newbury Park, CA: Sage, 1990), 329–362.

[38] Shanto Iyengar, Mark D. Peters, and Donald R. Kinder, "Experimental Demonstrations of the 'Not-So-Minimal' Consequences of Television News Programs," *American Political Science Review* 76 (1982): 855.

[39] Johnston, "Trends in Political Communication," 337.

[40] Shanto Iyengar and Adam Simon, "News Coverage of the Gulf Crisis and Public Opinion: A Study of Agenda-Setting, Priming, and Framing," *Communication Research* 20, no. 3 (1993): 368.

[41] Ibid., 376.

[42] Iyengar and Kinder, "More than Meets the Eye," 162.

[43] Zhongdang Pan and Gerald M. Kosicki, "Priming and Media Impact on the Evaluation of the President's Performance," 3–30.

[44] R. Lance Holbert, Owen Pillion, David A. Tschida, Greg G. Armfield, Kelly Kinder, Kristin L. Cherry, and Amy R. Daulton, "*The West Wing* as Endorsement of the U.S. Presidency: Expanding the Bounds of Priming in Political Communication," *International Journal of Public Opinion Research* 18, no. 2 (2005): 427, 440.

[45] Patricia Moy, Michael A. Xenos, and Verna K. Hess, "Priming Effects of Late-Night Comedy,' *International Journal of Public Opinion Research* 18, no. 2 (2005): 198.

[46] Ibid., 198.

[47] William A. Gamson, "News as Framing: Comments on Graber," *American Behavioral Scientist* 33 (1989): 157.

[48] Ibid., 157.

[49] Jim A. Kuypers, *Bush's War: Media Bias and Justifications for War in a Terrorist Age* (Lanham, MD: Rowman & Littlefield, 2006), 8.

[50] Michael Ryan, "Framing the War against Terrorism: US Newspaper Editorials and Military Action in Afghanistan," *Gazette: The International Journal for Communication Studies* 66, no. 5 (2004): 365. Ryan was quoting Robert M. Entman, "Framing: Toward Clarification of a Fractured Paradigm," *Journal of Communication* 43, no. 4 (1993): 53.

[51] Robert M. Entman, "Framing U.S. Coverage of International News: Contrasts in Narratives of the KAL and Iran Air Incidents," *Journal of Communication* 41, no. 4 (1991): 7.

[52] Ibid., 7.

[53] Paul D'Angelo, Matthew Calderone, and Anthony Territola, "Strategy and Issue Framing: An Exploratory Analysis of Topics and Frames in Campaign 2004 Print News." *Atlantic Journal of Communication* 13, no. 4 (2005): 200.

[54] Entman, "Framing U.S. Coverage," 7.

[55] Gladys Engel Lang and Kurt Lang, "The Media and Watergate," in *Media Power in Politics*, ed. Doris A. Graber (Washington, DC: Congressional Quarterly Press, 1984), 202–209.

[56] Graber, *Mass Media and American Politics,* 278.

[57] We believe this manipulation includes lack of press coverage. For example, numerous examples of press "blackouts" of controversial events potentially damaging to President Clinton have been documented and are available free of charge through the MediaWatch Archive, http://www.mrc.org/mainsearch/search.html

[58] Paul M. Sniderman, Richard A. Brody, and Philip E. Tetlock, *Reasoning and Choice: Explorations in Political Psychology* (Cambridge, UK: Cambridge University Press, 1991), 52.

[59] Thomas E. Nelson, Rosalee A. Clawson, and Zoe M. Oxley, "Media Framing of Civil Liberties Conflict and Its Effects on Tolerance," *American Political Science Review* 91, no. 3 (1997): 567.

[60] Zhongdang Pan and Gerald M. Kosicki, "Framing Analysis: An Approach to News Discourse," *Political Communication* 10, no. 1 (1993): 55–75.

[61] Ibid., 62.

[62] Ben Kauffman, "As You Were Saying . . . Evil Euphemisms Must Not Pass Our Lips Unexamined," *Boston Herald* (May 2, 1999), A28.

[63] In all fairness to the press, a majority of the papers examined did use these terms. However, enough depreciatory examples of naming exist to color the otherwise neutral descriptions.

[64] Pan and Kosicki, "Framing Analysis," 65.

[65] Jim A. Kuypers and Stephen Cooper, "A Comparative Framing Analysis of Embedded and Behind-the-Lines Reporting on the 2003 Iraq War," *Qualitative Research Reports in Communication* 6, no. 1 (2005): 1–10.

[66] Ibid., 2.

[67] Ibid., 6.

[68] Ibid., 6.

[69] Ibid., 7.

[70] Ibid., 7–8.

[71] Entman, "Framing: Toward Clarification of a Fractured Paradigm."

[72] Paul D'Angelo, "News Framing as a Multiparadigmatic Research Program: A Response to Entman," *Journal of Communication* 52, no. 4 (2002): 877.

[73] Ibid., 877.

[74] Ibid., 876.

[75] Kuypers, *Bush's War*; Steven D. Cooper, *Watching the Watchdog: Bloggers as the Fifth Estate* (Spokane, WA: Marquette Books, 2006); Kuypers and Cooper, "A Comparative Framing Analysis of Embedded and Behind-the-Lines Reporting on the 2003 Iraq War"; Jim A. Kuypers, *Press Bias and Politics: How the Media Frame Controversial Issues* (Westport, CT: Praeger, 2002); Jim A. Kuypers, *Presidential Crisis Rhetoric and the Press in the Post-Cold War World* (Westport, CT: Praeger, 1997).

[76] D'Angelo, "News Framing as a Multiparadigmatic Research Program," 878.

[77] L. Brent Bozell, *Weapons of Mass Distortion: The Coming Meltdown of the Liberal Media* (New York: Crown Forum, 2004); B. Goldberg, *Bias: A CBS Insider Exposes How the Media Distort the News* (Washington, DC: Regnery, 2002); S. Hannity, *Let Freedom Ring: Winning the War of Liberty over Lliberalism* (New York: Regan Books, 2002).

[78] Bozell, *Weapons of Mass Distortion*, 1.

[79] Ibid., 264.

[80] See as examples: Eric Alterman, *What Liberal Media?* (New York: Basic Books, 2003); Joe Conason, *Big Lies: The Right-wing Propaganda Machine and How It Distorts the Truth* (New York: Thomas Dunne, 2003); Al Franken, *Lies and the Lying Liars Who Tell Them* (New York: Dutton, 2005).

[81] Gallup Poll News Service. "Media Use and Evaluation" (2005). Retrieved 11 September 2007 from http://www.galluppoll.com/content/default.aspx?ci=1663

[82] Ibid.

[83] Pew Research Center, "Public More Critical of Press, But Goodwill Persists" (June 26, 2005). Retrieved 11 September 2007 from http://people-press.org/reports/display.php3?ReportID=248

[84] "Zogby Poll: Voters Believe Media Bias Is Very Real," Zogby International (March 14, 2007). Retrieved 11 September 2007 from http://www.zogby.com/news/ReadNews.dbm?ID=1262

[85] Ibid.

[86] Reported by Brent Bozell III, "Media and Politics: Overcoming the Bias," remarks given to The Union League Club (June 8, 2000). Figure on acceptance of homosexuality from "The People, The Press & Their Leaders" (Pew Research Center For The People & The Press, May 1995).

[87] This lopsided party affiliation continues when one moves beyond Washington: 44 percent of reporters polled nationwide considered themselves Democrats; 34 percent as independents; only 16 percent identified themselves as Republicans. Results are from a Freedom Forum sponsored poll of 1,400 journalists across the country by Indiana University professors David Weaver and G. Cleveland Wilhoit. Retrieved 13 September 2007 from http://www.mediaresearch.org/mediawatch/1992/watch19921201.asp

[88] These figures are rounded to the nearest percentage. Harris Poll, survey collection 911009 (June 1999), obtained from the Howard W. Odum Institute for Research in Social Science. http://www.irss.unc.edu/. A September 1990 Harris Poll (901106) obtained from the same source shows little change in these divisions: 36.9 percent conservative, 41.40 percent moderate, and 17.8 percent liberal. An October 1988 *USA Today* poll (study number 3108) found a smaller number of liberals and conservatives: 32.7 percent conservative, 48.1 percent middle of the road, and 13.7 percent liberal.

[89] Lydia Saad, "Independents Rank as Largest U.S. Political Group," Gallup News Service (April 9, 1999). 1999 figures show 28 percent Republicans, 34 percent Democrats, and 38 percent independents. http://www.galluppoll.com/content/?ci=3934

[90] Surveys by the Gallup Organization (April 1996). Reported in "Opinion Pulse: Issues," *The American Enterprise* (September/October 1996): 93.

[91] Data provided by The Roper Center for Public Opinion Research, University of Connecticut. Survey was conducted by the Gallup Organization, May 2001. http://www.ropercenter.uconn.edu/

[92] Lydia Saad, "Most Americans Would Soften U.S. Military's Rules against Adultery," Gallup News Service (June 13, 1997). http://www.galluppoll.com/content/?ci=4381&pg=1

[93] Gallup Poll Topic: Religion. http://www.galluppoll.com/content/default.aspx?ci=1690

[94] Norman Ornstein, Andrew Kohut, and Larry McCarthy, *The People, Press, and Politics: The Times Mirror Study of the American Electorate* (Reading, MA: Addison-Wesley, 1988).

[95] "The People, The Press & Their Leaders," Los Angeles: *Times Mirror* Center for The People & The Press, 1995.

[96] "National Survey of the *Roll of Polls in Policymaking*," The Henry J. Kaiser Family Foundation (June 2001), 27. Retrieved 11 September 2007 from http://www.kff.org/kaiserpolls/loader.cfm?url=/commonspot/security/getfile.cfm&PageID=13842

[97] Paul S. Voakes, "The Newspaper Journalists of the 90s," American Society of Newspaper Editors (October 31, 1997; updated January 12, 2000). Retrieved 11 September 2007 from http://www.asne.org/kiosk/reports/97reports/journalists90s/coverpage.html

[98] Joe Strupp, "New Survey Finds Huge Gap between Press and Public on Many Issues," *Editor & Publisher* (May 15, 2005). Retrieved 24 September 2007 from http://www.infoshop.org/inews/article.php?story=20050515203646455

[99] Pew Research Center for the People & the Press, "How Journalists See Journalists in 2004" (May 23, 2004). Retrieved 11 September 2007 from http://people-press.org/reports/pdf/214.pdf

[100] Christopher Hewitt, "Estimating the Number of Homeless: Media Misrepresentation of an Urban Problem," *Journal of Urban Affairs* 1, no. 4 (1996): 431–47; Robert Lichter, Stanley Rothman, and Linda Lichter, *The Media Elite* (Bethesda, MD: Adler and Adler, 1986).

[101] For examples see, Edith Efron, *The News Twisters* (Los Angeles: Nash publishing, 1971); M. Clancey and Michael Robinson, "General Election Coverage," in *The Mass Media Campaign '84*, eds. Michael Robinson and Austin Ranney (Washington, DC: American Enterprise Institute, 1985); Dennis T. Lowry and Jon D. Shidler, "The Sound Bites, the Biters, and the Bitten: An Analysis of Network TV News Bias in Campaign '92," *Journalism and Mass Communication Quarterly* 72, no. 4 (1995): 33–44; Robert Lichter and Richard E. Noyes, *Good Intentions Make Bad News* (Lanham, MD: Rowman & Littlefield, 1995); Paul J. Maurer, "Media Feeding Frenzies: Press Behavior during Two Clinton Scandals," *Presidential Studies Quarterly* 29, no. 1 (1999): 65–79.

[102] Kuypers, *Press Bias and Politics*.

[103] Tim Groseclose and Jeff Milyo, "A Measure of Media Bias," *The Quarterly Journal of Economics* 120, no. 4 (2005): 1191–1237. Retrieved 11 September 2007 from http://www.polisci.ucla.edu/faculty/groseclose/Media.Bias.pdf. This study is not without its critics. For example see, Mark Liberman, "Linguistics, Mathematics, Politics" (Language Log, December 22, 2005), retrieved 11 September 2007 from http://itre.cis.upenn.edu/~myl/languagelog/archives/002723.html; "Multiplying Ideologies Considered Harmful" (Language Log, December 23, 2005), retrieved 11 September 1007 from http://itre.cis.upenn.edu/~myl/languagelog/archives/002724.html

[104] "Media Bias Is Real, Finds UCLA Political Scientist," *UCLA News* (December 14, 2005). Retrieved 11 September 2007 from http://www.newsroom.ucla.edu/page.asp?RelNum=6664

[105] Ibid.

[106] Ibid.

[107] Ben H. Bagdikian, *The Information Machines: Their Impact on Men and the Media* (New York: Harper & Row, 1971); Thad Beyle, Donald Ostiek, and G. Patrick Lynch, "Is The State Press Biased?" *Spectrum: The Journal of State Government* 69, no. 4 (1996): 6–16; Brent Bozell, "How Can Liberals Deny the Media's Slanted Coverage?" *Philadelphia Inquirer* (5 October 1992), 9; Brent Bozell and Brent Baker, *And That's the Way it Isn't: A Reference Guide to Media Bias* (Alexandria, VA: Media Research Center, 1990); E. J. Dionne, Jr., "GOP Accuses Media of Bias Against Bush," *Washington Post* (12 August 1992), A1; Efron, *The News Twisters*; Richard C. Hofstetter and Terry F. Buss, "Bias in Television News Coverage of Political Events: A Methodological Analysis," *Journal of Broadcasting* 22 (1978): 517–530; Joseph Charles Keeley, *The Left-Leaning Antenna* (New Rochelle, NY: Arlington House, 1971); Lichter et al., *The Media Elite*; Lichter and Noyes, *Good Intentions Make Bad News*; Thomas E. Patterson and Wolfgang Donsbach, "News Decisions: Journalists as Partisan Actors," *Political Communication* 13, no. 4 (1996): 455–468; Stanley Rothman and Robert Lichter, "Elite Ideology and Risk Perception in Nuclear Energy Policy," *American Political Science Review* 81, no. 2 (1987): 383–404; William A. Rusher, *The Coming Battle for the Media* (New York: William Morrow, 1988); Larry Sabato, *Feeding Frenzy* (New York: Free Press, 1991), 86–92.

[108] Howard D. Doll and Bert E. Bradley, "A Study of the Objectivity of Television News Reporting of the 1972 Presidential Campaign," *Central States Speech Journal* 25 (1974): 254–263; Guido H. Stempel, "The Prestige Press Meets the Third-party Challenge," *Journalism Quarterly* 46 (1969): 699–706; Guido H. Stempel and John W. Windhauser, "Coverage by the Prestige Press of the 1988 Presidential Campaign," *Journalism Quarterly,* 66 (1989): 894–896; James Glen Stovall, "The Third Party Challenge of 1980: News Coverage of the Presidential Candidate," *Journalism Quarterly* 62 (1985): 266–271; James Glen Stovall, "Coverage of 1984 Presidential Campaign," *Journalism Quarterly*, 65 (1988): 443–449, 484.

109 Sandra H. Dickson, "Understanding Media Bias: The Press and the U.S. Invasion of Panama," *Journalism Quarterly* 71 (1994): 809–819; Daniel C. Hallin, *The Uncensored War: The Media and Vietnam* (Berkeley: University of California Press, 1989); C. Richard Hofstetter, *Bias in the News* (Columbus: Ohio State University Press, 1976); Keith Kennedy and Chris Simpson, "Was Coverage of the 1988 Presidential Race by Washington's Two Major Dailies Biased?" *Journalism Quarterly* 70 (1993): 345–355; James H. Kuklinski and Lee Sigelman, "When Objectivity Is not Objective," *Journal of Politics* 54, no. 3 (1992): 810–833; S. Robert Lichter, Daniel Amundson, and Richard Noyes, *The Video Campaign: Network Coverage of the 1988 Primaries* (Washington, DC: American Enterprise Institute Press, 1988); Michael J. Robinson and Margaret Sheehan, *Over the Wire and on TV: CBS and UPI Campaign in '80* (New York: Russell Sage Foundation, 1990); Rothman and Lichter, "Elite Ideology and Risk Perception in Nuclear Energy Policy"; James Glen Stovall, "Coverage of 1984 Presidential Campaign"; Lowry and Shidler, "The Sound Bites, the Biters, and the Bitten."

110 "Study: Kerry Gets Best Press Ever," The Center for Media and Public Affairs (2004). Retrieved 11 September 2007 from http://www.cmpa.com/documents/04.10.29.Kerry.Final.pdf

111 "No Second Honeymoon for Bush," The Center for Media and Public Affairs (2005). Retrieved 11 September 2007 from http://www.cmpa.com/mediaMonitor/documents/mayjun05.pdf

112 Emmett H. Buell, "'Locals' and 'Cosmopolitans': National, Regional, and State Newspaper Coverage of the New Hampshire Primary," in *Media and Momentum,* ed. Gary Orren and Nelson Polsby (Chatham, NJ: Chatham House, 1987); Peter Clarke and Susan H. Evans, *Covering Campaigns: Journalism in Congressional Elections* (Stanford, CA: Stanford University Press, 1983); Edwin Diamond, *Good News, Bad News* (Cambridge, MA: MIT Press, 1978); Audrey A. Haynes and Sarah G. Murray, "Why Do the News Media Cover Certain Candidates More than Others?" *American Politics Quarterly* 26, no. 4 (1998): 420–438; Kathleen Jamieson, *Dirty Politics: Deception, Distraction, and Democracy* (New York: Oxford University Press, 1992); Thomas E. Patterson and R. McClure, *The Unseeing Eye* (New York: Putnam, 1976); Thomas E. Patterson, *The Mass Media Election* (New York: Praeger, 1980); Robinson and Sheehan, *Over the Wire and on TV.*

113 Dhavan V. Shah, Mark D. Watts, David Domke, David P. Fan, and Michael Fibison, "News Coverage, Economic Cues, and the Public's Presidential Preferences: 1984–1996," *Journal of Politics* 61, no. 4 (1999): 914–943.

114 Mark D. Watts, David Domke, Dhavan V. Shah, and David P. Fan, "Elite Cues and Media Bias in Presidential Campaigns: Explaining Public Perceptions of a Liberal Press," *Communication Research* 26, no. 2 (1999): 144–175.

115 Entman, "Framing: Toward Clarification of a Fractured Paradigm," 52.

116 Dennis T. Lowry, "Measures of Network News Bias in the 1972 Presidential Campaign," *Journal of Broadcasting* 18 (1974): 387–402; Lowry and Shidler, "The Sound Bites, the Biters, and the Bitten"; Stephen A. Smith and Cherri D. Roden, "CBS, *The New York Times*, and Reconstructed Political Reality," *Southern Speech Communication Journal* 53 (1988): 140–158; Stempel and Windhauser, "Coverage by the Prestige Press of the 1988 Presidential Campaign."

117 . J. Liebling, *The Press* (New York: Ballantine, 1961); M. Cooper and L. C. Leviton, "All the Right Sources," *Mother Jones*, 15, no. 2 (1990): 20–27, 45–48; Martin A. Lee and Norman Solomon, *Unreliable Sources: A Guide to Detecting Bias in News Media* (Secaucus, NJ: Lyle Stuart, 1991).

118 For an example of this line of thought see Thomas J. Bico, "The Idea of a 'Moderate Independent' News Source," The Moderate Independent (April 15–30, 2003). Retrieved 11 September 2007 from http://www.moderateindependent.com/v1i1editorial.htm

119 David S. Broder, *Behind the Front Page: A Candid Look at How News Is Made* (New York: Simon & Schuster, 1987); Timothy E. Cook, *Governing with the News* (Chicago: University of Chicago Press, 1998); Dave D'Alessio and Mike Allen, "Media Bias in Presidential Elections: A Meta-Analysis," *Journal of Communication* 50, no. 4 (2000): 133–156; Everette E. Dennis, "How 'Liberal' Are the Media Anyway?" *Journal of Press/Politics* 2, no. 4 (1997): 115–119; Robert Entman, "Reporting Environmental Policy Debate: The Real Media Bias," *Journal of Press/Politics* 1, no. 3 (1996): 77–92; Edward Jay Epstein, *News from Nowhere: Television and*

the News (New York: Random House, 1973); Herbert J. Gans, "Are U.S. Journalists Danger-ously Liberal?" *Columbia Journalism Review* 2, no. 6 (1985): 29–33; Hofstetter, *Bias in the News*; James B. Lemert, *Criticizing the Media: Empirical Approaches* (Newbury Park, CA: Sage, 1989); David Niven, "Partisan Bias in the Media?" *Social Science Quarterly* 80, no. 4 (1999): 847–858; David Niven, "Bias in the News," *Press/Politics* 6, no. 3 (2001): 31–46; Robin-son and Sheehan, *Over the Wire and on TV*; Shah, et al., "News Coverage, Economic Cues, and the Public's Presidential Preferences: 1984–1996"; Peverill Squire, "Who Gets National News Coverage in the U.S. Senate?" *American Politics Quarterly* 16, no. 2 (1988): 139–156; Paul Waldman and James Devitt, "Newspaper Photographs and the 1996 Presidential Election: The Question of Bias," *Journalism & Mass Communication Quarterly,* 75, no. 2 (1998): 302–311; David H. Weaver and G. Cleveland Wilhoit, "News Magazine Visibility of Senators," *Journalism Quarterly* 51, no. 1 (1974): 67–52; G. Cleveland Wilhoit and Kenneth S. Sherrill, "Wire Service Visibility of U.S. Senators," *Journalism Quarterly* 45, no. 1 (1968): 42–48.

[120] R. Bauer, "The Obstinate Audience: The Influence Process From the Point of View of Social Communication," *American Psychologist* 19 (1964): 319–328; L. Becker and Gerald Kosicki, "Understanding the Message-Producer/Message-Receiver Transaction," *Research in Political Sociology,* ed. P. Blackburn (Greenwich, CT: JAI, 1995), 32–62; J. Duck, J. Terry, and M. Hogg, "Perceptions of a Media Campaign," *Personality and Social Psychology Bulletin* 24, no. 1 (1997), 3–24; Cecilie Gaziano, "How Credible Is the Credibility Crisis?" *Journalism Quarterly* 65, no. 2/3 (1988): 267–278; Cecilie Gaziano and Kristin McGrath, "Measuring the Concept of Credibility," *Journalism Quarterly* 63, no. 3 (1986): 451–462; Albert C. Gunther, "Attitude Extremity and Trust in Media," *Journalism Quarterly* 65, no. 2/3 (1988): 279–287; Albert C. Gunther, "Biased Press or Biased Public?" *Public Opinion Quarterly* 56, no. 2 (1992): 147–167; Seymour Martin Lipset and William Schneider, *The Confidence Gap* (Rev. ed.) (Baltimore: Johns Hopkins University Press, 1987); Tony Rimmer and David Weaver, "Different Questions, Different Answers," *Journalism Quarterly* 64, no. 1 (1987): 28–44; R. Vallone, L. Ross, and M. Lepper, "The Hostile Media Phe-nomenon," *Journal of Personality and Social Psychology* 49 (1985): 577–585.

[121] Paul Allen Beck, "Voters' Intermediation Environments in the 1988 Presidential Contest," *Public Opinion Quarterly* 55, no. 3 (1991): 371–394; Vallone, Ross, and Lepper, "The Hostile Media Phenomenon."

[122] Vallone, Ross, and Lepper, "The Hostile Media Phenomenon."

[123] Gunther, "Biased Press or Biased Public?"

[124] Kathleen M. Schmitt, Albert C. Gunther, and Janice L Liebhart, "Why Partisans See Mass Media as Biased," *Communication Research* 31, no. 6 (2004): 623–641.

[125] Vallone, Ross, and Lepper, "The Hostile Media Phenomenon," 578.

[126] Cindy T. Christen, C., Prathana Kannaovakun, and Albert C. Gunther, "Hostile Media Per-ceptions," *Political Communication* 19, no. 4 (2002): 423–436; R. Giner-Sorolla and S. Chaiken, "The Causes of Hostile Media Judgment," *Journal of Experimental Social Psychol-ogy* 30 (1994): 165–180; Richard M. Perloff, "Ego-involvement and the Third Person Effect of Televised News Coverage," *Communication Research* 16, no. 2 (1989): 236–262.

[127] Tien-Tsung Lee, "The Liberal Media Myth Revisited: An Examination of Factors Influencing Perceptions of Media Bias," *Journal of Broadcasting & Electronic Media* 49, no. 1 (2005): 43–64.

[128] Watts, et al., "Elite Cues and Media Bias in Presidential Campaigns."

[129] Graber, *Mass Media and American Politics,* 87.

The Internet Influence
Online Political News and Political Discourse

A candidate who can master the Internet will not only level the playing field; he will level the opposition.

—Larry Purpuro

The Information Revolution is likely to democratize politics by weakening the elites' grip on information.

—Richard Dunham

As society and technology change, so do the ways politicians campaign and govern. As a result, political rhetoric has undergone a fundamental change in both form and content. Barnet Baskerville argues in *The People's Voice*:

> Societal values and attitudes are reflected not only in what the speaker says but also in how he says it—not only in the ideas and arguments to be found in speeches of the past but in the methods and practices of representative speakers and in the role and status accorded speakers by the listening public. As public tastes and public needs change, so do speaking practices—types of appeal, verbal style, modes of delivery.[1]

Past to Present

The United States has a rich history of political oratory. For much of our history, public speaking provided the main avenue to public success and popularity. Politicians were expected to make frequent, lengthy, public orations. Political speeches were public spectacles with banners, bands, slogans, and fireworks. Shortly after the War between the States, political oratory slowly began to change; a trend toward brevity and simplicity developed.

133

There was, in the late 1800s, also a shift of public attention from politics to business. Those concerned with business espoused virtues of directness, conciseness, and pragmatism.[2] In the media, the number of magazine articles and newspaper stories increased while their length decreased. Political speeches followed those trends and became shorter, more colloquial, and less airy. In fact, political oratory became public speaking with an emphasis on the utility of messages and the sharing of information.

The introduction of radio in the 1920s signaled another shift in political oratory. It eventually led to lively discussion shows, news reports (unlike news stories), and time constraints on both the speaker and audience. Radio crossed ethnic and regional boundaries. The west coast was connected to the east coast. Public officials had to speak "at" audiences, not "with" audiences. The press became filters of, rather than vehicles of, political communication.

The third major change in political campaign rhetoric was caused by television. Kevin Phillips proclaimed that by 1974,

> in the age of the mass media, the old Republican and Democratic parties have lost their logic. Effective communications are replacing party organizations as the key to political success. . . . As the first communications society, the United States is on its way to becoming the first "mediacracy."[3]

The medium of television transformed the form and content of political discourse.

Today, we know our leaders only through the mass media. The days of impassioned, fiery oratory presented in packed auditoriums are over. Today, presidents invite themselves, through the medium of television, into the privacy of our homes or offices for informal "presidential conversations." Kathleen Jamieson argues that the illusion of interpersonal, intimate context created through television requires a new eloquence, one in which candidates and presidents adopt a personal and revealing style that engages the audience in conversation.[4]

This means shorter speeches crafted specifically for television, ones that are increasingly personalized and self-revealing. Ronald Reagan was the first to excel at this style, which stands in marked contrast to the conversational style of Franklin D. Roosevelt, for example. The strength of Reagan's rhetoric was that we felt we knew and understood him, while the strength of Roosevelt's was that he knew and understood us. Reagan's use of contractions—simple and often incomplete sentences, informal transitions, colloquial language, and frequent stories—transformed his formal Oval Office addresses into conversations with the people.[5] His skillful adaptation to the camera simulated direct eye contact with individuals in his audience. It had all the appearance of conversation, inviting the audience to conclude that it knows and likes presidents who use it.

Public officials adapt to the medium of television through higher levels of intimacy and expressiveness. The presumption of intimacy attempts to make the audience feel as if they know the official as a dear friend and to force the audience to render positive, personal judgments. Frequent conversations lead to friendship, trust, and intimacy with the nation. Issue disagreements are less important and are tolerated because of the appearance of friendship.[6]

While Reagan proved that television's intimacy could heighten audience identification, in the 1992 presidential campaign, Clinton introduced another context—the town-hall meeting, a format that epitomized "presidential mediated interpersonal conversation."[7] With Clinton, presidential conversation became the primary means of conveying policy orientations and image projection. His televised town-hall meetings and talk show appearances invited the viewing audience to look upon him as a friend. These one-on-one sessions, sometimes with viewer call-ins or with a live audience, seemingly moved the president one step closer to the public. Participation and interaction were encouraged. Settings gave the appearance of a casual interaction where the audience simply eavesdrops on the conversation.

Both the structure and the content of mediated presidential conversation differ from nonmediated conversation. For example, interviews on television differ greatly from those in print. The secret is a controlled response best suited for the medium of television. On television, *how* one responds is as important as the *content* of the response. Perceptions of personal characteristics conveyed through nonverbal communication have a distinct influence on viewer perception of specific presidential performances. Was there a hesitation, a shift of the brow, or perhaps an expression of emotion? In the infamous 1992 Richmond presidential candidate debate with Clinton and Perot, George H. Bush took a quick glance at his watch. The simple action communicated a rather callous, cavalier attitude toward the audience and the event. His glance dominated the headlines the day after the debate.

With each introduction of new technology, we have seen a corresponding effect on the way that politicians communicate with their audiences that embraces both the form and content of the communication. We are currently riding the crest of a new wave of communication technologies. Computers, fiber optics, satellites, and the Internet have introduced an era of high-speed and greatly enhanced communication that forcefully impacts the creation, collection, and dissemination of information; moreover, it promises to enhance the public's understanding of political issues and to motivate citizen participation. The new media also transcend the time and space constraints of traditional media. In the pages that follow, we focus on the Internet and its impact on U.S. politics. Specifically, we look at its influence on political news and political campaigns and then turn to a special consideration of blogs and politics.

The Internet, Political Campaigns, and Political News

The Internet is becoming one of the defining scientific and social innovations of the twenty-first century. The information superhighway, as labeled by politicians and the media, has the ability to link people and resources in a way previously impossible. Users can share data, communicate messages, transfer programs, discuss topics, and connect to computer systems all over the world. The potential of the Internet as a tool for retrieving information is almost limitless. As a result of the freedom of expression allowed on this unique network, the possibilities for learning and enrichment are endless. However, with a network so large (and a territory so uncharted), there is great concern about the material readily available to anyone accessing the Internet, from the most perverse pornography to instructions for building bombs.

Andrew Chadwick has suggested key themes revolving around the Internet and politics. Below we share with you six we feel most relevant to this chapter:

- *Decentralization*. The general idea behind this theme is that as the Internet continues to develop, it will see a corresponding decrease in the number of intermediaries (middlemen) who have had a significant role in social, political, and economic processes. In the political realm, the "Internet would provide the technology required to link a politically active cyber civil society and more formal decision-making processes once controlled by elite political gatekeepers. Such gatekeepers could find themselves automated out of existence by Internet-mediated opinion."[8] Although some displacement has occurred, most notably in the world of journalism, it does not yet appear that the new technology is supplanting established interests. Social, political, and economic gatekeepers still exist—many have just moved online. New intermediaries skilled in the use of the Internet are proliferating. One area where decentralization is taking hold, however, is the intersection of media and politics. Whereas public opinion was once shaped by communication professionals using traditional media, both individuals and small groups are using the power of the Internet to bypass these gatekeepers, thus decentralizing control of political information. Some of examples of this will be seen later in this chapter.

- *Participation*. The Internet is often viewed as a means of increasing political participation and combating citizens' political apathy. However, even though the Internet does allow for user interactivity—chat rooms, issue forums, political town-hall meetings, Listservs, and so forth—many of these have "been criticized for the poor quality of interaction they create as well as their tendency to produce a plurality of deeply segmented political associations. [In] the online world it is much more likely that we will seek out like-minded people and have our views reinforced rather than challenged by alternative perspectives."[9] As we will discuss later in this chapter, others point out that recent studies suggest online consumers of political news are actually exposed to a greater variety of positions and are more politically aware than consumers of traditional news media. These contradictory points of view will clash in upcoming political campaigns given that "a new form of online campaigning based on more interactive forms of communication, particularly blogs, creates a different sort of environment—one which appears to have lowered levels of apathy and increased citizen participation."[10]

- *Community*. One view of community on the Internet suggests that it is "medication for the perceived ills of modern society: isolation, fragmentation, competitive individualism, the erosion of local identities, [and] the decline of traditional religious and family structures."[11] Internet users blog, post messages in chat rooms, use special forums to post to online discussion boards, and develop personal Web pages. The argument runs that if one invents a strong community in cyberspace, that "greater levels of political participation will follow" in the real world. Contrary to this view is that the "ties that bind members of a virtual community are not as strong as the old ties of family, locality, religion, or even political structures [such as] local party and lobby group associations. The Net, in this view, takes the impersonality of modern society to a new level, substituting a diluted form of community . . . for the real thing."[12]

- *Rationalization*. This concept refers to "a set of ideas which inspired the emergence of rules-based organizations based upon rational calculation, planning, and control."[13] It has its roots in the computer revolution in the late 1950s and early 1960s. "Computing was seen as a part of the end of ideology because it held out the promise of information abundance as a pragmatic route to objectively better solutions to social and economic problems. These . . . would be guided by systematic knowledge rather than irrational ideological belief systems."[14] In short, those viewing the Internet from this perspective ask how the Net generates "new, more efficient forms of social control."[15] For example, online "behavior patterns can be used to generate tailored e-mail messages that mention policy issues in which a voter is interested. Special sections of candidates' sites that specifically cater to the press and broadcasters are now common."[16] In short, the Internet can be used to gather and process large amounts of data, which can then be used to target specific groups, even individuals, with specific messages designed to influence their behavior. Online political projects such as e-government and e-campaigns fall into the concerns express here.

- *Governance*. This theme covers the entire range of persons and institutions involved in governing our lives. A governance approach to looking at the Internet recognizes that "networks, interaction, and participation are increasingly important characteristics of contemporary politics. . . . The Internet is facilitating, reinforcing, and often reconfiguring these trends."[17] In short, since the Internet bypasses so much of the old controls on information possessed by governing agencies, we are now required to "think in terms of the diverse actors, new communities, interests, and interdependencies they foster."[18]

- *Libertarianism*. The Internet has long been seen as a space in which government control and intrusion are both unwelcome and minimal. However, this perspective encompasses a wide array of concerns. "Cyberlibertarianism as hatred of market regulation by government can be found throughout cyberspace yet so can cyberlibertarianism as distrust of political and corporate elites or fear of increases in public and private surveillance."[19] Importantly, "scientists and engineers involved in laying the foundations of its technologies may have had a vision of unfettered communication and information sharing, but their passion was matched by entrepreneurs that sought to make profits from the new medium."[20] We see no reason to believe that these tensions will be resolved anytime soon, nor that resolution is necessary.

There are, however, potentially negative effects as well. For example, some argue that much of what passes for political content on the Internet is actually information in a degraded form. That is to say, it is oversimplified, and very often aimed at producing a partisan effect, not broad political awareness. Additionally, the exchange of information on the Internet is based on a market economy; meaning, the news is sold, and what is relayed to Internet users is often based on the question: What sells? Another potential negative consequence of the Internet in politics is that it can increase social isolation. This may bode ill for any increase in civic engagement. Why, for instance, should one attend a town council meeting when one can simply send an e-mail after lurking in a chat room? The Internet can also provide unparalleled variety and amounts of news items. However, just because the Internet can provide large amounts of diverse information quickly does not mean that voters will be better *educated* on a particular issue. Finally, the Internet can lend anonymity to news sources; the information distributed can often be manipulated for partisan political effect as well. Spoofs and hoaxes aside, a partisan interpretation of an event or issue can be sent to hundreds of thousands of online users with next to no cost. This disinformation can then be passed along to others, potentially clogging the e-mail boxes of citizens as well as elected officials, often before the "news" can be verified.

News Use

The use of the Internet is only increasing. In 1997, 23 percent of adult Americans were going online. Just two years later, in 1999, approximately 41 percent were going online. By 2006, almost 75 percent of adults were online.[21] Although the Internet has a reputation for pornographic sites and uses, only 13 percent of users seek such sites.[22] Checking e-mail is the number-one online activity (91 percent of users); 68 percent are using the Internet to obtain news, and salient to this chapter, 58 percent are using the Web to find specific political information or news.[23]

As we see this rise in Internet use, we also see decreased consumption of broadcast news and local news. For example, in 1993 over 75 percent of

American adults regularly watched broadcast news and approximately 60 percent regularly watched their local news. By 1996, those percentages had dropped to around 65 percent and 40 percent respectively, even though online news consumption was only around 1 percent. Four years later, in 2000, broadcast and local news consumption had dropped to 55 percent and 30 percent, but online consumption had shot up to over 20 percent.[24] We see similar trends with print news as well. Undoubtedly some of those no longer using traditional media are turning to the Internet for their needs; however, it appears that a sizeable portion of those consuming Web-based news sources are doing so to supplement their traditional news consumption. There is an age gap associated with this usage as well:

> As large numbers of younger Americans turn to the Internet for news, the audience for traditional news media is aging. Nearly half of those under age 30 (46%) go online for news at least once a week, compared to just 20% of those age 50 and up. These older Americans are far more likely to say they watched TV news (67%) or read a paper (58%).[25]

Traditional news consumption is strongly correlated with political activity, and this appears to be the case among Internet news consumers as well. For those

> Internet users who are actively gathering political information and engaged in political deliberations and participations online, online information is helpful instead of misleading in making political decisions, the Internet is believed to improve instead of lower the quality of public debate, and the Internet encourages instead of discourages them to vote.[26]

In short, the "more that people use the Internet for political information, deliberation, and participation, the more positively they perceive the effects of the Internet on political life."[27]

The number of people who use the Internet for political news purposes is large and growing. For campaign 2004, 63 million used the Internet for political information, 43 million discussed politics via e-mail, and 13 million used the Internet to make political campaign contributions. Overall, 75 million Americans participated in at least one Web campaign contact or activity. Noticeably, 52 percent of those who voted indicated that information gathered from the Internet influenced their voting decisions.[28] All of this points to rapid growth and amazing possibilities. Yet for all of that, as mentioned above, online news is still a supplementary source of news. As Mark Jurkowitz points out, although

> online news has quickly emerged as a big part of the nation's increasingly diverse news diet, it is not yet, for most of us, the main course. That's largely because it takes reporters to produce a main course. And, at least for now, reporting remains very much a signature product of the traditional media.[29]

Even when this reporting hits the Web, not much changes. Jane B. Singer found that as mainstream news outlets move online, information-oriented functions, particularly those related to getting news out quickly, remain key components of their self-perceptions, especially in the political contest of furthering democracy. Like candidates and voters examined elsewhere, journalists do not see and are not enacting a fundamental change in this role as they move online.[30]

In short, as journalists move online, they are "normalizing" the use of the Web for news purposes, even maintaining their traditional gatekeeping functions.[31] They are not inventing new uses or innovative news functions; instead, they seek to augment what is provided in print. As Singer writes, news media

> material original to the Web was designed primarily to provide more and faster information. . . . [The] dominance of election night updates in editors' reflections may indicate too much emphasis on speed over what could be classified as true public-service political journalism.[32]

William P. Cassidy also found that one of the major differences between online and traditional print journalists was that the "online group rated getting information to the public as quickly as possible as significantly more important than the print group."[33]

Political Use

The role of the Internet in politics is still evolving and uncertain; however, it is a medium that no politician can ignore. Since 1992, with each successive campaign cycle, the roles and functions of the Internet grew. Dave D'Alessio found that before "1996, almost no political candidates were using the Internet for purposes of transmitting messages to large audiences." Moreover, only "6–10 percent of the electorate" sought out political information on the Web.[34] By the time of the 1998 midterm elections, somewhere between 50 percent and 63 percent of campaigns had put up a Web site.[35] These sites began simply as a source of candidate information, really only an online version of an informational brochure. By late 2003, this had changed. Though lagging far behind television and newspapers as the primary source of campaign news, the Internet had already forged ahead of radio "as a primary source of political information."[36] By the presidential election of 2004, the Internet had become a powerful tool and medium of persuasion and citizen action.[37]

Many early commentators suggested that the Internet would have a negative effect on democratic participation. By 2004, however, this view found challengers. Recent polling data suggest that Internet "users have greater overall exposure [to] political arguments, including those that challenge their candidate preferences and their positions on some key issues."[38] John Horrigan, Kelly Garrett, and Paul Resnick found that Americans with Internet access "hear more points of view about candidates and key issues than other citizens. They are not using the Internet to screen out ideas with which they disagree."[39] In this sense, the "Internet is contributing to a wider awareness of political views during [the] campaign season."[40] Although higher levels of education, interest in the campaign, and advancing age were also factors associated with exposure to different arguments, the role of the Internet clearly demonstrated that "Internet use predicts that people will have greater exposure to arguments that challenge their views."[41]

As hinted at above, campaign Web sites initially possessed a static form, often echoing the style of direct mail cards and pamphlets.[42] By the 2004 election cycle, *interactivity* was the norm on campaign Web sites. In going interactive, these Web sites

> attempted to engage voters not only through mechanisms [such as] user control, but also through fostering a spirit of interactivity through the content on campaign sites and blogs. Though blogs introduced unprecedented and streamlined features of interactivity, such as the ability to leave comments and contribute to campaign discourse, this was not done at the level purposed by popular press accounts.[43]

We would be remiss if we did not trace the beginnings of the revolution of online campaigning to Democratic presidential hopeful Howard Dean, his campaign manager Joe Trippi, and a host of young talent attracted to the initial excitement of the Dean campaign. The Dean campaign ushered in five dramatic online innovations:

1. *News-pegged fund-raising appeals*. The Dean campaign capitalized on the ability of the Internet to allow immediate action on the part of supporters. Short-term goals, often pegged to news events, were linked with appeals for donations.

   Contributions are sought to finance ads that will let a campaign respond fast and prominently to an opponent's assertion, or to stage a news event that will attract new coverage. The campaign can then thank the donors with evidence of the media play their dollars made possible.[44]

   John Kerry later used the same tactic. He asked his online supporters to make a statement on the day he accepted the Democratic Party's nomination for president, raising over $5.6 million.

2. *"Meetups" and other Net-organized local gatherings*. Through its home page, the Dean campaign allowed for sign-ups for group meetings. Dean supporters could invite like-minded others to meet at various places around the country. At the height of Dean's campaign, several hundred thousand supporters had signed up for this service.[45]

3. *Blogging*. Blogs allow for an immediacy in a campaign. In 2003 the Dean campaign posted 2,910 entries on its "Blog for America."[46] By way of reply, 314,121 user comments were posted.[47] Blogging allowed the Dean campaign the ability to immediately disseminate the campaign's take on the events to the day.

4. *Online referenda*. Perhaps the most memorable example of this was when the Dean campaign asked it supporters to vote online to decide whether or not Dean should decline public financing of his campaign.

Although the consensus is that Dean already knew he would opt out, the idea of asking his supporters for their direct and immediate feedback took hold. This also provided the campaign with a fund-raising opportunity to capitalize on the participation. Those who voted yes were sent a thank you e-mail from the campaign in which a request for a donation was made.[48]

5. *Decentralized decision-making*. Through the use of Web-based actions listed above, the Dean campaign enacted its campaign slogan: "You have the Power." Many ideas for campaigning were contained on Dean's Web site, but the day-to-day operations of local advocates remained theirs to decide.[49]

The Dean campaign's successes influenced both Bush and Kerry to adopt Web-based strategies. Steve Davis explains perhaps the largest contribution of the Web during the 2004 presidential race. He writes that both the Bush and Kerry camps in 2004 "used the Web to break down barriers to participation."[50] Not only did both candidates invite their respective party convention viewers to visit their Web sites, but the number of visitors to those sites rose sharply from the previous years: "from 9 million going to Bush in 2000 to 16 million to Bush in 2004, and from 7 million going to Gore in 2000 to 20 million going to Kerry in 2004."[51] Davis points out that both campaigns used a "peer-to-peer citizen model; they recruited volunteers, many of them via online, and asked *them* to personally press their candidates' case with others."[52] This was more than simply passing along a campaign e-mail; it was also an active commitment to personally speak with others. Both campaigns provided "online tools" to help with the grass-roots initiatives. Instructions for online invitations for house parties were posted, and supporters could download "walk lists" consisting of the names of neighbors whom supporters could then canvass and help register to vote. In another innovative example, the Bush campaign came up the idea of a Virtual Precinct. Davis writes that a "college professor like myself, for example, could sit in New York—a Kerry state from Day One—and create a Virtual Precinct of teachers in half-dozen swing sates, lobbying them by e-mail, phone call and letter—to vote for Bush."[53]

Just prior to the casting of votes in the 2004 elections, Michael Cornfield wrote that the "presidential campaign world today regards the Internet as an asset for fund-raising, voter-profiling, and insider communication, but not for advertising."[54] While generally true, there are signs that political advertising is creeping into the Internet. For example, the Democratic National Committee (DNC) found a novel way to use the Internet for advertising during the 2004 election. In effect, it created "a virtual spin room to enlist thousands of people in the postdebate rhetorical ritual."[55] The DNC placed ads on both local and national news Web sites following the presidential and vice presidential debates. These ads were designed to appeal to Internet users who were searching for additional news about the debates. Clicking on an ad would take the user to a "Debate Center" on the DNC Web site. Once there, users found Democratic talking points and an invitation to participate in various online polls. The Bush campaign followed suit. However, even when one enlarges the field to include other campaigns, very little political money found its way to online advertising.

> The presidential candidates, national political parties, and advocacy groups ("527s") spent a combined total of only $2.66 million for advertisements on the Web between January and August 2004. That is less than half of what the John Kerry campaign raised in contributions from the Internet in a single day: $5.7 million.[56]

In short, political online advertising saw only $1 spent for every $100 spent on traditional TV ads.

According to Lee Rainie, Michael Cornfield, and John Horrigan, one may conclude several important points about campaign 2004.

1. By 2004, the Internet had become "an essential part of American politics."[57]

2. Of those going online, just over half said that the Internet was "important in giving them information that helped them decide how to vote, and that it made a difference in their voting decision."[58]

3. Although convenience was the main reason cited by Americans for going online for political news, more than half who go online say they can obtain "information online that is not available elsewhere and because they do not get all the information they need from traditional news sources."[59]

4. Overall, Americans rendered a positive assessment about the overall impact of the Internet on the 2004 campaign, with 56 percent of those obtaining news online stating that 'the Internet has raised the overall quality of the debate' during the campaign."[60]

5. Those going online for political news are increasingly mainstream. For instance, by campaign 2004, the "Internet population had grown to 61% of the adult [U.S.] population and that changed the profile of the online political news consumer population [from being predominately upper-middle class white males] to include higher proportions of women, older Americans, and rural residents."[61]

In more general terms, Danielle Wiese and Bruce Gronbeck identified six major developments in cyberpolitics during the 2004 presidential campaign: the introduction of network software and theory to online campaign strategy; expanded database functions to enhance e-mail and wireless functions; incorporation of coproduction features to increase citizen participation in online campaigns; use of Web-video and Web-advertising for online campaign messages; evolution of candidate Web sites into a standard genre of Web-text; and the introduction of blogs to the political cyberscape.[62] They suggest that in light of the use of the Web in the 2004 presidential campaign, scholars should rethink some of the traditional assumptions of political communication theory. For them, a new rhetoric of cyberpolitics is emerging:

> Discourse in the era of televised politics is characterized by talk about candidates, coverage, demographics, and parties. Cyberpolitics thickens the discussion with a focus on alterations in the roles of sender and receiver and on such notions as political community, networks, organization, and mobility. In addition, the move to tie online politics with the always-on and always-available nature of the Net alters the tempo of campaign rhetoric, drawing attention away from the established markers of election events, even of what counts as an election event. The nightly news, the primary season, conventions, and the rest of the primary markers of political culture are reworked through the everyday politics of the Internet.[63]

Andrew Williams also focuses on the role of the Internet in the 2004 presidential contest. Williams agrees with Wiese and Gronbeck that the Internet had a major impact in this election cycle. All the campaigns took advantage of new developments with the medium to communicate with the electorate. For Williams, the most notable developments from a strategy perspective include third-party Internet use, Web-based political advertising by the campaigns, successful fund-raising, birth of influential blogs, e-mobilization, and the use of humor. Williams speculates that the primarily "pull" feature of the Web is now also capable of becoming a "push" medium as well. The blurring of the lines between the two classifications will continue in future elections.[64] As a "pull" medium, the individual personally and consciously chooses to go to a Web site and attune to only that information of interest. However, in becoming a "push" medium, a Web site can "move" someone to another one, as if being influenced by a banner or intrigued by a "tease," one will avail themselves beyond the initial site.

In July 2006 Democratic candidates participated in an unconventional format for preprimary debates. They answered questions submitted as videos to YouTube; videos were chosen from the more than 3,000 posted. The event aired on CNN and was moderated by CNN news anchor Anderson Cooper. Candidates answered questions "on an array of topics that Americans evidently think about but which panelists rarely broach in the button-down format of the traditional debate." [65] The format was evidence of "the Internet's rapid ascension to a place of prominence in American politics."[66]

Blogs, Podcasts, and Politics

If you do not know what a blog is, you are not alone. In 2005, 62 percent of Internet users did not know what a blog is.[67] In general, a blog is a single Web site, focused on self-publishing documents written by one individual or perhaps a small group. Those who write blogs are called bloggers. According to the Pew Internet & American Life Project, the "blog population has grown to about 12 million American adults, or about 8 percent of the adult Internet users and that the number of blog readers has jumped to 57 million American adults, or 39 percent of the online population."[68] Slightly more men than women have created blogs, and blogging "is very much the province of the young. Fully 19 percent of online Americans ages 18–29 have created blogs, compared to 5 percent of those 50 and older."[69] Robert MacDougall notes that

> [at their] best, blogs represent a new form of open-sourced/open-access partisan press. . . . At their worse, blogs represent the latest form of mass-mediated triviality and celebrity spectacle, with the potential to create and sustain insulated enclaves of intolerance predicated on little more than personal illusion, rumor, and politically motivated innuendo.[70]

Bloggers come in many different varieties. Some focus on entertainment, others on health issues, wine, economics, day care, and still others on media and politics. This latter group is the one that interests us here. Although as of 2006 only 11 percent of bloggers focused on politics and government, their impact has been great.[71] For example, several blogs generated headlines by debunking the forged documents touted by Dan Rather and CBS concerning President Bush's National Guard service. "The key contribution from the political bloggers in this case consisted of providing forums accessible to all Internet users in which facsimiles of the memos could be examined and discussed."[72] Bloggers also published very early exit poll information strongly favoring the Kerry campaign. By mid-afternoon Election Day, there was discussion about the polls and the race across the various media. Other bloggers are actually professional journalists, although they number in the minority. These bloggers, many listed on cyberjournalist.net, write columns for regular print papers and then expand those thoughts on their blogs. Those journalists who take up blogging are called *j-bloggers*. According to Singer, political j-bloggers show several defining characteristics:

> Although expressions of opinion are common, most journalists are seeking to remain gatekeepers even in this highly interactive and participatory format [the blogosphere]. Political j-bloggers use links extensively—but mostly to other mainstream media sites. At least in their early use [through 2004], journalists are "normalizing" the blog as a component, and in some ways an enhancement, of traditional journalistic norms and practices.[73]

In short, although mainstream news journalists are beginning to use blogs to supplement their regular columns, they are using them in such a manner that the traditional functions of the news media—agenda setting, gatekeeping, and agenda extension—are remaining intact.[74]

Although some argue that a portion of the growing influence of bloggers is derived from traditional journalists who have taken up the practice of blogging, we feel that the power of political blogs is derived "partly because a few dozen of them, known as the 'A-list' or 'political blogs,' [the top dozen or so with the most traffic] have been hailed as a new force in national politics."[75] According to Michael Cornfield and colleagues:

A-list bloggers occupy key positions in the mediascape. Journalists, activists, and political decision-makers have learned to consult political blogs as a guide to what is going on in the rest of the Internet. The bloggers are fast to spot items of interest; they link to sources so that items may be verified and inspected at length; and they embroider items with witty captions and frequently passionate commentaries. Accordingly, when bloggers buzz, the big mouthpieces of society notice."[76]

Examples of these A-list blogs include instapundit.com, michellemalkin.com, littlegreenfootballs.com, and mydd.com.

Gracie Lawson-Borders and Rita Kirk examined the use of blogs during campaign 2004. Their insightful essay found that studies of blogs that possessed a political communication function generally fell into three areas: blogs as a social narrative, blogs as organizing tools, and blogs as a form of civic journalism.[77] As a tool for *social narrative*, blogs give Internet users the opportunity to "share their thoughts and experiences on the Internet." In this sense, bloggers can share their point of view with others, and a conversation of sorts ensues. Researchers can track this conversational level, called buzz. "Tracking conversations occurring in the blogosphere provides real-time insight into the rise and fall of conversation topics and the intensity of that discussion."[78] Importantly, this can allow political strategists to "gain insight into how interested people are in talking about an issue and the stickiness of the message itself."[79]

As an *organizing tool*, political blogs show three characteristics. First, "blog-speech is short and emotive." In short, blog writing seems to follow a journalistic tradition, with bloggers using a headline to draw readers into the commentary that follows. Additionally, there is an emotional quality to blog posts. Blogs allow for the personalization of political news; they tell readers why and how political news matters to them. Second, blogs are used by campaigns as organizational tools and to encourage supporter involvement. Third, blogs are used by campaigns as a "participatory outlet."[80] This means that those reading a blog are often encouraged to "talk back" by commenting on the content of the blog; this in turn leads to others commenting and additional blog content.

As forms of *civic journalism*, political blogs allow citizens to bypass traditional media gatekeepers to both consume and produce news firsthand. In this way, more individuals are allowed into ongoing public discussions. Additionally, blogs "present a new context for understanding the role between journalists and their audiences in which the latter has the potential to become more involved, interactive, and a producer and not just a consumer of information."[81] Importantly, as Shayne Bowman and Chris Willis point out, blog postings, both individual blogs (one writer to many readers) and group blogs (many writers to many readers), "inevitably become part of what is now called the 'blogosphere' . . . the linking to and discussion of what others have written or linked to, in essence a distributed discussion."[82]

Another growing function of blogs is discussed by Stephen Cooper in *Watching the Watchdog: Bloggers as the Fifth Estate*. A central point made in this trenchant analysis is that

> if the people need a watchdog to make sure the institution of govern-
> ment does not abuse the power they have granted it, would there not be
> a need for a comparable check on the press, as a social institution with
> power in its own right?[83]

In short, Cooper asks how bloggers function as news media critics and focuses specifically on political news commentary. At the heart of his analysis, Cooper suggests four genres of criticism functioning within this potential Fifth Estate.

1. *Political blogs often challenge the accuracy of reports made by the main-stream news media.* Within their blogs, they check not only the factual accuracy of descriptions but also check the contextualization of quotations, authenticate documents, reinterpret statistics, and check the trustworthiness of "memes," which is blog-talk for "'a discrete idea that replicates itself.'"[84] For example, bloggers caught *New York Times* columnist Maureen Dowd intentionally misquoting a statement by President Bush in such a way as to make it appear that he had declared victory in the War on Terror. Cooper writes that in the "aftermath of this journalistic scandal, Dowd's name entered the lexicon of blogosphere jargon (Dowdification, n.d.). To dowdify, in blog-speak, is to selectively edit a quote in a way that distorts it meaning."[85] Perhaps the most infamous check of accuracy concerned the forged Bush National Guard memos highlighted on the news show *60 Minutes*. The story, supported by the content of the memos, cast a negative light on President Bush's National Guard service. CBS posted copies of the memos on its Web site, and these copies quickly came under close scrutiny by political bloggers. "In the end, the bloggers' doubts about the authenticity of the documents proved to be correct, and the mainstream outlet which had created the faulty report was forced to acknowledge this."[86]

2. Political news blogs act to dispute the mainstream news media frame, reframe an issue or event, or act to contextualize information when the news media fail to do so. As mentioned in chapter 6, framing is the process whereby communicators act—consciously or not—to construct a particular point of view that encourages the facts of a given situation to be viewed in a particular manner, with some facts made more or less noticeable than others.[87] For example, when mainstream news outlets framed a firefight in Iraq to highlight the strength of insurgents, political rantingprofs.com demonstrated that the same set of facts provided in the paper could have been framed in such a way as to demonstrate the overwhelming superiority of the responding U.S. troops as they crushed the insurgents.[88]

3. Political news blogs act to dispute the mainstream news functions of agenda setting and gatekeeping. As reviewed in chapter 5, gatekeeping is about story selection; who decides what stories shall pass through the media gate. In chapter 6 we saw how agenda setting goes a step beyond this; it shows that the amount of emphasis given to a particular event or issue raises awareness about that event or issue in the mind of the public. Because of this, the media sets an agenda of sorts concerning what is considered important to the public. Blogs challenge the mainstream news hegemony in this area by specifically raising awareness about events ignored by the mainstream news media. Blogs accomplish this through the questioning of the news judgment made by traditional journalists and editors, and also through the setting of alternate agendas.[89] For example, in the United States during the controversy over the publication of editorial cartoons depicting the Islamic prophet Muhammad, the mainstream news media effectively censored the images; only three newspapers and two broadcast outlets published one or more of the cartoons.[90] Contrast that number with the 146 bloggers who published the images, thus effectively bypassing the mainstream media's gatekeeping function. Some bloggers, such as Michelle Malkin, posted the cartoons and also closely scrutinized the role the mainstream media was playing in promoting acceptance of Muslim violence over depictions of the cartoons.[91] Another blogger, zombietime.com, posted links to Islamic depictions of the prophet, again bypassing the American mainstream media's information lockout on this issue.[92]

4. Political news blogs act to critique the mainstream news' general journalistic practices. This area concerns the actual reportorial practices of the reporters and editors. Specifically, blogs act to critique news gathering, writing, editing, and error correction practices. For example, during the Iraq war, the U.S. military began the practice of embedding reporters within military units. This was a popular practice, but immediately following the fall of Saddam Hussein's regime the practice fell off not, as one might assume, because the military was phasing the program out but rather because reporters discontinued their participation. Thus, coverage of the aftermath of the war took the form of "what some have termed 'hotel journalism'" . . . with journalists drawing on local stringers as much or more than their own direct observations of conditions and events in that area. For example, Cori Dauber of rantingprofs.com wrote:

> I remain mystified by the argument that, although reporters feel they can't leave their hotels in many instances, but must rely on barely trained or untrained Iraqi stringers to do the actual reporting, embedding is not an alternative because it would provide access to only one side of the story. Sitting in the hotel provides access to

no sides of the story—embedding would at least balance what the stringers are getting.

Does embedding permit higher quality journalism? My argument there has been that the work produced by papers such as the *North County Times* and the *Richmond Dispatch* suggests that it certainly can.[93]

This is just one example of a critique of mainstream press reportorial practices, something in the past left only on occasion to an individual paper's ombudsman and rarely creating national-level conversation.

Bloggers are not all-powerful, though. As pointed out by Michael Cornfield and colleagues, "the capacity of blog operators to make buzz and influence decision-makers, is circumstantial: dependent on the sorts of information available, and contingent on the behavior of other public voices."[94]

Podcasting is another area in which rapid change can occur. Audio and video programming can be downloaded to a user's iPod or computer for later listening or viewing. By the summer of 2006, approximately 7 percent of American adults had downloaded an audio podcast—over nine million.[95] Thus far, the supramajority of podcasts are produced by amateurs. We expect soon that commercial interests will invest in this format, as too will politicians looking to spread their messages.

Social Networks and Politics

Social networks are individuals or organizations tied together by common interests: values, beliefs, political perspectives, sickness or handicap, job or occupation, etc., to name a few. Members form rather unique communities involving a great deal of social interaction by way of chat, e-mail, file sharing, blogging, or discussion. The most popular today are MySpace, Facebook and YouTube. These sites naturally attract people who support specific candidates, political parties, or issue positions.

The political power and influence of these networks was particularly evident in the 2006 mid-term election. Perhaps the most widely noted incident occurred during Virginia's U.S. Senatorial campaign between Republican incumbent George Allen and Democratic challenger Jim Webb. During a campaign stop in far southwest Virginia, Senator Allen made reference to a twenty year old "tracker" from the Webb campaign who was videotaping his remarks. He referred to volunteer S. R. Sidarth—of Indian ancestry but born and raised in Virginia—as "Macaca."

This fellow here over here with the yellow shirt, Macaca, or whatever his name is. He's with my opponent. He's following us around everywhere. And it's just great. We're going to places all over Virginia, and he's having it on film and it's great to have you here and show it to your opponent because he's never been there and probably will never come. . . . Let's give a welcome to Macaca, here. Welcome to America and the real world of Virginia.[96]

The Webb campaign put the video on YouTube as well as their Web site and claimed the term was a racial insult referring to a genus of monkey or, even worse, a French and Spanish slang for excrement. The Allen campaign said that the Senator had messed up the word "Mohawk," the nickname staffers had given to Sidarth. After two weeks of intense criticism and literally hundreds of thousands of viewers of the video, Senator Allen apologized directly to Sidarth. However, the term had become a part of the political lexicon.

The lessons of the incident are threefold. First, campaigns could post unflattering comments and even past video on YouTube to draw attention away from mainstream media outlets. Second, it provided a forum to share opposition research and attack information that would feed material to sympathetic bloggers. Finally, it would provide a platform for candidates to share video statements or even commercials without cost to be viewed by thousands of people. In fact, by early 2007, there was a specific Web page in YouTube that would direct you to material for every Democratic and Republican candidate running for the party's nomination. On each candidate site, there is an introductory video as well as other ads, commentaries and opportunities to join the campaign and to share items with friends. The same is true for MySpace and Facebook. These social networking sites have become an integral part of state and national campaigns.

Summary

The history of new communication technology is a history of change. With each new technology, politicians have adapted to and used that technology to their advantage. We are now in the middle of an exciting period, with politics being influenced heavily by the impact of the Internet. Certainly, we will continue to see the use of the Internet for both regular news and political news. One promising area for online news lies in interactivity, which, according to Singer,

> offers interesting possibilities for significantly enhancing the democratic process. . . . By the early 1990s, a number of journalists believed it was extremely important to "give ordinary people a chance to express their views on public affairs." That is difficult, costly, and problematic in print; it is relatively simple, cheap, and desirable online.[97]

For instance, mainstream online news sites routinely run online polls and allow readers to submit comments that are then published below the original article. Some papers now even have their own ombudsmen blogs. Even with this interactivity, online users are pushing politics and news in new ways. For example, on September 22, 2006, a YouTube.com user posted a clip of a FOX News interview with former president Bill Clinton. Within two days, the clip was viewed over 850,000 times, and over 4,300 viewer comments were posted.[98]

One way of understanding new media is through the effects they have on consumers of political news. The potential positive effects on political participation are many. Whereas traditional media such as radio, television, and newspapers are considered unidirectional (that is, a one-way means of communication), the Internet allows for public comment on political topics. In this sense, the potential for great civic engagement is possible. Too, with the Internet one has the potential to find great numbers of alternative news sources. Because of e-mail, Listservs, blogs, and Web-based communities or town halls, the potential for increased interaction with other citizens increases (e.g., townhall.com). This can also lead to greater interaction with public officials, thus helping to reduce any perceived distance between members of the public and public servants. Another positive effect is that those seeking political news on the Internet are exposed to a greater variety of political arguments and points of view than those who rely only on traditional media.

We have seen that as the consumption of traditional news sources has declined since the early 1990s, the use of Internet-based news sources rose dramatically. However, it appears that the Internet is used to augment traditional news sources rather than supplanting them entirely; it is a place to find additional information. This use is growing across all demographic categories in the United States. Additionally, as traditional news sources move online, they generally adapt the Internet to the traditional formats. Exceptions to this practice do occur, but come from nontraditional sources, such as blogs and grassroots organizations.

The political use of the Internet has grown rapidly; the years 1996 to 2006 saw amazing growth, with each new election cycle showing the signs of the adoption of Web-based improvements. These changes, however, lag behind business uses of the Internet. Consider, for instance, that advertising on the Internet is a multibillion dollar industry. Even so, in campaign 2004, Bush and Kerry spent at a ratio of 100 to 1 on traditional advertising to Internet advertising. Increasingly the Internet is being seen as having a positive effect on political participation. This is in part due to campaigns and politicians reaching out to Internet users, but also to the exposure that Internet news consumers have to a variety of political ideas and issues.

Blogs are an exciting new aspect to Internet politics. We have seen their growth coming from traditional sources such as mainstream news and political campaigns and also from a new category of journalists, the A-list bloggers. The traditional news sources appear to be using blogs as an extension of traditional news functions, while political campaigns are using the blog format to lend an immediacy to their campaigns and to increase voter involvement. A-list bloggers and others of similar intent are actively challenging the mainstream media's role in U.S. politics and may be on their way to developing into a Fifth Estate.

Although research to date is only speculative regarding the role the Internet will play both in politics and in future elections, one thing is certain: the online political audience will continue to grow. In 1996 only 4 percent of the general public and 22 percent of regular Internet users went online to obtain news about the elections that year. In 2004, 29 percent of the general public and 52 percent of regular Internet users went online to obtain news about the elections.[99] With this rate of growth, no politician can afford to ignore the Internet any longer.

Notes

1 Barnet Baskerville, *The People's Voice* (Lexington: University of Kentucky Press, 1979), 4.

2 See, for instance, Walter Dill Scott, *Influencing Men in Business* (New York: The Ronald Press Company, 1911).

3 Kevin Phillips, *Mediacracy* (New York: Doubleday, 1974), v.

4 Kathleen H. Jamieson, *Eloquence in an Electronic Age* (New York: Oxford University Press, 1988), 166.

5 Robert E. Denton, Jr., *The Primetime Presidency of Ronald Reagan* (Westport, CT: Praeger, 1988).

6 Robert Cathcart and Gary Gumpert, "Mediated Interpersonal Communication: Toward a New Typology," *Quarterly Journal of Speech* 69 (1986): 267–277.

7 Robert E. Denton, Jr. and Rachel L. Holloway, "Clinton and the Town Hall Meetings: Mediated Conversation and the Risk of Being 'In Touch,'" in *The Clinton Presidency: Images, Issues, and Communication Strategies*, ed. Robert E. Denton, Jr. and Rachel L. Holloway (Westport, CT: Praeger, 1996), 17–41.

8 Andrew Chadwick, *Internet Politics: States, Citizens, and New Communication Technologies* (Oxford: Oxford University Press, 2006), 22.

9 Ibid., 25.

10 Ibid., 26.

11 Ibid., 26.

12 Ibid., 26.

13 Ibid., 30.

14 Ibid., 30.

15 Ibid., 30.

16 Ibid., 31.

17 Ibid., 32.

18 Ibid., 32.

19 Ibid., 36.

20 Ibid., 32.

21 "Percentage of Adults Online," Pew Internet & American Life Project Surveys, March 2000–2006. Retrieved 12 September 2007 from http://www.pewinternet.org/trends/Internet_Adoption_ 4.26.06.pdf

22 "Internet Activities," Pew Internet & American Life Project Surveys, March 2000–2006. Retrieved 12 September 2007 from http://www.pewinternet.org/trends/Internet_Activities_ 7.19.06.htm

23 Ibid. Numbers refer to December 2005 and November 2004, respectively.

24 "Internet Sapping Broadcast News Audience," Pew Research Center for the People & the Press (June 11, 2000) 1.

25 *Internet Sapping,* 2

26 Yan Tian, "Political Use and Perceived Effects on the Internet: A Case Study of the 2004 Election," *Communication Research Reports* 23, no. 2 (2006): 135.

27 Ibid., 135.

28 Andrew Paul Williams and John Tedesco, "Introduction" in *The Internet Election: Perspectives on the Web in Campaign 2004*, ed. Andrew Paul Williams and John Tedesco (Lanham, MD: Rowman & Littlefield, 2006), 1.

29 Mark Jurkowitz, "Now in Its Adolescence, the Internet Evolves into a Supplementary News Source," *Journalism.org* (August 1, 2006), 3. Retrieved 12 September 2007 from http://pewresearch.org/pubs/42/now-in-its-adolescence-the-internet-evolves-into-a-supplementary-news-source

30 Jane B. Singer, "Campaign Contributions: Online Newspaper Coverage of Election 2000," *Journalism & Mass Communication Quarterly* 80, no. 1 (2003): 50.

31 William P. Cassidy, "Gatekeeping Similar for Online, Print Journalists," *Newspaper Research Journal* 27, no. 2 (2006): 6–23.

32 Singer, "Campaign Contributions," 50.

33 William P. Cassidy, "Variations on a Theme: The Professional Role Conceptions of Print and Online Newspaper Journalists," *Journalism and Mass Communication Quarterly* 8, no. 2 (2005): 264.

34 Dave D'Alessio, "Adoption of the World Wide Web by American Political Candidates, 1996–1998," *Journal of Broadcasting & Electronic Media* 44, no. 4 (2000): 556.

35 Ibid., 564.

36 "The Internet Is Playing a Growing Role in Politics," Pew Internet & American Life Project (January 12, 2004), 1.

37 For a more detailed chronology of the use of the Internet by political campaigns see, Philip N. Howard, *New Media Campaigns and the Managed Citizen* (New York: Cambridge University Press, 2006), 6–18.

38 "More Americans Get Campaign News Online and the Internet Helps Them Become Aware of a Wider Range of Political Views," Pew Internet & American Life Project (October 27, 2004), 1.

39 John Horrigan, Kelly Garrett, and Paul Resnick, *The Internet and Democratic Debate*, Pew Internet & American Life Project (October 27, 2004), 1.

40 Ibid., 2.

41 Ibid., 3. (Italics in original removed.)

42 John C. Tedesco, "Changing the Channel: Use of the Internet for Communication about Politics," *Handbook of Political Communication Research*, ed. Lynda L. Kaid (Mahwah, NJ: Erlbaum, 2004), 507–532. Some scholars have suggested ways to formally evaluate a campaign Web site. For example, see Pamela J. Benoit and William L. Benoit, "Criteria for Evaluating Political Campaign Web Pages," *Southern Communication Journal* 70, no. 3 (2005): 230–247.

43 Kaye D. Trammel, Andrew Paul Williams, Monica Postelnicu, and Kristen D. Landreville, "Evolution of Online Campaigning: Increasing Interactivity in Candidate Web Sites and Blogs Through Text and Technical Features," *Mass Communication & Society* 9, no. 1 (2006): 42.

44 Michael Cornfield, "The Internet and Campaign 2004: A Look Back at the Campaigners," Commentary on the Impact of the Internet on the 2004 Elections, Pew Internet & American Life Project (March 6, 2005), 1–2.

45 Ibid., 2.

46 For an in-depth examination of the Dean campaign's Blog for America see, Matthew R. Kerbel and Joel David Bloom, "Blog for America and Civic Involvement," *Press/Politics* 10, no. 4 (2005): 3–27.

47 Cornfield, "The Internet and Campaign 2004," 2.

48 Ibid., 3.

49 Ibid., 3.

50 Steve Davis, "Presidential Campaigns Fine-Tune Online Strategies," *Journalism Studies* 6, no. 2 (2005): 242.

51 Cornfield, "The Internet and Campaign 2004," 4.

52 Davis, "Presidential Campaigns Fine-Tune Online Strategies," 242

53 Ibid., 242.

54 Michael Cornfield, "Presidential Campaign Advertising on the Internet," Pew Internet & American Life Project (October 3, 2004), 1.

55 "Political Online Advertising Update," Pew Internet & American Life Project (October 15, 2004), 1.

56 "First-Ever Systematic Study of Online Political Ads: The 2004 Presidential Campaigns Have Virtually Ignored the Internet as an Advertising Medium," Pew Internet & American Life

Project (September 29, 2004), 1. Retrieved 12 September 2007 from
http://www.pewinternet.org/PPF/r/134/report_display.asp

[57] Lee Rainie, Michael Cornfield, and John Horrigan, "The Internet and Campaign 2004," Pew
Internet & American Life Project (March 6, 2005), vii.

[58] Ibid., ii.

[59] Ibid., vi.

[60] Ibid., ii.

[61] Ibid., iii.

[62] Danielle Wiese and Bruce E. Gronbeck, "Campaign 2004 Developments in Cyberpolitics," in
The 2004 Presidential Campaign: A Communication Perspective, ed. Robert E. Denton, Jr.
(Lanham, MD: Rowman & Littlefield, 2005), 217–239.

[63] Ibid., 233.

[64] Andrew Williams, "The Main Frame: Assessing the Role of the Internet in the 2004 U.S.
Presidential Contest," in *The 2004 Presidential Campaign: A Communication Perspective*, ed.
Robert E. Denton, Jr. (Lanham, MD: Rowman & Littlefield, 2005), 241–254.

[65] Christi Parsons and John McCormick, "Blunt Voters Steer Debate," *Chicago Tribune*, July 23,
2006, p. 6.

[66] Steve Johnson, "Substance Overcomes Novelty," *Chicago Tribune*, July 24, 2007, p. 6.

[67] Lee Rainie, "The State of Blogging," Pew Internet & American Life Project (January 2, 2005),
1. Retrieved 12 September 2007 from http://www.pewinternet.org/report_display.asp?r=144

[68] "Blogging Is Bringing New Voices to the Online World," Pew Internet & American Life
Project (July 19, 2006), 1.

[69] "New Data on Blogs and Blogging," Pew Internet & American Life Project (May 2, 2005), 1.

[70] Robert MacDougall, "Identity, Electronic Ethos, and Blogs: A Technological Analysis of
Symbolic Exchange on the New News Medium," *American Behavioral Scientist* 49, no. 4
(2005): 575.

[71] "Blogging is Bring New Voices to the Online World," 1.

[72] "Innovative Study Suggests Where Blogs Fit into National Politics," Pew Internet & American Life Project (May 16, 2005), 1.

[73] Jane B. Singer, "The Political J-Blogger: 'Normalizing' a New Media Form to Fit Old Norms
and Practices," *Journalism* 6, no. 2 (2005): 173.

[74] The final item in this list, agenda extension, is not derived from Singer's essay; rather, it represents the observations of the authors.

[75] Michael Cornfield, Jonathan Carson, Alison Kalis, and Emily Simon, "Buzz, Blogs, and Beyond:
The Internet and the National Discourse in the Fall of 2004," Pew Internet & American Life
Project (May 16, 2005), 3. Retrieved 12 September 2007 from http://www.pewinternet.org/ppt/
BUZZ_BLOGS_BEYOND_Final05-16-05.pdf

[76] Cornfield et al., "Buzz, Blogs, and Beyond," 5.

[77] Gracie Lawson-Borders and Rita Kirk, "Blogs in Campaign Communication," *American
Behavioral Scientist* 49, no. 4 (2005): 548–559.

[78] Ibid., 552.

[79] Ibid., 553.

[80] Ibid., 555.

[81] Ibid., 556.

[82] Shayne Bowman and Chris Willis, *We Media: How Audiences are Shaping the Future of News and
Information.* The Media Center at the American Press Institute (posted September 21, 2003).
Retrieved 12 September 2007 from http://www.hypergene.net/wemedia/weblog.php?id=P38

[83] Stephen D. Cooper, *Watching the Watchdog: Bloggers as the Fifth Estate* (Spokane, WA: Marquette Books, 2006), 13.

[84] Ibid., 97.

[85] Ibid., 54. See specifically, 47–54.

[86] Ibid., 76–77. See especially, 54–76.

[87] See chapter 1 in Jim A. Kuypers, *Bush at War: Media Bias and Justifications for War in a Terrorist Age* (Lanham, MD: Rowman & Littlefield, 2006).

88 Cooper, *Watching the Watchdog,* 106–108.

89 Ibid., 121–152.

90 This is our informal count.

91 Michelle Malkin, "Support Denmark: Why the Forbidden Cartoons Matter" (January 30, 2006). Retrieved 12 September 2007 from http://michellemalkin.com/archives/004413.htm

92 Retrieved 23 February 2007 from http://www.zombietime.com/mohammed_image_archive/

93 Cori Dauber, "There are Benefits to Embedding," (April 21, 2005; italics in original). Retrieved 12 September 2007 http://www.rantingprofs.com/rantingprofs/2005/04/there_are_benef.html

94 Cornfield et al., "Buzz, Blogs, and Beyond," 1.

95 "What Is Podcasting," *Journalism.org* (July 19, 2006), 1–4. Retrieved 12 September 2007 from http://journalism.org/node/1899

96 Retrieved 12 September 2007 from http://www.youtube.com/watch?v=r90zOPMnKwl

97 Singer, "The Political J-Blogger," 51

98 "Bill Clinton Freaks Out." Retrieved 24 September 2006 from http://youtube.com/watch?v=3UwJabtvSUQ

99 Rainie, Cornfield, and Horrigan, "The Internet and Campaign 2004," i.

Campaign Planning, Management, Strategies, and Tactics

Plans are useless. Planning is essential!

—Dwight D. Eisenhower

The notion of "campaign" comes from a military vocabulary. In a general context, a campaign is a connected series of operations designed to bring about a particular result. It involves planning, strategy, competition, and of course, winners and losers. In 1994, former Republican Speaker of the House of Representatives Newt Gingrich, in motivating candidates for the Republican takeover of the House for the first time in 40 years, observed that "politics and war are remarkably similar systems. . . . War is politics with blood; politics is war without blood."[1]

The United States holds more elections, more often, than any other modern nation; with well over 500,000 elected officials, there are over a million elections held in every four-year cycle.[2] Just 40 years ago, volunteers and party activists conducted campaigns, with face-to-face canvassing essential to winning. Beginning in the 1960s, new communication technology and improved methodologies of social science changed the way one conducted and ran campaigns. The changes in campaign technologies continue to evolve. Today, political campaigns are major, expensive, and intense events. According to longtime political operative Ed Rollins:

> The modern campaign . . . is a high-tech, high-maintenance, high-anxiety, high-concept monstrosity where response time is instant. The candidate may have never held office. The manager is a professional political consultant who may be juggling three other races. The pollster samples public opinion every night for weeks. The press is frantically looking for

157

dirt on the candidate and his or her every relative, dead or alive. The television budget may be larger than the gross national product of Niger. And if your ads don't slash and burn, you'll lose.[3]

Daniel Shea and Michael Burton argue that campaigns have moved from an "old style" to a "new style" of campaigning in four ways: new players, new incentives, new tactics, and new resources.[4] In the old style, parties ran candidates for office. Between 1830 and 1960, campaigns were party driven, and maintaining voter contact was the role of party activists. Today, individuals run for office. The party has less control over who runs, especially in cases of primaries. Individuals with money, for instance, Steve Forbes in 1996 or Ross Perot in 1992, or perhaps with name recognition but no or little political experience, now may run, self-identifying with a particular party. Once nominated, the individual carries the campaign function with little else but party endorsement. Of course, television and changes to the nomination process to include primaries contributed to today's "candidate-centered" campaigns.

Simultaneously, the political consultant industry began. Campaign professionals replaced volunteers; campaign management and services became an industry. For consultants, political ideology or public policy are less important than the number of clients. By the end of the 1970s, there were 30 different campaign professional specialties, such as media relations, advertising, and speech writing. By the spring of 2006, *Campaigns & Elections* magazine identified 75 different categories of campaign professionals.[5] The traditional notion of a citizen-legislator is replaced with the professional, career politician, often viewing government service as providing a path to corporate jobs and big money. Prior to the 1970s, successful party officials and campaign workers would perhaps be placed in government jobs or on the elected official's staff. However, in the age of consultants, the professional's goal is continuous employment. Top consultants in a national or even high-profile state campaign can literally earn millions of dollars.

Old style politics involved traditional strategies of group-based appeals with traditional party messages. The goal was voter education and broad mass appeal. Today, the strategies and tactics are more narrowly defined and targeted. Voter preferences are revealed through scientific research. Messages are targeted to voter segments. New tactics correspond to new communication technologies, which include the proliferation of cable stations, satellites, fiber optics, and wireless technologies. As seen in the last chapter, campaigns are now investing heavily in and adapting to Internet technologies. Methods and frequency of voter contact continue to expand.

Much of the change, of course, comes at the higher levels of electoral politics. There still are true "citizen-politicians" at the state and local level; however, there is an increasing professionalization of political campaigns, even at the local levels. As Shea and Burton note:

> Even city council races are starting to use expensive, high-tech methods, and the newfound tricks of the 1980s were considered passé a decade

later. Instead of large-scale polls, narrowly targeted focus groups came into vogue. By the mid-1990s, it was normal to see videotapes distributed en masse. Satellite feeds were replacing smoke-filled rooms, and blast faxes rendered hand-distributed press releases obsolete. Of course, the advent of the World Wide Web brought about fundamental changes in daily campaign communications.[6]

Today campaign workers and money come from outside the geographic area of the race. Money rules the day in terms of staff, advertising, and the use of campaign technology. Of course, money has always been the lifeblood of politics, and this is even more so today. Outside and special interest groups now contribute millions of dollars to influence electoral outcomes.

Today, the "uses and gratifications model" of campaign effects is increasing in popularity. This model basically argues that campaign effects upon voters depend upon the needs and motivations of the individual voter. Voters may turn to campaign messages for information, issue discussion, or pure entertainment. There are a variety of motives, therefore, for exposure to campaign communication.

Campaign Planning

Campaigns as Exercises in Communication

As we argued in chapters 1 and 2, politics is primarily a communication activity. William Sweeney, Jr., thinks "a political campaign is fundamentally a communications exercise about choices . . . between the aspirants for public office and the audience of voters."[7] A communication approach to campaign analysis challenges the basic assumption of behaviorists that political campaigns play a minor role or have little influence in election results. Communication scholars argue that too much emphasis of campaign research has been focused on voter conversion. Such research tends to ignore the long-term, subtle effects or cumulative effects of politics and political campaigns.

Campaigns are exercises in the creation, re-creation, and transmission of significant symbols through communication. Communication activities are the vehicles for action—both real and perceived. It is true, however, as Samuel Becker argues, that "any single communication encounter accounts for only a small portion of the variance in human behavior."[8] He characterizes our communication environment as a "mosaic."[9] The mosaic consists of an infinite number of information "bits" or fragments on an infinite number of topics scattered over time and space. In addition, the bits are disorganized and exposure is varied and repetitive. As we find these bits to be relevant or to address a need, we attend to them. Thus, as we attempt to make sense of our environment, our current state of existence, political bits are elements of our voting choice, worldview, or legislative desires. As voters, we must arrange these bits into a cognitive pattern that comprises our mosaic of a candidate, issue, or situation. Campaigns, then, are great sources of potential information and contain, however difficult to identify or measure, elements that impact decision making. Information bits can replace other bits to change or modify our worldview, attitudes, or opinions.

Jonathan Robbin, chairman of the Claritas Corporation and pioneer in the field of geo-demographics, recognizes the important role of communication in successful campaigns. "The essence of political campaigning is communications. A majority is built by repeatedly contacting voters and persuading them to register, turn out, and cast their ballot for the 'right' candidate or side of an issue."[10] For him, market data alone will not guarantee electoral success; rather, how the market data are applied is critical to the campaign process. "The efficiency of a campaign depends on accurate delivery of elective communications."[11] Noted political strategist Dick Morris, consultant to Bill Clinton's 1996 presidential campaign, claims that everything he writes, "a speech, an ad, a memo, a tract—[are] all text with a mission to convert, a goal to persuade."[12]

According to Shea and Burton, it is essential for every campaign to have a theme. "A good theme is a carefully crafted merger of what the voters want, what the candidate has to offer, and what the opponent brings to the table."[13] Consistency and repetition of the campaign theme are critical considerations. Campaign themes are most effective for voters who go beyond party or incumbent status to make voting decisions. Bush was effective in 2004, for example, in portraying Kerry as a "flip-flopper." Campaign slogans often reflect campaign themes. Examples could include: "A strong voice for (place name or issue here)" or "It's time for a change" or "Proven leadership for the future." Public opinion polling helps in theme development to find a message that sums up voter concerns. Campaign themes try to be as inclusive or broad as possible. Challengers tend to have more latitude in theme selection. However, incumbents are more restricted because they have a record to defend or exploit[14] and prior rhetorical postures from which deviation is difficult.

Finally, in campaigns, there are two basic types of issues. *Positional issues* are those that have well-defined sides and require definitive positions. Issues such as abortion, gun control, embryonic stem cell research, and homosexual marriage are examples of positional issues. *Valence issues* are more general concerns about which most persons agree. Who would be against a strong national defense, good schools, safe roads, and affordable health care? Campaigns express and communicate more valence issues than positional ones.[15]

Communication Functions of Campaigns

Using a communication perspective, Bruce Gronbeck has constructed a "functional model of campaign research." The model, consistent with the uses and gratifications model, assumes that "receivers are active human beings who are subjecting themselves to communicative messages because certain needs can be satisfied and hence certain gratifications can be gained from exposure to those messages."[16] In campaigns, there are both *instrumental* functions and *consummatory* functions. One of three instrumental functions is behavioral activation. Campaigns serve not only to reinforce voter attitudes or convert voter preference but also to motivate voters to vote or to help in a campaign. Another instrumental function of campaigns is cognitive adjustments. Campaigns, by discussing issues, may stimulate awareness of issues, reflect candidate views, or result in voter position modification. Finally, campaigns function to legitimize the new leadership and the subsequent rules, laws, and regulations.

Consummatory functions are those embodied in the communication processes that go beyond candidate selection and legislative enactments. They help create the meta-political images and social-psychological associations that provide the glue that holds our political system together. One of two consummatory functions of campaigns is that they provide *personal involvement* in many forms: direct participation, self-reflection and definition, social interaction and discussion, and aesthetic experiences of public drama and group life. The second is that campaigns provide the *legitimization of the electoral process*, reaffirming commitment to our brand of democracy, debate, and political campaigning.

There are five basic functions of political campaign communication.[17] Every communication activity addresses one or more of these functions. (1) *Name identification* is more important in local, state, or low-profile races. High name recognition can save the campaign money and provide an advantage when participating in a primary. Outdoor and television advertising are the best mediums to increase name recognition. (2) *Candidate image* may, in some races, be more important than any given issue. Candidate image includes all the attributes and impressions of the candidate. Once formed in the mind of the public, personal image is very difficult to change. (3) *Issue development and exploration*, which together, are perhaps the most visible functions of political campaign communication. The majority of campaign communication deals with issue definition and explanation. (4) *Attacking the opposition* entails challengers assailing incumbents in order to generate reasons for voters to abandon the perhaps better-known incumbent. Radio and direct mail, especially in state and local races, are the best mediums for attack. (5) Finally, there is the *defense function* of political campaign communication. Defense can take several forms: denial, explanation, general response, or counterattack, to name a few.

The communication function of campaigns acts, then, on many levels. Campaign communication influences, reinforces, motivates, increases enthusiasm, and converts. As Gronbeck argues, campaigns

> get leaders elected, yes, but ultimately, they also tell us who we as a people are, where we have been and where we are going; in their size and duration they separate our culture from all others, teach us about political life, set our individual and collective priorities, entertain us, and provide bases for social interaction."[18]

Political Marketing

Politics is a complicated, high-tech, big business. Many aspects of politics are becoming more scientific with each election. Especially with the supreme importance of the mass media, politicians are utilizing marketing techniques and research tools. Gary Mauser argues that candidates and marketers have the same basic problems and goals.[19] Both compete for the support of a specified, target group under the constraints of time, money, and personnel. It is rather natural, then, for politicians to utilize the techniques of product marketing for election campaigns.

This development, according to Jack Honomichl, reached a new high during Ronald Reagan's 1979 presidential campaign.[20] It was, from a marketing standpoint, the most sophisticated and well-funded research program in the history of U.S. politics and provided the blueprint for the 1984 election and for Bush Sr.'s 1988 campaign. Reagan's 1979 presidential bid was based on a marketing plan developed by Richard Wirthlin, president of Decision Making Information (DMI). He developed a 176-page strategy statement that became the bible of the campaign.

However, for Bruce Newman, it was Clinton's 1992 presidential contest that fully implemented contemporary marketing concepts and strategies. He argues:

> The Clinton campaign organization resembled the best-run marketing organizations in this country, such as Proctor & Gamble, McDonald's, Quaker, and others. And as in these finely tuned marketing-driven organizations, Clinton's campaign organizers kept their finger on the pulse of the consumer, the voter. Just as McDonald's uses marketing research to decide where to open up new restaurant locations, Bill Clinton's pollsters used the same technology to determine which states to target with commercials. Just as Quaker uses focus groups to decide which new products to bring to the marketplace, Bill Clinton's researchers used focus groups to decide on how best to communicate their message of change about the economy to the American people.[21]

Political marketing is now a global phenomenon. Business and commercial techniques and strategies have permeated the political arena. This is the result of less party influence, more independent voting, a better educated and informed electorate, and mediated candidate-centered elections.[22] We have witnessed the emergence of the "market-oriented party," "a party no longer tied to historical ideology . . . but one more focused on developing a credible product with which to satisfy its core electoral market"[23] Darren Lilleker and Jennifer Lees-Marshment argue that the global public is thinking and behaving like a consumer in all areas of life, including in campaigns and elections. They and others call this "Americanisation," "Coca-Cola-isation" or "McDonaldisation" of the world.[24]

Bruce Newman and Richard Perloff define political marketing as

> the application of marketing principles and procedures in political campaigns by various individuals and organizations. The procedures involved

> include the analysis, development, execution, and management of strategic campaigns by candidates, political parties, governments, lobbyists and interest groups that seek to drive public opinion, advance their own ideologies, win elections, and pass legislation and referenda in response to the needs and wants of selected people and groups in society.[25]

According to Lilleker and Lees-Marshment,

> As an activity, political marketing is about political organizations (such as political parties, parliaments and government departments) adapting techniques (such as market research and product design) and concepts (such as the desire to satisfy voter demands) originally used in the business world to help them achieve their goals (such as win elections or pass legislation).[26]

Instead of analyzing political parties from their historical, ideological, or policy platforms, they are considered in terms of their market standing or competitive position. In marketing terms, political parties are market leaders, challengers, followers, or "nichers" (narrowly defined groups seeking a distinctive mix of benefits).[27] The political party is viewed as the company, and the vote is the purchase. As already mentioned, market research in politics is conducted using opinion polls or focus groups that provide a snapshot of the electorate's views. When a political party is the market leader, its strategies are to expand the total market, increase its market share further, and defend its market share. Of course, the market leader is always under attack. The problem of increasing market share involves balancing the appearance of stability and dominance with the impression of innovation and being open to new ideas and constituencies. To achieve this balance requires a blend of product (policies) and promotion (communication). The primary strategy is to maintain market share by reinforcing the existing image among supporters and to provide reasons for remaining loyal to the party.[28]

At the heart of the marketing concept is the exchange between a buyer and seller, most often the exchange of money for products or services. Applying this concept to the political process is rather straightforward. The politician offers political leadership through policies advocated and a vision for the country in exchange for the vote of confidence revealed in public opinion polls (approval ratings). In a campaign context "a market orientation then requires that research and polling be done to help shape the policies of the politician, which become the product through which the exchange is consummated."[29]

This analogy between business and politics takes us only so far. Newman and Perloff argue that there are two major differences between business marketing and political marketing.[30] First, there is a difference in philosophy. The goal in business is profit. In politics, the ultimate goal is the successful operation of democracy. One can win in politics by just the slimmest of margins. In business, the difference between winning and losing is based on large variations. The second difference is that in business, marketing research is closely followed. The implementation of political marketing research depends upon the philosophies and inclination of the politician. Business and politics are similar, however, in that they utilize the same marketing practices, tools, and techniques.

For Nicholas O' Shaughnessy, political marketing has come of age and defines governing today.

> Marketing fundamentally involves the integration of some total "offer" into an overall strategy, and political marketing has advanced beyond issue and image advertising and into strategy itself (although strategy also has evolved independently from other, historical resources); beyond this, it has become a total way of conceptualizing government, a core organizing force.[31]

Key Elements of a Campaign

Six elements are crucial to developing an understanding of the political campaign process: the strategic environment, organization, finance, public opinion polls, candidate image, and media. Each of these functions independently as well as interactively. That is, they have both an independent effect on the rhetorical strategies and tactics of the candidates and they also affect one another. In chapter 11 we demonstrate the interaction effect when considering presidential campaigns. The interaction of the elements establishes clear expectations of the campaign process. A brief overview of these elements follows.

Strategic environment.   In 1980, Nelson W. Polsby and Aaron Wildavsky coined the term *strategic environment* in their seminal work, *Presidential Elections*. For these authors, the strategic environment includes voters, interest groups, political parties, finances, control over information, television, and the issue of incumbency. The strategic environment is the broad context within which the electoral process is played out. The elements of the context are those unalterable by the candidate, the opponent, or anyone else. Such elements include the candidates' status, the candidates' qualifications, opponents' qualifications, the media market, and national trends, to name only a few. Ultimately, all strategies, tactics, and campaign messages originate from the surrounding context. Importantly, the context varies depending on the electoral phase.

Four general areas of concern must be kept in mind when thinking of the strategic environment.[32] First, there are *political concerns*, which include party identification, party nomination rules, number of likely opponents, incumbency, and voter behavior and attitudes. For example, elements of voter behavior such as turnout, group ties, and partisanship will have very different strategic implications during the primary versus the general election phase of a campaign.

Second, there are *social concerns*, which include dominant social issues, issues created by candidates, and unforeseen or unexpected events. Some social issues may dominate a campaign such as the economy, crime, or abortion. For example, post-9/11 concerns of security became a consideration of campaigns. If gas prices are high, as they were the first three quarters of 2006, then they become an issue to address. Candidates, of course, hope to own issues, or at least to be recognized as possessing unique positions on issues. Issue importance varies, however. For example, the broad issue of family values was salient in the presidential campaign of 2000, but it was markedly less important in 2004, when the war in Iraq dominated voter concerns.

Third, *electoral laws* are also important as broad determinants of candidate behavior. In the preprimary period, they are a factor as candidates decide which races to enter and which to avoid; getting on the ballot may require a strong enough organization to obtain requisite signatures and may require an early decision. During the primary period, these laws govern the allocation of delegates to state and national conventions. The allocation procedure is not neutral and will inevitably favor some candidates or some types of candidacies above others. Finally, in the general election for presidential contests, the Electoral College is a crucial determinant of candidate strategy. All candidates naturally want the largest vote total they can amass, but because of the peculiar arithmetic required by the Electoral College, candidates are inclined to spend less time in safe states and in those they have given up for lost and instead concentrate their efforts on close state races, or on those where they are likely to succeed.

Fourth, a candidate's rhetorical strategies are also affected by the *partisan structure of the race*. This structure determines the strategy to the degree that it requires the candidate to appear centrist, right, or left wing. The structure during the preprimary and primary is clearly different from that of the general election, for the relevant electorate is also different. Similarly, volatility and expected turnout will affect candidate strategy, for candidates design appeals to those most likely to vote. In a very real sense, support only matters to the extent that it can be measured in the voting booth.

Elections do not occur in a vacuum. Citizens bring their histories, beliefs, attitudes, and values to the voting booth. The social and political contexts of elections greatly influence strategic considerations. Political consultants and activists are quick to note that no two campaigns are alike. What worked in one cycle will not likely be successful in the next electoral contest.

Organization.   In any campaign effort, the organization of a candidate is vital. At the presidential level, campaign organizations are large, specialized, and complex. At a minimum, most campaigns have a director who coordinates all activities and acts as a liaison among the candidate, the organization, and the party; a campaign manager who oversees the day-to-day activities; division chiefs for specialized tasks such as polling, media, issues, fund-raising, and so on; and geographic coordinators living in and assigned to regional territories down to congressional district levels within states. From a macro perspective, the organization plans, develops, and implements campaign strategies and tactics.

This organization is both internal and external. Internally, the organization consists of all the advisors and strategists—those people who plan the strategy, coordinate the effort, and manage the overall campaign. According to political scientist John H. Kessel, this internal organization can be broken up into two specific groups: the core group and the strategy group.

> The core group consists of the candidate's own confidants, persons he has known well or worked closely with for some years. . . . The strategy group is made up of those persons who are making the basic decisions about the campaign. Its membership is quite restricted, and should not be confused with a publicly announced "strategy committee."[33]

The majority in the strategy group, and some would argue the most critical members of a campaign staff, are the paid political consultants. Political consultants have come to dominate the presidential election scene and, in the process, have become political actors of some note themselves. Consultants are important in their own right as well as because of their input into other strategic considerations. Larry Sabato notes:

> The consultants successfully recruited by a candidate have become status symbols. . . . Through the consultant he is purchasing acceptance from other politicians, insurance that his campaign will be taken seriously, and a favorable mention by journalists. He is also buying association with a consultant's past clientele, particularly the winners. He is securing access to the web of relationships that a consultant and his firm have developed. Finally, he is accepting the public services of a surrogate.[34]

The external candidate organization is also very important, although it is becoming less essential as the mass media and new technologies increasingly dominate the electoral scene. Such an organization is more important in some locations than in others and certainly in local races. The rule of thumb is that the larger, more urban, more heterogeneous the state, the more likely it is that candidates will rely more heavily on media appeals than on the precinct workers of old. National campaigns rely on state and local partisan "get-out-the-vote" efforts.

Finance. Along with organization, campaign finance is a critical element in any campaign. A long-standing maxim is that money is the lifeblood of politics; there is a strong correlation between electoral success and campaign expenditure. Financial concerns are more than just raising funds. There are also considerations of where to obtain funds, how to obtain funds, how to allocate funds, and how to insure compliance with complex legal requirements of political fund-raising. Such concerns have strategic and tactical implications. Money is most critical early in a campaign and for those less known to the general public. Early money is needed for candidates to hire consultants, conduct polls, and pay for travel. In contemporary presidential politics, the size of the war chest is often the determining factor of whether or not to enter the race.

New regulations governing campaign finance insure that raising money is increasingly problematic and time-consuming. Instead of relying on fat cats or political parties for money, candidates are turning to professional fund-raisers and the technologies of direct mail and the Internet. This has resulted in the replacement of individual contributors who give large sums with small, grassroots contributors and Political Action Committees.

No one can discuss modern campaign finance without including a discussion of Political Action Committees (PACs) and the 527s. Because PACs can raise and disburse large amounts of money, candidates simply cannot ignore them. Yet, relying heavily on PAC money can reduce a candidate's strategic and rhetorical options, and the candidate risks being identified as the candidate of special interests. Under section 527 of the campaign finance reform of 2002, groups can organize and are allowed to raise unlimited and undisclosed amounts of money. The advocacy groups are free to influence elections through voter mobilization efforts as well as by running issue ads. In the 2004 presidential election, 527 groups spent nearly $600 million on television spots alone.[35] Even at the state level, political parties, PACs, and interest groups provide the most money for candidates.

Public opinion polls.   Harry S. Truman said of polling:

> I wonder how far Moses would have gone if he'd taken a poll in Egypt? What would Jesus Christ have preached if he'd taken a poll in Israel? Where would the Reformation have gone if Martin Luther had taken a poll? It isn't polls or public opinion of the moment that counts. It is right and wrong leadership—men with fortitude, honesty, and belief in the right that makes epochs in the history of the world.[36]

Much has changed since Truman expressed his sentiments. Political public opinion polls have become an essential element of both campaign management and news coverage. Technology has increased the types, frequency, and sophistication of opinion polls. Opinion polls evolved into their central role in campaigns through three historic eras. First, was the *pioneer era*, from the 1930s through 1967. George Gallup dominated this period. The primary challenge for the early pollsters was developing techniques to forecast public opinion and to project the outcomes of races. By 1960s, polling organizations aligned their services by party affiliation. Second was the *technician era*, 1967–1978, when pollsters developed increasingly sophisticated methods of tracking opinion and experienced more accuracy of findings. This was largely due to door-to-door interviewing. Third, the current *strategic era*, introduced the use of telephone interviewing. National polling firms created large, in-house phone banks. In the 1980s, the introduction of workplace computers stimulated a proliferation of polling firms. Attention was also given to questionnaire construction and further refinement of data interpretation and analysis. Focus groups, borrowed from advertising and marketing research, became a mainstay of testing political ads and message themes: "The increasingly rapid turnaround of surveys and the depth of analysis allowed strategic decisions based on current information to be used at every step in the campaign."[37] There are numerous data collection techniques: phone surveys, door-to-door surveys, mail surveys, dial-900 surveys, and focus groups, to name just a few.

From a campaign perspective, polls provide much needed information about voters: who they are, what they think, how they feel, and how they will behave in the voting booth. In addition to providing information on voters, polls also provide valuable feedback to the campaign allowing for message adjustments and refinements. During the course of a campaign, the primary types of polls include benchmark, follow-up, panel surveys, and tracking.

A candidate's standing in the polls is a crucial determinant of that candidate's ability to raise money, so it comes as no surprise that campaigns usually spend between 5 and 10 percent of their budgets on polling.[38] As already noted, polls have several uses: they allow candidates to identify constituencies and issues, to tailor their image, to target their opponents' weaknesses, to allocate resources, and to influence media strategy.

In addition to candidate-sponsored polls, there has been an incredible growth of news media public opinion polls. During the campaign season, major news organizations release weekly polls at the national and state levels, and these polls can dramatically impact election coverage. According to Diana Owen, the reporting of poll results "represent news manufactured by journalists themselves through the production of statistical data that can be reported as fact. News stories that contain polls gain a heightened aura of authenticity by assigning a numerical figure to a political trend."[39] Polls influence how candidates are covered, how much airtime they will receive, which reporter will be assigned to cover them, and the portrayal of a candidate's campaign. Some scholars argue, however, that media polls lead to biased reporting and misrepresentation. To simply report who is ahead provides very little in the way of understanding issues or reasons for voting. In addition, most of the reporting on polls tends to favor one candidate over the other.

There are direct and indirect impacts of polls in campaigns beyond organizational strategic considerations. They influence voters, politicians, political elites, opinion leaders, and members of the media.[40] For example, media polls influence candidate image, status, momentum, funding opportunities, candidate performance expectations, volunteer help, and so on. From a voter perspective, polls may influence interest in or support for a candidate, as well as motivation to seek out additional candidate information. Polls may also influence voter turnout.

Candidate image. Campaigns involve a multitude of persuasive messages from diverse sources. Citizens select, sort, prioritize, and attend to messages that develop images of candidates. Some studies find that voters are more persuaded by their cognitive responses to messages than by the messages themselves. Kenneth Hacker claims, for instance, that voters often respond more to their perceptions than to objective realities about campaigns and candidates. "Voting behavior," according to Hacker, "occurs in relation to the ways in which voters perceive the election, their own circumstances and concerns, the messages and behaviors of the candidates, and how commentators and other voters talk about the candidates."[41]

Image is more than public perceptions of a candidate. As Stephen Wayne observes, "It is difficult to separate a candidate's image from the events of the real world."[42] As noted in chapter 4, the three factors that influence voters most are issues, partisanship, and candidate attributes. Today, candidate image is more than a reflection of one's political-philosophical orientation or issue positions. In our media age, it includes such elements as personality, job performance, dress, character, lifestyle, to name a few. Today's mode of campaigning and new technologies provide more opportunities for candidates to create, to reinforce, and even to reinvent their public persona and image. Every American can cite a list of desirable traits that make a "good" president. Candidates compete to demonstrate that they meet public expectations of presidential performance.

Some scholars argue that candidate image is that set of attributes given to a politician by the electorate; others argue that candidate image is created by a candidate. Regardless, a key factor in determining a candidate's standing in the polls is image, and designing a viable one is the chief and most controversial task of the political consultant. According to Keith Melder:

> Political images are specialized applications of image-making. They serve as devices of shorthand identification, distortion, appeal, and illusion—inevitable elements of modern political persuasion. Like language itself, images create a symbolic universe. In the world of commerce, they are fabricated in order to produce results in the marketplace. Similarly, political images are most effectively applied in that marketplace of politics, campaigns, and elections.[43]

However, as Sidney Blumenthal notes: "Image-making, no matter how manipulative, doesn't replace reality; it becomes part of it. Images are not unreal simply because they are manufactured."[44]

There is at least some evidence that "perceptual defenses are lower during the primaries than in the general election, and hence images of the candidates formed during the primary season, especially early on, are more likely to be stimulus-determined."[45] This means that the earlier candidates begin to communicate an image, the more control they—and their organization—have over the image-building process. Obviously, however, this process does not occur in a vacuum, no matter how early the candidate begins, especially on the presidential level. Most presidential contenders have been in public life, and in the public eye, for many years. They cannot create new images out of whole cloth, but must design images that are appropriate for both their presidential bid and their public past.

Increasingly, character is becoming an important part of candidate image, as candidates as diverse as Robert Dole as being mean, Gary Hart's revealed affair, and Joseph Biden's plagiarism in 1988; Bill Clinton in 1992 and 1996 for allegations of affairs; Bush in 2000 with the revelation of his DUI arrest; and Kerry in 2004 with revelations about his military service. Candidates' private lives are no longer considered sacrosanct by the media, and posing with spouse, kids, and family dog no longer constitutes sufficient evidence of moral integrity. It is not enough merely to design a presidential image and hope for the best; the candidate must also be careful not to undermine that image through inappropriate or inconsistent behavior.

Candidate image is an important element, if not to create, at least to control through paid media, news coverage, campaign events, speeches, and debates. Most Americans do not cast their vote based on a single issue, but rather they vote for an individual. Likability has become a critical factor for swing voters.

Media.   Campaigns are essentially mass media campaigns. In fact, Matthew Kerbel finds television

> brokering the relationship between candidate and voter to an unprecedented extent. . . . It is not by design, but television has come to function as a political institution. By this I mean that television is structured in such a way and newsgathering is conducted in such a fashion as to have an enduring role in American political decision making.[46]

The media, in all of its forms (broadcast and print, news and entertainment, free and paid) are the principle means of conducting campaigns.

There have been incredible changes in the realm of media in the last two decades that impact politics. Cable television has become king over the traditional networks. Talk radio has brought new voices to the airwaves and challenged traditional media in terms of news values. Of course, the 24/7 news cycle places unique demands on campaigns—they have only hours to respond to attacks rather than days. The divide between news programming and entertainment has become less clear. Finally, with each election cycle, the role and influence of the Internet continue to grow.

The mass media have caused both quantitative and qualitative changes in elections. Daily news coverage of the campaign, debates, political ads, and pseudo-events produce more campaign messages than ever before. From a qualitative standpoint, the media demand more sophisticated techniques of presentation, message creation, and targeting.

Media coverage can make or break a candidacy, as candidate organizations are painfully aware. Although few candidacies are planned solely around media strategies, all candidate organizations plan with a view toward media interpretations of events. These interpretations are most important during the early stages of a campaign, when the standards of victory are less clear (as in multicandidate primary races) and the level of information is low. As the level of information increases and the competition is more clearly defined, making decisions becomes easier. The role of the media as interpreter diminishes correspondingly.

The media do not lack for powerful roles as the race continues, however. These roles include agenda setting and the defining of candidate images. Much of their ability to perform these roles depends on access to the candidate, and campaigns can, within limits, control coverage by controlling access.[47] Candidate organizations also use staged events and similar techniques in their effort to control and dominate the news.

In his classic study, Matthew Kerbel found that television coverage of elections encompasses five distinct themes: horserace, issue, process, image, and nonissues.[48] Horserace coverage alludes to stories of who is on top, who is ahead, and in the case of presidential races, the electoral status of the race. Issue coverage is stories about policy concerns and positions of the candidates. Process stories actually focus on the news media's role of covering the election; that is, news media coverage of the news media coverage. Image stories focus on the personae of the candidates. Their concerns are more than candidate resume items and also include aspects of character, deeds, and past actions. Nonissue coverage are those unplanned, unexpected, and surprise elements and events of campaigns. They may be dramatic moments, campaign crises, or breaking stories that dominate news interests. In 1996 such items included speculation about Clinton's health-care records or Dole's tumble off the podium, or in 2000 the revelation of Bush's DUI arrest years earlier. For Kerbel, each theme becomes part of the television story or portrayal of a campaign.

Although candidates and elected officials are frequently criticized for trying to manage the news, it is equally true that candidates and elected officials who fail to manage the news are not likely to be candidates or elected officials for very long. A presidential candidate, in particular, must communicate a strongly focused image to gain success in the polls and at the polls, maintain an organization, and raise needed funds. No candidate can afford to rely on the media to safeguard their image, attempts at controlling the news is the logical result.

Although each of the six elements highlighted above is important in its own right, the synergy of the interaction between the elements is critically important. This dynamic process is played out over time in a roughly predictable fashion. An analysis of the time periods that provide context for this process appears in chapter 11.

Campaign Management

Campaign management today is a profession, not a hobby. Campaign professionals are used in races at all levels. Political consultants are the new power in U.S. politics. As already noted, in the days before consultants, the old party bosses served as the link between electoral politics and campaigns. Their job was to generate support, control conflict, and reinforce party discipline. Today, political consultants have access to the candidate and develop local campaign strategies and tactics from offices miles away. As political consultants have gained in influence, the role of state and national political parties has declined. "Campaign finance reform, the proliferation of political action committees, the creation of the political consulting industry, and the rise of the candidate-centered campaign all were important factors in the declining importance of political parties."[49] As a result, political parties are primarily concerned with fund-raising and distribution of funds to candidates.

When the general public thinks of a politician they are usually referring to an elected official or a candidate running for an elected office. Some may also include visible party leaders who serve over a period of time in various administrations. Few, however, consider the new campaigners as professional politicians. The new campaigners include consultants, pollsters, television producers and directors, fund-raisers, speechwriters, and direct marketers—all professionals who shape the true character of modern political campaigning in the United States.

Larry Sabato, one of the first scholars to recognize the growing role and importance of using professionals in campaigns, defined a political consultant as "a campaign professional who is engaged primarily in the provision of advice and services (such as polling, media creation and production, and direct mail fund-raising) to candidates, their campaigns, and other political committees."[50] David Dulio expands the definition to represent a broader range of activities consultants perform today. Political consultants are

> an individual or firm that provides campaign services on a fee-for-service basis during an election cycle for more than one candidate, political party, organized interest group, or initiative and referendum campaign for more than one election cycle. These services include, but are not limited to: strategic advice, survey research, focus-group research, opposition research, media production, targeting analysis, direct mail creation, or fund-raising assistance (including events, political action committees, or direct mail).[51]

Because of the sophistication and technological advancement of mass communication and persuasion techniques, the trend is toward segmenting campaign activities into areas of specialization. The professional politician today, then, is more likely to be a specialist focusing on one activity of a campaign endeavor.

The number of firms and individuals who earn a living working on campaigns is increasing. Today, there are over 3,000 firms in the United States that specialize in campaigns and elections with more than 50,000 campaigns per year managed by campaign professionals.[52] Most firms, however, are rather small, often employing five to seven people. During a campaign the more specialized tasks of polling, advertising, and fund-raising are subcontracted to firms specializing in such activities. Most political consulting firms are owned and operated by a well-known, successful professional. Being associated with winning campaigns is vital to the professional political consultant. Matt Reese, a well known consultant, states that the "trinity of necessity" for a political consultant consists of winning (or the reputation of winning), working for people whose names are well known, and winning when you're not supposed to.[53]

Beyond big-name consultants are literally thousands of political junkies, who work on numerous campaigns, and the staffs of elected officials. Within a political season, such people may change jobs and titles many times. Some will work on an elected official's staff—until the next election, when they will move to the campaign staff only to return to the official's staff after the election.

Today's professional politicians are politicians only insofar as they earn their living working for political candidates and campaigns. They are professionals in the sense that they possess unique skills and knowledge relevant to human motivation and mass communication technology. They are experts and specialists first and are political in the traditional use of the word second.

Political Consultants

Who was the first political consultant? Well, it's impossible to say. But Robert Friedenberg speculates that perhaps it was the individual who in 1758 suggested to a candidate of the Virginia Colonial Assembly that he should provide refreshments for the voters. The candidate, based upon this advice, bought 160 gallons of beverages for the voters and won the race. The candidate was George Washington.[54]

Dan Nimmo effectively asserts that today's political consulting industry is a direct descendant of the public relations profession that matured during the 1920s.[55] Their task was to "propagandize" the activities of U.S. business. It is not surprising that the skills and techniques of advocacy became the mainstay of U.S. politics.

Edward Bernays, cited in *Time* magazine as "U.S. Publicist Number One," is considered the father of public relations. In the 1920s, Bernays introduced the "engineering of consent," scientific approach to public opinion formation and dynamics. President Calvin Coolidge was the first president to benefit from his skills. The press of the day portrayed Coolidge as "cold and aloof." To counter this image, Bernays invited Al Jolson and 40 other vaudevillians to a White House breakfast. The next day *The New York Times* headline read "Actors Eat Cakes with the Coolidges . . . President Nearly Laughs." This was, according to Sidney Blumenthal, the "first overt act initiated by a media advisor for a President."[56] A decade later, Bernays called for the creation of a cabinet position titled Secretary of Public Relations.

The first political consulting firm was created by Clem Whitaker (a newsman and press agent) and Leone Baxter (a public relations specialist) in 1933.[57] In that year the California legislature passed a bill authorizing a flood control and irrigation project. Pacific Gas and Electric Company viewed the project as a direct threat to the company and thus initiated a campaign to reverse the decision. In turn, proponents of the project hired Whitaker and

Baxter to develop a campaign that would defeat the electric company's effort. With a budget of $39,000 the team was victorious in stopping the opposition. Soon after the effort, Whitaker and Baxter formed Campaigns, Inc. Between 1933 and 1955 they won 70 out of 75 campaigns they managed. They developed many of the techniques and strategies used in political campaigns today.

Whitaker believed that most Americans do not seek information during a campaign and have no desire to work at being good citizens. Thus, he argues that

> there are two ways you can interest [citizens] in a campaign, and only two that we have ever found successful. Most every American loves a contest. He likes a good, hot battle, with no punches pulled. So you can interest him if you put on a fight! Then, too, most every American likes to be entertained. He likes fireworks and parades. So if you can't fight, put on a show.[58]

By 1950, advertising agencies handled national election campaigns. However, by 1970, advertising agencies realized that handling campaigns was not as profitable as other products. A political campaign ends in a few months whereas selling soap, cars, or clothes goes on for years; additionally, selling soap is less stressful. The last advertising agency campaign was Nixon's 1968 presidential race, well documented in Joe McGinniss's *The Selling of the Presidency*. He writes of the role advertising played in creating and recreating a "new Nixon."

Public relations specialists were a permanent part of every campaign effort by 1960. Between 1952 and 1957, about 60 percent of all public relations firms had some kind of political account.[59] Part of John Kennedy's campaign staff included a research group, speech-writing group, and publicity group all comprised of public relations personnel. Within two decades, firms emerged completely focused on political campaign management. Every serious candidate at the national and statewide levels was using professional consultants. In the 1990s, even candidates for office below the statewide level were using professional consultants.[60]

Today, consultants coordinate the activities of media, advertising, public relations, and publicity. They understand both the new technologies and the unique requirements of campaigning. It is that blend of expertise and experience that makes them a sought-after commodity, even after the campaign is over.

Campaign consultants differ from party operatives. First, although both are professionals, consultants choose their clients. Party staffers are to assigned candidates and campaigns. Second, consultants are compensated by a "fee-for-service" and must recruit clients. Campaign folks are salaried employees of the national or state party. Third, party staffers usually do not get involved in primaries. They do not wish to take sides. However, consultants will work primaries for clients.[61]

Just who are today's consultants? One survey revealed that the vast majority are men and disproportionately white, well educated, young, and wealthy. Thus, as a group, they do not reflect the demographics in the United States. About 95 percent of the principal political consulting firms are white. The average age of a consultant is 46. Many consultants, about 44 percent, worked their way up by working for a political party, and a majority, about 53 percent, worked for an elected official. In terms of education, 40 percent have completed some form of advanced degree (i.e., Masters, J.D. or Ph.D.). The average income reported in this study was $102,000. Finally, 90 percent of consultants work for one party or the other. Indeed, political beliefs and ideology provide motivation for getting into the industry for 53 percent of the consultants surveyed.[62]

There are several reasons why political officeholders and candidates need the services of campaign specialists. The modern campaign requires the performance of many specialized tasks that include advertising, issue research, strategy development, polling, and fund-raising. Each of these tasks is complex, requiring training, experience, and knowledge of the industry. It is unrealistic to expect a candidate for public office to have the technical expertise in each of these areas or even to have the time to manage these activities in addition to campaigning or governing. As Johnson observes, "Modern campaigns, increasingly sophisticated and technologically complex, are being taken over by professional consultants, and because of that professionalization, there is little room for the amateur or volunteer campaign worker."[63]

Another reason for campaign specialists is the impact of behavioral and social science concepts and theories concerning human motivation. The scientific approach to opinion formation and dynamics has become an essential element of every campaign. Predicting public attitudes and behavior is key to the development of campaign strategy. The measurement, tracking, and analysis of demographic and psychographic data form the bases for issue positions and public appeals. Social science has provided the necessary tools and methodologies for monitoring public beliefs, attitudes, and values.

The electoral process itself places unique requirements on candidates and campaigns. Historically, Americans value the notion of candidates meeting the public and discussing issues. However, as our society has become larger, more diverse, and more complex, so too have the requirements of campaigning. For most campaigns, extensive direct voter contact is impossible. At the national level, each primary becomes an individualized contest requiring professional help and analysis.

Of course, the greatest reason for the need of consultants is the role of mass media in our society. Every requirement and characteristic of the mass media impacts the nature of political campaigning. Reaching the public through the media requires money, news exposure, and 30-second discussions of issues. Actions and statements are carried beyond the immediate audience. Television especially likes drama, a contest, and often favors an underdog. A mistake is recorded forever and subject to instant replay without contextual explanation. The media serve as a source of information, persuasion, and presentation of reality. To use a medium requires knowledge of that medium—its strengths, weaknesses, and nature. The growth and necessity of political consultants and professional politicians are directly related to the growth of the mass media and communication technologies.

Political consultants are also needed today because of what Blumenthal calls "the permanent campaign." The permanent campaign, a direct result of the new technology in the age of information, has become

> the steady-state reality of American politics. In the new politics, issues, roles, and media are not neatly separate categories. They are unified by the strategic imperative . . . the elements of the permanent campaign are tangential to politics: they are the political process itself.[64]

Political consultants are permanent, and politicians are ephemeral. With the decline of party structure, discipline, and workers, television commercials and media appearances not only mobilize voters, but they also act as devices used for governing the nation. Governing the nation, then, becomes a perpetual campaign where the public is constantly addressed and its support continually solicited. Ronald Reagan brought into the White House some of the most sophisticated marketers, pollsters, and media advisors to ever work for a president. Much of his success in opinion formation, information control, and law enactment is a result of his use of the new technologies. Bill Clinton utilized polls, not only to direct public policy but also to provide insight into how to generate public support. In the end, according to Dick Morris, "we created the first fully advertised presidency in U.S. history, which led to an extensive record of legislative accomplishment."[65]

A Campaign Plan

An important function of political consultants is the management of an entire campaign. They first establish the campaign organization consisting of professionals, committed party regulars, and citizen volunteers. Complete campaign management requires the implementation of campaign strategies and the allocation of a candidate's time, money, and talent. Today, even in congressional races, campaigns employ a team of consultants.

A campaign plan is essential to any campaign. Money alone or tireless energy is not enough. According to Daniel Shea and Michael Burton

> A campaign plan defines *what* is to be done, *when* it should be done, *who* should be doing it, and *what* will be needed to finish the job. Good plans divide responsibility, integrate work, and offer a step-by-step blueprint of the election.[66]

A campaign plan is a reference tool, a timetable, that delegates responsibilities and keeps staffs focused on campaign tasks. The plan is a concrete document, although its sections and parts may differ depending on the level of the race or consultant. The plan serves as a strategic blueprint for the campaign. A good plan reflects research, analysis, and reflection.

Elements of a campaign plan differ. Shea and Burton suggest several key elements:

- *District profile*—The profile includes the district or territory's geographics, industry, housing patterns, community organizations, transportation infrastructure, and other fixed assets. Such information is useful in planning key areas of travel and contacts.

- *Demographic profile*—The voting population is segmented by a large variety of variables: age, sex, race, income, party affiliation, religious affiliation, and other group memberships such as unions, VFW, and so forth. The information is summarized with numerous tables of data collection.

- *Candidate and opponent profiles*—For both candidates, key information includes professional background, experience, committees, social group affiliations, bill sponsorship, appointments, and so forth. Opposition research elements are also included in this profile with backup details and documentation in reference material.

- *Electoral history*—This is a general summary of electoral history of the district or area with very detailed summaries from the past two or three elections. The more recent analyses are broken down to the precinct level with past voting behaviors to include general and primary elections as well as any party affiliation data.

- *Public opinion*—Relevant polling information is provided. Most often, the plan contains an overview of voter concerns, key issues, and social topics. A polling plan is also often included.

- *General strategy*—This contains the basic themes, issues, and candidate positioning in the campaign. How will the candidate be portrayed? Who are the key targets? What is the rationale of the campaign? Why should citizens vote for the candidate?

- *Communications strategy*—Usually the plan provides separate rate schedules and buys for each medium: television, radio, newspaper, etc. It also lays out a strategy for news coverage and summaries of issue positions complete with prepared questions and answers for "rapid-response" purposes for media interviews or questions.

- *Grassroots*—This is also referred to as "Get Out The Vote" (GOTV) efforts. It includes plans for grassroots efforts such as "door-to-door" voter contact as well as election-day activities to maximize vote.[67]

Most plans also address resources and staffing issues focusing on budget and organizational items. Budget considerations include a fund-raising plan, schedule of key fund-raising activities and visits, and targeted allocations by area. It is important for the staffing requirements to detail both organizational needs as well as duties and expectations of staff members.

Campaign Research

Campaign research is a highly specialized function and provides the basis for strategy development and execution. Campaign research provides a great deal of the data in the overall plan including voting patterns, voter turnout, demographic correlates of voting, voter attitudes, opinions, issues, registration, and election projections, to name a few. Dennis Johnson argues that it is important to note that political campaign research is very different from traditional academic social science research.[68] Campaign research is applied research. Its purpose is to provide information that one can use in a variety of ways during a campaign. It does not attempt to be objective or reflect both sides of an issue. The information is selective; however, the information should be accurate and genuine. When campaigns claim opponents' facts or information is wrong, in reality, it's the interpretation of the facts and information that is usually problematic.

Most campaigns prepare a "bible" that summarizes the relevant issues of the campaign; profiles friendly voters; analyzes the opposition's strengths, weaknesses, and strategy; and provides local data for campaign stops. Like campaign planning and strategy development, research is a continual process, especially as election day approaches.

Thousands of hours are spent on campaign research. There will be thousands of pages and items noted and recorded. Ironically, probably 95 percent of the material will never be used. However, one never knows what will be needed in the heat of the campaign.[69]

Research is first conducted on one's own candidate. Incumbent or not, this research is essential and it reveals potential problem areas as well as a list of accomplishments. The accomplishments are normally identified by key constituent groups; by media market; by issue and subject areas, and in the case of incumbents, by year in office; and by names of individuals, groups or organizations that benefited from the vote or work.

An important element of campaign research today focuses on the opposition. Opposition research is more than simply finding dirt on one's opponent. It is detailed information that covers every aspect of an individual's private and public life. The key is how to interpret, apply, and communicate a particular piece of information.

The first major and systematic effort of oppositional research that provided the blueprint for future endeavors was during the 1984 presidential campaign. The Republican National Committee formed the Opposition Research Group with a $1 million budget. The goal was simple: gather every piece of information on the democratic contenders as possible. The research team tapped over 2,000 sources and amassed more than 400,000 documents.[70]

The first step entailed the review of thousands of documents such as newspaper and magazine articles, Congressional Record statements, campaign speeches, broadcast transcripts, to name just a few. As the items were reviewed, readers looked for direct quotes by the candidates—quotes attributed to them and quotes about them. Key excerpts became the data that were entered into the mainframe computer that contained an issue dictionary with over 600 separate and distinct categories. By the start of the general campaign between Ronald Reagan and Walter Mondale, there were approximately 75,000 items, and nearly 50,000 quotes covering the entire career of Mondale. During the campaign, the database was updated every 24 hours.[71]

Additionally, an electronic communications network connected all state party headquarters as well as all the dedicated spokespersons in each media market. The system could provide instant and up-to-date talking points, issue papers, and speech drafts. The internal staff generated over 1,000 benchmark issue papers, most between 5 and 30 pages. They would discuss the key aspects of Mondale's record, including any outrageous statements, shifts in positions, contradictions, and so on.[72]

These issue papers became the primary resource for the debates. The database helped in predicting Mondale's charges and responses as well as in developing attack themes and postdebate material for the media. The research team provided a 200-page debate briefing book for study and preparation.[73] After each debate, the team would work all night preparing detailed analyses and responses to Mondale's statements made during the debates for the media.

Finally, the Opposition Research Group reviewed videotapes of Mondale and vice presidential candidate Farraro. They provided clips for study. Some have called the Opposition Research Group and its computer system the Republican's "secret weapon" in the 1984 presidential race.[74] One thing is for sure; it forever changed the nature of campaign research.

Opposition data may reveal past actions and behavior that disqualify a candidate for selection or it may provide a basis to predict future behavior or attitudes about specific policies that may be contrary to prevailing public desires. Opposition research is usually presented in two parts. The first is simply a compilation of data and information under several categories: incumbent legislative record and candidate voting record, property records, court records, interest group ratings, resume verification, newspaper searches, government budget analysis, statements of economic interest, and review of campaign finance disclosure statements. The second part is the analysis and interpretation of the raw information. Such analysis provides themes for attack strategies and messages.[75]

The information found in opposition research is usually broken down into four categories. *Political information* consists of activities undertaken by a candidate while in an elected position or previous statements made in campaigns. The information comes from past voting records, absenteeism or key missed votes, various bill sponsorships, various committee and leadership assignments, support of pork or very wasteful spending projects, review of mailings, public office and staff expenses, exotic or personal travel at public expense, verbal gaffes or misstatements, and issue or position contradictions. *Campaign finance information* may generate all types of potential attack issues. Where are the donations coming from, citizens or businesses? Who are the key "big" donors, individuals, or special interests? Are all the rules and regulations being followed? *Career information* reviews prior professional or business activities either public or private. Key considerations include resume inflation or questions of accuracy, questionable business practices, and dubious past associates or business partners. Finally, there is *personal information* gathered from very public and legitimate sources, such as court records, media interviews or citations, meeting minutes, professional associations, among others.[76]

For some, the use of opposition research has harmed the electoral process by making campaigns too personal and mean-spirited. It also leads to distortion of views, redirects public attention from important issues, and contributes to the spiral of public cynicism about contemporary campaigns. However, many consultants claim the use of opposition research is good for the democratic process. They claim that such data make candidates more accountable and make campaigns more open and honest. At a minimum, it is important that any opposition information be true and obtained in a legal manner.[77]

Campaigns today have more to be concerned with than just their opponents. There are third parties who attempt to influence the electoral outcome. Outside organizations run their own commercials and distribute literature in local and national races. In 2004, they were the notorious 527s that greatly influenced the campaigns both locally and nationally. Thus, the research is valuable at several stages of a campaign. It provides the basic framework of the strengths and weaknesses of the candidate and the opponent. Research also provides information and ideas to be tested through focus groups to generate issue positions and message points. More detailed information is used in the creation of specific direct mail and PAC literature, especially those targeted to a specific group. As the campaign unfolds, the research is critical in fact-checking media advertising of both incumbent and challenger advertising. Later in the campaign, the research material becomes invaluable in preparing for debates. Finally, research material is vital in the day-to-day point and counterpoint exchanges of charges and countercharges. It helps in the much-needed rapid response of the new 24/7 media environment.[78]

Campaign Strategy

Every campaign needs a strategy or a blueprint for winning an election. A strategy is how to position the candidate and allocate resources to maximize the candidate's strengths and to minimize the candidate's weaknesses. According to Ron Faucheux, the "message is the reason you give voters to select you over the opposition. How and when you communicate that message (sequence, timing, intensity, persuasion) and how and when you mobilize your resources are the strategic components of every campaign, large and small."[79]

According to Shea and Burton, there are three main goals of campaign strategy: reinforcement, persuasion, and conversion. Reinforcement is keeping core or base voters committed to the campaign. Persuasion is gaining the support of swing or undecided voters. Conversion is bringing opponent supporters over to your side. Generally, campaigns reinforce their own partisans, persuade the toss-ups, and convert partisans of the opposition. Of course, it is easier to reinforce or persuade voters than to convert them.[80]

Message strategies may be based on the personal virtues or vices of the candidate (e.g., (in)experience, (in)competence, integrity or lack thereof, compassion, and so forth); ideological or partisan differences (e.g., liberal, conservative, libertarian, etc.); or some combination of the two. The main point is that the campaign message must draw a line of distinction between the candidate and the opposition by framing a clear choice for voters.[81]

Faucheux argues that every campaign needs four strategies.[82] A *message sequence* strategy identifies the order of presenting arguments to voters. A *timing and intensity* strategy specifies when the candidate acts and at what pace. A *mobilization and persuasion* strategy targets voter preferences and allocates resources to specific favorable voting groups. An *opportunity* strategy finds ways to exploit situational events or obstacles.

An overall campaign strategy will answer several basic questions: Who is the target audience? What is the message? What resources are needed to reach the target audience? When will the target audience be reached? How will the audience be reached? Although rather simple and straightforward, the answers to each question are complex and multidimensional. It is important to remember that strategies must be compatible with the candidate. In implementation of strategy, you should remember that campaign messages should be consistent, coherent, and coordinated.

Channels of Communication and Communication Strategy

There are four basic communication channels: electronic media, print media, display media (e.g., billboards), and personal contact. It is a most difficult task to determine the best combination of media to reach the potential audience and which best communicates the desired theme. In addition, timing, money, and distribution are also important considerations. Candidates must decide when and where they will concentrate their communication efforts, making sure they do not peak too soon or spend too much money in areas of little consequence.

To determine the communication strategy, the target audience, which includes both committed loyalist and potential voters, must be identified and segmented. Next, most campaigns attempt to map voter perceptions. The goal here is to identify the ways voters classify the candidates and issues viewed as important in the decision process. As already demonstrated, a great deal of time is also spent identifying and characterizing the competition. By mapping voter preferences, candidates can better identify specific strengths, weaknesses, and likely patterns of competition. From all of this information, various strategies can be identified, discussed, and evaluated. Ultimately, a budget is allocated, a strategy is determined, the timing and content of appeals are isolated, and a detailed media and marketing plan is established.

Despite all this activity, there is a high degree of homogeneity in the political perceptions of the American people. It is difficult for well-known politicians to radically alter their image once it has become fixed in the minds of the public. There is little advertising can do to drastically change or convert voter perceptions, beliefs, and attitudes, especially in the middle of the general campaign period. Thus, most strategies seek to reinforce and link campaigns to existing perceptions, beliefs, and attitudes.

There is a standard, well-known marketing and advertising dictum: Products compete best against each other as long as they are perceived as being similar to each other. As Gary Mauser observes, "The patterns of competition for any new product can be predicted from its pattern of perceived similarity with the other products in the markets."[83] Thus, challengers must appear presidential, and presidents must act presidential. With this in mind, Mauser argues that the following communication strategies are probably most effective: Stress the importance of features that are most attractive to the target electorate; avoid, or state euphemistically, the features that are deemed to be undesirable; coordinate all information and advertising to reinforce the most important features of the candidate; and, if possible, attempt to move the candidate along those dimensions that can place him or her in an advantageous position.[84]

Negative and Attack Strategies

There has been concern expressed about the growing influence of attack or negative campaigns. Actually, there is naturally an attack phase to every campaign. This is when candidates are engaged in comparisons and contrasts of records, visions, policy goals, and outcomes. However, campaigns are more likely to turn to negative advertising when going up against a well-funded and well-known incumbent, when the opponent has done something clearly and unquestioningly wrong, and when candidates have less name recognition.[85] There are two primary negative tactics campaigns use against one's opponent. *Guilt by association* is an attempt to question the character, competency, or honesty of the opponent by pointing to his or her association with others whose character is questionable. For example, when Gore was linked to Clinton (who had been involved in an extramarital affair) in the 2000 presidential campaign or when all incumbent Republicans were linked to "the failed policies of the Bush administration" during the 2006 mid-term congressional elections. *Red herring* is using a side of an issue or argument that is unrelated to the campaign to introduce fear among voting groups. Democrats often claim Republicans will end social security, thus influencing senior citizen voters. Of course, there are strategies for dealing with negative

Response to Attack:

attacks: admit publicly to incriminating information before it is released by an opponent, attack the opponent for introducing negative and personal information, deflect the attack with humor, deflect it with sorrow, admit the mistake and ask for forgiveness, deny the charges and demand an apology, or simply ignore the attack.[86]

Campaign Tactics

A tactic is a method or tool of implementing strategy. Because campaigns are exercises in communication, campaign tactics are the methods and tools of communicating with constituent groups. We will review four of the more common methods and will add more detail about specific campaign communication in subsequent chapters.

Advertising

Political advertising is the most recognized and controversial service provided by consultants. It is also, perhaps, the most important. In the 2004 presidential contest, Bush and Kerry spent over $600 million on television advertising, with another $1 billion spent by third parties and special interest groups.[87] The media adviser was once primarily a technical adviser not privy to the overall strategy and tactics of the campaign. Today, however, the media consultant is a key member of the staff often responsible for a campaign's total advertising and communication strategy.

Nearly two decades ago, Richard Armstrong recognized that nothing changed the business of political advertising more than the advent of video.[88] Video allows for quicker spot production as well as lower cost. The result was more ads that were different, more ads running, and because of the fast turnaround time, more reactive or response ads to counter opponents or to reflect a change in voter attitudes. In 2004, the Bush campaign produced 59 ads and Kerry ran 111 ads for the general campaign period (this does not include those sponsored by the Republican and Democratic Parties).[89] Interestingly, 49 percent of all political advertising took place online. There were five political ads for every campaign news story in 2004.[90]

Of course, modern political advertising is a far cry from the distribution of flyers and campaign buttons of the 1800s. As radio and television became the primary means of communicating to a large number of people, it was natural for politicians to seek access to the media. Utilizing the commercial, business format of advertising as a way to gain voter acceptance was an evolutionary process, however. For Joe McGinniss, the process was also a natural one. He wrote in 1968 that

> politics in a sense, has always been a con game. . . . Advertising, in many ways, is a con game too. . . . It is not surprising then, that politicians and advertising men should have discovered one another. And, once they recognized that the citizen did not so much vote for a candidate as

make a psychological purchase of him, not surprising that they began to work together.[91]

Although in 1948 only 3 percent of the population owned a television, Harry Truman produced a spot encouraging citizens to vote. It wasn't until 1952 when about 45 percent of the nation owned a television set that political ads became commonplace events. In that presidential contest, the Republicans spent $1.5 million and the Democrats only $77,000. Eisenhower's advisers felt television spots could be more controlled and counter his "stumbling press conference performances."[92] Accounting for inflation, Eisenhower's television budget was greater than that spent in the 1980 presidential campaign.[93]

The dominant format of early political ads featured the candidate speaking directly to the camera. For media specialists, this format was lacking. It did not utilize the full capabilities of the medium and was certainly boring to the general public. Later, in a more creative use of the medium, entire campaign events were broadcast live. Live events are, however, difficult to control and staged interactions soon followed. In addition to 30- and 60-second spots, extended half-hour documentaries and telethons were a popular format from 1960 to 1972 but are much too expensive to broadcast today.

Contemporary political ads are creative, fully utilizing the medium of television with color, music, and a variety of technological manipulations. Lynda Kaid and Dorothy Davidson, in their 1986 study of political ads, found two very distinct videostyles that still hold true today.[94] The incumbent videostyle uses an announcer, includes more testimonials, stresses competence, focuses on the candidate's positive qualities, depicts more formal dress, and intersperses more slides with printed messages,;. The challenger videostyle uses more opponent-negative focus, talking head ads, cinema vérité style, more eye contact with the audience, more casual dress; and the challenger most often speaks for him- or herself in the ads.

There are numerous functions of political ads: to create interest in a candidate; to build name recognition; to create, soften, or redefine an image; to stimulate citizen participation; to provide motivation for candidate support; to reinforce support; to influence the undecided; to identify key issues and frame questions for public debate; to demonstrate the talents of the candidate; and to provide entertainment. The content, approach, and thrust of an ad are based on several considerations. A few of these are the strengths and weaknesses of the candidates; the strengths and weaknesses of the opponent; availability of funds; the nature of news coverage of the candidate; public information and views of the candidate; and the general artistic and aesthetic inclinations of the consultant.

Although there are numerous specific advertising formats and strategies, there are four basic political advertising messages. (1) Positive messages are those designed to promote the positive attributes of the candidate and to link the candidate to voters in a positive way. Such efforts range from rather basic biographical spots to more myth-evoking, "product of the

American Dream" spots. (2) Negative messages are specifically designed to attack the opponent; they focus on personal weaknesses, voting record, or prior public behavior. (3) Comparative messages are still designed to attack the opponent but tend to focus on issue positions. The most effective comparison ads give the appearance of providing a two-sided argument, but the presentation is always slanted to favor the candidate sponsoring the ad. Some comparisons are implied and thus never specifically refer to the opposition. Audience interpretation favors the candidate sponsoring the ad. (4) Finally, there are response messages designed to directly answer challenger charges, allegations, and attacks.

Today, political advertising utilizes the same concepts of product advertising and marketing. The context, the political campaign, is different. The basic principles include the following:[95]

- *The 80/20 rule*—Generally, 80 percent of sales are made by 20 percent of a firm's customers. This informs where to focus one's advertising messages. Thus, one should focus most of the campaign activities on those most likely to vote, those who are the strongest believers in the message, and those who support the candidate.

- *Market segmentation and target markets*—Campaigns segment voters into various categories based on demographic and psychographic variables. Consumers of toothpaste, for example, are grouped into categories based upon goals of users, such as cavity fighters, tooth whiteners or brighteners, breath fresheners, stain removers, tartar fighters, sensitive teeth/gums, and specialty items for children (colorful, contains sparkles, etc.). In terms of voters, they may be segmented by race, age, sex, income, education, religion, etc. We know, for example, that Republicans targeted evangelicals, Hispanics, and married women in the 2004 presidential contest. George W. Bush noticeably improved his numbers in those categories. Voter segmentation goes well beyond that of issues.

- *Positioning*—Products are positioned in terms of image and what consumers think of when the product is mentioned. Think of all the automobiles manufactured by just one automaker. Each model is positioned for a different market segment. In terms of General Motors, the Cadillac is a prestige car communicating success, the Chevrolet Corvette is the classic American muscle car with speed and power, and Saturns serve as an alternative to well-priced foreign-made vehicles. In terms of campaigns, politicians position themselves as either an experienced incumbent, an outsider who will reform government, or the common person who represents the average citizen, to name just a few.

- *Consumer benefits*—all products offer benefits: saves time, made from high-quality materials, easy to operate, long-lasting, and the list rolls on. Political candidates offer emotional and rational benefits to targeted groups: more and better jobs, return to traditional values, improved education, elimination of certain taxes, and so on.

Specific ads may serve a variety of functions or purposes. Interestingly, however, there is a chronology of their use during a campaign.[96] Early in a campaign, advertising seeks to create name recognition and candidate identification. As previously noted, biographical spots are most common during this phase. The next strategic use of commercials is to generate arguments detailing the candidate's themes of the campaign often targeted to a particular demographic voting group. During the argument phase of the campaign, issues are treated in emotional terms, seeking the approval and interest of voters. Following argument ads are attack commercials or what some call negative ads. The focus of these is on the opponent and is seldom delivered by the candidate. Campaigns attack opponents to gain momentum, to move undecided voters, and to motivate people to vote against the opposition. Depending on voter response and polling data, campaigns may simultaneously run positive messages to mitigate backlash to negative ads. Finally, by the end of the campaign, ads of resolution appear. In these spots candidates attempt to sum up the issues, their positions, and provide reasons for voting for them. Usually these ads are in the last week of the campaign and have the candidates speaking directly to the audience.

Many journalists and scholars argue that there seems to be an increasing trend toward negative campaigns in recent history at all electoral levels. Although there have always been negative ads, Richard Armstrong argues that the elections of 1986 marked a new stage in electoral politics, a stage he calls "reactivity."[97] New technologies allowed candidates to respond to opponents, public attitudes, and situations much faster, thus becoming more reactive, resulting in what appears to be more negative campaign activities. Today's technology has developed a kind of punch-counterpunch campaign. Through her analysis, Lynda Kaid finds the 1988, 1992, 1996, 2000, and 2004 elections characterized by the growing amount of negative advertising by both incumbents (if one existed in the campaign) and opponents.[98]

In 1997, Karen Johnson-Cartee and Gary Copeland provided an extensive review of research findings on the effects of political advertising.[99] More recently, Lynda Kaid provided an update of findings.[100] Based on their reviews of the literature, we provide summary findings of the effects of advertising in terms of awareness, emotions, voting, issues, image and negative or attack advertising.

In terms of *cognitive or awareness effects* of political advertising:

- Political advertising leads to more general knowledge about issues and candidates.
  - Name identification is the most important knowledge effects.
  - Ad exposure influences voter recall of candidate issue positions.
  - Viewing television news generates higher levels of learning.
  - Ads have greater influence on those with low campaign involvement.

- There seems to be a point where information gain from political spots does not increase with increased exposure to the ads.
- Individuals who watch moderate levels of political advertising demonstrate the same level of information gain as heavy viewers of political advertising.
- Political advertising influences issues that are most salient to voters during a campaign.

Among the more important *emotional effects* of political advertising:

- Political advertising influences individual evaluation of candidates in terms of attractiveness, credibility, and status.
- Political advertising generates positive and negative emotions or feelings about a candidate.
- Issue-oriented ads increase a candidate's perceived leadership skills and feelings of warmth.
- Exposure to ads leads to greater positive affect toward candidates.
- Candidates are less persuading when expressing their own opinions than are newscasters and retired politicians.

Determining how political advertising influences voting behavior is complex and difficult to isolate. Sometimes, findings of various studies seem to contradict each other:

- Most people report that political advertising does not influence their vote.
- There is a positive relationship between money spent on political advertising and voter turnout and electoral outcome.
- Increase in political advertising tends to encourage voter ticket splitting (i.e., voting for members of different parties during an election).
- Political ads have often been identified as an important criterion affecting an individual's vote in an election.
- Impact of political advertising tends to be the strongest in "low-level," or more "low-involvement" local races as well as in primary nomination campaigns, nonpartisan races, and state races.
- Political ads have greater influence on undecided and late-decider voters.

Political advertising is also very important in influencing candidate issues and image. Both notions are multidimensional and can be very subtle. Candidate image deals with attributes of a candidate's character. Issues are matters of public concern or potential policy positions of candidates. In terms of issues, broadly defined, research indicates:

- The majority (60–80 percent) of ads in races usually mention some issue or issues.
  - It is increasingly difficult to distinguish between image and issue ads.
  - Historically, candidates are more successful when using issue ads.

- While ads may discuss an issue, the candidate's position on those issues may not always be presented in the ad. More often, the "favorable" stance is assumed.
- When mentioned, issues are usually treated in rather superficial and broad manner.
- When issues are clearly identified in ads, they tend to be targeted to specific demographic voting groups.

Candidate image is a broad theoretical construct rather than a specific concrete variable. Studies investigating image have ranged from considering how a candidate looks to the personal moral behavior of candidates. In reviewing empirical studies on candidate image and advertising, findings indicate:

- Television has increased the importance of how a candidate looks more than it has increased the importance of issue positions.
- Personal characteristics of candidates are more important to a large number of voters than candidate issue positions.
- The way issues are treated in political ads influence image perceptions of candidates.
- The most common image appeals in political ads include experience, competence, special qualities, honesty, leadership, and strength.
- Candidate image influences how favorably voters view the candidate.
- Political ads contain a great deal of emotional content such as pride, trust, hope, etc.
- Image-oriented ads are best for content recall and candidate name recognition.
- Principal verbal styles in spots include optimism, activity/action, realism and certainty.
  - Winners use more words indicating activity and optimism than losers.

Findings on negative advertising include:

- Term includes various types.
- Negative ads impact information and learning in campaigns.
  - Negative ads generate higher levels of audience recall.
  - Negative ads can enhance issue knowledge.
- Negative ads have the potential of backlash or backfire.
- Negative ads are more effective when sponsored by a third party.
- Attacks on opponent's issue positions are more effective than attacks on character.
  - Attacks are effective if they focus is on issues of competence or experience
- Inoculation can provide protection against attacks.

- Negative ads work better for challengers than for incumbents.
- Negative ads contribute to lower voter turnout and voter cynicism.

Campaign ads from any election, whether a mayoral race or a presidential race, provide a capsulated form of the basic issues, strategies, and tactics of a campaign. Together they target the psyche of the public—their likes and dislikes, their concerns and worries, their hopes and dreams. They indeed provide future historians snapshots of U.S. politics.

Public Opinion Polling

The art and science of polling have become the major influence in strategic decision making in modern political campaigns. Polling is used during all stages of campaigns. Pollsters gather data, suggest strategy, monitor campaign status, and evaluate communication tactics.

The *Harrisburg Pennsylvanian* published in 1824 contained the first political opinion poll in the United States.[101] It consisted of a survey of presidential preferences of the constituents between Andrew Jackson and John Quincy Adams. Jackson won the straw vote two to one. But scientific polling did not begin until the 1930s. Mrs. Alex Miller was the first candidate to use polling by her son-in-law George Gallup. She became the first female secretary of state in Iowa by utilizing sampling techniques that Gallup developed in his doctoral thesis. He founded the polling industry in 1935. Franklin Roosevelt's use of public opinion polls was to gauge his popularity and not to form issue or policy. Although Eisenhower's advertising agencies consulted Gallup in the development of themes to use in the 1952 television ads, extensive use of polling did not begin until 1960. John Kennedy used Louis Harris to analyze public opinion in key primary states. Upon Harris's urging, Kennedy, a Catholic, entered the West Virginia primary—and West Virginia is a heavily Protestant state. Kennedy nearly lost the primary and lost faith in Harris's predictions.

Political polls most often focus on three major variables: the candidate, the public, and specific issues or topics. In terms of the candidate, polls assess electoral viability, strengths and weaknesses of personality characteristics, profile matches with voters or specific voter groups, and current status of the election. In terms of the public, polls seek to identify what kinds of people plan to vote for the candidate and against the candidate, what they are thinking, why they are thinking the way they are, and how their thinking will impact the election. Finally, polls attempt to reveal issue positions in terms of support, strategy development, and electoral impact. For example, focus group and public opinion testing was a major factor in every public pronouncement and decision of the Clinton White House.

> Every State of the Union speech, every presidential address, and every major campaign announcement is pretested, topics are emphasized or disregarded, words and phrases are used or avoided, depending upon what the public wants to hear. Polls and focus groups concluded that

> Clinton's affair with Monica Lewinsky was a private matter; when it was
> finally time to address the nation, six times in a four-minute speech, Bill
> Clinton uttered the resonating word *private*.[102]

Private campaign survey research varies widely, depending on such factors as: competitiveness of the race, funds available, whether or not there is a primary, size of the electorate, demography of voters, and the basic dynamics of the campaign.[103] In a campaign, polls are used to assess name recognition, issue preferences of voters, distribution of knowledge or beliefs about particular topics, and underlying attitudes about social and political values as well as to test hypotheses or issue positions among voter groups.

Shea and Burton identify six major types of polls in political campaigns.[104] *Focus groups* consist of small number of individuals talking about their beliefs, attitudes, and values; the purpose of these groups is to help formulate strategy, test message points or themes, test strategic moves, and fine-tune tactics.

The *benchmark poll* is the most basic and extensive piece of research of an entire campaign. The survey has five main elements: (1) survey the political mood of voters on all types of items such as evaluations of the candidates, the economy, and the direction of the nation; (2) survey attitudes on numerous issues in order to discover those most favorable to the electorate; (3) attempt to reveal how voters perceive the candidates based on personal attributes; (4) test potential candidate weaknesses in order to gauge the magnitude of impact and how to answer criticisms; and (5) focus on themes or issues that will work against the opponent.

Tracking polls are conducted on a regular basis to identify trends and to follow the status of the campaign. While limited in scope, they usually attempt to track name recognition, candidate support (including favorable and unfavorable impressions), issue support, and effectiveness of campaign activities and ads. Somewhat similar, campaigns may conduct quick response polls intended to assess the effect of specific events, usually those that are unplanned such as a barrage of attack ads.

Dial groups and *mall intercepts* are close cousins of focus groups. Dial groups are usually used for television spots. Participants are identified by specific characteristics (male, female, young, old, etc.), and they use a control knob to indicate higher or lower levels of agreement or satisfaction. This allows a second-by-second analysis to pinpoint the strengths and weaknesses of message points. The mall intercept method is when an interviewer approaches a subject who meets certain criteria and asks certain questions. This helps to fine-tune message points for TV spots and direct mail. Both of these techniques are usually done in public spaces such as malls.

Finally, according to Shea and Burton, *push polls* are usually done in the final days of a campaign. Their sole purpose is to "push" voters away from the opponent. "Push polls disguise voter persuasion as survey research. . . . Push polls simulate an interview on the telephone, but they often do not involve genuine data collection." Highly negative information is introduced such as, "If X had been arrested for drunk driving, and as a teen, for the use of heroin, would you still be inclined to vote for X?" It is important to note that the Association of Political Consultants does not endorse the use of push polls and considers them unethical.

Of course news organizations conduct many polls, and these are much less informative than campaign polls. They tend to have higher margins of error and are much more limited in scope. Their sample may not be representative of actual voters in general. Campaigns generally employ professional polling companies so that the information from the polls is reliable and useful.

Bill Hamilton notes three new related trends in polling.[105] First is the increasing use of marketing techniques in testing advertising material. Second is the testing of radio spots or audio tracks through telephone interviews. Finally, flash polls are becoming popular. Instead of asking questions to a large sample, just one or two questions are posed to a small group of individuals. This allows the campaign to get quick and cheap confirmation of an issue or message theme.

Although polling has become very sophisticated and scientific, it still remains problematic despite its popularity. Critics claim that polls do not distinguish between awareness of an issue and intensity of opinion. There is often no link between an attitude and subsequent behavior. In addition, formulating a reliable sample is becoming more difficult. Those who use only cell phones are not sampled and refusal and hang-up rates are growing. In close races, high margins of error, such as plus or minus 5 percent or higher, are virtually useless. However, by far the greatest concern is that polls alone become the basis for decision making. Nevertheless, political opinion polls, unlike public polls of Gallup and Harris, are more tools of persuasion, image control, and image creation, than reports of information. They are, simply put, an important element of a consultant's service arsenal.

Direct Mail

Of all the services provided by consulting firms, the public is probably less aware of the importance and role direct mail plays in a campaign. As a relatively new industry, direct mail has rapidly become the cornerstone for mounting a political campaign. In fact, if one considers all levels of political campaigns from presidential to school board elections, more money is spent on direct mail than television. Also, in general, campaigns normally spend about 20 percent of direct-mail budgets in places where the candidate is the strongest or weakest and about 80 percent in swing areas.[106]

Richard Armstrong claims that direct mail

> utterly revolutionized American politics ... it has drastically changed the role of the national parties ... created an enormous shadow government of special interest groups ... completely revolutionized the nature of campaign finance ... abetted the rise of political action

committees . . . created a new form of political advertising . . . changed
the way incumbents communicate with their constituents . . . and dramatically altered the nature of lobbying.[107]

Direct mail is a powerful and persuasive communication medium. Larry
Sabato refers to direct mail as "the poisoned pen of politics,"[108] and Armstrong writes, "like a water moccasin, persuasion mail is silent, it is poison-
ous, and it has a forked tongue."[109] As the fastest growing advertising
industry, direct mail utilizes the latest technology and theories of social science research.

In terms of politics, it was the 1972 presidential campaign that first demonstrated the power and effectiveness of direct mail.[110] George McGovern
was generally unknown and had great difficulty obtaining endorsements from
party regulars, wealthy supporters, or organized groups. He was forced to use
direct mail to generate funds from individual citizen supporters. Even in a
difficult campaign, by 1972 direct mail was bringing in over $200,000 a month.

Republicans have benefited most from direct mail. In 1974, following
Nixon's resignation, Congress enacted legislation that set a $1,000 limit on
individual political contributions. Republicans immediately began developing a sophisticated direct mail program utilizing the latest technology; they
consistently raised four or five times as much money using direct mail than
did Democrats.[111] According to Richard Viguerie, Republicans and conservatives were forced to use direct mail because of the need to bypass the liberal mass media. It became, for them,

a way of mobilizing our people, it's a way of communicating with our
people; it identifies our people, and it marshals our people. It's self-liq-
uidating and it pays for itself. It's a form of advertising, part of the marketing strategy. It's advertising.[112]

Viguerie discovered that direct mail responders are more interested in principles than in winning elections. During the 1980s, he churned out direct mail
solicitations concerning one hot issue after another. The "new right" began
to generate more and more money. Conservative causes used direct mail to
finance campaigns and sympathetic PACs through direct mail solicitation.

Thus, fund-raising is the primary function of direct mail in political campaigns. Candidates use direct mail to supplement federal financing of elections. Fund-raising objectives include reaching new contributors as well as
continual contact with previous ones. Other uses of direct mail include targeting voters, developing issues, recruiting volunteers, molding opinions,
getting out the vote, and laying the groundwork for future campaigns by
establishing a list of donors and supporters.

Direct mail tends to work best for both fund-raising and general advertising purposes when campaigns expect a low voter turnout, when the district
or geographic area is not part of a major media market, or if the race is second tier or "down-ballot" in an expensive media market. In other words, if
you are running for attorney general in a state election, most attention will

be on the governor's race. Thus, lower on the ticket means more reliance on direct mail and even radio.

Direct mail is powerful because the message can be carefully constructed to distill complicated issues. Direct mail has the option to use graphic language, a longer format, and a personalized message that targets specific voters. Placed on the outside of the envelope is a teaser or attention-getting statement that leads the reader to open the correspondence. The letter usually begins with a startling or dramatic statement by the politician or a celebrity and continues in a conversational and personal style, using a lot of "I's" and "you's." There is an early identification of an enemy that is the opponent, a group, or an issue position. The situation is described as being critical, desperate, and urgent. Of course, most letters conclude with an appeal for support and financial assistance. In short, the copy must get attention, arouse interest, stimulate desire, and ask for action. At the heart of political direct mail is emotional isolation. The target is an angry person who is politically frustrated. Direct mail acknowledges the anger and shows that someone or some group cares.

Techniques of emotion and motivation are well known by the professionals. They know that a letter is more likely to generate funds if the letter is very specific as to what the money will be used for, such as television advertising. Experts know that participation devices stimulate interest and focus concentration on the issues or action discussed. Many mailings include opinion surveys, boxes to be checked, or sample ballots to be marked. In terms of fund-raising, the size of a contribution will be greater not only if the amount is specified but also if the suggested amounts start with the largest (i.e., $500, $250, $100, $50, rather than $50, $100, $250, $500). Ironically, a two-page letter is more likely to be read than a one-page letter, and the signature should be in blue ink and appear to be personally signed.

The timing of a mailing is critical to its impact and success. Generally, it is best to send a mailing just before or after an announcement of candidacy, before a primary or general election, and to coincide with a major media blitz.

Finally, experts know that direct mail donors are more committed to the candidate and issues than single-event donors. Single-event donors are usually one-shot contributors who like being near the candidate or at a party, whereas the direct mail donor will be responsive even in tough times. Thus, the list of contributors is a valuable commodity.

Usually, there is coordination between direct mail efforts and phone efforts. Such efforts have three phases. The first, which occurs about two months before election day, is a *sensitizing* phase where voters get a short and direct phone call asking for support and to be on the lookout for something coming in the mail. Within a day or so, the voter receives a piece of direct mail from the campaign. The second phase, which is usually four to six weeks before the election, is called *identification*. This phase attempts to identify those who favor the candidate or lean toward voting for the candidate. The phone call identifies the campaign and proceeds to ask several questions to determine if there is support for the candidate and the reasons for or against. This information allows for the creation of a specific and tailored piece of direct mail personalized for the voter. One week to 10 days out, the phone call targets voters by specific issues to nail support for the candidate as well as to motivate the person to vote. For example, the call may target senior citizens with a message of support for social security. The final phase is *get-out-the-vote*, where identified supporters are called at least twice within a couple of days of the election. The call is straightforward, not so much asking for support but urging the individual to go to the polls.[113]

There are several advantages to the direct mail medium. There is more complete control, not only over the construction of the message but also over who receives the message and where the message will be sent. The message appeals can be tailored and targeted, tell the full story, and present a detailed issue position. The message is not limited to 30 seconds. In direct mail there is wider coverage, personalized and guaranteed contact, and the ability to capitalize on current events. It is also less costly and very effective. The importance and impact of direct mail techniques will continue to be a factor in every campaign endeavor.

New Technologies

In the late 1990s, new campaign technologies included computerized interactive telephone calls, continued cable segmentation of audiences with nearly a hundred channel offerings, the use of satellites for distance media interviews and conferences, and the use of video press releases for local media and video mail targeted to specific constituent groups or geographic areas. The Internet was just beginning to play a role in politics. In 1996, just 25,000 of the more than 100,000 candidates who ran for public office posted home pages on the World Wide Web.[114] By 2004, 63 million online political news consumers used the Internet for political information, 43 million discussed the election by e-mail, 13 million even used the Internet to make a political contribution, and 52 percent of online users indicated that information obtained from the Internet influenced their vote.[115] Nearly half of all campaign ads appeared online, campaign e-mails were routine, and blogs gained importance for both campaigns and media outlets as a means of interactivity with constituents.[116] Innovation of activity on the Web follows new technological software and hardware. The impact, influence, and potential of the Internet were discussed in great detail in the last chapter.

With each election cycle new uses and innovations of technology are adapted to political campaigns. Craig Varoga, CEO of the public affairs firm Varoga & Rice, predicts the use of a couple of new technologies in campaigns in the future.[117] Digital billboards will be able to display a different message every eight seconds, tailoring messages to the time of day. Extended video and text messages will be able to be accessed in a 24/7 environment by small, portable hand-held devices. The usefulness of any new technology for campaigns is the ability to target constituents with customized or personalized messages, resulting in voter mobilization and activation.

Summary

Political campaigns are communication events: communication of images, characters, and persona. Most campaign strategies are designed to do more than get votes. They are designed to project a certain image, alter a perception, or counter the opposition. Political campaigns are long and expensive. They offer numerous messages about our past, future, and current situations. As primarily communication phenomena, they influence and impact our behavior in both obvious and subtle ways. Their importance transcends the preference of one individual over another.

One cannot consider the role of the new politician without also considering the impact upon our political process of new technologies and media consultants. For some, consultants are now kingmakers and are at the heart of our electoral process. Consultants, of course, believe that they are actually making the electoral process more democratic. They claim that they cannot control votes as the old political bosses did through the patronage system. Also, consultants can't enforce voter discipline or the voting behavior of elected officials. Consultants further argue that they make elections more open and provide access for reporters to candidate strategy, views, and campaign information.

Of course there is nothing inherently wrong or evil in the use of new technologies or even the desire of politicians to present their best attributes to the public. However, the pressure of winning for both the candidate and the consultant cannot be ignored. Therein lay the potential for abuse. For consultants to get business, they must continue to win elections. They are more likely, then, to accept only sure bets, and once in the throes of battle, they may not recognize any limits to winning. The fact is most candidates are willing participants. They seldom question the advice or strategy of consultants. Those who do, often lose. Candidates are paying a great deal of money for consultant services, and they seldom understand the new technologies or have the time to develop the necessary expertise to become a full partner in media decisions.

In the demise of political parties, consultants have taken their place in generating supporters, motivating voters, and raising money. For major elective offices, consultants rather than parties have become the intermediaries between politicians and the public and the press. The consequences are the continuing decline of party organizations; emphasis of images over issues; candidate independence from party ideology; more narrow elections with a focus on single issues that can be packaged; dissemination of communication tools and techniques to political action committees or issue groups; resorting to factual inaccuracies, half-truths, and exaggerations; using deceptive and negative advertising resulting in voter distrust and apathy; emphasis on emotional themes over rational discussion of issues; and drastically increasing the cost of elections.[118]

The professional politicians of today are not the political officeholders, for the latter are paid for governing while the former are paid for managing and winning elections. For professional politicians, politics is a permanent, continual campaign and not the process of governing. Political consultants possess the tools, skills, and techniques of mass communication and human motivation. The functions and services of political consultants, while communication based, have a profound effect upon our electoral process.

Notes

[1] Ron Faucheux, "Strategies that Win!" *Campaigns & Elections*, 18, no. 10 (1998): 26.

[2] Dennis Johnson, *No Place for Amateurs* (New York: Routledge, 2001), xiii.

[3] Ibid., 15.

[4] Daniel Shea and Michael Burton, *Campaign Craft,* 3rd ed. (Westport, CT: Praeger, 2006), 9–12.

[5] Ibid., 10.

[6] Ibid., 3–4.

[7] William Sweeney, Jr., "The Principles of Planning," in *Campaigns and Elections American Style*, 2nd ed., ed. James Thurber and Candice Nelson (Boulder, CO: Westview Press, 2004), 17.

[8] Samuel Becker, "Rhetorical Studies for the Contemporary World," in *The Prospect of Rhetoric*, ed. Lloyd Bitzer and Edwin Black (Englewood Cliffs, NJ: Prentice Hall, 1971), 21.

[9] Ibid., 21–43.

[10] Jonathan Robbin, "Geodemographics: The New Magic," in *Campaigns and Elections*, ed. Larry Sabato (Glenview, IL: Scott Foresman, 1989), 106.

[11] Ibid., 107.

[12] Dick Morris, *Behind the Oval Office* (New York: Random House, 1997), xiii.

[13] Shea and Burton, *Campaign* Craft, 127–129.

[14] Ibid., 130–131.

[15] Ibid., 131.

[16] Bruce Gronbeck, "Functional and Dramaturgical Theories of Presidential Campaigning," *Presidential Studies Quarterly,* 14 (Fall 1984): 490.

[17] Jay Bryant, "Paid Media Advertising," in *Campaigns and Elections American Style*, 2nd ed., ed. James Thurber and Candice Nelson (Boulder, CO: Westview Press, 2004), 90–108.

[18] Ibid. 496.

[19] Gary Mauser, *Political Marketing: An Approach to Campaign Strategy* (New York: Praeger, 1983).

[20] Jack Honomichl, *Marketing Research People: Their Behind the Scenes Stories* (Chicago: Crain Books, 1984), 67.

[21] Bruce Newman, *Marketing of the President* (Thousand Oaks, CA: Sage, 1994), xv.

[22] Darren G. Lilleker and Jennifer Lees-Marshment, "Introduction: Rethinking Political Party Behavior," in *Political Marketing: A Comparative Perspective*, ed. Darren Lilleker and Jennifer Lees-Marshment (Manchester, England: Manchester University Press, 2005), 1.

[23] Ibid., 1.

[24] Ibid., 3.

[25] Bruce I. Newman and Richard Perloff, "Political Marketing: Theory, Research, and Application," in *Handbook of Political Communication Research*, ed. Lynda Lee Kaid (Mahwah, NJ: Erlbaum, 2004), 18.

[26] Lilleker and Lees-Marshment, "Introduction: Rethinking Political Party Behavior," 6–7.

[27] Neil Collins and Patrick Butler, "Considerations on Market Analysis for Political Parties," in *The Idea of Political Marketing*, ed. Nicholas O'Shaughnessy (Westport, CT: Praeger, 2002), 2.

[28] Ibid., 6–8.

[29] Ibid., 19.

[30] Newman and Perloff, "Political Marketing," 9.

[31] Nicholas O'Shaughnessy, *The Idea of Political Marketing* (Westport, CT: Praeger, 2002), xiii.

[32] Stephen Wayne, *The Road to the White House 1992* (New York: St. Martin's Press, 1992), 56–84.

[33] John Kessel, *Presidential Campaign Politics* (Chicago: Dorsey, 1988), 88.

[34] Larry Sabato, *The Rise of the Political Consultants* (New York: Basic Books, 1981), 20.

[35] Shea and Burton, *Campaign Craft*, 140.

[36] "Out of the Past," *People* 17 (February 16, 1981), 74.

[37] Bill Hamilton and Dave Beattie, "Modern Campaign Polling," in *The Manship School Guide to Political Communication*, ed. David Perlmutter (Baton Rouge: Louisiana State University, 1999), 96.

[38] Ibid., 97.

[39] Diana Owen, *Media Messages in American Presidential Campaigns* (Westport, CT: Greenwood Press, 1981), 91.

[40] Michael Traugott, "The Impact of Media Polls on the Public," in *Media Polls in American Politics*, ed. Thomas Mann and Gary Orren (Washington, DC: Brookings Institution), 126–146.

[41] Kenneth Hacker, *Candidate Images in Presidential Elections* (Westport, CT: Praeger, 1995), xii.

[42] Wayne, *The Road to the White House*, 207.

[43] Keith Melder, "Creating Candidate Imagery," in *Campaigns and Elections*, ed. Larry J. Sabato (Glenview, IL: Scott Foresman, 1989), 6.

[44] Sidney Blumenthal, *The Permanent Campaign* (New York: Touchstone Books, 1980), 5.

[45] Herbert Asher, *Presidential Elections and American Politics*, rev. ed. (Homewood, IL: Dorsey Press, 1980), 250.

[46] Mathew Kerbel, *Edited for Television* (Boulder, CO: Westview Press, 1994), xiv, 208.

[47] George Edwards and Stephen Wayne, *Presidential Leadership,* 2nd ed. (New York: St. Martin's Press, 1990), 34–38.

[48] Kerbel, *Edited for Television*, 4–6.

[49] Johnson, *No Place for Amateurs*, 21–22.

[50] Sabato, *The Rise of Political Consultants*, 8.

[51] David Dulio, *For Better or Worse?* (Albany: State University of New York Press, 2004), 44.

[52] Johnson, *No Place for Amateurs*, 9, xiii.

[53] As cited in Sabato, *The Rise of Political Consultants*, 18.

[54] Robert Friedenberg, *Communication Consultants in Political Campaigns* (Westport, CT: Praeger, 1997), 1.

[55] Dan Nimmo, *The Political Persuaders* (Englewood Cliffs, NJ: Spectrum Books, 1970), 36.

[56] Blumenthal, *The Permanent Campaign*, 40.

[57] Sabato, *The Rise of Political Consultants*, 11–13.

[58] Blumenthal, *The Permanent Campaign*, 164.

[59] Sabato, *The Rise of Political Consultants*, 12.

[60] Johnson, *No Place for Amateurs*, 9.

[61] Dulio, *For Better or Worse?*, 43.

[62] Ibid., 45–49, 51.

[63] Johnson, *No Place for Amateurs*, xvi.

[64] Blumenthal, *The Permanent Campaign*, 10.

[65] Morris, *Behind the Oval Office*, 145.

[66] Shea and Burton, *Campaign Craft*, 20.

[67] Ibid., 20–22.

[68] Johnson, *No Place for Amateurs*, 61.

[69] Ibid., 76.

[70] Michael Bayer and Joseph Rodota, "Computerized Opposition Research," in *Campaigns and Elections*, ed. Larry J. Sabato (Glenview, IL: Scott Foresman, 1989), 20.

[71] Ibid., 21.

[72] Ibid., 22.

[73] Ibid., 23–24.

74 Ibid., 25.

75 John Bovee, "Opposition Research," in *The Manship School Guide to Political Communication*, ed. David Perlmutter (Baton Rouge: Louisiana State University, 1999), 108–112.

76 Shea and Burton, *Campaign Craft*, 66–73.

77 Ibid., 60–65.

78 Johnson, *No Place for Amateurs*, 76–77.

79 Ron Faucheux, "Strategies that Win!," 25.

80 Shea and Burton, *Campaign Craft*, 123.

81 Faucheux, "Strategies that Win!," 25.

82 Ibid., 26–32.

83 Gary Mauser, *Political Marketing*, 276.

84 Ibid., 276.

85 Bike, *Winning Political Campaigns*, 2nd ed. (Juneau, AK: The Denali Press, 2001), 44.

86 Ibid., 44–50.

87 Lynda Kaid, "Videostyle in the 2004 Presidential Advertising," in *The 2004 Presidential Campaign: A Communication Perspective*, ed. Robert E. Denton, Jr. (Lanham, MD: Rowman & Littlefield, 2005), 284; and "By the Numbers," *Campaigns and Elections*, August 2006, 14.

88 Richard Armstrong, *The Next Hurrah* (New York: William Morrow, 1988).

89 Kaid, "Videostyle in the 2004 Presidential Advertising," 286.

90 Kaid, "By the Numbers," 14.

91 Joe McGinniss, *The Selling of the President* (New York: Trident Press, 1969), 26–27.

92 Sabato, *The Rise of Political Consultants*, 113.

93 Patrick Devlin, "An Analysis of Presidential Television Commercials: 1952–1984," in *New Perspectives on Political Advertising*, ed. Lynda Lee Kaid, Dan Nimmo, and Keith Sanders (Carbondale: Southern Illinois University Press, 1986), 25.

94 Lynda Kaid and Dorothy Davidson, "Elements of Videostyle," in *New Perspectives on Political Advertising*, ed. Lynda Kaid, Dan Nimmo, and Keith Sanders (Carbondale: Southern Illinois University Press, 1986), 199–208.

95 Thomas Peters, "Political Campaign Advertising," in *The Practice of Political Communication,* ed. Guido Stempel III (Englewood Cliffs, NJ: Prentice Hall, 1994), 101–106.

96 Edwin Diamond and Stephen Bates, *The Spot* (Cambridge, MA: MIT Press, 1984), 303–345.

97 Armstrong, *The Next Hurrah*, 18.

98 Kaid, "Videostyle in the 2004 Presidential Advertising," 285, 289.

99 Karen Johnson-Cartee and Gary Copeland, *Inside Political Campaigns* (Westport, CT: Praeger, 1997), 149–183.

100 Lynda Kaid, "Political Advertising," in *Handbook of Political Communication Research*, ed. Lynda Kaid (Mahwah, NJ: Erlbaum, 2004), 155–202.

101 Sabato, *The Rise of Political Consultants*, 69.

102 Johnson, *No Place for Amateurs*, 89–90.

103 Ibid., 90.

104 Shea and Burton, *Campaign Craft*, 105–108.

105 Cited in Johnson, *No Place for Amateurs*, 55.

106 Bike, *Winning Political Campaigns*, 3.

107 Armstrong, *The Next Hurrah*, 28.

108 Sabato, *The Rise of Political Consultants*, 220.

109 Armstrong, *The Next Hurrah*, 60.

110 Sidney Blumenthal, *The Permanent Campaign*, 242–244.

111 Armstrong, *The Next Hurrah*, 116.

112 As cited in Blumenthal, *The Permanent Campaign*, 245.

113 Walter Clinton and Anne Clinton, "Telephone and Direct Mail," in *The Manship School Guide to Political Communication*, ed. David Perlmutter (Baton Rouge: Louisiana State University, 1999), 137–146.

[114] Robert Friedenberg, *Communication Consultants in Political Campaigns* (Westport, CT: Praeger, 1997), 204.

[115] Andrew Williams and John Tedesco, "Introduction," in *The Internet Election* (Lanham, MD: Rowman & Littlefield, 2006), 1.

[116] Kaid, "By the Numbers," 14; and see Kaye Trammell, "The Blogging of the President," in *The Internet Election* (Lanham, MD: Rowman & Littlefield, 2006), 133–146.

[117] Craig Varoga, "Campaign Doctor," *Campaigns & Elections*, August 2006, 68.

[118] Sabato, *The Rise of Political Consultants*, 313.

Presidential Campaigns

> *The strategies of all the participants in presidential elections are to a certain extent constrained, and to a certain extent driven, by the ways in which actors are situated with respect to conditions that are for them given and hard to manipulate.*
>
> —Nelson Polsby and Aaron Wildavsky

In chapter 8 we noted that political campaigns are complex communication activities with a growing influence of communication specialists in every level. There are numerous channels of campaign communication that include: public appearances (speeches, rallies), interpersonal exchanges (luncheons, meetings with opinion leaders), organizational dynamics (party machines, workers), display media (buttons, posters, and billboards), print media (campaign literature, ads, newspapers), auditory media (radio, telephone), and television (advertising, new coverage, programs). Interestingly, some local campaigns are as complex, long, and expensive as national campaigns. Local and state campaigns differ only in scope and money spent—not in basic task requirements. However, the U.S. presidential contest is the most unique in the world. Because of the magnitude of the office, every presidential election is historical and impacts upon the rest of the world.

The formal criteria for becoming president as set forth in Article 11, Section I of the Constitution are threefold: natural born citizen, at least 35 years old, and a resident of the United States for 14 years. But the informal criteria are numerous and include: political experience, personal charisma, fundraising capabilities, and audience adaptation. Today, the presidential contest extends beyond the traditional three-month campaign between Labor Day and November every four years. In fact, the contest has become continual and, for some participants, a matter of lifelong training and maneuvering. The right person for the job is not just found but is created, demonstrated, and articulated to the U.S. public. The distinction between being a president and being a presidential candidate has virtually disappeared. The presidential election campaign is no longer simply the way a president is chosen, but the process actually influences the kind of person chosen and the priorities that person will have as president. Thus, the strategies and tactics presidential candidates use to present themselves and to communicate with the public are of vital importance and are the focus of this chapter.

The Process

Since World War II, our political system has undergone a fundamental change in how candidates for the presidency have been selected. In fact, one of the most striking features of our presidential nomination process is its constant change of rules, financing regulations, and primaries. Changes to the electoral process have resulted in longer campaigns and increased influence of media coverage. Some reforms impact the process in ways not known at the time. Many of the changes involve the role of the public. The citizenry, rather than party activists, increasingly determine which candidates will meet in the general election. Since 1968, presidential primaries have become the critical factor in capturing nominations, and the public have become the true power brokers. We have, in effect, blurred the distinction between nominating and electing candidates.

Historically, we have experienced three presidential nominating systems. The congressional caucus system existed between 1800 and 1824. Successful candidates had to appeal to congressmen and the national political elite. Party congressmen controlled the nomination, and the role of party grassroots voters and the press was minimal.

The brokered convention system, 1832 to 1968, emerged as a result of the deaths of the founding fathers, general population growth and movement to the west, and the initiation of more democratic political customs. Within this system, nominations occurred at national conventions involving a great deal of bargaining. Popularity with state and local officials as well as with major officeholders was critical for the successful candidate. Although presidential primaries began in 1908, regular party leaders and national officeholders controlled the nomination. As late as 1968, Hubert Humphrey won the Democratic Party nomination without contesting in a single presidential primary. Once again, party grassroots voters and the press had little influence on candidate selection.

The system of popular appeal began with the 1972 presidential election. The old systems functioned under the philosophy of *consent of the governed* and the new system operated under the auspices of *government by the people*. National conventions normally ratify state primaries, conventions, and caucuses. Candidates have to maintain popularity with party voters, activists, and media representatives. The new system, initiated by the Democratic Party, was heralded as open, democratic, deliberative, and responsive to popular preferences. The presidential nomination system of popular appeal raises several concerns and issues:

1. Officeholders are at a disadvantage seeking nominations because of the need for full-time personal campaigning for years prior to a general election.

2. The role of political parties decreases, diminishing peer review of candidates and weakening the ties between campaigning and governing.

3. The primary in some states is now more important than in others, based on such factors as size, time of primary, and so on.

4. Rules for delegate selection vary from state to state.

5. Voter eligibility rules differ among states.

6. Sequencing of primaries changes the number and candidate choices in later primaries.

7. Most citizens learn very little about the candidates during the primary process.

8. General public opinion seldom corresponds to those of specific or important state primaries.

9. Convention delegates are not representative of the general public.

10. Journalists play a major role in the campaigns.

11. The current system favors people who have a burning desire for power and who can campaign full time.

We tend to focus on and to think of two or three candidacies for the presidency. In reality, there are numerous candidates on the ballot. In 2004, for instance, there were over 175 official presidential candidates on the ballot in at least one or more states.[1] The largest number of candidates historically comes from the U.S. Senate. However, especially in the twentieth century, governors have had better success seeking the office. Only two presidents (Harding and Kennedy) were elected directly from the Senate to the White House in that century. Since 1974, 22 Democratic and 12 Republican Senators have run along with five Democratic and six Republican House members.[2]

Phases of the Presidential Campaign

From a communication perspective, campaigns are exercises in the creation, re-creation, and transmission of significant symbols. Political campaigns are an essential part of our national conversations, conversations about our national goals, social objectives, national identity, and future courses of action. Scholars have identified various stages or phases of presidential campaigns. For example, Trent and Friedenberg identify the stages as surfacing, primary, convention, and general election.[3] Each phase is distinct, and various communication functions differ within each of the stages.

The Surfacing Phase

During the surfacing stage, candidates must achieve visibility, establish credibility or fitness, and begin to build a viable organization.[4] In this early phase, images are framed, altered, and reframed; much discussion centers on who will and who won't be running; and the debate is characterized by uncertainty. This period is important because the public begins to establish expectations of the candidates important issues surface, and front-runners emerge. The activities of this phase begin three to four years before the election. Indeed, some candidates begin their run for the White House immediately after the inauguration address of a new president.

Dennis Johnson argues that during the preprimary or surfacing phase, three considerations are vitally important.[5] First, adequate fund-raising is essential. In 2004, altogether the candidates raised $684 million, up from $350 million in 2000. Second, candidates must attempt to gain attention, support, and endorsements. Candidates call in favors and line up as many elected officials as possible. Finally, candidates want to gain positive media attention and be portrayed as viable. Usually this means appearing on all the Sunday morning talk shows and cable political shows.

The dominant elements of this stage of the campaign are finances, polls, and organizational considerations. Fund-raising and organizational development are critical and time-consuming at this point of the campaign. Key donors provide the necessary funding to identify early staff members and to pay for modest travel. Potential large-sum donors and contributors are personally contacted, consulted, and courted. The campaign identifies and begins to work with likely sympathetic or supportive Political Action Committees. Immediate financial support is needed as well as a structure for future fund-raising efforts.

From an organizational perspective, state coordinators and congressional district supporters are identified. A campaign organization is needed in every state. Nomination politics impacts the duties and behind-the-scenes activities of grassroots supporters. Candidates must wheel and deal with party bosses. Again, as with fund-raising, although the actual number of supporters may be low, the structure must be established at this phase of the campaign. Campaigns need a small but highly skilled professional staff. By the primary season, it's too late to hire important, high-level staff members.

Although one can argue that political opinion polls are always critical to candidates, they serve a dual function in the surfacing (or preprimary) period. Straw polls provide legitimacy for the candidacy to the media as well as to potential key donors. For the media, early polls create candidate performance expectations, front-runner status, and initial candidate image and issue positions. For candidates, early campaign polls aid in surveying issues and developing positions.

The strategic environment is characterized by a lack of formal rules, emphasis on many candidates, and talk of various factions needing appeasement within the political parties. This lack of clear context means that the media have an important role. Known to candidates as the "Great Mentioner," the media provide predictions of candidate viability and/or potential weaknesses. The importance of labels cannot be underestimated. At this stage, few candidates have a well-defined image but are in the process of defining and shaping their image portrayal.

Arguably, there are numerous important elements that candidates must acknowledge if they are to be successful, but the most important task in the surfacing period is announcing the candidacy and emerging as a viable choice. There is always the risk of entering the race too soon or too late. In the former case, public apathy may result, and in the latter case there may be too little time to raise funds and generate adequate support. Another important consideration involves how the collective media set the agenda for the surfacing period, and this may help or hurt a candidate's early image. The reputation of a candidate will dictate the frequency, slant, and tone of coverage. In addition to routine struggles of garnering favorable free media coverage, candidates use paid media spots to position themselves for the forthcoming primary season. Candidates must also develop and articulate the campaign theme as part of their campaign's rhetorical vision. This theme extends beyond specific issues and allows the candidate to share their vision of the United States and the American Dream. The candidate's rhetorical vision also includes key issues that will be emphasized during the campaign. These issues, of course, are based on poll results and in the early campaign are localized to maximize impact. Of course, unexpected events outside the campaign may suddenly influence the strategic environment. National or international events may dominate the headlines and force candidates to respond.

Campaign rituals during this period include fund-raising events, speaking engagements, and countless parties and dinners. These rituals function to create media attention, introduce the candidate to the voters, build group support, and help the candidate to sharpen skills for the primary period that follows.

Perhaps the most difficult element of building candidate image in the preprimary phase is the need to demonstrate that the candidate is presidential material. It is essential that the candidate be perceived as diplomatic and credible. Candidates attempt to convey this by exhibiting knowledge and expertise as well as by taking trips abroad or introducing legislation. Image in the surfacing period involves creation, definition, and demonstration rather than reinforcement or expansion. As already mentioned, the media play a major role in this early phase of candidate image definition.

Dennis Johnson identifies four trends during the surfacing phase of presidential campaigns.[6] First, the amount of money a potential candidate needs to raise continues to increase with each election cycle. Most observers agree that successful candidates must enter the primary season with $40 million or more. Second, media interest is on the horserace nature of the season rather than on issues or policy. Third, with each cycle, primaries are earlier and closer together. This front-loading of primaries makes early fund-raising and early primaries most important. Finally, Internet and online communications are becoming increasingly important in this phase.

The Primary Phase

This phase of the presidential election process has changed the most in the past hundred years. Until the twentieth century, primaries were not a part of the presidential campaign. By 1916, however, 26 states were holding primaries as part of the presidential election process. It was not until the 1970s and 1980s, however, that primaries played an important role in the nomination process. Before 1968, party bosses controlled delegate selection; candidates had no option other than to lobby party leaders to win the nomination. Winning primaries was not necessary, and entering them was often a sign of weakness rather than strength. Delegate selection was not necessarily connected to electoral strength and was not representative of the overall population.[7] Women and minorities in particular were largely excluded from the process.

Televised news events such as the Vietnam War and the civil rights demonstrations in 1968 created an informed and activism-minded public. The networks covered the same stories, so that the public's exposure was essentially identical. Candidates soon realized that they could reach the entire public via the network news, and the nomination system quickly became nationalized. Party leaders were soon seen as out of touch with their constituency and were less able to influence that constituency's behavior. The lack of representativeness in the nomination process and the newly informed public led the Democratic Party to reform their delegate selection process.

In 1971 the McGovern/Fraser Commission of the Democratic Party implemented many changes in delegate selection. The two most important changes were: (1) a quota system for delegate selection that required a certain percentage of minorities, women, and young people; and (2) the party published uniform rules for all delegate selection.[8] These changes made primaries more important by attempting to take away the power of party bosses and making the process more representative. Holding primaries was the easiest way for states to comply with the new rules.

In 1976, the Democrats implemented a percentage rule calling for the elimination of winner-take-all primaries. Candidates who received some percentage of the vote would earn a proportional number of delegates to the national convention. This rule further stressed the importance of running in the primaries and caucuses. Thus, by 1976 the nominating system was based almost entirely on elections, with most of the convention delegates selected in primaries and bound by those results.

As the Democrats made their reforms, the Republicans were swept into the new system. Most of the Democratic election reforms were passed into law, which required Republican compliance as well. All of these rule changes during the early 1970s helped to create and magnify the importance of primary and caucus elections as a means of determining delegate selection. Since 1968, the number of primaries and caucuses has gone from 16 to 55. Candidates could no longer win the nomination as John F. Kennedy or Hubert Humphrey had done. State-by-state primaries and caucuses were the only way to the nomination.

The three dominant elements of this phase of the campaign are the news media, the campaign organization, and the strategic environment. *News media* become the gatekeepers of access to the public as well as judge and jury of electoral performance. Campaigns are simplified, dichotomies are created, winners and losers are labeled. As a result, front-runners emerge more quickly from media analyses and labels than from actual votes. Media expectations often determine the magnitude of candidate success or failure. The news media become active participants in shaping the strategic environment by reporting polls, candidate issues, images, and strategies.

Media reports can greatly impact poll results that influence future primary elections and caucuses. Poll results justify media labels and become the mainstay of most primary-period coverage. The public uses polls to assess candidate viability and electability. Polls also help candidate name recognition and even provide momentum for candidacies. From the candidate perspective, targeted media, such as radio and direct mail, are particularly valuable, since the relevant electorate is small, and it is relatively easy to tailor candidate appeals directly to them. In the primary season, voters are developing personal perceptions of the candidates. First, they form relational perceptions about the candidate's personal qualities such as warmth, integrity, sincerity, to name a few. Later they form perceptions of candidate viability and potential competence.[9]

A strong *organization* is vital to primary success. The candidate's strategy team must decide which contests to enter and develop an appropriate strategy for each. These strategies must be designed specifically for each state or region, and yet, because of the nationalization of the election process, must also be consistent across states and regions. A sound strategy will reinforce specific images in every contest, help avoid direct contradictions, and focus on relatively few themes. The result is often grand-sounding mush, potentially effective on television but relatively free of policy content. At this point, early financial support is needed for specific state campaigns. Availability of funds will dictate primary strategies. In many ways, beyond advertising and day-to-day operations, finance has less impact on candidate image. The media have greater influence in determining success potential, amount of news coverage, and so on. Organization outside of the immediate staff is also crucial, for these are the people who wear the buttons, listen to the speeches, place the yard signs, and carry the placards. They are also the ones who are instrumental in getting out the vote, and they are critical in a primary, when voter turnout is low.

The *strategic environment* is fully energized at this point. In a contested nomination battle, candidate organizations must be ready to respond to new issues, charges, or allegations. The contest feeds the media, which impact candidate polling numbers, issue positions, and candidate image. In many ways, candidates are more concerned with image, leadership, and personality qualities than issues—especially in terms of media coverage. For instance, Kathleen Kendall argues that advertising is especially influential during the primary season. This is true because candidates may not be well known to the general public. Advertising spots also allow for quick strategy adaptation or changes.[10]

New Hampshire traditionally runs the first primary, a position enshrined in that state's constitution. Since 1972, Iowa holds a caucus a week or 10 days before the New Hampshire primary. Nelson Polsby and Aaron Wildavsky argue that from a historical perspective, one ignores the Iowa and New Hampshire primaries at his or her own peril.[11] The two are linked in the media; Iowa sets the stage for New Hampshire. To ignore one or the other removes the candidate from the spotlight. In addition, although winning one primary or the other does not insure nomination, losing badly tends to end a candidacy.

Especially since 1980, the front-loading of primaries has become an issue. In 2004, for example, 41 of 55 primaries were held between January and March. The front-loading of primaries has two main effects. First, it gives advantage to those who win the preprimary period in terms of endorsements and amount of money raised. Second, for those candidates who are successful, front-loading magnifies media exposure.[12]

The Convention Phase

Today, political nominating conventions are simply media events. They no longer serve as decision makers but instead as ratifiers of the party's nominees. Larry David Smith and Dan Nimmo characterize conventions as "a week-long hyped, publicized, televised spectacle that recognizes politics for what it is as currently practiced. . . . Teleconventions . . . showcase what is normally a concealed side of the contemporary conciliation of interests."[13] In essence, conventions are four-day-long partisan political commercials. However, conventions do provide some drama and follow a pattern.[14] First, there is some conflict either over the nomination or various platform positions. Second, party leaders generate some compromises among the various factions. Next, the big celebration focuses on the candidate and the pending campaign. Finally, the media pass judgment and begin forecasting the race. Conventions serve several functions:[15] they provide legitimization of the nomination process and the party's nominees; they provide an opportunity for the party to show unity and showcase party principles; and they provide the opportunity for candidates to share their social agenda and issue positions. Thus, party conventions are highly orchestrated events resulting from the "process of give-and-take among party members, the news media, and various governmental institutions."[16]

The dominant elements of the convention phase of the campaign are organization and media. The soon-to-be-nominated candidate's campaign organization plans the convention. Maximum control of all events and no surprises are the operative goals of convention management. The length and tone of media coverage become strategic concerns. The "prime-time" segment becomes the venue for noted speakers, rallies, and events to insure a large audience and promote the positive reception of party messages. Media judgment and interpretation impact both tracking polls and projections of nominee viability, long after the convention. The nominee's organization attempts to maximize the traditional convention lift in polls and positive reporting, hoping to frame the political agenda and environment for the fall campaign. A successful convention will lead to increased fund-raising support. By this time, candidate image and issue positions are set in the public's mind. In fact, many voters have already made up their mind concerning who they will support.

We know that conventions are TV events, scripted down to the second. The actual layout of the convention hall itself is designed for television coverage. Conventions are planned in order to sell the party and its ticket to the national audience. In 1996, for the first time, the three major networks were less than happy about their coconspirator role in bringing the carefully scripted events into American homes. In fact, Ted Koppel of ABC's *Nightline* left the Republican convention on the second day, declaring the proceedings were "more of an infomercial than a news event" and concluding "nothing surprising has happened. Nothing surprising is anticipated." Today, networks cover conventions primarily during the morning shows, nightly newscasts, and perhaps one- or two-hour prime-time wrap-ups of the day's highlights. In 2004, network coverage reached an all-time low, just one hour each of three nights between 10:00 PM and 11:00 PM. Of course, cable news networks covered the entirety of conventions with various preproduced and analysis segments inserted from time to time.

The General Campaign Phase

This phase is the shortest and most intense of the entire election cycle. The political parties are mobilized, the electorate is finally interested (or becoming so), and the context is national rather than state or regional.

The dominant elements in this final phase of presidential campaigns are strategic environment, news media, and organization. The *strategic environment* is critical to all decision making. It is dominated by the peculiar calculus demanded by the rules of the Electoral College. Candidates write off some states as irretrievable, minimize the attention given to others, and focus on building the largest coalition possible given the requirements of securing 270 electoral votes. Candidates need to campaign in states with large numbers of votes. States that almost always go for the opponent's party receive less attention. Indeed, the presidential campaign one experiences depends on where one lives. Candidates tend to spend more time in Michigan, Missouri, Ohio, Illinois, Pennsylvania, Florida, and California. Issue positions and image maintenance are also concerns of the strategic environment. If one is behind in the race, corrective positions and strategies will be developed.

Of course, the *news media* are the primary means of reaching the voters in two ways: paid advertising and news coverage. How campaigns are covered impact public perceptions of the status of the candidates and the race. The coverage and general consensus among reports of how the race is shaping up impact the strategic environment and the candidate's standing in the polls. Above all, there is a sense that time is running out—a sense that is heightened and reinforced by polls that repeatedly announce the candidates' standings. Much of the campaign money is earmarked for television. Media usage during the latter stages of the campaign is concentrated on reinforcing existing images and motivating the potential electorate. Negative or attack ads attempt to push undecided voters into the candidate's camp—as well as to detract support from opponents. Candidate images are, by this phase, established. Voters pretty much know who the candidates are and what they stand for. Candidates stress empathy above identification, for voters must be motivated at all costs. Advertisements become more emotional and less issue-based than they were before.

The *organization* is running at full speed. Although day-to-day operational concerns are primarily event planning and coordination, finances are also important—when to spend, what to spend on, and where to spend are the big questions, made increasingly difficult as the laws governing spending limits and disclosure become more complex. Thus, the main focus is on where to spend money, not on raising it. The new campaign finance reform legislation implemented in the 2004 presidential campaign resulted in massive independent spending for television advertising. The spending by these groups outnumbered candidate spending for ads. For the first time, independent groups impacted the election in major ways. Overall, funding attacks against Bush surpassed those against Kerry. However, the Swift Boat Veterans for Truth ads that attacked Kerry's Vietnam service were powerful and hurt his image. Unless there is new legislation, third-party and outside independent group influence will continue to grow and become another element for the campaign of the candidate to manage.

Strategies and Campaign Communication

As discussed in chapter 8, there are four basic communication channels: the electronic media, the print media, display media (i.e., billboards, etc.), and personal contact. Decisions about the best combination of media to communicate the desired theme and to reach the potential audience depend on factors such as timing and money. In determining communication strategy, the target audience must be identified and segmented; simultaneously, the competition must be identified and characterized. Most strategies link campaigns to existing perceptions, beliefs, and attitudes.

Public Statements about Strategy

There is a rather clear distinction, as Henry Ewbank observes, between campaign strategies and public statements about campaign strategies.[17] Public statements about campaign strategies can come from three sources: the candidate, the candidate's spokesman, or an opponent. Often strategy statements result from a direct challenge by an opponent, the news media, or a specific voting bloc of citizens. Sometimes, in an effort to gain media attention or redefine the campaign issues, a candidate will provide a statement articulating a position or campaign strategy. Most public strategy statements deal with specific actions to be taken if elected, feelings relevant to the current state of affairs, and intentions relating to the execution of the campaign. The latter serves to establish appearances of fairness, open-mindedness, and honesty. The themes of most public statements about strategy are twofold: consistency and uniqueness. Consistency is related in terms of how the candidate will meet the needs and expectations of the public; uniqueness is related in terms of how the candidate will provide new leadership and new solutions to old problems. For Ewbank, strategy statements can be classified in five ways according to apparent intent: offering an interpretation of a past great event, offering an explanation of current campaign events, offering a description of the future, soliciting reaction to some aspect of the campaign that may serve as a trial balloon for future reference, and constructing a desired perception of an event or issue position that is about to become a visible part of a campaign.[18]

The most public view of strategy, from a communication standpoint, is candidates' discussions of issues. Critics and scholars claim that with each contemporary campaign, true issues become less salient and less understood, but this is simply not the case. Even in political ads, issue content is a major component. In fact, in reviewing the verbal content in ads from 1952 to 1996, Lynda Kaid and Anne Johnston found that most of the focus was on issues.[19] In 2004, for example, 85 percent of Bush's ads and 79 percent of Kerry's ads focused on issues.[20]

Issues, from a communication perspective, should not be viewed as abstract or complicated constructions. They are simply what concerns the voters illustrated in concrete examples. Jean Elshtain is correct when she argues there is no difference between real or symbolic/rhetorical issues:

> To claim, then, that candidates are trafficking in nonissues because they immerse themselves in weighty symbolism is to presume that which does not exist—a clear-cut division between the symbolic and the real, between issues and emotional appeals. . . . Thus, the speeches and symbols and rhetorical acts of our presidential candidates are coauthored by "we the people," depending upon how we receive their efforts.[21]

Additionally, one cannot distinguish between *rational* issues and *emotional* issues because, for example, even the issue of abortion may be based on the tenets of a religion or interpretation of the Constitution. The key to understanding issues is audience response, with the real question being whether or not citizens understand the scope, complexity, or relevance of some issues such as the Minute-Man missile, Star Wars, support of the Contras, or the war on terror. Perhaps, as Elshtain observes, the way issues are constructed becomes the issue.

In politics, the goal is to win the election. To do this, of course, requires getting individuals to become committed to one's candidacy, and then, of equal importance, to prompt them to vote in the election. This is indeed a long, complicated process. No single variable, issue, event, or personal characteristic can motivate enough people to become committed and to vote in sufficient numbers to win an election. Likewise, no single strategy can win an election. We argue, however, that there are a limited number of communication approaches or strategies in which to articulate and motivate voters. Importantly, whether or not the candidate is an incumbent or challenger does impact strategy.

Incumbent Strategies

Judith Trent and Robert Friedenberg have provided a comprehensive overview of incumbent strategies.[22] They argue that incumbents have many more strategy options than challengers. Some of the strategies involve maximizing the symbolic, subtle aspects of the office. Incumbents are certain to surround themselves with the purely symbolic trappings of the office. Such trappings include the use of the presidential podium and seal, "Hail to the Chief," and various official backdrops. Such devices communicate the strength and grandeur of the office. They serve to remind the audience that they are listening to the President of the United States and not just an average citizen.

In addition to the physical artifacts that enhance the prestige of the incumbent, the office itself provides a sense of legitimacy, competency, and charisma. Any individual who holds the office is generally perceived as rational, intelligent, and worthy of respect. The pageantry, history, and majesty of the office are transferred to its occupant. In a campaign, such perceptions are worth a great deal.

Presidents have immediate and almost total access to the media. It is very easy for them to create pseudoevents for the purpose of gaining favorable media exposure. Such pseudoevents include making special announcements, appointments, or proclamations that have more political impact than policy impact.

During the campaign period, presidents make many appointments to jobs and special committees. This is a way to line up supporters early in the campaign, tap talent for the reelection bid, and identify people for key positions after the election. Also, reports of special task forces are usually revealed during the campaign period. Task forces can be used effectively to address special issues or concerns of the voters without committing resources or personal support. The very act of forming a task force communicates concern about an issue and the promise of future action. Furthermore, it allows the candidate to postpone taking a stand on controversial issues while at the same time making an appeal to a particular group of voters. An incumbent president will appropriate billions of dollars to cooperative public officials for cities and projects in return for support. By the 1980 election, Carter had given over $80 billion in the form of federal grants. In 1992, Bush Sr. granted government contracts in states where jobless rates were higher than the national average. Clinton, in 1996, provided targeted appropriations to local police departments to hire additional officers.

Without doubt, incumbent presidents will visit world leaders during an election year. Such trips provide great drama and show the president as a world leader respected by other countries. The foreign visits also provide a repertoire of future references that can be worked in debates and discourse to reinforce notions of leadership and experience. But more importantly, most trips are television spectacles, providing video not only for news but also for future spots.

Incumbent presidents have the opportunity to manipulate domestic issues. This is done in two ways. First, presidents can divert or lessen the impact of news by creating competing pseudoevents. Of course, good news comes from the White House, and bad news is released with little notice from related agencies. Another way to manipulate domestic issues is to take short-term actions that will provide at least a temporary impact. This is especially true in the economic realm. Usually, by election time, interest rates and inflation are down. In fact, the stock market has gone down only six times in the 25 years in which presidential elections were held since 1900. Administrations in the final two years of a term tend to focus on economic expansion to enhance the party's reelection endeavors.

A strategy that is especially useful for incumbent presidents is to obtain public endorsements from locally respected, successful, and well-liked politicians. Here the candidate is trying to link himself with already established leaders. Along these same lines, presidents can also use surrogates to campaign for them. Popular members from the administration, or locals who are part of the administration, can have a very positive effect on a campaign. Simply because of the daily job requirements, all presidents now must rely on the help of others during the campaign season. In 1972, Nixon used over 50 surrogates, and in the midterm elections of 1982, the Republican National Committee developed a program called "Surrogate 82" where all cabinet members were required to give 15 days to campaign activities. During the 1980 presidential campaign, Carter was forced to use surrogates because of his statement that he would not campaign while Americans were still held as hostages in Iran. As their length of captivity lengthened, Carter had to rescind his statement. Family members, both close and rather distant, all hit the campaign trail attempting to cover as much of the country as possible. However, there is a limit to the use of surrogates. The public expects candidates to travel and press the flesh—up to a point. An incumbent president must not appear to be neglecting the job of running the country. Thus the use of surrogates best complements the campaigning of an incumbent president rather than replacing it.

Somewhat related, most incumbents try to create the image that they are above the political battle and removed from the day-to-day charges and countercharges of politics. Early presidents, as already noted, seldom actively participated in campaigns or even attended the party conventions. Such participation appeared undignified and unstatesmanlike. In contemporary times, the extreme of such a strategy is called the Rose Garden strategy. Very strong candidates can stay at the White House, appearing presidential, committed, and serious. Only until close to election day will incumbents enter the campaign full time.

Nearly all presidents claim that reelection will communicate to the world a sense of stability. Most incumbents intensify their description of foreign policy problems to create an illusion of crisis to motivate voters to rally around and support the administration. Franklin Roosevelt was most successful using this strategy. History has shown that regardless of the crisis, Americans support rather than condemn their leaders.

Finally, the major strategy of every incumbent president is to emphasize the administration's accomplishments. The president must demonstrate tangible results to promises made or problems solved, deny that a problem is in fact a problem or clearly place blame for a problem on a single individual or group. Actions often speak louder than results. To propose a constitutional amendment to balance the budget even though such a proposal would never be taken seriously is to at once fulfill a campaign promise and to place blame if not accepted. For every action, there is an official interpretation that must be provided.

Despite the appearance of an almost limitless number of strategy options, Trent and Friedenberg are correct in claiming that there are several major disadvantages of incumbency campaigning.[23] First, as already mentioned, presidents must run on their record. All actions or interactions must be explained and justified. Naturally, the challenger will blame the incumbent for all ills and problems of the nation. As the total presidential campaign period lengthens, challengers literally have years to question, second-guess, and negate the efforts of the current president. In the real world and especially in politics, there seldom are complete victories. Most victories are partial and it becomes demoralizing for every effort to be criticized or questioned. Finally, the news media create a climate of expectations, conflict, and excitement during a campaign. There is a great deal of pressure associated with being the incumbent. The United States traditionally favors the underdog and a good fight. Thus, there are more restrictions on behavior and performance pressure associated with the incumbent than with the challengers.

Challenger Strategies

When campaigning against an incumbent president, challengers must take the offensive position in a campaign. Every action, issue, and stance of the president is questioned, challenged, and sometimes ridiculed. This often goes beyond simply attacking the record of the incumbent. Moreover, probing and questioning seldom result in the presentation of concrete solutions. John Kennedy never provided the details about the New Frontier, nor did Nixon elaborate on how he would end the war in Vietnam, nor did Reagan outline how he would end inflation. In fact, being too specific can lead to counterquestions and attacks. For example, in 1972 McGovern provided the details of a tax plan and guaranteed income that caused many problems. Mondale's call for higher taxes virtually ended any hopes for a close race in 1984. Clinton promised universal health care, with specific plans to follow. In 2000, George W. Bush and Al Gore spoke in grand terms of how to save social security. In fact, most contemporary candidates articulate broad policy hopes and desires and avoid offering specific policy details.

Most of the time, challengers call for a change in direction and leadership. They emphasize optimism for the future and share a vision of future prosperity and peace. According Trent and Friedenberg, an equally important task is to persuade voters that the challenger is indeed the candidate most likely to generate change and favorable policies.[24]

Challengers focus their appeals on traditional values, as did Carter in 1976 (honesty, self-rule, humility, morality); Reagan in 1980 and 1984 (free enterprise, capitalism, democracy, and moral courage); Clinton in 1996 (stronger families, smaller and more efficient government, and strong economy); and George W. Bush in 2000 (favor amendment against same-sex marriage, favor parental consent for abortions, against partial birth abortion, favor faith-based initiative). Challengers must also attack the records of the incumbent and take offensive positions on issues. The latter is simply "probing, questioning, challenging, attacking, but never presenting concrete solutions for problems."[25]

Finally, challengers must create constituency groups and will always claim to speak for the forgotten American, the silent majority, and middle America. This transforms into a strategy of articulating the values and feelings of an average American; the philosophical center is the road to follow.

The Campaign Promise and Issues

An important feature of U.S. politics is the campaign promise. In theory, an elected official is obligated to fulfill promises made during a campaign as a result of the electoral mandate. Despite jokes about campaign promises, each election generates countless promises from candidates. To demonstrate the seriousness with which they are made, Carter's transition team compiled a 114-page listing of his 1976 campaign promises. But promises are difficult to keep or fulfill. In 1980 Reagan promised to reduce federal spending, to cut federal taxes, to reduce inflation, to balance the federal budget, and to increase defense spending. By 1984, Reagan's federal budget had the highest deficit in U.S. history. In fact, all presidential candidates have promised to balance the federal budget since 1976. Only Bill Clinton, in the budget year 1999 was able to achieve this promise with the help of a Republican-dominated Congress. In 2000, Bush made good on his promise of tax cuts. However, his efforts to address the issue of social security in 2004–2005 met with stiff resistance.

Some might argue that the fulfillment of three out of five major campaign promises is not a bad record. Of course, a .600 batting average would be incredible; on the other hand, for test purposes 3 out of 5 represents a score of 60 percent—a failing mark by most standards. Others would argue that even to promise reduced federal spending and a balanced budget reflects supreme naivete. Regardless, keeping campaign promises is a difficult task, and their fulfillment depends upon the cooperation of others. Few promises can be met with a simple presidential declaration. The public today recognizes that politicians as a group seldom deliver their promises.

With the length of today's campaigns, candidates must develop issue positions and alternatives nearly two years out from an election. Most campaigns develop an issue notebook prepared by policy experts, former officials, and academics. When events happen, revisions and updates are made.[26]

From a communication perspective, there are four observations about campaign promises. First, the degree of importance attached to a promise depends on how much the fulfillment of the promise affects each of us. Thus, of the promises made during a campaign, only those relevant to us as a group or as individuals are to be remembered. Second, what constitutes fulfillment of a promise is likely to be an attempted action rather than a complete fulfillment of the promise. To lower inflation by 1 percent is to fulfill the promise of lowering inflation but may be of little real value in economic terms. The issue of what determines fulfillment of a campaign promise, then, is a matter of interpretation and campaign debate. Third, it is best not to make specific promises that may come back to haunt the candidate in future elections. That's why value statements are better than issue statements. Finally, there is indeed a rhetoric of campaigning that differs from a rhetoric of governing. One is the rhetoric of hope, promise, and certainty; the other is one of negotiation, persuasion, and compromise.

The Basic Stump Speech

Local appearances by candidates demand a few appropriate remarks. With the frequency of travel and the nature of national campaigning, candidates develop a series of speech modules resulting in a basic campaign speech, often called the "stock speech."[27] The stock speech is not just one speech. Rather, it contains *units* tailored to the specific audience, but the core themes remain the same for each speech.

Campaigns will generally develop a speech module on each of the major issues or likely policy questions confronting candidates. For example, in 1992, the Clinton campaign developed over 30 speech modules on topics ranging from AIDS to welfare reform.[28] Each module is an independent two- to seven-minute speech unit that can easily be incorporated into a larger speech. According to Robert Friedenberg, most modules are organized around three key points and follow a similar pattern.[29] They open with a typical attention-getting device or identify a problem, which is followed by a brief discussion of the problem; they conclude with a presentation of the candidate's proposed solution to the problem. Often, as part of the solution phase of the module, candidates will visualize the problem—along with a full exploration of its detailed impact.

The basic campaign speech has four purposes.[30] First, the basic speech defines the crucial issues of the campaign. Most issues fall within the areas of policy issues, personal issues, or leadership issues. Issues in campaigns also display similar characteristics. They tend to be very broad, be small in number, lack definition, and are seldom defined in terms that will arouse controversy. Also, campaign issues are often linked to claims about the personal qualities of the opponent. Finally, some issues are localized; for instance, education for the South, unemployment for the Northeast, farming for the Midwest, and environmental protection for the West.

The second purpose of a basic campaign address is to identify and emphasize the failures of the opposition. Here the opponent's past issue positions, actions, and voting records are used to demonstrate either a lack of ability to lead or a lack of proper issue positions. The speech must at least attempt to show why the opponent should not obtain or no longer hold the office. Statements concerning actions, positions, or personal characteristics are offered as evidence of failure.

Another important purpose of the basic campaign speech is to appeal to the audience. This is achieved through style and substance of the address. Stylistically, the candidate hopes to use common words and phrases unique to the geographical area. The goal is to give the appearance of being one of the locals, sharing their concerns and speaking their language. Dress is also a part of this process. When speaking to farmers, candidates often wear jeans and shirts without ties.

Finally, the basic campaign speech offers a vision of the future. The vision is usually a carefully constructed articulation of the American dream: a world of peace, prosperity, justice, and equality. The vision often involves evoking a sense of duty and obligation to make the future better than the present for the sake of our children and grandchildren. The vision portion of the speech need not be logical but rather uplifting and inspiring.

For the basic speech, the speechwriter will depend upon poll data or intended audiences for guidance to determine the important issues. Focus groups can be used to test key ideas and phrases as well as to discover the best ways to handle certain issues rhetorically. Often the speechwriting staff will include an audience analysis unit and a research unit.

Although the major issues of the campaign have long been decided, the basic stump campaign speech is truly a localized affair; this is in part because meeting the public face-to-face has become an important part of presidential politics. For the local population attending the campaign event and hearing the candidate in person, the information is new and appears spontaneous. Such events, however, hold little interest for the national news reporters traveling with the candidate. They hear the basic speech hundreds of times. What interest them most are the question-and-answer exchanges that follow most addresses. Here the candidate may show unexpected emotion, share a new statement or position, or stimulate some newsworthy event. This means that, although the basic speech is given over and over again, the national audience is unlikely to hear it. Nevertheless, with an eye toward coverage in the evening news, the candidate may begin the address with offering a timely retort or challenge to the opponent. Journalists, therefore, pay attention to the beginning of each speech for any new charge, allegation, or issue discussion, and wait for their chance for the give-and-take of post-speech question-and-answer sessions.

It is important for candidates to stay on message, especially in today's 24/7 news environment. It is also important for candidates to deliver the stump speech with great enthusiasm each and every time delivered. They are always facing a new audience, with cameras and reporters waiting for a misstatement or some anomaly. They need to be fully involved at all times.[31] In fact, according to Nelson Polsby and Aaron Wildavsky, the news media, not the public, are the immediate audience for much of what candidates say and do while campaigning. Democratic media consultant, Robert Squier, recalls,

> if you discount travel time, I'd say that the media take a third of a candidate's entire day. It's not just the news conferences, but one-on-one interviews, hotel room press briefings, radio and TV shows, editorial board discussions, back-of-the-car interviews and conversations.[32]

Candidates must always try to get positive media attention. Oftentimes, the amount of coverage, tone, or slant of a story depends on how reporters regard the candidates. Working relations with staff and reporter impressions do impact coverage. Polsby and Wildavsky observe:

> Little things, such as phasing news to meet the requirements of both morning newspapers and the evening network news shows, or supplying reporters with human-interest material, can be helpful to candidates. The personality of the candidates, their ability to command the respect of the sometimes rather jaded men and women assigned to cover them, may count heavily.[33]

News Media Considerations

We have already examined news media in great detail, primarily in chapter 5. However, there are several special considerations when considering the role of the print and broadcast press in presidential campaigns. Although there is a three-way interaction among candidates, journalists, and voters, news coverage of political campaigns are ongoing negotiation among key actors. This includes journalists, editors, and owners on the one hand, with candidates, campaign staffers, and party activists on the other.[34] Each actor desperately wants to control the news story: the questions, the responses, the hook or slant. John Zaller theorizes that the more a candidate's campaign attempts to control the coverage, the more journalists will resist and report something different.[35] Zaller refers to this process as "the rule of product substitution." Journalists want to create and sell a product, but when the candidate attempts to control coverage, the journalists substitute the product with their own.

Voters prefer direct exposure to the candidates rather than news punditry or filtered and reworked sound bite versions of the candidate's remarks. Television focuses more on strategy and provides more analysis and interpretation than newspaper coverage. In the past 20 years, there has been a distinct rise in interpretive reporting in both print and television coverage. From the reporters' perspective, they are attempting to provide context, more thorough information for audience understanding. With the 24/7 news environment of today's cable news networks, entire programs are developed around talking heads offering opinions and commentary. Wayne Steger found that media have the most influence in the primary phase of campaigns when voters are seeking candidate information. He also found that front-running candidates receive more media coverage than others.[36]

Finally, especially in presidential campaigns, media generated polls drive coverage. According to June Rhee, all too often, news organizations would treat very small changes in poll numbers as major changes reflecting on candidate status. She also found that the larger the changes in poll numbers, the more media attention ensued, and when poll data are used, the more likely the focus of the story is on campaign strategy.[37] Neither, however, increases voter knowledge or information in comparing candidates.

Debates

Presidential debates are an expected element of presidential campaigns. Historically and mythically, the Lincoln–Douglas debate of 1858 provided the precedent for the debating of political issues. But the Kennedy–Nixon debates of 1960 firmly established the debates as a part of presidential politics. In fact, the 1960 presidential debates attracted the largest television audience (at that point in history) of over 100 million viewers. Historically, incumbent presidents viewed debating opponents as too risky. Gerald Ford became the first incumbent president to debate his opponent, Jimmy Carter. Four years later, Carter also debated his challenger, and the tradition has continued until today. However, it is interesting to note that incumbents Ford, Carter, and George H. Bush lost their reelection bids with only Reagan, Clinton, and George W. Bush winning a second term. Both Reagan and Clinton performed well in their debate challenges. Debates were more challenging for George W. Bush. In fact, most news pundits awarded 2 of 3 debate victories to both Al Gore and John Kerry over George W. Bush, thus proving that while important, one can still win the election without "winning" the debates.

Television has had the greatest impact on the form and content of presidential debates. According to Susan Hellweg and her colleagues:

> The demands of television have dictated the structure and formats of contemporary debates and . . . the visual content of presidential debates plays an important role in the way candidates exercise influence in televised debates. Television manifests a unique symbol system, which fundamentally shapes what is communicated to receivers, apart from content, and has changed the very nature of presidential debate discourse.[38]

Thus, today's debates are an interesting combination of the old and the new.[39] The common audience, opposing candidates, time limits, right to rebut, and agreed-upon rules are vestiges of traditional debate. Multiple topics, question-and-answer formats, and use of interrogating reporters are contributions from press conferences. Television technology has contributed various production techniques and time constraints as well. Television does more than simply carry the debate, the medium is an element of the debate.

By the 1980s, there were numerous complaints about debates and the traditional format: lack of time for sufficient depth of discussion, lack of direct interaction among candidates, less relevant questions from journalist, and insufficient time for follow-up questions. Some more recent innovations in format include: a single moderator, a town-hall format with citizen participation, and roundtable candidate conversations. Citizens tend to prefer a single moderator, a focus on issues of relevance to general public, and the town-hall format.[40]

Debates have several benefits for the electorate. They provide an opportunity to compare the personalities and issue positions of the candidates in a somewhat spontaneous setting. They also invite serious consideration and attention to the campaign and the candidates, thus stimulating voter interest in the election. Finally, they certainly increase candidate accountability. What candidates say, support, and promise becomes a matter of record for future evaluation. However, contemporary presidential debates are not as freewheeling or spontaneous as most voters think. They are as planned, rehearsed, and constructed as any other speech, commercial, or public presentation. The candidates place a great deal of importance on the debates. Image definition and confirmation is supreme to issue development and debate. Campaign staff lobby hard with news organizations to insure no surprises for their candidates.

To get candidates to even debate requires a great deal of negotiation. In the debates of 1976, the issues of lighting, staging, position of cameras, use of reaction shots, camera movement, and the height of the podiums became major points of discussion and negotiation between the candidates prior to agreeing to debate.[41] In the 1980 debates, an issue of discussion was whether or not the candidates would sit or stand. Carter favored sitting while Reagan favored standing. The compromise was to have stools for both candidates such that if seated the candidate would still appear to be standing. In 1992, the Commission on Presidential Debates suggested a new format, 90-minute debates with a single moderator. President George H. Bush preferred the traditional panel of questioners. In the end, there were three debates with three different formats: a panel of reporters, a talk show format with audience questions, and the combination of single moderator and panel of reporters.[42] One of the major issues of negotiation for the 1996 presidential debates was whether or not to allow independent candidate Ross Perot to participate. Dole wanted to debate Clinton one-on-one, while Clinton was more concerned about utilizing the town-hall format for the debates. In the end, both candidates got their wish. Perot was barred from the debates and the town-hall format was used for one of the two confrontations.[43] This last example demonstrates the immense power of the news media to determine viable presidential candidates; Perot had taken 19 percent of the vote in the previous presidential election. In 2000, Gore wanted three 90-minute debates to be carried on all networks. Bush countered that Gore had said "anywhere, any time," and suggested one debate on NBC with one moderator, another debate with Larry King on CNN, and a final debate in the traditional format Gore wanted. In 2004, the Bush and Kerry campaigns issued a 32-page memorandum of understanding detailing the ground rules of the debates. One of the rules restricted television cutaway shots to any candidate not responding to a question. However, the networks ignored the provision. In fact, the cochairs of the Commission on Presidential Debates refused to sign the memorandum, calling the document "unenforceable."[44] Campaigns will always want to control as much as possible, but in the future, the question is who becomes the enforcer of rules—campaigns, networks, or the Commission on Presidential Debates?

Are such issues, irrelevant to running the nation and fixing current problems, really important? Most campaign organizations believe they are, and there is a growing body of research to support such conclusions. For example, one study of the 1960 presidential debates reports that those listening to the debates on the radio thought neither candidate won the debates but those watching the debates on television thought Kennedy clearly won the debates.[45] Robert Tiemens, in investigating factors of visual communication in the 1976 presidential debates, found that differences in camera framing and composition, camera angle, screen placement, and reaction shots seemingly favored Carter.[46] In 1992, George H. Bush's lack of adaptation to the more informal town-hall debate format and the lack of awareness of camera shots greatly hurt perceptions of his debate performance. To the audience, he appeared distant and even impatient. Of course, Clinton was master of the town-hall format. He would walk away from the podium, approach the person asking a question and make eye contact, with the camera following every move.

Debate preparations are elaborate, especially since 1980. Many months in advance, most campaigns form a Debate Task Force that negotiates formats, prepares briefing materials, conducts research, develops debate strategies and tactics, and provides professional consultation on presentational aspects of the debates. Candidates usually spend two to three days prior to the debates practicing in front of knowledgeable panelists. At the debates, campaigns establish an Operations Center where as many as 50 researchers carefully monitor each statement to see if errors are committed or if contradictory or false statements are made. Throughout the debate, the Operation Centers print out statements for the press of any misstatements by the opponent.

Edwin Diamond and Kathleen Friery argue that perhaps the media coverage is more important than the actual debates. Debates attract a large quantity of news coverage and analysis. Diamond and Fiery identify five media themes of debate coverage.[47] First, the media begin weeks in advance "signaling the big event." Issues, strategies, preparation, and negotiation are discussed in print and broadcast. There is a great deal of speculation as to the role and importance of the debates. The week before the event all the networks engage in a lot of self-promotion in coverage and analysis. The countdown begins and dominates all newscasts and front pages of national and local newspapers. Second, the media spend a great deal of time "picking the winners and losers." They speculate on who won and why and what impact the outcome will have. This analysis function has led to the development of the use of spin doctors, campaign professionals who attempt to shape media interpretation of campaign events. After debates, each candidate places spinners in front of TV cameras, proclaiming victory and stressing points scored. The third media theme is that of "assessing the candidate's appearance." This includes special stories on the candidates' performances on such items as oral competence, personality, and image. Even such aspects as candidate nervousness and ability to handle questions are noted. The focus of such stories is on the style of performance rather than the issues discussed. A fourth theme tends to focus on the "debate as theatre." Journalists want excitement, drama, and confrontation. The language of reporting the event reflects the need for vivid commentary. Comments using such terms as "stinging-attacks," "dullness," and "striking a death blow," are common. The athletic, fight image of the event pervades most commentary. Finally, Diamond and Friery add the theme of "avoiding the facts." The press is so concerned with reporting impressions of the debate that it fails to report enough facts of the debate. Television is an especially poor medium for the presentation of facts and pure information. Diamond and Friery's general concerns about the coverage of debates include the inability of reportage to advance knowledge of what is said, separating the viewer from the central enlightening purpose of debates, and a general lack of balance coverage.

From a strategic perspective, the most successful debaters are those most able to:

- direct their remarks at highly targeted audiences;
- develop an overall theme throughout the debate;
- avoid specifics and make use of proven safe responses;
- present themselves as vigorous, active leaders;
- foster identification of themselves with national aspirations;
- foster identification of themselves with the dominant political party/philosophy; and
- personify themselves as exemplifying a desirable characteristic.[48]

From the famous Nixon–Kennedy debates of 1960, much research has been done on the impact or effects of presidential debates. Some of the findings are contradictory. However, it is important to remember that debate effects are more than the outcome of any specific debate and cannot be viewed outside the context of the total campaign environment. Nevertheless, the principle effect suggests that they play more of a confirmatory than persuasive role in voter decision making. Predebate preferences tend to crystallize opinions and confirm voting decisions. Preference reinforcement tends to be the major effect when candidates amplify major themes, when viewers discuss the debate with others, and when candidate performance corresponds to poll position and public expectations of candidates. Thus, few voters change their opinions to favor a different candidate after a debate.

However, they can be most important during the primary season when citizens are less committed to specific candidates. Some research indicates that debates may have influence on undecided voters and provide some issue information, but most voter impressions revolve around candidate image and character rather than issue stances. In addition, postdebate analysis by the media generates the most influence on voter perceptions of winners and losers.

Most scholars agree that debates do focus audience attention on the pending election and increase audience attention of the candidates. For some voters, debates can increase knowledge of issues and issue positions of candidates. Other findings in the research literature include:[49]

- Debates have more influence in races where one of the candidates is unknown, when voters are undecided, when races are close, and when party allegiances are weak.
- Debates have more influence with voters who are highly interested in the race.
- Debates are information-rich and provide issue knowledge to viewers. However, studies show that most issue learning occurs from the first debate with less knowledge acquired from subsequent debates.
- Debates influence viewer perceptions of candidate character or image traits.

- Debate viewing promotes civic engagement and the electoral process.
- Between Labor Day and Election Day, debate-related news stories are among the most frequent of all campaign stories.
- Newspapers better reflect content and exchanges in debates than television news.
- News reports about the debate are more influential than the actual debate in terms of impact on public perceptions of who won and who lost.
- Debates force candidates to focus their message, respond to opponents' charges, and encourage them to be more introspective.
- There are fewer candidate attacks in the town-hall debate format.

There are numerous strategies and tactics one can use during debates. Each one must be carefully analyzed to assess the potential gain or loss for the candidate. Trent and Friedenberg identify several debate strategies.[50] Prior to the debate, campaigns attempt to *lower expectations* of candidate performance. It is better to exceed media predictions and public expectations of performance than to do well but be expected to do well. Related to this strategy, campaigns engage in *mind games* to set up their opponent. Public statements about debate strategy or issues are often designed to mislead or misdirect opponents and influence their debate preparations and expectations. In the meantime, campaigns determine their primary audience and message points. Candidates will then spend several days preparing for the debate, practicing potential questions and responses to opposition attacks. During the debate, candidates want to make sure they *continually mention their issues and campaign themes*. They also want to *reinforce images of leadership, create opportunities of audience identification, and reflect desired character personality traits*. After the debate, surrogates for the candidates *proclaim victory* and attempt to put their special "spin" on the debate.

Summary

As we noted in chapter 8, political campaigns are primarily communication events. Presidential campaigns are a long, nearly continuous version of these communication events. The burden is on the candidate to appear presidential, capable, and worthy of trust and confidence.

The preprimary is when most of the candidate creation takes place. During this period the public is more susceptible to the ideas and arguments of future candidates. The groundwork for the campaign is carefully planned and constructed during this period. For most Americans, though, the political season really begins during the primary period. The period tests the fabric of the candidates, the depth of their views, and the dimensions of their persona. Election interpretations and presentations are most important during this period.

Presidential campaigns follow rather predictable patterns. There are a limited number of issues, images, tactics, and strategies that are available for any campaign. Today, as never before, the tools of marketing and research are the instruments of electoral victory. American presidential politics is not based on issue development as much as on specified images, visions, and persona targeted to identified and segmented audiences.

Most campaign strategies are designed to do more than get votes. They are designed to project a certain image, alter a perception, or counter the opposition. Communication is at the heart of every campaign strategy. Strategies can be grouped according to whether the candidate is an incumbent or challenger. In terms of presidential politics, the incumbent has many more strategy options than challengers. From the strategies, the promises, the basic speeches, and even the acceptances of victory and defeat, the rhetorical patterns are predictable in both form and content. In the end a president is elected who must confront new communication challenges.

The challenge for the future was clearly articulated in a press conference the day after the landslide defeat of Walter Mondale in 1984. In running against Reagan, Mondale acknowledged the day after the election at a press conference that he was at a distinct disadvantage in the television age.

> Modern politics requires mastery of television. I think you know that I've never warmed up to television, and it's never warmed up to me. By instinct and tradition I don't like these things [said while twisting the television microphones in front of him]. I don't believe it's possible to run for president without the capacity to communicate every night.

Mondale continued his observations about the impact of television on the quality of a presidential campaign:

> American politics is losing its substance. It is losing the debate on merit. It's losing the depth that tough problems require discussion. More and more it is those 20-second snippets. I hope we don't lose in America this demand that those of us who want this office must be serious people of substance and depth and must be prepared not to handle the 10-second gimmick that deals with things like war and peace.

Despite the problems and ills of our presidential election process, it's still important for citizens to participate and vote. Whether we like it or not, the results of every election impact our future. Presidents determine foreign and domestic policy, appoint justices to the Supreme Court that influence public policy for decades, and set our national agenda. Pragmatically, every election is important, and every vote counts.

Notes

[1] Dennis Johnson, "First Hurdles: The Evolution of the Pre-primary Stages of American Presidential Elections," in *Winning Elections with Political Marketing*, ed. Philip Davies and Bruce Newman (New York: The Haworth Press, 2006), 184.

[2] Ibid., 184–185.

[3] Judith S. Trent and Robert V. Friedenberg, *Political Campaign Communication*, 5th ed. (Lanham, MD: Rowman & Littlefield, 2004), 21–36.

[4] Ibid., 22.

[5] Johnson, "First Hurdles," 187.

[6] Ibid., 179.

[7] Scott Keeter and Cliff Zukin, *Uniformed Choice* (New York: Praeger, 1983), 6.

[8] Ibid., 8.

[9] Kathleen Kendall, *Communication in the Presidential Primaries* (Westport, CT: Praeger, 2000), 93.

[10] Ibid., 92–93.

[11] Nelson Polsby and Aaron Wildavsky, *Presidential Elections*, 11th ed. (Lanham, MD: Rowman & Littlefield, 2004), 100.

[12] Ibid., 108.

[13] David Smith and Dan Nimmo, *Cordial Concurrence: Orchestrating National Party Conventions in the Telepolitical Age* (New York: Praeger, 1991), 218.

[14] Ibid.

[15] Trent and Friedenberg, *Political Campaign Communication*, 54–60.

[16] Smith and Nimmo, *Cordial Concurrence*, xiv–xv.

[17] Henry Ewbank, "Public Statements Concerning Campaign Strategies." Paper presented at the Annual Central States Speech Association Convention, Lincoln, NE, April 8, 1983.

[18] Ibid.

[19] Lynda Kaid and Anne Johnston, *Videostyle in Presidential Campaigns* (Westport, CT: Praeger, 2001).

[20] Ibid., 287.

[21] Jean Elshtain, "Issues and Themes in the 1988 Campaign," in *The Elections of 1988*, ed. Michael Nelson (Washington, DC: Congressional Quarterly Press, 1989), 111, 126.

[22] Trent and Friedenberg, *Political Campaign Communication*, 81–99.

[23] Ibid., 98–99.

[24] Ibid., 99.

[25] Ibid., 101.

[26] Polsby and Wildavsky, *Presidential Elections*, 147.

[27] Robert Friedenberg, *Communication Consultants in Political Campaigns* (Westport, CT: Praeger, 1997), 74.

[28] Ibid., 76.

[29] Ibid., 76–77.

[30] Lenny Reiss and Dan Hahn, "The Dichotomous Substance and Stylistic Appeals in Kennedy's 1980 Basic Speech." Paper presented at the Annual Convention of Eastern Communication Association, Pittsburgh, PA, April 24, 1981.

[31] Polsby and Wildavsky, *Presidential Elections*, 174.

[32] As cited in Ibid., 143.

[33] Ibid., 153.

[34] Girish Gulati, Marion Just, and Ann Crigler, "News Coverage of Political Campaigns," in *Handbook of Political Communication*, ed. Lynda Kaid (Mahwah, NJ: Erlbaum, 2004), 237.

[35] As cited in Amy McKay and David Paletz, "The Presidency and the Media," in *Handbook of Political Communication*, ed. Lynda Kaid (Mahwah, NJ: Erlbaum, 2004), 317.

[36] As cited in Ibid., 320.

[37] As cited in Ibid., 320.

[38] Susan Hellweg et al., *Televised Presidential Debates* (Westport, CT: Praeger, 1992), xxii.

[39] Kathleen Jamieson and David Birdsell, *Presidential Debates* (New York: Oxford University Press, 1988), 118.

[40] Mitchell McKinney and Diana Carlin, "Political Campaign Debates," in *Handbook of Political Communication Research*, ed. Lynda Kaid (Mahwah, NJ: Erlbaum, 2004), 220.

[41] Robert Tiemens, "Television's Portrayal of the 1976 Presidential Debates: An Analysis of Visual Content," *Communication Monographs* 45 (1978): 362–370.

[42] Robert Friendenberg, "The 1992 Presidential Debates," in *The 1992 Presidential Campaign: From a Communication Perspective,* ed. Robert E. Denton, Jr. (Westport, CT: Praeger, 1994), 91–92.

43 Robert Friedenberg, "The 1996 Presidential Debates," in *The 1996 Presidential Campaign: From a Communication Perspective*, ed. Robert E. Denton, Jr. (Westport, CT: Praeger, 1998), 101–103.

44 Robert Friedenberg, "The 2004 Presidential Debates," in *The 2004 Presidential Campaign: A Communication Perspective*, ed. Robert E. Denton, Jr. (Lanham, MD: Rowman & Littlefield, 2005), 97.

45 Elihn Katz and Jacob Feldman, "The Debates in the Light of Research," in *The Great Debates*, ed. Sidney Kraus (Bloomington: Indiana University Press, 1962), 173–223.

46 Tiemens, "Televisions Portrayal of the 1976 Presidential Debates," 370.

47 Edwin Diamond and Kathleen Friery, "Media Coverage of Presidential Debates," in *Presidential Debates*, ed. Joel Swerdlow (Washington, DC: Congressional Quarterly Press, 1987), 43–51.

48 Friedenberg, "The 1996 Presidential Debates," 104.

49 McKinney and Carlin, "Political Campaign Debates," 203–219.

50 Trent and Friedenberg, *Political Campaign Communication*, 283–292.

Congressional and Senatorial Campaigns

In my experience, the vast majority of members of Congress are there because they want to make America a better place, but most Americans ... believe they're there to enrich themselves. Just as important, people aren't interested in hearing only about problems; they also want to hear about solutions. So know what you want to accomplish and be straightforward about it—Americans can spot phoniness amazingly quickly.

—Lee Hamilton, member of Congress for 34 years

Congressional and senatorial campaigns have become highly professional. Much of the structure, tasks, strategies, and tactics of presidential campaigns are utilized in congressional and senatorial campaigns. Thus, the campaign basics presented in chapter 8 on campaign planning, management, and strategies as well as the tactics of presidential campaigns in chapter 9 are applicable to legislative campaigns. Likewise, some of the activities discussed in the next chapter, focusing on local and state campaigns, are also used in congressional campaigns as well. In this chapter we highlight some of the more unique features of legislative electoral contests.

Congressional contests are actually very local races for a national office. Candidates are persons you may see on local or national television as well as at your neighborhood grocery store. Serving in Congress is a difficult job. While in Washington, representatives review and enact legislation. While at home, they attend countless functions, explain their votes, and continually raise funds. They attempt to portray themselves as working on behalf of their constituencies; sometimes, they attempt to separate themselves from the more common national views of politicians and the institution of Congress.

Campaigns are very important to the outcomes of congressional elections. As Paul Herrnson argues, "National conditions are significant, but their impact on elections is secondary to the decisions and actions of candidates, campaign organizations, party committees, organized interests, and other individuals and groups."[1] In addition, candidates themselves, not political parties, ideologies, or (rarely) national issues are the focus of congressional campaigns. This is why party fortunes infrequently influence specific congressional races. Some argue that this forces congressional candidates to focus on issues and themes of their constituencies rather than those of party leaders or even the president. Thus, above all else, congressional races are candidate-based.

Candidate-Centered Campaigns

The very nature of congressional races makes them candidate centered. Herrnson argues that a successful congressional candidate is likely to be one with "strategic ambition."

> The combination of a desire to get elected, a realistic understanding of what it takes to win, and an ability to assess the opportunities presented by a given political context, is one such characteristic that distinguishes most successful candidates for Congress from the general public.[2]

Yet, despite the money spent on congressional campaigns, voters base their decision on considerably little information. For instance, in most races, only 20 percent of voters can recall the names of the candidates.[3] Of course, incumbents enjoy the major advantage of name recognition among voters. Most voters base their decision on three factors: incumbency, partisanship, and the relative state of the nation, which for some translates to presidential approval.[4] In general, if the public is content, incumbents, regardless of party, are very safe. If the public is not, as in the 2006 elections, incumbents dangle in the wind.

Incumbents

For most congressional elections, the question for voters is simply whether the incumbent should be removed from office. In effect, all elections are referendums on the incumbent. However, unlike most all other elections, congressional elections are the most predictable. Incumbents win in large numbers. The number of competitive congressional contests has declined, especially since 1996. However, the margin of party control in both houses has narrowed as well. As a result, party organizations, political action committees (PACs), and special interest groups focus their attention and support on fewer and fewer races. Naturally, the most activities are targeted for those races that would potentially influence party control of the Congress (or Senate).[5]

One major reason for such stability is redistricting. Every 10 years states must reapportion or redistrict House seats based on population growth and shifts. The party in power in the state legislature can enhance their prospects for new seats or preserve current incumbents. The Republicans did such a good job in 2000 that many congressional seats have remained stable. Of course, in 2006, Democrats took back the House and the Senate. The Iraq war and the unpopularity of President Bush played a large role in changing control of the legislature.

Another reason for the stability is what Michael Burton and Daniel Shea call "retrospective voting," the notion that elections depend on precampaign events.[6] Congressional representatives are always campaigning. They "do not draw a clean line between time in office and time on the campaign trail."[7] In reality, incumbents are more concerned about maintaining and reinforcing their lead than attempting to gain new voters. Interestingly, most incumbents begin the race with a core vote of 65 percent. According to Herrnson, incumbents who are more likely to be in trouble are those who represent marginal districts, have been implicated in a scandal, failed to keep in touch with voters, or cast too many votes out of line with the desires of their constituencies.[8]

As already mentioned, another important feature of congressional campaigns is that they remain largely "candidate centered." As Gary Jacobson observes, "although national parties have recently expanded their efforts to recruit and finance candidates, most serious congressional aspirants operate, out of choice and necessity, as individual political entrepreneurs."[9] They must instigate their candidacies, have money or raise what's needed, and put together their own campaign organizations. Even given the favorable conditions for Democrats in the 2006 congressional elections, success still relied on the skills of challengers and how they effectively exploited the national mood in the local campaigns. Thus, candidates tend to be self-selected in congressional races rather than selected by the political parties. The candidates themselves are the major focus of congressional campaigns, and they bear the primary responsibilities of the campaign.[10]

Ironically, the members of the House of Representatives are not representative of the American people in terms of income, occupations, religion, gender, or race. Those from law and public service sectors are numerous in number. Those who are wealthy and can afford both the time away from work and self-financing of campaigns are also overrepresented in Congress. For instance, as of 2004, about one in four members of Congress and one in three members of the Senate were millionaires.[11] Only about 1 percent of the general population can lay claim to that level of wealth. Whereas in 2004 the median *household* income in the United States was $43,389,[12] the "current salary (2006) for rank-and-file members of the House and Senate is $165,200 per year."[13] In addition, congressional candidates tend to be much older than the general population.[14]

Challengers

Challengers or nonincumbents who decide to run for Congress tend to fall into several distinct groups. The obvious are prior local or state officeholders. They often have the advantages of name recognition, proven electoral viability, and a constituency base. The "unelected politicians" are those who have significant prior political and campaign experience, but who have never run for public office. These include campaign consultants, former staffers, state and local party officials. Finally, "political amateurs" are those with very little political experience but who run out of a sense of civic duty or because of feelings about a specific issue.[15]

Increasingly, both political parties report difficulty in recruiting candidates for a variety of reasons. Among those most mentioned are the rough and tumble of contemporary campaigns, character assassination, impact on family, the enormous cost of elections, and the general lack of respect for national elected institutions. Although incumbents begin elections with 65 percent of the vote, challengers begin with only 27 percent of potential vote. Thus, challengers must mount aggressive campaigns, build name recognition, give voters reasons for support, and overcome the early advantages of incumbent opponents.

Strategic Context

Increasingly, fewer Americans vote in congressional elections, especially during off-presidential election years. In fact, voter turnout generally drops about 13 percent in off-year congressional elections. Even in presidential election years, voting for congressional offices are 5 percent lower than for the top of the ticket.[16]

We have already acknowledged the importance of incumbency. The fact of the matter is that citizens are reluctant to vote for candidates they do not know anything about. Studies show that the simple knowledge of who candidates are influences candidate choice.[17] As a result, one reason incumbents do so well is partly because voters are more likely to at least remember their names. In addition, because name recognition is so important in terms of voting, a strong correlation exists between money spent in congressional campaigns and who wins. The more spent, the more likely a candidate will become known to voters. This is especially critical for challengers. Generally, those who have sufficient resources to contribute to a challenger recognize the odds of victory and thus are less likely to offer financial support.

Perhaps the major advantage of incumbency is the control of numerous resources for reaching, communicating, and serving constituents. Herrnson argues, "Congress has adapted to the career aspirations of its members by providing them with resources that can be used to increase their odds of reelection."[18] The resources include free postage, multiple district offices, and subsidized travel, not to mention pork-barrel projects for the district, to name just a few items. Meeting district and constituent demands provides opportunities for building credit with constituents. Likewise, incumbents have access to PACs and major donors, resulting in constant and continual fund-raising in nonelection years.

Another advantage of incumbency is the role it plays in discouraging potential opponents. Incumbents discourage opposition or challengers by maintaining an active and visible presence in the district, maintaining the electoral coalition that won the first election, and by frequent contact and friendly gestures to potential rivals. Thus, for incumbents, according to Jacobson, "elections are not merely discrete hurdles to be cleared at regular two-year intervals."[19] Rather, they are "a series of connected events that form part of a 'career in the district' that parallels the career in Washington."[20]

In addition, most incumbents face inexperienced and reluctant challengers who are underfunded and lack the organization to mount a major campaign. Jacobson thinks this is because "politically skilled and ambitious nonincumbents follow rational career strategies."[21] In open-seat elections, those without an incumbent, about half of the candidates have previously held an elective office, while less-experienced candidates comprise a quarter of those challenging incumbent. Furthermore, experienced challengers are more likely to run against incumbents who survived close races in the last election or who are facing their first reelection campaign.[22]

Given such odds favoring an incumbent, why would anyone offer a challenge? In most cases they want to provide some opposition, to make sure the party is represented in the election. Some people run to build name recognition and a following for future races. Others are true believers and run to promote strongly held beliefs and ideological values. A more self-serving motive is to advertise their professions, thinking a run for office generates more subsequent business. Finally, some candidates find the process itself rewarding, providing the opportunity to express views, to meet people, and to participate in the democratic process in an active way.[23]

In congressional campaigns, there are several elements of the social and political contexts that are very influential. The geographic sizes of congressional districts vary greatly. Some districts, such as those in urban areas like New York City, may be as small as less than 10 square miles, while those in rural areas or in states like Alaska could span hundreds of thousands of miles. Thus, the physical size of a congressional district may well present unique challenges. Likewise, the density of population may vary greatly as well. Population spread over large areas makes it challenging to meet voters and to campaign in a traditional way. The geographic size and population of districts impact methods of campaign communication. Some districts may cover several media markets while others a single one. Those encompassing two or more media markets increase the costs of advertising and make voter contact via the media more difficult. The economic base of a congressional district may be an important issue of consideration as well. Within a district, there may be only one major employer or industry while others may have more heterogeneous economies. The economic makeup of the district may well influence issue positions and voting to protect certain jobs and industries. Similarly, the average income of the district influences a host of issue positions from minimum wage to health care, to virtually all government entitlements. Finally, the ethnicity of districts generally determines who runs and who is elected.[24]

With this in mind, Burton and Shea argue that the principal rule for congressional campaigns is "know your district." Candidates must know the district inside and out and "collect data such as electoral histories, survey results, census materials, industrial profiles, reports on local housing patterns and more."[25] They further suggest that the most important electoral features of a congressional district include local political personalities, social demographics, partisan composition, economic conditions, local issues and ideologies, and available political resources.[26]

> [Consultants] take account of electoral histories, ballot design, partisan leanings, social geography, national trends, candidate biographies, policy preferences, issue climates, financial resources, the distribution of media outlets, advertising costs, party organizations, bases of political support, and a host of other political features that are normally deemed relevant to understanding an electoral district.[27]

We have already mentioned the role of redistricting in stabilizing districts for incumbents. However, redistricting can also provide opportunities for challengers because it creates new House seats and changes district boundaries. As a result, some districts become more competitive or less so. The process encourages retirements and thus creates more opportunities for competitive races.[28]

We have also mentioned that in midterm elections, especially when presidents are unpopular or in their second terms, there are better opportunities for challengers. Incumbents of the president's party are blamed for the "sins" of the president. In the wake of Watergate, Republicans lost 49 seats in the House in 1974. Similarly, Democrats lost 52 seats in the House in 1994 largely due to the public's sense of Clinton being out of touch with the American people. In 2006, as already mentioned, the Iraq war and low approval ratings for George W. Bush resulted in Republicans losing control of both houses of Congress.

Finally, congressional elections in presidential contest years also present opportunities for challengers, especially if voters' stances on national issues favor one party over another. During the later 1960s and early 1970s, Vietnam dominated several elections. Over the decades, races have been influenced by such national issues as civil rights, the economy, gender issues, and war. The generally higher voter turnout in presidential years is also a factor in the competitiveness of congressional races.[29]

Campaign Organization

It wasn't until the 1970s that congressional campaigns became more professional in terms of using consultants and specialists.[30] Today virtually all races are managed by paid, professional campaign consultants. In addition, the functions of communication (polling, advertising, etc.), fund-raising, and opposition research are hired positions. Incumbents tend to use the same organization members and structure from previous campaigns. Congressional staffers often take leaves of absence from their jobs to work on campaigns and return to their regular positions after the election. Most of the field activities are conducted by the national political parties, PACs, and trusted volunteers.[31]

Challengers may have only one or two paid staff members and therefore depend primarily on family, friends, and partisan volunteers to serve in organizational functions. If a challenger mounts a viable campaign, state and national party organizations may provide assistance. Specific ways in which state and national parties help congressional candidates are discussed in the next section.

Strategies and Tactics

From a strategic perspective, one usually starts with election day and then "reverse-engineers" the campaign victory

> by designating the week prior to the election for the GOTV [get out the vote] and the week prior to that as an opportunity to refine the campaign's voter lists, and so forth, until the plan reaches back to the present moment in time.[32]

Of course, continuous adjustments are necessary because the political terrain or electoral environment constantly changes.

According to Burton and Shea, "a political professional apprehends a voting district as a conglomeration of voters, demographic characteristics, media markets, neighborhoods, partisan and ideological preferences, long-standing political alliances (and disputes), and other electorally significant features."[33] Electoral rules for successful campaigns include: building strong connections with the electorate, hammering home the opponent's weak points, defying conventional wisdom, gaining the center without losing the base, and preempting the challenge in the first place.[34] Campaign strategy is more important today than it was just several decades ago. As Burton and Shea observe, "with partisanship declining, media consultants on the rise, and campaign operations seeming to pay more and more attention to the demands of the voting public, strategy may well play a heightened role in deciding electoral outcomes."[35]

Communicating with Voters

Most congressional campaigns spend nearly 75 percent of their budget on communicating with voters. Of this amount, nearly 20 percent is allocated for television and an equal percentage to direct mail. Radio expenditures account for about 10 percent and newspaper about 5 percent of the communication budget. The remaining is spent on candidate travel, billboards, yard signs, campaign literature, and get-out-the-vote efforts.[36] In the heat of the campaign, ground war tactics include personal contact along with mail, telephone, and e-mail activities.[37] Direct mail is the mainstay; in competitive races well over a dozen pieces per candidate are sent. In addition, special interest groups may conduct several mailings independent of the candidates running for office.

According to Herrnson, the focus of most advertising in House campaigns is on the candidate's issue positions (45 percent) followed by the candidate's image (25 percent). Surprisingly, just over 10 percent of advertising focuses on the opponent's image (12 percent) or issue positions (11 percent). Of course, these allocations vary greatly depending on whether the candidate is an incumbent, challenger, or running in an open-seat race. For example, challengers focus more on opponent image and issues (21 percent).[38]

Chapters 8 and 9 detailed the strategic use of media during campaigns. There are more considerations and constraints of media usage in congressional campaigns. Television, of course, is the best medium for image presentation and agenda setting. However, television is expensive, and congressional districts may cross several media markets or none at all; yet, nearly 70 percent of House campaigns use television. Radio is a major medium for congressional campaigns. Radio allows candidates to target voters based on listener profiles. Newspaper ads are used primarily for announcing campaign events and last-day get-out-the-vote efforts. Congressional campaigns usually spend more on direct mail than any other form of advertising. Direct mail is used to raise funds, attack the opponent, and to deliver a specific message to a highly targeted group of supporters or likely voters. Counter to popular belief, the most negative and vicious attacks occur in direct mail advertising rather than through television advertising.

Congressional campaigns work hard to generate free coverage of the candidate and the campaign by the news media. Coverage depends on many factors: competitiveness of race, market, news focus of the outlet, and so forth. Among the most common activities in which campaigns engage in their attempt to gain coverage include a steady stream of press releases, press conferences, and editorial board meetings, to name a few. Newspapers and radio are more likely to devote extensive coverage to congressional races than is television. Nevertheless, when candidates participate in events that are visually interesting and action oriented, they are more successful in attracting the attention of local news outlets, especially television.

Candidates who walk through neighborhoods or long distances or who wear special clothing gain media notice. Most people in Virginia remember Oliver North's plaid shirt senatorial campaign of 1994 where he was attempting to appeal to the "average citizen." (Most people had seen Lieutenant Colonel North only in his military uniform.) Likewise, former Senator George Allen, wearing cowboy boots and hat and throwing a football to members of a crowd, provided good video. Witty sound bites are guaranteed to be used in print and broadcast. The media love drama, conflict, and a good fight. Thus, consistent and constant attacks on one's opponent will garner media attention and coverage (both good and bad). Finally, the release of new information or sharing very creative perspectives on issues and topics of concern will likely gain widespread media mentions.

Direct voter contact is especially important for congressional races. Although it may be less efficient in reaching large number of voters, it is very effective on a per voter basis. In fact, it appears that any direct request for support tends to be effective. Even the candidate's family members, friends, volunteers, and party and interest group activists are effective in soliciting voter support. According to Shea, there are several reasons why direct voter contact is valuable. First, contact with the candidate brings the voter to a different cognitive level than other communication contacts. The voter becomes more engaged and attentive when meeting with the actual candidate. Second, direct contact allows two-way communication. Voters value the opportunity to not only meet candidates, but to interact with them. Third, voter interaction humanizes the candidate. Media portrayals of campaigns are less real than face-to-face interaction. Finally, direct voter contact brings more commitment and enthusiasm to a campaign.[39] More detailed strategies and tactics of voter contact will be discussed in the next chapter.

In considering issues, most congressional candidates identify with valence issues such as good schools, strong economy, job growth, safe streets, national security; these issues and positions possess universal agreement. Candidates avoid more controversial or wedge issues. Challengers will often make one issue the centerpiece of their campaign. Economic issues drive congressional races, whether it's positive—low inflation and good jobs—or negative—high unemployment and increased taxes. In general terms, Democrats tend to discuss economic issues in terms of fairness; Republicans center their conversations on growth and opportunity. Political reform is a mainstay of both parties.[40]

Candidate image is important in any campaign. The public will already have some image of an incumbent, based on his or her record, prior speeches, actions, and published statements. Challengers are, of course, less well known than incumbents; however, this provides an opportunity for them to construct a positive public persona. Style is a factor of today's candidate-oriented campaigns as well. How the candidate looks and acts are important in defining the candidate's image. How something is said, how a candidate responds to criticism, and the total demeanor impact candidate image. A third factor influencing candidate image is the political environment. Issues may indeed influence perceptions of candidates, especially from an ideological perspective. For example, close identification with specific issues may portray a candidate as liberal or conservative.

In congressional races, the most successful campaigns incorporate the candidate's persona and policy positions into thematic messages. It is important to link the candidate to common, everyday values of hard work, honesty, and loyalty. Personal anecdotes about accomplishments and professional successes, as well as anecdotes about family, childhood, and life experiences connect with voters. According to Herrnson, good campaign messages are "clear and easy to communicate, short, convey a sense of emotional urgency, reflect voters' perceptions of political reality, establish clear differences between the candidate and the opponent, and are credible."[41] Consultant and strategist Peter Hart identifies the seven "P's of Strategy: performance, professional experience, positioning, partisanship, populism, progressivism and positivity."[42]

Campaigns for open seats create a very different political landscape. Individual candidates are more likely to have survived a heated primary or caucus to achieve the party nomination. Depending on the electoral history of the district, the major campaign could well be the one for the nomination rather than for the general election. In open-seat elections, the candidates do tend to have some experience in elective office and more likely to have sufficient financial backing because both parties are highly involved. Thus, candidates for open seats are generally better known and liked than those candidates who are challengers against incumbents. Party affiliation, national trends, and presidential coattails play a larger role in open-seat elections.[43]

Incumbents and Challengers

Burton and Shea consider congressional incumbents as campaign professionals who are always in the campaign mode, which for them "is a way of life more than a point of discussion." They define the campaign mode as "as state of mind that combines a visceral drive to win with a strategic thinking that maximizes the prospects of electoral victory."[44] The visceral drive is the operative's passion that runs a political race day and night with an intense commitment to electoral success. They define strategic thinking as "the capacity to relate the knowledge of political terrain and campaign rules, often by combining a forward-looking plan with a reverse-engineered vision of electoral success."[45] For them, it is as much an art as a science.

In terms of campaigns, incumbents project a personal home style that is more about relationships than about issues or policy positions. On display is demonstrating a sense of identification with constituents, mutual trust, and continual accessibility. This style of campaigning stresses how issues are addressed as being more important than the issue itself.[46] For this reason, polls generally show that citizens do not like Congress as an institution but love their own congressperson. A standard tactic of incumbents is to completely ignore the opposition; don't mention their names, refuse to debate (or perhaps only once), and never agree to joint appearances. If the challenger grows in strength, the incumbent will attack the inexperience, lack of qualifications, and general naiveté of the challenger. Naturally, it is routine for incumbent campaigns to make frequent references to things done for the district, the value of experience, and seniority in Washington.

The main objective of challengers is to convince voters that they are qualified to serve in office. Some take advantage of any scandal that can be linked to the incumbent, whether excessive junketing, individual political failings, or lack of attention to district concerns. Most often, they attempt to demonstrate that incumbents are simply out of touch with district needs and the citizens.[47] The incumbent is part of "that mess in Washington" and is clearly "out of touch" with the people, needs, and values of the district. Not surprising, challengers portray themselves as caring, hard working, and bringing common sense and experience to the job.

The Republican and Democratic National Committees are somewhat limited in the amount of support they can offer congressional candidates. There are, however, two national party organizations (the Democratic Congressional Campaign Committee and the Republican Congressional Campaign Committee) that help local congressional campaigns with money, services, and advice. These congressional campaign committees offer more direct support. They primarily offer candidate training seminars, providing "talking points" and party platform information. At the national level they raise money, set priorities for the party, recruit candidates, and provide some direct help to specific campaigns.[48]

The committees focus on competitive races. They provide help first to incumbent races facing serious challengers. Second in priority are races perceived as winnable by party challengers. Generally, if the president is popular, the party committee of the president tends to invest more in challenger and open-seat races. The out-party committee tends to allocate more resources to incumbent races. In general, in-party committees tend to take a defensive posture favoring incumbent races and out-party committees tend to be more aggressive favoring challenger races. The list of targeted races are continually reevaluated and revised throughout the campaign season. As a result, some campaigns may lose support while others may gain help.

Committees use several criteria when considering making contributions to a race: competitiveness of district, incumbency, strength of candidate, and if an open seat, to name a few. Of course, committees closely monitor races, and over the course of a campaign, some candidates may receive help throughout the race, while others who received early help may receive less support toward the end of the campaign.

Committees serve as a major source of information for local candidates. They keep lists of consultants and preferred vendors for all campaign activities. They also are involved in training seminars for potential candidates. Historically, the most assistance campaigns receive from national committees is public opinion polling. National committees commission hundreds of polls during a campaign season. They often allocate a few questions for local candidates. As noted in chapter 8, a good showing in a party poll will increase fund-raising potential. Finally, increasingly, national committees provide opposition research for party contestants as well.

Political Action Committees and Special Interests Groups

Outside of campaign technology, the role of PACs has the greatest impact on congressional campaigns. Special interests groups form PACs to provide direct financial support to candidates in order to influence electoral outcomes and, hence, the formation of public policy. PACs tend to fall within four main categories: corporate, labor, trade (includes health care industry), and "nonconnected" (no sponsoring organization—the PAC is the organization itself).

The goal of most PACs is to have access to legislators, especially powerful ones who are in leadership positions on various committees and can impact legislation of interest to the sponsoring organization. Some PACs are ideological, hoping to increase the number of legislators who share their values and views on social issues. From these two broad motives, PACs follow several strategies of influence. Ideological PACs tend to give most of their money to candidates in close races where they have the best chance of influencing the outcome. Access-oriented PACs tend to contribute most of their funds to incumbents and open-seat races.[49] During the 1970s, most PAC support followed rather strict partisan lines. Corporate and trade PACs largely supported Republican candidates and Labor PACs backed the Democrats. Over time, business-oriented PACs have become more concerned about issues of access than issues of ideology. Although limited to donations of $5,000 to each candidate or candidate committee per election, national PACs may make other monetary contributions per calendar year to state, district, and local party committees; to national party committees; and to any other political committee.[50] PACS therefore wield influence in numerous congressional races—often distributing well over $10 million nationwide per election.[51] It is interesting to note the shift in support when leadership changes in the House. The party in power receives the most funding support. With the Republican control resulting from the 1994 elections, PACs gave most of their funds to Republicans, reversing their previous contribution pattern of giving. With the Democratic takeover of Congress in 2006, we should see contribution patterns switch to their favor.

Independent groups, or what we refer to today as the new 527s, were more likely to contribute to Democratic candidates. Among the most loyal groups to the Democrats include MoveOn.org, unions, pro-choice groups, and environmental groups. Republican-leaning groups are medical, pro-life, and business organizations, as well as the NRA and the Club for Growth.[52]

Summary

Although congressional candidates seek a national office, they participate in contests that are very locally oriented. In addition, they are candidate-driven campaigns. Incumbency is the greatest predictor of electoral viability above all else. David Magleby and colleagues find four key characteristics or regularities of contemporary congressional elections.[53] First and foremost, incumbency matters. It brings more advantages to congressional elections than it does to even presidential races. Second, ideological interest groups, such as the Christian Right, face the dilemma of supporting candidates who fully support their positions, but in doing so become less desirable for the general election. Third, local issues still dominate despite national issues or trends. Congressional contests are much more local than senatorial or certainly presidential races. Finally, for candidates who emerge as winners of intense intraparty primaries, the chances of winning the general election are not great—the primary process damages the ultimate winner when facing the general election challenge.

Darrell West and Sandy Maisel conclude that today there is a much wider diversity of organizations that communicate with voters in congressional campaigns. Candidates use to be the dominant communicators, but now there are numerous interest groups and national organizations that get involved.[54] For them, a potential disturbing trend is the ever-increasing targeting of select audiences rather than attempts to communicate to broader segment of voters. They fear broad public interests may be ignored in favor of narrow appeals to special-interest segments of voters. This leads to more parochial appeals and thus may not serve the best interests of a representative democracy.[55]

Also troubling is both parties are finding it more difficult to recruit candidates for local, state, and national offices. Campaigns are time-consuming and difficult activities. Yet, the quality of our government is directly related to the quality of our elected officials.

Notes

[1] Paul Herrnson, *Congressional Elections*, 2nd ed. (Washington, DC: Congressional Quarterly Press, 1998), 2.

[2] Ibid., 30.

[3] Ibid., 158.

[4] Ibid., 160.

[5] David Magleby, J. Quin Monson, and Kelly Patterson, *Electing Congress: New Rules for an Old Game* (Upper Saddle River, NJ: Pearson/Prentice Hall, 2007), 140.

[6] Michael Burton and Daniel Shea, *Campaign Mode* (Lanham, MD: Rowman & Littlefield, 2003), 39.

[7] Ibid., 39.

[8] Herrnson, *Congressional Elections*, 250.

[9] Gary Jacobson, *The Politics of Congressional Elections*, 4th ed. (New York: Longman, 1997), 5.

[10] Herrnson, *Congressional Elections*, 6–7.

[11] "Millionaires Fill U.S. Congress Halls," (June 30, 2004). Retrieved 13 September 2007 from http://www.commondreams.org/headlines04/0630-05.htm

[12] "Median Household Income," Infoplease.com. Retrieved 21 September 2006 from http://www.infoplease.com/ipa/A0104688.html

[13] "Salaries and Benefits of U.S. Congress Members." Retrieved 13 September 2007 from http://usgovinfo.about.com/library/weekly/aa031200a.htm

[14] "Congress." http://www.c-span.org/questions/weekly69.asp

[15] Paul Herrnson,*Congressional Elections*, 2nd ed. (Washington, DC: Congressional Quarterly Press, 1998), 35.

[16] Jacobson, *The Politics of Congressional Elections*, 86.
[17] Ibid., 93.
[18] Herrnson, *Congressional Elections*, 19–20.
[19] Jacobson, *The Politics of Congressional Elections*, 43.
[20] Ibid., 43.
[21] Ibid., 34.
[22] Ibid., 35.
[23] Ibid., 46–47.
[24] Ibid., 14–15.
[25] Burton and Shea, *Campaign Mode*, 3.
[26] Ibid., 8.
[27] Ibid., 8.
[28] Herrnson, *Congressional Elections*, 20.
[29] Ibid., 21.
[30] Ibid., 59.
[31] Ibid., 60–64.
[32] Burton and Shea, *Campaign Mode*, 6.
[33] Ibid., 7.
[34] Ibid., 13.
[35] Ibid., 32.
[36] Herrnson, *Congressional Elections*, 68–69.
[37] Magleby et al., *Electing Congress*, 133.
[38] Herrnson, *Congressional Elections*, 172.
[39] Burton and Shea, *Campaign Mode*, 182–183.
[40] Herrnson, *Congressional Elections*, 172–174.
[41] Ibid., 170.
[42] Ibid., 170.
[43] Ibid., 77.
[44] Burton and Shea, *Campaign Mode*, 5.
[45] Ibid., 5.
[46] Jacobson, *The Politics of Congressional Elections*, 74.
[47] Ibid., 70–71.
[48] Herrnson, *Congressional Elections*, 75.
[49] Ibid., 116.
[50] Federal Election Commission, "Contribution Limits Chart 2007–08." Retrieved 13 September 2007 from http://www.fec.gov/pages/brochures/contriblimits.shtml
[51] Magleby, et al., *Electing Congress*, 16–17.
[52] Ibid., 17.
[53] Ibid., 140–141.
[54] Darrell West and Sandy Maisel, "Conclusion: Discourse and Beyond," in *Running on Empty*, ed. Sandy Maisel and Darrell West (Lanham, MD: Rowman & Littlefield, 2004), 231.
[55] Ibid., 230.

Local and State Campaigns

Politics—good politics—is public service. There is no life or occupation in which a man can find a greater opportunity to serve his community or his country.

—Harry Truman

Running for office at any level is challenging, demanding, exciting, frustrating and, quite simply, life changing. Win or lose, families make sacrifices and there are endless demands on the candidate. Of course, running for office provides the opportunity to provide leadership, address issues of concern, and perform a civic duty. As noted in an earlier chapter, there are over a half million elective offices in the United States. A great deal of attention is given to national and statewide candidates and elections. However, local races follow the same flow, requirements, and considerations of larger state and national elections.

Right or wrong, there is a hierarchy of interests in political campaigns. Not surprisingly, the most attention and interest starts with presidential campaigns, then U.S. senatorial contests, followed by statewide and large-city mayoral races, and then all the rest. In terms of news media coverage, most U.S. congressional races receive little attention compared to other races. Not only does coverage and voter interest vary by the level of the race, so too does the actual voting. According to Daniel Shea and Michael Burton, "Lower-level offices can suffer more than a 40 percent drop-off from the top of the ballot."[1]

Shea and Burton also argue that voters have very distinct and clear expectations of how candidates should act, how they should look, and what issues they ought to address. "Voters seem to match issues to offices and offices to candidate qualities."[2] For executive posts, citizens expect candidates to have leadership skills and abilities to implement programs. In contrast, legislative candidates are expected to relate to the voters. Good constituent service and loyalty to the needs of the locality are valued over general good of the nation as a whole.[3]

Local and statewide politics are retail politics. This means it's about
direct voter contact. It's about meeting voters, talking to voters, and shaking
as many hands as possible: the more local the race, the more retail the
expectation. Direct voter contact is invaluable for several reasons. First,
direct contact with a candidate makes the voter more committed to the candidate and engaged in the campaign. Second, it allows for two-way communication and interaction. Voters can express concerns and ask questions,
thus making them feel important while generating interest in the candidacy
and campaign. Face-to-face contact also humanizes the candidate, allowing a
firsthand observation and evaluation. Studies also show that people are
more likely to vote for a candidate they meet in person, regardless of party
or even issue positions.[4]

In this chapter we highlight some of the unique characteristics, strategies, and tactics of local and statewide campaigns. The basic assumptions
and functions of campaign communication shared in chapter 8 are still true
for lower-level campaigns. However, some communication activities and
objectives differ.

Context of the Race

There are three types of local races: partisan candidate races, nonpartisan candidate races, and issue-based races. Partisan races usually involve primaries or caucuses for candidate selection. And, as the name implies, the
candidate runs with the blessing of the local Democratic or Republican
Party. In nonpartisan races, candidates run independent of local or regional
political party support. The candidate runs on his or her platform and positions on issues. Usually, a nonpartisan race occurs only in the fall election,
and the winner is the one with the most votes. Issue-based races may be generated by a governing body or by a citizen initiative process. These races do
not involve candidates but concern referenda, perhaps to recall an official,
propose a constitutional amendment, or support a bond issue to build a
school, for example.[5]

For Shea and Burton, "no other contextual element has a greater bear-
ing on the outcome of the election than incumbency status."[6] However, the
higher the profile of a race, the less advantage incumbency has. Lower-level
races tend to be less competitive in terms of the number of candidates and
success of challengers. Local and statewide races incorporate more relevant
and specific campaign themes and messages. The themes and messages create relationships with voters and provide a rationale for support. In local
races, issues and candidate positions are directly related to the jurisdiction
of the office. For example, national defense policy has nothing to do with
running for the state legislature or the school board. It is not surprising,
therefore, that the issues and themes in a local race are more specific and
tailored to constituents.

Campaign Organization

The campaign team varies depending on the level and scope of the race, the funds, and the general inclination of the candidate. Some campaigns are virtually a family affair with very little outside help.

Most local and even state-level campaigns form a *campaign committee*. It serves as a support group for the candidate and campaign efforts, as well as being the primary source of expertise. The committee is an insider group consisting of the candidate, the campaign manager, noted community leaders, those who will contribute to the campaign, and trusted friends. This select group offers advice, provides criticism, and serves as a sounding board for strategies and campaign efforts. The number of committee members is usually under 10. The committees often meet weekly, early in the week to provide a look back and forward to activities. The campaign manager leads the meetings.[7]

Generally, the number of full-time staff for most campaigns, ranging from the most local up to congressional, is between five to eight workers. For large-city mayoral, senatorial, and gubernatorial races, paid staff may well reach 20 members.[8] The candidate usually has a secretary—an assistant or aid—who travels with him or her at all times. This person is helpful in recording requests and the names of individuals met, as well as keeping the candidate on time.

Whether a campaign is built around running for president of the United States or for a position on the town council, the campaign manager is the most important position in the campaign. In local races, the campaign manager may be on salary or be a volunteer. Increasingly, campaign managers are being paid and have the only paid position of the campaign. The manager interacts with a variety of groups, people, volunteers, and even the local media. Thus, good communication skills are vital. The manager travels with the candidate to all public functions; serves as confidant, supporter, critic, and top motivator; coordinates all campaign activities; oversees the creation of all campaign literature and advertising spots; helps establish and supervises fund-raising efforts; and develops the overall campaign strategy and message themes.

Volunteers are the lifeblood of local campaigns; they tend to be party loyalists and most have worked on numerous campaigns. They can assist in passing out literature, stuffing envelops, making phone calls, delivering yard signs, and working to keep the headquarters open.

Potential candidates often build alliances many months prior to the actual election. Candidate and staff identify community leaders and organizations that would naturally support the candidacy because of shared views and values. They also identify leaders who are not part of the "natural" base, thereby hoping to expand the candidate's voter block. Such alliances assist in providing advice, financial support, and forming citizens' committees that lend credibility and legitimacy to the campaign.

If volunteers are the lifeblood of local campaigns, money is the required fuel. All campaigns need money, but the size of the campaign budget is critical to local and state elections. Studies continually reveal that in most cases, campaigns with the most money win. From a pragmatic perspective, money allows campaigns to contact or "touch" more voters. Money also allows candidates to hire more and better campaign professionals. In addition, candidates who raise more money are viewed as successful, legitimate and worthy of support. From a tactical perspective, a large war chest discourages challengers.[9]

Usually, key donors and money from PACs and formal organizations provide the start-up and early money necessary to establish a team and organization. The more local the race, the more individual candidates fund the majority of their own campaigns. Campaigns at least start with a budget, ranging from minimum to best-case scenario. They tend to be as comprehensive as possible to include operational costs, organizational costs, campaign activity costs, advertising expenses, and the all important GOTV costs.

Especially in local and state races, direct contact by the candidate requesting financial support from individuals remains the quickest and most effective way to generate funds. This is especially true when soliciting the big, major donors. Candidates routinely set aside dedicated time each day to make solicitation calls. For some candidates, this is the most difficult, even most distasteful part of the campaign. However, direct solicitation of funds is an essential task of all candidates.[10] Some folks will contribute because of personal friendship with the candidate. However, such contributions are framed in terms of issues, goals, and initiatives rather than in terms of a personal favor.

Of course, nearly all campaigns use direct mail to solicit funds. "Reply cards" accompany the solicitation for support; they facilitate donations of time and money. Individuals can volunteer to place yard signs, call friends, stuff envelopes, and so forth.

Campaign Activities

Campaign activities at the local level have three primary purposes: fundraising, volunteer recruitment, and generating voter support. While the activities identified below are part of all campaigns, they are more important and of greater influence in local elections.

- *Special events*—Although these are pegged as "campaign-sponsored activities intended to raise money and support for the campaign,"[11] Shaw notes that special events actually raise very little money and are very time-consuming. Most are attended by supporters, thus lending little assistance in gaining undecided or independent voters. However, if done well, the events may generate publicity, strengthen bonds among volunteers, and generate subsequent commitment to the candidate.[12]

  In order for special events to be successful, they need a defined purpose. Is it to raise money, thank supporters, attract endorsements, etc.? Not only is it important to consider all the details and arrangements, promoting the events will insure a good turnout. A poorly attended event is embarrassing to the candidate and communicates a lack of candidate interest and support.[13]

- *Public appearances*—Potential candidates hit the speaking circuit, visiting local clubs and groups long before any announcement of the forthcoming election. The specific speech topic is not important. The act of speaking before public groups aids name recognition and credibility and, from a pragmatic perspective, allows the candidate to practice speaking to diverse groups and audiences.

Interestingly, William Bike recommends that candidates should dress for where they are going, not where they are. Thus, their attire should normally be business dress for such events. He even thinks it's a mistake for candidates to dress down to match the crowd. "An audience of truck drivers or waitresses is not going to vote for someone just because they dress like they do. But everyone wants to vote for someone who looks like a winner."[14]

- *Dinners*—For local campaigns, sponsored dinners are a traditional and very effective means of fund-raising. Often, a restaurant will provide the dinners at their cost and the campaign sells tickets for usually twice retail price. In contrast to larger campaigns, local ones tend to sponsor several smaller dinners rather than one large event. This allows for more individual contact with the candidate. Dinners hosted by individuals in their homes are also common and effective. Usually a well-known individual from the community will host a high-end, catered meal at his or her own expense. These events are selective in terms of invitees, and the ticket costs are high. A private dinner may well generate several thousand dollars. Well-known state or other local leaders may attend the dinner as incentive for others to attend.[15]

- *Coffees*—Coffees are another excellent way to fund-raise as well as to motivate and activate supporters. Sponsors are usually well known or local leaders who greatly enhance attendance. The primary advantage of coffees is that they can be used throughout the campaign cycle and can be hosted at various times throughout the day, usually mid-morning, late afternoon, or early evening. As with dinners, local campaigns have numerous coffees with a reasonable number of attendees rather than very large ones that limit access and time with the candidate. In addition to fund-raising, coffees provide a great opportunity to solicit volunteers and distribute yard signs to the campaign's most loyal supporters.[16] At coffees, candidates usually explain why they are running, ask attendees for support, answer questions, and inquire about concerns and issues of interests to the guests.[17]

- *Press conferences*—There tend to be fewer, if any, press conferences in local races. The higher the level of the race, the more likely there will be press conferences. Press conferences are useful at all levels as long as they are not overdone. They are most effective when used to announce major themes or programs, to respond to major allegations, or to issue challenges to the opponent. Even in small media markets, a press conference may generate local radio and newspaper coverage. The danger for new or less-experienced candidates is that they may not be fully prepared for the many questions that members of the media will ask. Thus, it is important for candidates to know their subject very well and to "practice" answering anticipated questions. If the candidate is not well prepared, the press conference may actually hurt the candidate.

• *Debates*— Issue information is the primary goal of the debate event. Debates and candidate forums are an essential part of all campaigns and are more numerous in lower-level races. However, the candidates tend to have less experience in such settings, especially with the local media likely in attendance. It is important for candidates to express issue positions clearly; demonstrating an understanding of local issues and telling audience members what he or she will do upon being elected are much more important than simply attacking opponents. In local races, candidates are neighbors and have many friends in common with the voting population. Being too negative will generally backfire. If a candidate decides to attack an opponent, the facts and information disclosed should be true, without any doubt. Thus, coming across as informed while projecting an image of confidence and leadership is most desirable. Of course, today, all candidates have to be ready to be criticized and perhaps even attacked. Prior to any debate, or even campaign, candidate weaknesses are generally well known. No candidate should be caught off-guard. Problematic elements should be addressed and responses practiced as part of any debate preparation. As with national races, local candidates should practice questions and responses prior to any debate.

• *Phone banks*—Phone banks are used throughout a campaign for a variety of purposes: fund-raising, yard sign placements, solicitation of volunteers, and as part of the campaign's GOTV efforts. (We will have more to say about "GOTV" efforts at the end of the chapter.) Usually, volunteers work between one and two hours making phone calls. Each caller has a general script to follow. To avoid receiver aggravation, most calls are made between and 7 and 9 PM. Normally callers complete 20 to 30 calls per hour.

• *Neighborhood walks*—Neighborhood walks include several activities. Canvassing is targeting specific precincts. Using voter lists, the campaign may target voters of the same party, those of the opposition party, or those identified as independent. Targeting those households of the same party is useful to motivate partisans for the candidacy.

Targeting those of opposing party and independents attempts to increase share in a specific precinct. There are two types of canvassing: a "knock" and a "drop." The candidate may or may not participate. Candidates may conduct the walk by themselves or with a volunteer. Candidates should focus their time in "swing" neighborhoods. Candidate walks begin mid- to late summer and continue up to election day. Volunteers usually participate in groups of four, two per house. The "knock" is simply approaching the house and speaking with one or more of voting-age household members. The "drop" is simply leaving a brochure or doorknob flyer at the door.

- *Op-eds and letters to the editor*—Potential candidates and community leaders often write op-ed pieces and letters to the editor even years before running for some local office. This provides visibility for the individual and also frames the person as a community opinion leader. As the campaign progresses, campaign staff members and friends write letters of support for publication in local outlets. Newspaper editors attempt to be fair in publishing letters in terms of relatively equal numbers for all candidates. It is most useful for letters to reinforce key issue positions or address concerns or charges against a candidate. Readers may not recognize the author as a partisan or affiliated with the candidate. The lack of supporting letters in the news outlets generates the appearance of lack of support for a candidacy. Thus, most local campaigns enlist specific individuals throughout the campaign to write letters.

- *Endorsements*—According to Bike, "two or three good endorsements may be worth a thousand campaign speeches."[18] Local and state candidates often seek endorsements from civic groups (Rotary, Chamber of Commerce, Lions, etc.), interest groups (arts, business, anti or pro gun, unions, seniors, etc.), media (primarily local newspapers), political action committees, political officials, organizations, party committees, and community leaders.[19] Shea and Burton report that incumbents generally receive newspaper endorsements and in one study in 2002, 85 percent of all incumbents benefited from newspaper endorsements.[20] The traditional wisdom is that endorsements are more valuable in local and statewide elections and are worth the effort to obtain.

Campaign Literature

The more local the race, the more campaigns rely upon traditional literature to raise name recognition and motivate voters.

- *Brochures*—For local campaigns, a generic brochure is the fundamental piece of campaign literature. It serves as an introductory piece with a short biography, several photos, and key issues of the campaign. For incumbents, the brochure highlights past accomplishments.[21] Brochures are used in neighborhood walks, in direct mail, and as handouts at debates or other activities. Studies still show that red, white and blue are preferred colors by voters and enhance trust and confidence in candidates. Of course, there are good reasons not to use a variation of red, white, and blue. For example, a candidate running in a predominantly ethnic area may select the colors representative of the people's heritage. Another example may be using the colors of a nearby college, university, or high school.[22]

Photos are an important part of the brochure. There is at least one photo of the candidate, several "action" or candidate at work photos, as well as some of the candidate interacting with specific constituent groups—women, workers at a factory, parents, etc.

The message is simple and clear, covering just a few basic themes. Most local campaigns have just one brochure; thus it must provide a quick background of the candidate and an issue or two to motivate support. The challenge is to include enough information to be informative without making it too cluttered with too much copy.

- *Lawn signs*—Lawn signs serve as billboards in local campaigns. They can create a "bandwagon" effect if numerous signs appear in neighborhoods and surrounding areas. Large-format signs are useful at key strategic areas such as major intersections, along busy roads, in front of commercial establishments, and on fences in rural areas. These "field signs" are more permanent and long lasting than yard signs. They usually go up at the beginning of the campaign.

Two critical factors about lawn signs are placement and maintenance. Incumbents have an advantage. They have records of the locations of previous lawn and field signs. Once someone is willing to place a lawn sign, the person will usually do so again. Challengers must ask people if they are willing to place a sign on their lawn; a candidate may approach people when conducting neighborhood walks. Although aggravating to campaigns, signs disappear. Some will be taken by rival supporters, but most disappear just by random acts of removal. In fall campaigns, Halloween pranks often result in the destruction of lawn signs.[23] Most campaigns have volunteers who serve as a "maintenance crew" and travel around at least weekly to check on signs. It is their responsibility to replace or repair signs as needed.

In terms of general strategy, campaigns increase the number of signs as Election Day nears. This creates the "bandwagon" effect. In addition, campaigns have numerous signs at every campaign event, large or small.

- *Bumper stickers and buttons/tags*—Bumper stickers act as mini-billboards. They are an inexpensive way to build name recognition and generate the impression of broad support. Buttons or stickers serve as personal testimonials and endorsements. They are available for distribution at all campaign events.

Media Considerations

There are two types of media: paid and unpaid. Paid media are primarily ads that campaigns pay for. Paid media provides the ability to control the message. Unpaid media or "earned media" is coverage of the campaign on television, on radio, and in the newspapers. Shea and Burton argue that, "successfully obtaining news coverage is one of a campaign's most important goals."[24] Of course, campaigns not only want to get the media to cover the candidate and campaign but also desire that the coverage be "positive." They also observe that the higher the office, the greater press scrutiny. From a reporter's perspective, "federal candidates will be expected to have a grasp of national issues, state contestants should know about state issues, and local office seekers should understand community concerns."[25] Shea and Burton also suggest that the scrutiny of personal and professional lives varies with the office—the higher the office, the more scrutiny.[26] Some activities are certain to be covered by the news media, such as debates or candidate forums. However, campaigns also try to entice news coverage with a variety of activities ranging from press conferences to press releases.

Even in local and especially in statewide elections it is important to have a mix of media advertising utilizing print (newspapers and direct mail), television, radio, and outdoor signage. Generally, in county and small-town elections, newspaper and radio are most common outlets. Higher-level races will incorporate television, which can be very expensive.

- *Television*—What makes television powerful is the combination of the visual and audio elements. In most races, a television presence communicates legitimacy and electoral viability. As a result, even in more modest races, some television advertising, if only on cable, may be desirable. In fact, placing ads on cable stations is not only more affordable than placing them on one (or more) of the major network stations, it also allows for targeting audience viewers by demographic, socioeconomic, and lifestyle characteristics. Most campaigns buy time during or close to newscasts. Those who view news programs are voters. Likewise, community-access cable is a good value, and viewers are community leaders and activists—voters for sure.[27]

- *Radio*—Next to direct mail (discussed below), radio provides the best opportunities for targeting messages based on demographic and psychographic variables. In addition, production costs are the least expensive of all the media and allow flexibility and immediacy in terms of timing, scheduling, and presentation.[28] For local elections, a radio-based strategy is low in cost, easy and quick to produce, and thus offers the potential to have numerous ads addressing a variety of issues and constituencies.

- *Newspapers*—Although television, regardless of market size, is the primary source of political information, newspapers still provide a good outlet for campaign advertising and information. Newspaper readers tend to be more educated, the most likely to vote, contributors to charities, and members of the middle and upper classes.

  Newspaper political advertising can be effective, especially in local elections. Visuals and photos may elicit emotion among readers. Newspapers provide opportunity for long-copy, informational material. Unlike television, radio, or cable, ad space is always available. Newspapers do not run out of inventory—all ads are laid out first, then the news content is placed. In effect, the length of newspapers is dictated not by all the news worthy to print, but the number of ads). More recently, newspapers allow market segmentation by printing sections of the paper for specific geographic or neighborhood areas. Finally, in very local elections, newspaper ads help with name recognition and may well influence coverage of the campaign.

  There are several rather standard formats used in newspaper ads. One of the most popular mimics a news story layout or an opinion column. The candidate's photo is prominent with a bold headline and copy alongside. The campaign slogan is also in bold, and its font distinguishes it from the rest of the copy. Each ad usually focuses on just one issue. This format can be standardized, allowing for different issues and topics to be inserted to correlate with the timing of the race or the paper's readership.

  Next in popularity are testimonial or endorsement ads containing positive remarks made by prominent citizens, such as social and business leaders. These ads are an effective way to gain support from those who are less familiar with the candidate or the campaign.

  Just as in television advertising, ad placement is also an important consideration. Very different people will be exposed to an ad that appears in the sports section compared to one in the business section. As a result, campaigns target newspaper ads by section, based on the potential readers' occupation, interests, and gender.[29]

- *Direct mail*—Direct mail allows for the creation of a relationship between candidate and voter but can also serve to create identification with issues and, early on, help raise funds. In addition to general precinct or general voter mailings, direct mail can be sent to specific groups such as teachers, members of particular social organizations, civic club members, etc.

  Solicitation appeals in direct mail contain several elements. The letter uses "flattery" to make the reader feel he or she is special. The recipient is a "patriotic American" who has given support in the past. The mail piece hints of "insider status" for the reader, who is being provided information not available to the general public. Letter recipients are often invited to a special dinner or event in order to "rub shoulders with party dignitaries." They are told that they are part of an "army fighting the good fight" against the opposition. Letters solicit "opinions and viewpoints" from the reader. And, of course, there is always the "asking for money."[30]

The issue or issues addressed in a direct mail piece will be based on the constituent group targeted. The key is to target the message to the potential voter—the more specific the message, the more effective the piece. For example, a direct mail piece going to teachers would address issues of education, pay raises, and school safety. Behind every good direct mail effort is a good mailing list, a list that is accurate and reflects the desired characteristics of the targeted group.

Finally, direct mail is used to attack or "hit" opponents. The "hit" is based on opposition research. If running against an incumbent, "hits" may be on the opponent's poor attendance record, certain key votes, over-budget spending, lack of effectiveness, and so forth. Such attacks are direct, simple, and clear. Attack direct mail is most effective a week away from the election. This reduces time for the opponent to challenge or respond. In fact, some of the most negative direct mail pieces arrive the Saturday before Tuesday's election.

GOTV

According to Shea and Burton, "Get-out-the-vote (GOTV) efforts can be the most important activity undertaken during a campaign."[31] Of course, every activity of a campaign attempts to get people to favor the candidate or campaign and to vote. However, GOTV activities are specifically tailored to motivate and activate supporters so they will go to the polls and vote. Identifying how undecided and swing voters will vote is "voter ID." Getting campaign supporters out to vote on Election Day is "GOTV."[32] By Election Day, most voters have decided who to support. GOTV is not about increasing general election turnout but is about increasing the turnout of supporters for a specific candidate or campaign.

Activating a campaign's base or core constituency increases voter turnout. A campaign's base consists of party loyalists who always vote and most often display lawn signs. They need very little encouragement to go to the polls. Prior to Election Day, campaign organizations have analyzed precinct turnout data from past elections. They know the areas of strength and support. For the campaign's dedicated voters, a simple "drop piece" the day before the election is enough to stimulate voting. However, campaigns must motivate those who are supporters but are somewhat lazy when it comes to voting. These voters need several contacts in the days leading up to the election: canvas (neighborhood walk), direct mail, telephone call, and final direct mail piece the day before the election is the normal sequence of contacts. Interestingly, the voters most difficult to motivate to vote in local and state elections are those who may support a candidate but reside in areas dominated by members of the other political party or by supporters of the opposition candidate. These individuals need the most contacts of all supporters. Usually, an additional phone call is made the day before or on Election Day to these voters.

There are a variety of methods to identify voters. Usually, campaigns start with a list of registered voters. The list is broken down to the neighborhood area. Either by phone interviews or neighborhood walks, after each contact the name is listed as "supporting," "leaning support," "undecided," "leaning no support," or "not supporting." The first three categories determine the method and frequency of contact by the campaign. Those who are identified as genuinely undecided voters through phone calls or neighborhood canvassing should also receive at least both pieces of direct mail and a preelection phone call. Needless to say, those who are identified as nonsupporters do not warrant any contact. For the campaign, contacting nonsupporters would be a waste of time, energy, and money.[33] According to Bike, the undecided and ticket-splitters receive about 80 percent of a campaign's efforts.[34]

Although very labor intensive, poll watching is a valuable technique in local elections to aid in GOTV. Individuals have a list of supporters by precinct. Poll watchers are equipped with clipboard, the list of supporters, and a cell phone. As the name of voters is called out to the recorder, the poll watcher checks the list of supporters. Every couple of hours, poll watchers report to phone banks or campaign headquarters the names of those who have not voted. These individuals are then called and encouraged to vote. Callers may even offer supporters a ride to the polls if needed.

Summary

We started this chapter recognizing that while local and statewide races generally follow the same strategies and tactics of upper-level races, they are much more "retail," requiring more levels and frequencies of voter contact. The communication activities and objectives differ. And the use of media are more limited but also more targeted. In this chapter we highlighted some of the unique characteristics, strategies, and tactics of local and statewide campaigns.

Catherine Shaw provides the "ten commandments" of local campaigns: honor your base, stay on message, money is your savior, never tell a lie, aim at the souls that can be saved, never waste a donor's money, do not commit adultery, start early, be prepared in all things, know who you are. For Shaw, the "cardinal sins of campaigning" include: being caught in a provable lie, committing a crime, having a relationship with a member of your staff, committing adultery, and declaring bankruptcy.[35] These "commandments" and "sins" are just as true for upper-level campaigns as well.

Notes

[1] Daniel Shea and Michael Burton, *Campaign Craft*, 3rd ed. (Westport, CT: Praeger, 2006), 35.

[2] Ibid., 32.

[3] Ibid., 33.

[4] Ibid., 182–183.

[5] Catherine Shaw, *The Campaign Manager*, 3rd ed. (Boulder, CO: Westview, 2004), 1–2.

[6] Shea and Burton, *Campaign Craft*, 36.

[7] Shaw, *The Campaign Manager*, 7–9.

[8] Edward Schwartzman, *Political Campaign Craftsmanship* (New Brunswick, NJ: Transaction Publishers, 1989), 4.

[9] Shea and Burton, *Campaign Craft*, 137.

[10] Shaw, *The Campaign Manager*, 89–90.

[11] Ibid., 81.

[12] Ibid., 81.

[13] Ibid., 87–89.

[14] William Bike, *Winning Political Campaigns*, 2nd ed. (Juneau, AK: Denali Press, 2001), 64.

[15] Shaw, *The Campaign Manager*, 82–83.

[16] Ibid., 84.

[17] Bike, *Winning Political Campaigns*, 43.

[18] Ibid., 20.

[19] Ibid., 20–21.

[20] Shea and Burton, *Campaign Craft*, 34–35.

[21] Shaw, *The Campaign Manager*, 21–22.

[22] Bike, *Winning Political Campaigns*, 31.

[23] Ibid., 119–125.

[24] Shea and Burton, *Campaign Craft*, 3.

[25] Ibid., 33.

[26] Ibid., 34.

[27] Bike, *Winning Political Campaigns*, 5–6.

[28] Ibid., 8.

[29] Shaw, *The Campaign Manager*, 213–226; Shea and Burton, *Campaign Craft*, 163–164.

[30] Dennis Johnson, *No Place for Amateurs* (New York: Routledge, 2001), 157–159.

[31] Shea and Burton, *Campaign Craft*, 191.

[32] Shaw, *The Campaign Manager*, 322.

[33] Ibid., 325–331.

[34] Bike, *Winning Political Campaigns*, 39.

[35] Shaw, *The Campaign Manager*, 5.

The Presidency

> *Style is the President's habitual way of performing his three political roles: rhetoric, personal relations, and homework. . . . A President's world view consists of his primary, politically relevant beliefs, particularly his conceptions of social causality, human nature, and the central moral conflicts of the time. . . . Character is the way the President orients himself toward life.*
> —James David Barber

For years, scholars have noticed the increasing difference between campaigning and governing. Today, scholars are noting a new form of leadership, one based on style and public popularity rather than on performance and accomplishment. In this chapter we review the current trend toward symbolic executive leadership and how the president governs by focusing on the role of communication in creating, defining, and sustaining our relationship with the institutional presidency.

Executive Leadership

Certainly in the last 25 years we have seen a transformation or a transition in terms of the roles and functions of the U.S. presidency—not so much from a constitutional perspective, but from a cultural and sociological one. Today, the presidency is a social institution; it interacts with the public and the public interacts with the institution.

Public expectations and perceptions are created through a president's rhetoric, use of symbols, rituals, and sense of history. In essence, the office is created, sustained, and permeated through interaction comprised of campaigns, socialization, history, and myth. Certainly, from a public perspective, the presidency had evolved to become a very different office since the Nixon era. Watergate caused a fundamental reappraisal of the beliefs about the presidency and its role in U.S. democracy.

The 11 presidents of the post–World War II era have certainly not enjoyed political good fortune despite the power and majesty of the office. From Harry Truman to George W. Bush, two declined to run again because of unpopular wars, one was assassinated, two survived assassination attempts, two faced the possibility of impeachment and conviction, one was impeached by House vote but survived the trial, and three failed to be elected as incumbents. Additionally, despite public job approval ratings, President Clinton enjoyed the lowest personal character rating of any president since such polls were taken, and successor George W. Bush sustained the second lowest job approval ratings for nearly a year. In short, we witnessed the transformation of the American presidency from the heroic leadership model of governing to a more managerial model of governing, from a parental model of leadership to a CEO model of management.

Presidential scholar Barbara Kellerman argues that conceptions of leadership and management have converged as we continue to enter the twenty-first century. Leaders in the business community have become more similar to those in government or politics in terms of activities, skills, and demands. She predicts that as we go forward into this new century, leaders will move from business into politics, and from politics into business, more easily and more frequently.[1]

Leadership as a concept is many things: a process, a product, a method, a style, a group of behaviors or skills, to name just a few characteristics. Rather than focusing on the content of leadership, let us reflect on how presidents lead. Presidents lead by words, deeds, action, and the symbolic vestments of the institution. By words, we mean public discourse; by deeds, we mean their specific legislative agenda; by action, we mean, their personal character, personality, and habits of behavior; and by the symbolic dimensions of the office, we mean the historical, mythic, public expectations of the institution. These components, that is words, deeds, action, and symbolic dimensions of the presidency, generate a public impression, or orientation to the occupant's management style.[2]

"Good leadership," from Kellerman's perspective, "is said to be the result of good fit between leaders and followers and between leaders and the tasks at hand."[3] Theodore Sorensen, an advisor to President Kennedy, renewed the argument for a strong and powerful presidency in the mid-1980s. He believes,

> Congress can legislate, appropriate, investigate, deliberate, terminate and educate—all essential functions. But it is not organized to initiate, negotiate, or act with the kind of swift and informal discretion that our changing world so often requires. Leadership can come only from the presidency.[4]

It is, however, much easier to call for strong leadership than it is to define the concept.

Dan Nimmo argues that political leadership "actually refers to a particular relationship that exists between a leader and his followers in specific settings."[5] The focus of much modern leadership theory is on the willingness of followers to follow. Americans have generally denied hero status to contemporary politicians, unlike that granted to sports figures and Hollywood stars. Our revolutionary heritage and democratic institutions have perpetuated a general mistrust toward governmental and centralized authority.

James Kouzes and Barry Posner have studied leadership in a variety of contexts and situations for years. Through their interviews and research, they find that the *content* of leadership *does not change*, however, the context does change for all types of reasons: technology, world events, cultural and social demands, to name a few. Through their years of research, surveys, and interviews, they found five practices of exemplary leadership: model the way, inspire a shared vision, challenge the process, enable others to act, and encourage the heart.[6] Generally speaking, then, leaders should be a "model" for how they wish others to act. They should "lead" by inspiration, by challenging, by providing a clear direction for future actions or behaviors. By challenging the process, leaders are pioneers, taking us toward new directions, new issues, and new challenges. We expect our leaders to be enthusiastic, energetic, and positive about the future. Inspiring leaders provide meaning and purpose in our lives; they encourage us to believe that our best moments lie ahead of us. A leader's vision articulates goals and objectives and communicates the beliefs and values that influence and shape the cultural and behavioral norms. Similarly to Kouzes and Posner, historian Stephen Ambrose finds that the qualities of a great public leader are vision, integrity, courage, understanding, the power of articulation, and profundity of character.[7]

The difficulty for leaders, argues Bert Rockman, is balancing governing with legitimacy in that leaders must use their power to confront and solve problems but must also be accountable to various groups and constituencies. Achieving an acceptable balance can be difficult, because while we demand inspired leadership we also hold a basic lack of trust and respect for autocratic decision-making and formal institutions. Many politicians traditionally run against government, and this has contributed to a shift of focus from issues and policies to candidates and officeholders.

Several scholars have noted this trend. Theodore Lowi calls today's presidential government a "plebiscite," a government based on "popular adoration."[8] The inability to meet expectations of performance were masked by shows of personal popularity. Lowi suggests, for example, that Reagan was so good at creating the appearance of success that he earned the distinction of possessing the "Teflon presidency." His popularity literally protected him from political scandal or inefficiencies of his administration. Dennis Simon and Charles Ostrom argue that "maintaining public support has become a key instrumental goal of the modern president," and the officeholder must actively engage in the "politics of prestige." They conclude that "the value of public support reveals that presidents have an incentive to manage, manipulate, or otherwise control how they are evaluated."[9]

George Edwards also recognizes that the "greatest source of influence for the president is public approval,"[10] and Raymond Moore predicts that "the leadership style most likely to win in the future will be 'political presidents' who exhibit a high degree of salesmanship but low managerial skills."[11] Barbara Kellerman describes today's "presidential politicking" as a process of "transactional leadership" based on private bargaining and public interaction. The result is a personalized presidency that requires an engaging personality, an endless campaign, the maintenance of public relations activities, and public approval.[12]

Rockman speculates that the reasons we lean toward the personalization of the presidency are the slack between these major elements: the social system (the public dimension) and the political system (the operational, organizational dimensions), the American culture of individualism, the structure of institutions that stress individual autonomy, and the contemporary role of political polls and public opinion.[13] There is a cost, however, in personalizing the presidency. Presidencies based solely on public approval and popularity will have a positive impact upon the legitimacy and prestige of the office but will have little influence on party cohesion or legislative programs. In contrast, a president who is elected based on political reputation and bargaining skills has a better chance of impacting society through legislative enactments.

The Postmodern Presidency

For Ryan Barilleaux, the trend toward the personalization of the presidency and Reagan's success of maintaining personal popularity established a new era of presidential leadership and government. He argues, "The office occupied by Ronald Reagan and his successors is not merely an extension of the modern presidency created by Franklin Roosevelt, but is sufficiently different to warrant a new label."[14] He calls it the "postmodern" presidency. Although Reagan did not create the postmodern presidency, he consolidated and maximized efforts and activities that have revised the institution and its occupant forever. There are several key characteristics of the postmodern presidency: revival of presidential prerogative power; governing through public politics; a large, specialized and centralized staff; policy making through public support and staff appointments in the courts and various regulatory agencies; the president serving as chief whip in Congress; and the vice president serving as a key adviser, envoy, and surrogate. Barilleaux poses a relevant question: "How do postmodern presidents govern in this environment?" The answer is that they do not: "The postmodern presidency does not govern, but is the premier part of a governing system."[15]

For some scholars and political observers, it was Clinton who ushered in the

> postmodern presidency . . . where the organizing themes of modern American politics—the heroic presidency, the Cold War, the conflict between Democratic liberalism and Republican conservatism—are

superseded by fleeting images and issues that do not produce any consistent or coherent political understanding.[16]

In this era, a "postmodern character" refers to "a political actor who lacks a stable identity associated with ideological and partisan values and who is, thereby, free to move nimbly from one position to another as political fashion dictates."[17]

According to Shawn Parry-Giles and Trevor Parry-Giles, "postmodern" American politics are dominated by "the image" and a "hyperreal" depiction of candidates and leaders. Such politics largely rejects historical norms and expectations of leadership. Postmodern politics "simultaneously rejects and embraces existing presidentialities while it seeks to craft a new presidentiality for a hyper-mediated, hyper-visual, hyperreal time."[18] As a result, following their analysis:

> Voters and citizens are constructed as more targeted, more fragmented, more scopophiliac [voyeuristic], more skeptical than ever before. They are repeatedly told that their political system does not work, that their leaders are dishonest and solely motivated by money and special interests, and that little or nothing can be done to solve intractable problems facing the nation. They are also conditioned to believe that politics is artificial, and they long for a real, genuine, authentic politics, as if such a community has ever existed or will ever be possible.[19]

Given this "postmodern" environment, Clinton is portrayed by many academics as simply a victim of contemporary politics. For example, Parry-Giles and Parry-Giles posit that Clinton was forced to confront the impact of the "ghosts of Nixon, Johnson and JFK." As the argument goes, Clinton embodied not only the angst related to the presidency but also related to the larger cultural tensions inherent in his generation. As the first baby-boomer president, he was forced to deal with the "ambiguity, confusion, and irony" associated with such issues as the Vietnam War, the military draft, drugs, casual sex, divorce, among others.

> Thus, even as Clinton uttered his first words on the campaign trail, even as he took the oath of office, his bid for the presidency as well as his performance in office were shaped by the ideological dissonances of the larger political culture.[20]

A major Clinton apologist, journalist Joe Klein, concurs with the above:

> It seems likely, in retrospect, that Bill Clinton was a compendium of all that his accusers found most embarrassing, troubling, and loathsome about themselves, especially those who come of age, as he did, in the deep, narcotic prosperity that enveloped the nation after World War II. On the most superficial level, his excesses reflected the personal excesses—sexual and material—of his generation.[21]

All these various scholars are acknowledging that today, presidential communication activities are a source of tremendous power: power to define, justify, legitimize, persuade, and inspire. Everything a president does or says has implications and communicates "something." Presidents surround themselves with communication specialists. Every act, word, or phrase becomes calculated and measured for a response; every occasion proclaims a need for utterance.

The Rhetorical Presidency

James Ceaser, with several other colleagues, argues that three factors have attributed to the rise of the "rhetorical presidency."[22] The first factor is the modern doctrine of presidential leadership. The public expects a president to set goals and provide solutions to national problems. To be a leader is a cherished concept and a political expectation and, hence, a necessity for our presidents. The second factor giving use to the rhetorical presidency is the development of the mass media. The mass media have increased the size of the audience, provided immediate access to the public, and changed the mode of communicating with the public from primarily the written word to the spoken word delivered in dramatic and mediated forms. The final factor contributing to the supremacy of the rhetorical presidency is the modern electoral campaign. Contemporary presidential campaigns require national travel, public performances, image creation, issue definition, and the articulation of problem solutions. A "common man" can become known and win an election. Competition for communication opportunities is great.

Craig Allen Smith and Kathy Smith[23] identify six features of presidential leadership that point to presidential persuasion as the essential element:

1. The presidency today is fundamentally different from the presidency envisioned by the founders.
2. The presidency is actively engaged in policy making and the legislative process.
3. Presidential leadership entails the creation, mobilization, transformation, and maintenance of coalitions.
4. The creation, mobilization, transformation, and maintenance of coalitions requires presidents to influence a variety of other citizens: the Congress and the courts, political parties and interest groups, reporters and pundits, the powerful and the powerless, foreign and domestic groups, public opinion, and posterity.
5. Presidents attempt to influence those other citizens by informing them, by bargaining with them, by persuading them—in short, by communicating with them.
6. The effectiveness of a president's leadership depends heavily on persuasive abilities.

Since Franklin Delano Roosevelt, each president has communicated with the public more than his predecessor. Just think about it. A president today delivers at least one speech or statement every day. That takes time, staff, practice, meeting with people before and after the event, and travel, to name just a few of the demands associated with simply "speaking." Interestingly, in the nineteenth century, presidents spoke little in public and were seldom seen. In the early years of our nation, individuals did not "run" for office; rather, they were nominated because of their resumes, life experience, sacrifice, or public service. According to Jeffery Tulis, Woodrow Wilson ushered in the new style of presidential leadership, one based on public discourse, to mobilize votes and influence public opinion on national issues: "Popular or mass rhetoric has become a principal tool of presidential governance. Presidents regularly 'go over the heads' of Congress to the people at large in support of legislation and other initiatives."[24] In short, presidents today attempt to govern by means of direct rhetorical appeals. One result is the constant tracking of the president's job and personal approval ratings— the more popular a president, the less conflict with Congress and the more passage of favored legislation. As an example of this, consider that when President Bush's approval rating was above 70 percent, he had no difficulty moving legislation through Congress; when it fell below 40 percent, the legislation that his office supported moved slowly, if at all.

Thus, the rhetorical presidency refers to more than a collection of speeches delivered by any one president. It refers to the communicative attributes of both the institution and its occupants. The Presidency is an office, a role, a persona, constructing a position of power, myth, legend, and persuasion. Within such an environment, as Clinton Rossiter notes, the president becomes "the one-man distillation of the American people reflecting their perceived dignity and majesty."[25] Today, we often refer to the president as "the voice of the American people."

Roderick Hart argues that because

> the rhetorical dimensions of the presidency are now so pronounced, and because each speech requires emotional and physical stamina from the chief executive, many presidents come to feel that *to have spoken about a matter is to have done something* about the that matter.[26]

Presidential communication is a very large requirement of the job.

The Institutional Presidency

Of all the major clauses in the Constitution, the one governing the presidency is the shortest. The members of the Constitutional Convention simply did not delineate in great detail the powers and responsibilities of the presidency. According to Rossiter, eight key decisions were made at the convention that really created the form and structure of the American presidency:[27]

1. A separate executive office should exist apart from the legislature.
2. The executive office should consist of one man called the president of the United States.
3. The president should be elected apart from the legislature.

4. The executive office should have a fixed term subject to termination by conviction of impeachment for high crimes or misdemeanors.

5. The president should be eligible for reelection with no limit as to the number of terms.

6. The president should derive power from the Constitution and not simply from Congress.

7. The president should not be encumbered with a specified body from which to seek approval for nominations, vetoes, or other acts.

8. As president, one may not be a member of either house of Congress.

These key decisions created the office, but they contain little information as to what the office entails. Nearly half of Article II simply deals with tenure, qualifications, and election of the president. Section 2 of Article II states that the president "shall be Commander in Chief"; "shall have power to grant reprieves and pardons"; "make treaties, provided two-thirds of the Senators present concur"; "appoint Ambassadors, other public Ministers and Consuls, judges of the Supreme Court, and all other officers of the United States . . . by and with the advice and consent of the Senate"; and "shall have power to fill all vacancies that may happen during the recess of the Senate." Section 3 adds that the president "shall from time to time give to the Congress information of the State of the Union"; "convene both Houses . . . on extraordinary occasions"; "shall receive Ambassadors and other public Ministers"; and "shall take care that the laws be faithfully executed." These, then, are the duties as specified in the Constitution. On the surface, they appear rather simple and straightforward. It is, however, the fulfilling of these functions that complicates the office.

Contemporary scholars, when addressing presidential functions, seldom delineate constitutional provisions. Rather, they group presidential tasks into broad, general categories. These categories, of course, differ in number. For Thomas Cronin, the job description of the president involves six major functions:[28]

1. symbolic leadership that must generate hope, confidence, national purpose;

2. setting national priorities and designing programs that will receive public attention and a legislative hearing;

3. crisis management, which has become increasingly important since 1940;

4. constant legislative and political coalition building;

5. program implementation and evaluation, which has also become increasingly difficult in modern times; and

6. general oversight of government routines, which forces the president to be responsible for governmental performance at all levels.

Somewhat related to Cronin's categories are Bruce Buchanan's four generic functions of the presidency: national symbol, policy advocate, mediator among national interests, and crisis manager.[29] George Reedy believes, however, that what a president must do can be boiled down to two simple fundamentals: resolve policy questions that will not yield to quantitative, empirical analysis; and persuade enough citizens that decisions are viable and will not destroy the fabric of society.[30]

From this brief discussion of presidential functions, the Constitution as a job description is vague and general. A president clearly does more than what is outlined in the Constitution. Even as commander-in-chief, the president may undertake crisis management, legislative and political coalition building, and so on. It is how one meets or carries out the functions that provide insight into how the institution influences behavior.

Edward Corwin was the first to mention presidential roles as sources of power. A president's power is based on five constitutional roles: chief of state, chief executive, chief diplomat, commander-in-chief, and chief legislator.[31] These roles are roughly analogous to the various areas of responsibilities outlined in the Constitution. A president who creates additional roles, and hence additional power, approaches a dangerous "personalization of the office."

As chief of state, the president functions as the ceremonial head of government not unlike the monarch of England. Some would argue that the majority of presidential activity is ceremonial. Projected on the president is the symbol of sovereignty, continuity, and grandeur. As chief executive, the president is manager of one of the largest "corporations" in the world. Whether the president likes it or not, he or she is held responsible for the quality of governmental performance ranging from a simple letter of complaint to military preparedness. In event of war, the president as commander-in-chief must ensure strategic execution and victory. Within past 70 years, the field of foreign relations has become extremely important. The formulation of foreign policy and the conduct of foreign affairs force the president to serve as the nation's chief diplomat. Finally, by providing domestic leadership, the president must guide Congress by identifying national priorities for legislation. These legitimate, constitutional roles are obviously interrelated. Yet, the various hats a president wears require rather distinct approaches, strategies, and temperament. Even these, however, may be bound to the particulars of any given situation.

Clinton Rossiter, building on Corwin's analyses, argues that five extra-constitutional roles must also be recognized: chief of party, protector of the peace, manager of prosperity, world leader, and voice of the people.[32] Rossiter, like Corwin, believes that the source of presidential power lies in the combination of the various roles. Rossiter, at least, recognizes the expanding nature of the presidency. These extra roles resulted from the growing activities of a president plus the growing expectations of the public. When speaking of presidential roles, most scholars cite Rossiter's classic *The American Presidency*. Hence, the list of roles is fairly stationary. Yet, as the functions or duties of the presidency grow, so do the roles. To complicate matters, as the various tasks become more complex, numerous roles may be required to carry out one function. One should also note that each role may require very different skills and techniques. Roles, then, are more numerous than functions. They are labels or character traits that people see, and each has a distinct mode usually congruent with public expectations that will be developed later. Finally, if a role set is good or successful, the set may become a model. The model may thus serve as an overall approach to the fulfillment of the functions. The role set, as a model, may be praised, condemned, imitated, or may serve as a guide to performance. For instance, President Bush's performance immediately following 9/11 received high praise. However, the public then expected the same "set" of behaviors from the president in other crises, for instance, following Hurricane Katrina. By not responding in the same manner to Katrina as he did to 9/11, President Bush, deservedly or not, met with condemnation.

The Symbolic Presidency

Most political scholars recognize that the presidency is both an institution and a role. As such, the presidency has a great deal of influence on those who occupy the office as well as on the general public. Certainly, the American presidency has established a rather clear traditional role set. However, the title of president implies more than simply a job description. We know, for example, that behavioral expectations and restrictions are attached to all social positions. Thus, to know that a person is president is to know, in a very general way, how the individual is likely to behave and how others will behave toward the individual. The title not only provides a means for anticipating a range of behaviors but also confines the range of behaviors possible.

Noted presidential advisor and historian, Emmet Hughes, in his classic *The Living Presidency*, states that a president faces two constituencies: "the living citizens and the future historians."[33] This certainly is not an easy task. Nearly all scholars agree that any American president inherits a vast, complex set of role expectations. Roles create expectations but societal expectations can also create political roles. Public expectations also evoke a specific political role and self-conception for those individuals who accept the role in question. When Alfred deGrazia speaks of "the myth of the President," he is referring to "a number of qualities [that] are given to every President that are either quite fictitious or large exaggerations of the real man."[34] He further notes, "The myth is not alone the property of the untutored mind, but of academicians, scientists, newspapermen, and even Congressmen."[35]

Thus, the office of the presidency has grown because of interaction—interaction of the office with the public and the public with the office. As public expectations increase, so does the job. Concurrently, the job is forced to expand to meet the wide-ranging public expectations.

There appears to be a growth in public expectations of the presidency. However, today's presidents, because of the use of mass media, have encouraged the public to identify with the candidate and the potential of the office. Historian Theodore White asserts that especially since 1960, our idea of government consists of promises—promises to take care of people, the cities, the sick, the old, the young, and so forth. According to White, "by 1980 we had promised ourselves almost to the point of national bankruptcy."[36] Consequently, the public has responded by holding the president accountable for meeting various demands.

Citizen expectations of a president tend to revolve around the office itself and also around the individual who holds the office. Thus, the public has expectations for how a president handles issues that directly affect them. These issues are vast and complex, ranging from gasoline prices to the quality of education to natural disasters to the cost of health care—to name just a few examples. Many of these expectations include hoped-for results that lie outside presidential control. Even so, if the president fails to handle them in a way that is satisfactory to the public, the public becomes disappointed in the president's performance.

The public's expectations (realistic or not) encouraged presidents to attempt more than they can accomplish in any term of office. Thus, expectations invite presidents to overpromise and overextend themselves. This, in turn, creates the need for image-making activities, which in some cases, become the major task or work function of an administration: As Thomas Cronin argues:

> The public-relations apparatus not only has directly enlarged the Presidential workforce but has expanded public-relations expectations about the Presidency at the same time. More disquieting is that, by its very nature, this type of press agency, feeds on itself, and the resulting distortions encourage an ever increasing subordination of substance to style.[37]

Many attitudes about the presidency stem from messages received in childhood about the virtues of various presidents. Through the political socialization process and history lessons in schools, the president is ordinarily the first public official to come to the attention of young children. Long before children are informed about the specific functions of the presidency, they view individual presidents as exceptionally important and benign. Children tend to stress personal characteristics of the president that include honesty, wisdom, power, goodness, and benignity. Generally, by the age of nine, virtually every American child has some detailed awareness of the presidency and can identify the incumbent president. Thus, esteem and respect for the office independent of the occupant is established at a rather early age. Every year since World War II, the majority of the 10 most admired men and women are involved in national politics; the president, regardless of performance, is usually among them. As citizens, we tend to selectively extract information about a president's personal image that is beyond the media content focusing on issues. Voters form perceptions of candidates in two stages of primaries. First, the public forms "relational perceptions" about the candidate's sincerity, honesty, and caring qualities. Then the public assesses job competencies based on mediated statements and appearances.[38] Thus, we perceive and evaluate the president as a person in addition to the policies generated and skills demonstrated while in office.

Another result of childhood socialization is the heavy dependency for leadership on the presidency, especially in times of national crisis. In times of national emergency, we discard skepticism and return to childhood images of the presidency. As adults, we still desire to see the president as a combination of Washington, Jefferson, and Adams, making wise decisions and working harder than the average citizen to preserve the quality of life. Recall the high approval ratings of President George W. Bush in the aftermath of the attacks of September 11, 2001. He was perceived as a strong and comforting leader during the postcrisis period.

A presidential campaign emphasizes the childhood visions and qualities of the office. Hence, campaigns themselves perpetuate the mythic and heroic role demands of the office. To mobilize a nation is indeed a somewhat mysterious process. Although a campaign may be rather contentious and even disorderly, the process allows the opportunity to assess and project presidential qualities on the candidates.

Media advisers must project appropriate images of the candidates that are always simplified depictions of reality. The best image is one that is vague enough for voters to complete in a manner to see something they like. In the simplest terms, this means that conservatives should be able to see the candidate as conservative and, likewise, liberals should be able to see the candidate as liberal. We also like to have a sense of identification with presidential candidates; that is, we want to know that they understand us in terms of our lifestyle, values, and goals. Above all, this should be done without seeming contradictory or insincere. In his campaign for the 2008 Democratic nomination, John Edwards ran into difficulties when news of his 28,000-square-foot mansion and $400 haircuts came out at the same time he was stressing poverty reduction as a campaign theme.

By inauguration day a candidate has emerged as president. A tremendous transformation, at least in the eyes of the public, has occurred. Americans want and even need to believe that the common person they elevate to the presidency is a Washingtonesque bearer of infinite wisdom and benevolence. The perceived qualities are confirmed as soon as the candidate takes the oath of office.

The public's relationship with the presidency is more than a search for the fulfillment of childhood notions of the office. For some time empirical and clinical evidence has shown that the office provides, for a large portion of the population, an outlet for expression of deep, often unconscious, personality needs and conflicts. Harold Lasswell, in his 1930 classic *Psychopathology and Politics*, argues that private needs become displaced onto public objects and rationalized in terms of general political principles.[39] Greenstein, a student of Lasswell, continually investigated these phenomena in relation to the presidency. He recognizes six major psychological uses of the presidency for the population.

1. The office serves as a cognitive aid by providing a vehicle for the public to become aware of the functions, impact, and politics of government.

2. The presidency provides an outlet for feelings and emotions. The office serves as a focal point of pride, despair, hope, as well as frustration. It can easily be responsible, in the eyes of the public, for all that is bad or for all that is good.

3. The office serves as a means of vicarious participation. The president becomes an object of identification and consequently presidential efforts become citizen efforts resulting in a sharing of heightened feelings of potency.

4. Especially in times of crisis or uncertainty, the presidency functions as a symbol of national unity. When a president acts, it is the nation acting as one voice expressing one sentiment.

5. Likewise, the office serves as a symbol of stability and predictability. We assume that the president is knowledgeable and in control of events, thus minimizing danger or surprise.

6. Finally, the presidency serves as a lightning rod or as an object of displacement. The office is the ultimate receptacle for personal, which becomes national, feelings and attitudes. The president becomes either idealized or the ultimate scapegoat. Truman's cliché, "The Buck Stops Here," is true—at least in the minds of the public.[40]

Of all the political myths of the nation, Theodore White argues that the supreme myth is the ability of the citizens to choose the *best* person to lead the nation. From this belief follows the notion that the office will ennoble anyone who holds it—that the office would "burn the dross" from the president's character and that the duties of the office would by their enormity make the president a superior being able "to sustain the burden of the law, wise and enduring enough to resist the clash of all selfish interests."[41] Thus, the presidency is a combination of symbol and reality. However, the symbolic dimensions of the office are increasingly becoming more important as the role of mass media has become both "maker and breaker" of presidents. In fact, the manipulation of salient symbols clouds issues and blurs situations resulting in emotionally charged but nebulously defined symbols.

Perhaps the forefathers were aware of the fact that the most practical method of unifying people is to give them a symbol with which all could identify. When the symbol is manifested in a person, the efficacy of uniting a nation is greatly enhanced. Clearly, the president of the United States is the focal point of our political system. Every action by the president is symbolic, not only as an executive act but also as a carrier of meaning. What the individual symbolizes to each person or group depends on the system of interpretation of the person or group. In many ways, the president becomes the lens through which we interpret the quality of American life—good or bad times, success or failure, and so on.

The very potency of the presidency as a symbol gives the office purpose and pragmatic nature. Americans expect presidents to prod, to unite, as well as to provide direction and a sense of purpose. As such, the presidency fulfills the parental functions of supreme leader, guide, and teacher. It is important to note, however, that symbolic power is the precondition of pragmatic power. Much legislation and many programs have failed because they were not symbolically acceptable. The key to success, of course, is presidential leadership. Not surprisingly, the most frequent complaint of the presidency since the Vietnam War is the lack of leadership. But leadership, from an interactionist perspective, is more than effective management and the ability to isolate and derive solutions to problems.

Recognizing the symbolic importance and dimensions of leadership is not to support the old notion that one is born a leader or that leadership is simply a matter of charisma. Instead, those who follow grant true leadership; it is comprised of their own unique perceptions, needs, and expectations.

Generally, most presidential scholars, although using somewhat different terminology, believe that the American people expect three major aspects of presidential behavior. First, the president is expected to be a competent manager of the vast machinery of government. Second, the American people expect the president to take care of their needs by initiating programs, legislation, and safeguarding the economy. Finally, the people want a sense of legitimacy from the president. The office, while providing symbolic affirmation of the nation's values, should faithfully represent the opinions of the public as well.

We cannot overemphasize the importance of presidents meeting the expectations of the public. For example, Carter was very successful in rising from obscurity in 1976 to becoming president of the United States. As a presidential candidate, Carter was most successful in presenting himself as a common man and as a man of the people. Carter also effectively articulated the traditional values of an average U.S. citizen. Carter's campaign rhetoric reflected how Americans wanted to conceive of themselves and the myth they wanted to live by as evident in Carter's slogan of "a government as good as its people." A vote for Carter became a vote for us reaffirming our national values and virtues in the wake of Nixon's disgrace.

But an interesting paradox of the American presidency is that once elected we demand uncommon leadership, great insight, and vast knowledge from our presidents. A president must appear presidential as defined by history, culture, and status of the position. Carter was often criticized for his lack of presidential behavior, dress, and demeanor: he wore a blue suit for his inaugural ceremony rather than a morning coat and top hat; took the oath of office as Jimmy Carter rather than as James Earl Carter; he walked down Pennsylvania Avenue rather than rode in a limousine; he prohibited the playing of "Hail to the Chief"; he sold the presidential yacht *Sequoia*; he sent his daughter, Amy, to a public school; he carried his own luggage; and he wore blue jeans in the White House.

In July 1977, Carter received a 64 percent positive rating on the question of restoring public confidence in government. Just one year later, however, Carter received a 63 percent negative response to the same question.[42] There is evidence to suggest that the public soon resented and rejected Carter's attempts to reduce the perceived stature and dignity of the presidency. Carter, as evidenced in his memoirs, realized this much too late:

> In reducing the imperial Presidency, I overreacted at first. We began to receive many complaints that I had gone too far in cutting back the pomp and ceremony, so after a few months I authorized the band to play "Hail to the Chief" on special occasions. I found it to be impressive and enjoyed it.[43]

Ronald Reagan was largely successful because he reestablished the "heroic presidency" and reinforced perceptions of American myths and values.[44] He believed most Americans are good, moral, hardworking, and optimistic about the future. For him, the heritage of the United States is one of freedom, faith, courage, commitment, determination, and generosity. With Reagan, Americans saw the president of an idealized past who defined the citizens in textbook terms of "patriotism, motherhood, and apple pie."

Reagan also carefully managed the symbolic vestments of the presidency. His public presentations were carefully planned and orchestrated. Image control was of prime importance to his staff. Reagan appeared in press surrounded by flags, with dignitaries, in splendid locations, or "at work." Reagan conformed to the form and content demands of television to take his message to the people. His acting skills, cinematic language, and orchestrated settings resulted in the election and reelection of one of the most popular presidents in contemporary U.S. history.

The Clinton presidency challenged many assumptions about the institution: the role of leadership versus management, private versus public behavior, and the degrees of telling the truth or depending upon the meaning of what "is," "is." Some would argue that the nation's mythic, symbolic expectations of the office are no longer apropos to meet the challenges or realities of the twenty-first century. Too, political cynicism has been on the rise for more than a decade. Yet the office has a rich history, and every occupant leaves some "fingerprint" on the institution. Nevertheless, the presidency is both our administrative office and our ceremonial office. Our president must meet and entertain other kings and rulers of nations. The office, and hence the individual, embodies the hopes, desires, dignity, and values of our nation.

Governing

It has become a truism in political science literature to recognize the distinction between campaigning and governing. For the rest of the chapter, we consider the more operational or pragmatic communication concerns of t' institutional presidency.

Communication

Presidential communication follows a continuum ranging from full control to virtually no control over content, timing, or context. For example, a presidential address offers the most control while evening newscasts offer the least amount of control. Of course, every White House wants as much control over presidential communication as possible, especially in terms of news coverage and presentation. As a result, there are three presidential institutions that attempt to influence news coverage and public reception of presidential communication: the White House Office of Communications, the press secretary, and press conferences.

The White House Office of Communications

Richard Nixon created the Office of Communications to combat the White House press corps whose coverage was a constant source of frustration and irritation. According to John Maltese, the goal of the office is to set the public agenda, to make sure all elements of the executive branch stay on the specified agenda, and to promote the agenda through mass marketing.[45] More specifically, the office is responsible for long-term public relations planning, dissemination of the "line of the day," and the circumvention of the White House press corps by orchestrating direct appeals to the American people. On a daily basis, the office is usually responsible for media relations, public affairs activities, speechwriting, and research.

Each subsequent president has retained the office. More recent administrations separated the communications and press functions into individual units with informal links of connection. In some cases, as with Reagan and Clinton, the press office was under the communications office. However, it was the Reagan White House that strategically used the office in a proactive way to carefully manage public images and portrayals of Reagan.

According to Richard Perloff, Reagan advisors decided to "sell the country on Reagan the man—the charming political leader."[46] They developed several rules of information management: plan ahead, stay on the offensive, control the flow of information, limit reporters' access to the president, talk about the issues *you* want to talk about, speak in one voice, and repeat the same message several times.[47] The communication team also developed the strategy of the "line of the day." Each morning, staffers would decide on a major theme they would emphasize that day with every encounter with members of the press corps. This strategy also included considerations of how to get the president and the selected message point in the evening news and next-day newspapers. All officials were instructed to speak only about the selected theme to insure coverage and consistency of message. The communication staff also paid very close attention to visuals, the backdrops and positioning of the president for television and photo opportunities. Nothing was left to chance. Virtually every moment of an event was planned, every word was carefully scripted, and everywhere the president would stand or move was clearly marked.[48] Finally, the Reagan administration perfected the notion of White House spin control, concerted efforts to provide their interpretation of events and actions. From press releases to public statements by cabinet officers, the Reagan White House would bombard the press with "official" accounts and reactions of the day's national and international news. Such orchestrated efforts reduced the likelihood of presidential gaffes and improved consistency of message and favorable portrayals of the president.

Although successive presidents have attempted to utilize many of the Reagan strategies, Presidents George H. W. Bush and Bill Clinton were less successful. President Bush simply did not see the full value of such concerted efforts of news management. He preferred more informal meetings with the press and was comfortable with his public persona. Although the Clinton Administration wanted to emulate the Reagan successes in media management, the staff was disorganized and simply less experienced. Complicating matters, Clinton was more difficult to keep on script, and he would speak on many issues rather than just one or two. After the midterm elections of 1994, staffers determined that Clinton was actually "overexposed." He was too accessible to media and the public through the informal town-hall meetings. His casual approach had eroded the dignity and stature of the presidency. As a result, the staff increased the ratio of press conferences to other appearances in order for Clinton to appear more "presidential."[49] Then, when he came under attack during the Lewinsky affair and impeachment hearings, his press exposure was more restricted and limited.

George W. Bush entered the White House with more experience dealing with the media than any other previous president. According to James Mueller, he managed press relations through a combination of personal charm, message discipline, and the rigid control of press access and internal leaks.[50] However, as President Bush's popularity continued to decline because of the Iraq war, access to the "mainstream media" was even more restricted, and internal leaks increased.

Press Secretary

The press secretary is the primary spokesperson for the president. The secretary releases news and information, as well as provides the official interpretation of events, words, and actions of the president. "How" something is said is as important as "what" is said. Without exaggeration, the words of the press secretary become the words and expressions of the president. The job is difficult and challenging. In addition to balancing policy and political demands, the press secretary must also accurately reflect the thoughts and positions of the president. Press secretaries must also maintain the trust and confidence of the press corps.

Usually before noon, the press secretary conducts the daily news briefing that includes announcements about pending policy issues, presidential appointments for the day, and any other items of interest. During the typical "question and answer" portion of the briefing, press secretaries provide the White House interpretation on topics of interest.[51]

It is important for press secretaries to stay informed on a wide range of issues and to know the president's views, positions, and perspectives on the issues. Most successful press secretaries are those who have total access to the president and are part of the inner circle, including participation in senior staff meetings.[52]

Press Conferences

Presidential press conferences have become major national media events. They provide presidents with a national audience, an opportunity to express their views, and the chance to frame the political debate on issues of importance to the public. According to Carolyn Smith, "The presidential press conference has evolved into a semi-institutional, quasi-spontaneous, inherently adversarial public encounter between the president and the press."[53] For her,

> the main obligation of the president in this dialogue is to persuade. The main obligation of the press is to hold the president accountable for his policies and his actions. These contrary obligations produce a delicate but natural tension—a balancing act, if you will—that should be played out in each and every good press conference exchange.[54]

While not a constitutional requirement, press conferences have become institutionalized. Presidents differ in the number and frequency of press conferences. Usually, the longer a president is in office, the fewer formal press conferences will be conducted. Press conferences are used to make a special announcement, to sustain policy momentum, or to make a diplomatic response.[55]

Presidents vary greatly in their views of press conferences and skill in handling the press during the exchanges. Richard Nixon did not like the press and often openly confronted reporters. Ronald Reagan and John Kennedy enjoyed the exchanges and performed well. George H. W. Bush was "adequate" in his dealings with the press; he developed personal relationships with members of the press corps by meeting with them "on background," taking them on boat rides, and having them to dinner. Bill Clinton was also very attentive to the press and was at ease during exchanges.[56] George W. Bush dislikes press conferences, believing that they provide a platform for reporters to make news rather than provide an opportunity for sharing.[57]

Press conferences are risky because there is limited control over the questions and agenda. After the opening statement, regardless of any prior agreements with the press, reporters are free to ask virtually any question. Many reporters want to be called on to ask a question of the president that will generate interest and headlines. Some reporters, like Dan Rather and Sam Donaldson, build a reputation for asking tough questions that lead to better career opportunities. In fact, most network news anchors were White House correspondents.

Presidents must prepare for a variety of questions, ranging from soliciting an attitude about a policy or situation, to seeking specific information, to putting the president "on-the-record," thereby forcing the president to take a public stand on an issue. The phrasing of some questions may advocate positions that are often counter to that of the administration. In each case, the president must remember who the ultimate audience is—the American public. Once again, from a political perspective, how a president responds to questions is as important as the content of his response. For Smith, the best questions at a press conference are the ones that elicit new information about the president's public self, the administration, and policies.

> The best presidential *answers* are those that enhance the president's leadership image to the American people. The best press *exchanges* are those which reveal that the president is exercising legitimate leadership and the press is exercising its legitimate watchdog role.[58]

It is important for the president to demonstrate a broad knowledge of issues, to use humor, and to connect with the viewing audience. From a strategic perspective, a president hopes to avoid controversy and to gain a lift in the polls and approval ratings. Press conferences have declined in importance in recent years. Networks find them too scripted and less informative. Presidents experience less control over the agenda and endure more hostile questions.

The News Media

We have already noted how the news media have impacted how candidates run for office. It is also important to recognize the impact of the media upon governing. Prior to television, presidents governed by accommodating broad coalitions and interests groups; leadership in the age of television, however, requires the mobilization of public opinion. Public opinion has become a critical element of political influence.

Today, there are over 2,000 credentialed White House correspondents. Usually between 100 and 150 will travel with the president on any domestic trip and over 300 go on international visits.[59] It seems every move, statement, and action of the president is worthy or *potentially* worthy of public attention. However, do we really need to see the president or hear something from the White House *every day*? From network perspectives, news coverage of the White House is: profitable, does not conflict with local news programming, fulfills FCC requirements for public affairs programming, is easy and cost-effective to produce, and advances the careers of White House correspondents.[60]

According to Doris Graber, the media perform four broad and major functions in terms of the presidency. First, they inform the executive branch about current events and public issues. By highlighting some issues and events, they may focus executive attention or actions. Second, they help the executive branch stay informed of and in touch with public opinion and concerns. Mirroring public concerns helps provide an agenda for action. Third, the media provide the means for presidents to communicate with the public. Finally, the media provide accountability by keeping the president in full public view in action, words, and deeds.[61]

The institutional presidency relies on the news media to communicate strategically to a variety of audiences: the general public, opinion leaders, members of the other branches of government, and the international community, to name only a few. Timothy Cook identifies three reasons why presidents use the news media as a strategic tool for governing the nation.[62] First, just making news can be making policy itself. For example, at the noon White House briefing, public statements about a whole range of issues become "official" policy that influences subsequent actions and behaviors. Especially in the international arena, presidential statements become the basis for negotiation and terms of our relationships with other nations. Second, making news is a way the president can call attention to preferred issues and frame public debate. Publicity about issues influences the public's demand for action. Finally, making news is itself a form of public persuasion. News coverage of an event influences public opinion in several ways. Media provide very basic information and facts about issues necessary for opinion formation. The tone of coverage may influence public perceptions about issues. The duration or frequency of coverage of an item influences the sense of urgency or magnitude of an issue.

There are several techniques presidents use to achieve their objectives with the news media. The most basic is to allow or deny access to the president and other White House officials. Sometimes journalists agree to some basic guidelines of topics that may or may not be addressed. Off-the-record interviews are ways the White House can raise trial balloons or release information to test public reactions. Secrecy is often used, justified on grounds of national security or executive privilege. Of course, secrecy is difficult to maintain. The primary technique the White House uses is the attempt to control the timing of information release. Positive information is released easily and early. More negative information is released on a Friday, late in the afternoon or early in the evening, thus ensuring that the news is exposed to small weekend audiences.[63]

There is a rather clear cycle to media coverage and cooperation with the White House regardless of being a Democratic or Republican administration. Grossman and Kumar identify three stages of a relationship between a newly elected president and the media.[64] First, in the alliance stage, there is a high degree of mutual cooperation between the media and the president. Next follows the competition phase of the relationship where both sides are attempting to get their specific views heard. Manipulative strategies and more aggressive tone characterize this stage of the relationship. Finally, late in a president's administration, the detachment stage develops, where the relationship is rather formal and very structured. After much competition and contentiousness, both sides settle into a pattern or routine of interaction.

In a similar fashion, Fredic Smoller writes about the "four seasons of presidential news."[65] Each season is distinguished by the content and tone of news coverage. In general, coverage proceeds from being positive in tone to being negative in tone. The first stage of coverage is a personal profile of the president, staff, and family. These tend to be the most favorable, highlighting past accomplishments and unique events in the lives of the first family. The second stage moves to coverage of the president's legislative agenda and policy initiatives. The tone becomes increasingly negative as the press focuses on the president's persuasive attempts to push programs through Congress. In the third stage, the legislative program and initiatives are prematurely evaluated. The press judges the competency and the effectiveness of programs long before the programs can be implemented or the impact of any specific piece of legislation can be felt. During this stage, the media also focus on internal staff conflicts or scandals. Washington elites pass judgment, and opposition members of Congress are granted greater access to the news media. In the final stage of coverage, the president is reevaluated. The skills and competency of the president are openly questioned. The portrayal is now one of crisis, failure, and decline. According to Smoller, "In short, the president is profiled, and then his policies are examined; these policies are evaluated, and then the president is reevaluated."[66]

Richard Perloff identifies five characteristics of presidential news.[67] First, it tends to be very cynical. Journalists, especially since Watergate, have become less trusting and more adversarial in dealing with all issues of politics and with politicians in general. Second, presidential news tends to focus on very narrow political issues. As noted in previous discussions, complex issues are reduced to winners and losers, right or wrong, and just two sides. The third characteristic of presidential news is that it focuses on conflict and controversy. Audience attraction to and need for drama encourages such an approach to covering politics. On television, this conflict takes on an especially visual component. Finally, as recognized by Smoller, presidential news tends to be personal.

Speech Making

Presidents invite us, through the medium of television, into the privacy of their living rooms or offices, for informal, "presidential conversations" rather than addressing large crowds gathered in auditoriums. This change, of course, did not occur overnight. Radio signaled the change from flamboyant oratory to a more conversational style. Franklin D. Roosevelt initiated the fireside chats and brought live presidential communication into American living rooms. As Roosevelt's style became institutionalized, and as politicians became accustomed and adapted to the new medium, public addresses increasingly took on the style and tone of conversation. Speeches became talk. Television furthered this process, rendering presidential speech more intimate and conversational. The visual dimension of television also reinforced the apparently casual, intimate exchange between leaders and the citizenry. Cathcart and Gumpert classify such exchanges as "media simulated interpersonal communication."[68] Kathleen Jamieson argues that the interpersonal, intimate context created through television requires a "new eloquence," one in which candidates and presidents adopt a personal and revealing style that engages the audience in conversation.[69] Characteristics of "eloquence conversation" and research about nonverbal communication inform our understanding of the transformation of presidential communication strategies in the age of television. At the same time, television shapes the interaction in ways different from actual interpersonal communication contexts. With all of this in mind, we find that the interaction of the television audience is thus "parasocial"[70]

Presidents who increasingly rely on the medium of television are forced to play the communication game by television's rules. This not only means that speeches are shorter, it also means they are crafted specifically for television.[71] Presidential speech is increasingly familiar, personalized, and self-revealing. Reagan's use of contractions, simple, often incomplete sentences, informal transitions, colloquial language, and frequent stories transformed his "formal" Oval Office addresses to conversations with the American people.[72] His skillful adaptation to the camera simulated direct eye contact with individuals in his audience. It had all the appearance of conversation. This conversational style "invite[s] us to conclude that we know and like" presidents who use it.[73] Ronald Reagan first excelled at this style, which stands in marked contrast even to the conversational style of Franklin D. Roosevelt, for example. The strength of Reagan's rhetoric is that we feel we know and understand him; the strength of FDR was that he knew and understood us. Bill Clinton, through his mediated conversational style accomplishes both, especially in the town-hall meeting format. For Clinton, the town-hall meetings best represent the power and potential of successful mediated conversation as a strategy of public discourse and persuasion in the age of telepolitics.[74]

Presidential discourse. Roderick Hart provides the most systematic and detailed study of presidential discourse.[75] He and his colleagues coded every address from the Truman through the Reagan administrations. He found that the presidents during this time period averaged 20 speeches per month, ranging from Eisenhower's low of 10 to Ford's high of 43. Interestingly, in his first year, each new president gave more speeches than the previous president and more speeches were given in the second year of each presidency than in the first. The speech sample reveals that 37.5 percent were ceremonial in nature, 26.5 percent were briefings, 15 percent were given at political rallies, 10.3 percent were given at organizational meetings, with the remainder delivered at miscellaneous speaking activities.[76] Hart's analysis also finds that presidential language is more optimistic, contains more realism, is less complex, and contains more self-references than language of other leaders.[77] When comparing media versus non-media appearances, Hart found that presidential television language has more self-references, familiarity, human interest, and optimism than the language of personal appearances.

Richard Perloff argues that the rhetorical presidency is a broad theoretical construct, for example:[78]

- presidential addresses can be as important as policies;
- the words of presidents are deeds since they bring the force and majesty of the office with them;
- even presidential directives will not achieve their goals if presidents cannot persuade the public and the press to support their aims;
- presidents have a variety of ways to influence opinions, including speeches, press conferences, and the news;
- presidential messages are the outgrowth of modern marketing techniques.

From a strategic perspective, presidential discourse is required because:[79]

- presidential persuasion is no longer a private game, but a very public endeavor;
- presidents are increasingly appealing to the public for support;
- going public can take different forms, including public addresses, presidential appearances, political travel, and the use of new technologies.

The process of speech making.   Throughout history ghostwriters have lived in the shadows of public awareness, at least since a Sicilian named Corax received payment to coach awkward orators over 2,500 years ago. Academics such as Plato might later quarrel about the presumptuous ethics of teachers and writers who would help "the weaker look the stronger." But the existence of republican government has always required coaching in the art of rhetoric. Like other arts, political persuasion must be learned. The propriety of using a collaborator is arguably as acceptable as the relationship between mentor and apprentice, legal counsel and client, or expert and layman.

But there is a threshold that is crossed at some risk. Most Americans know that a high proportion of the president's rhetoric originates in the minds of subordinates. Few journalists even bother to inquire about the writers who assisted in preparing a particular message. Although this sharing of a political burden is an accepted folkway, public figures must not seem to relinquish control over what is issued in their name. Collaboration cannot be capitulation. With the presumption of authorship comes the burden of responsibility.

A romantic but not entirely inaccurate view of the presidency is that it once nurtured a grandiloquent rhetorical tradition. Washington's Inaugural, Jefferson's First Inaugural, Jackson's popular challenges to Calhoun on the issue of nullification, and Lincoln's wartime and emancipation statements have all become part of America's political literature. The sonorities and spaciousness of eighteenth- and nineteenth-century rhetoric vividly recall the heyday of the orator, but also what seems at first glance to be an old art in a state of advanced decay. The conciseness and ordinary prose of today's political rhetoric often renders it incapable of provoking the range of emotions that a Lincoln–Douglas debate could muster in the mid-1800s. Its metaphors and images are more mundane—taken from the broken rhythms and incomplete sentences of conversation rather than the fuller images of the printed word. Whereas orators of old drew images from Shakespeare and the Bible, Presidents Reagan and George H. W. Bush found models in Hollywood characterizations of Knute Rockne and Dirty Harry ("Let's win one for the Gipper," "Make my day," "Read my lips").

The potential for rhetorically altering the nation's climate of opinion has never been greater. With the evolution in the 1920s of mass radio audiences for a single speech, presidential utterance was rendered cautious and tactical rather than spacious and all-encompassing. Through the mass reach of radio, Franklin Roosevelt addressed the rough equivalent of all of Jefferson's presidential audiences in just one 15-minute "fireside chat." Changed most dramatically by radio, oratory that previously had to be suited to only the immediate audience on hand (and a secondary audience of newspaper readers) suddenly had to suit a nation of diverse constituents and accidental listeners held together by the invisible thread of the radio network. The temptation to use this medium and to widen the appeal of key speeches made the speechwriter an attractive addition to the White House staff. By allowing a writer to undertake what had been for Woodrow Wilson and Theodore Roosevelt an immensely time-consuming task of speech drafting or dictation, a president not only saved time but also gained the confidence of knowing that someone was available to flag an ill-conceived remark.

The broadcasting of presidential addresses and increased reporting of all public appearances naturally meant that political rhetoric had to be adapted to a wider audience than ever before. The risks of an unintended slur were increased and meant that others would not intervene in what had been to most presidents the task least able to be delegated. As a public document having the widest possible distribution, it was thought a speech could no longer risk the candor expected by a gathering of a limited size. Presidents after Theodore Roosevelt were largely unwilling to jeopardize their political power by depending on their own memories or on their skills at speaking "off the cuff." The broad dissemination of virtually every message now meant that too much was at stake.

The growth in the number of special assistants and aides concerned with public relations and speech writing is what presidential scholar Thomas Cronin considers "one of the more disquieting aspects of the recent enlargement of the presidential establishment."[80] The first speechwriter hired to assist a president was Judson Welliver, who joined the Harding administration with that designated role in 1920.[81] By any standard Harding needed all the help he could get to defend what became an increasingly troubled and corrupt administration after the Teapot Dome and Justice Department scandals in the early 1920s. Even earlier, in the 1880s, Chester Arthur employed a friend named Daniel Rollins to help draft a number of presidential messages clandestinely from New York. Perhaps because ghostwriting would have been an unthinkable sharing of responsibilities at the end of the nineteenth century, Rollins went to great pains to keep his help to the ailing Arthur a total secret.[82]

To a large extent speechwriters were to remain a rarity until the administration of Calvin Coolidge in 1923. Prior to Coolidge, the White House worked at whatever pace its officeholder set. Theodore Roosevelt not only answered the phone on occasion but relished the chance to write speeches on as broad a range of topics as a president has ever claimed to conquer. War, physical fitness, politics, conservation, human rights, corporate monopolies, and natural history were frequent topics heard from his "bully pulpit." For Woodrow Wilson, who followed William Howard Taft in 1912, speeches remained a high priority. Trained by a Scots Presbyterian minister who placed the highest value on his son's oratory, Wilson spent hours perfecting what still remains as some of the most thoughtful and coherent of all presidential rhetoric.

Calvin Coolidge managed to vastly increase the number of presidential speeches through the continued aid of Judson Welliver and others, thereby establishing both an important precedent and a harmful liability for the publicity-conscious executive branch. The precedent was that the enlarged staff became known to the public and perceptions of the office changed accordingly. With the Coolidge administration, Americans began to think of a president in the contemporary sense: as a leader whose fate was determined by the quality of his staff as well as by his own efforts. The liability was that rarely again would an executive's words reflect the undiluted visions and attitudes of just one person.

"Silent Cal" had managed to double the number of addresses over his eloquent predecessor, but at a heavy cost. No longer would presidents be content to write their own speeches, offer them for review and comment to close friends and advisers, and then deliver them. The emerging pattern was to be a reversal of that process for all except the most important statements. Others would write early drafts, with varying degrees of guidance, while only the president would do the editing.

This basic pattern remains today. Officials in the Speech Writing Office compose over 650 remarks for public events each year.[83] Though presidents occasionally write sections of important addresses such as convention acceptance speeches, inaugurals, and portions of state of the union addresses, they now more usually function as final editors of drafts written elsewhere. The highest praise that one usually hears from aides working with a president is not that the commander in chief is a good cowriter but is a good editor. The president's ability to quickly rework an aide's manuscript so that it represents an authentic copy of the president's own rhetorical signature—what is characteristic of the president in terms of idiom, ideas, and style—is a major test of the president's editorial skill. The result is the synthetic duplication of a rhetorical style that only approximates what a president might produce.

Today, staff members will use focus groups and polling data to fashion sound bites and key message points. In the recent past, key writers of important speeches have usually had a comparatively long association with the president, often in many capacities other than as speechwriter. When pondering a major speech, a president will typically seek out whoever has been a reliable writer among his closest aides. These selected members initiate the first draft and edit others in what has become an elaborate process of bureaucratic review.

Another way that presidential speeches are written reflects the inevitable tie between policy and the way it is articulated; it also demonstrates how a neat organizational chart outlining staff responsibilities misses the fact that key policy makers regularly function to write major addresses. What better method is available to insure that a presidential good intention is translated into a firm commitment than to write the script of that commitment on behalf of the president? As a matter of routine, new policy initiatives in foreign and domestic affairs are in effect sponsored by a cabinet head or presidential staffer with a deep interest in that initiative's success.

Lesser speeches usually involve one or two subordinate speechwriters serving nominally under a senior aide and writer. These second-line staffers may also work on press releases, important mail, and reports. An assignment will usually come with advice on who should be contacted for background information. If a minor message directly involves a shift or new development in policy, a first draft or an outline of "talking points" is usually requested from the agency responsible for the area. If the address is political, it may incorporate the suggestions of a supportive member of Congress.

Only on rare occasions will a president be involved before several drafts have been refined and edited by senior writers. Normally the president is given a final draft from a few days to several weeks before the speech is delivered. It may be rejected, sending the staff into frantic high gear to produce something new in a short period of time; more commonly, the draft is edited by the president, sometimes with the request to clean up or alter one or two passages.

Surprisingly, however, there is little evidence to suggest that writers chosen for a routine speech are selected because of their expertise on the topic. The mundane realities of office work, such as who has the time, may be more important in determining an assignment than who will produce the best draft. What emerges from various memoirs and accounts is that anybody from as many as five or six writers might produce a first draft. There is also little support for what would seem to be the natural conclusion that a president at least oversees the assigning and outline of a speech. The memoirs of most presidents contribute to this false impression. They frequently speak of "the need for a speech" to the National Association of Broadcasters, the V.F.W., the National Press Club, or thousands of other potential audiences. In fact, the decision to appear before a group—and the secondary step of assigning a writer—may well fall to one of several of the president's chief political advisers.

Richard Perloff thinks presidential oratory is indeed important. However, just what is the impact of presidential discourse? Does it work? In attempting to answer these pragmatic questions, he observes:[84]

- presidential speeches do not always increase public support for the president.
- presidential speeches are unlikely to influence public opinion if the president fails to make a clear and convincing case for the policy recommendations, and if the rhetoric is inconsistent with the chief executive's public image.
- presidential speeches will fail if they do not mobilize elite members of the president's political party.
- presidential speeches can change political cognitions.
- presidential speeches can influence people's feelings and attitudes.
- presidential speeches can help a president hold together a fragile political coalition.
- presidential speeches help to preserve the institution of the presidency.
- presidential speeches can change the nature of public discourse.
- presidential speeches can influence public policy by mobilizing powerful interest groups and by capitalizing on favorable press coverage.

Summary

The American presidency is a center of ever-accumulating functions, roles, obligations, and expectations. It is a universe unto itself that is constantly growing and expanding. From a distance one notices only singular "planets." On closer inspection, however, a strong interdependence of the planets is revealed. As an individual interacts with the constitutionality of the office, roles develop. These roles not only constrain individual behavior but also help create expectations of specified behavior. As expectations grow, so does the job. The public's perceptions of the office are institutionalized into models, myths, history, and textbooks. Unrealistic demands and expectations produce reliance on style rather than on substance, on image rather than on issues. A president must appear active, moral, fair, intelligent, and common. Yet, we know that appearances are deceiving and paradoxical. For how can one be both active and passive, both common and uncommon, both impotent and powerful?

Such ambiguity attests to the symbolic nature of the presidency. As an institution, the presidency is synthetic, believable, passive, vivid, simplified, and ambiguous. The office is our symbol of justice, freedom, equality, continuity, and national grandeur. The presidency is itself a significant symbol, comprised of many levels and elements. The institution reflects the beliefs, attitudes, and values of the public already established through socialization. All occupants, therefore, must demonstrate that they possess the perceived qualities of the office. presidential authority is largely a matter of impression management. presidents run and lead through a variety of communication activities and behaviors.

Notes

[1] Barbara Kellerman, *Reinventing Leadership* (Albany: State University of New York Press, 1999), 208.

[2] See Robert E. Denton, Jr., *Moral Leadership and the American Presidency* (Lanham, MD: Rowman & Littlefield, 2005), 1–45; and Robert E. Denton, Jr., *Symbolic Dimensions of the American Presidency* (Long Grove, IL: Waveland Press, 1982), 37–66.

[3] Barbara Kellerman, *The Political Presidency* (New York: Oxford University Press, 1984), 349.

[4] Theodore Sorensen, *A Different Kind of Presidency* (New York: Harper & Row, 1984), 10.

[5] Dan Nimmo, *The Political Persuaders* (Englewood Cliffs, NJ: Prentice-Hall, 1970), 8.

[6] James Kouzes and Barry Posner, *Leadership Challenge*, 4th ed. (San Francisco: Jossey-Bass, 2007), 14.

[7] Stephen Ambrose, "Dwight D. Eisenhower," in *Character Above All*, ed. Robert A. Wilson (New York: Simon & Schuster, 1995), 61.

[8] Theodore Lowi, *The Personal President* (Ithaca, NY: Cornell University Press, 1985), xi.

[9] Dennis Simon and Charles Ostrom, "The Politics of Prestige," *Presidential Studies Quarterly* 18, no. 4 (1988): 755.

[10] George Edwards, *The Public Presidency* (New York: St. Martin's Press, 1983), 1.

[11] Raymond Moore, "The Constitution, the Presidency and 1988," *Presidential Studies Quarterly* 18, no. 1 (1983): 60.

[12] Kellerman, *The Political Presidency*.

[13] Rockman, *The Leadership Question* (New York, Praeger, 1984), 177–178.

[14] Ryan Barilleaux, *The Post-Modern Presidency* (New York: Praeger, 1988), 2.

[15] Ibid., 77.

[16] Bruce Miroff, "Courting the Public," in *The Postmodern Presidency*, ed. Steven Schier (Pittsburgh: University of Pittsburgh Press, 2000), 106.

[17] Ibid., 106.

[18] Shawn J. Parry-Giles and Trevor Parry-Giles, *Constructing Clinton* (New York: Peter Lang, 2002), 5.

[19] Ibid., 15.

[20] Ibid., 158.

[21] Joe Klein, *The Natural* (New York: Doubleday, 2002), 184.

[22] James W. Ceaser, G. E. Thurow, Jeffery Tulis, and J. M. Bessette, "The Rise of the Rhetorical Presidency," *Presidential Studies Quarterly* 11 (1981): 158–171.

[23] Craig Allen Smith and Kathy Smith, *The White House Speaks* (Westport, CT: Praeger, 1990), 16.

[24] Jeffrey Tulis, *The Rhetorical Presidency* (Princeton, NJ: Princeton University Press, 1987), 4.

[25] Rossiter, *The American Presidency* (New York: Mentor Books, 1962), 16.

[26] Roderick Hart, *The Sound of Leadership* (Chicago: University of Chicago Press, 1987), 196.

[27] Rossiter, *The American Presidency*, 72–75.

[28] Thomas Cronin, *The State of the Presidency* (Boston: Little, Brown, 1975), 250–256.

[29] Bruce Buchanan, *The Presidential Experience* (Englewood Cliffs, NJ: Prentice-Hall, 1978), 29.

[30] George Reedy, *The Twilight of the Presidency* (New York: World, 1970), 29.

[31] Edward Corwin, *The President: Office and Powers*, 3rd ed. (New York: New York University Press, 1948), 20–23.

[32] Rossiter, *The American Presidency*, 28–37.

[33] Emmet Hughes, *The Living Presidency* (New York: Penguin Books, 1972), 26.

[34] Alfred deGrazia, "The Myth of the President," in *The Presidency*, ed. Aaron Wildavsky (Boston: Little, Brown, 1969), 50.

[35] Ibid., 50.

[36] Alvin Sanoff, "A Conversation with Theodore H. White," *U.S. News and World Report*, July 5, 1982, 59.

[37] Cronin, "The Presidency Public Relations Script," in *The Presidency Reappraised*, ed. Rexford Tugwell and Thomas Cronin (New York: Praeger, 1974), 168.

[38] Michael Pfau et al., "Relational and Competence Perceptions of Presidential Candidates during the Primary Election Campaigns." Paper presented at the International Communication Association Convention, Washington, DC, May 1993.

[39] Harold Lasswell, *Psychopathology and Politics* (Chicago: University of Chicago Press, 1930).

[40] Fred Greenstein, "What the President Means to Americans" and "Popular Images of the President," in *The Presidency*, ed. Aaron Wildavsky (Boston: Little, Brown, 1969), 121–147; 287–295.

[41] Theodore White, *Breach of Faith* (New York: Antheneum, 1975), 324.

[42] Victor Lasky, *Jimmy Carter: The Man and the Myth* (New York: Richard Marek, 1979), 16.

[43] Jimmy Carter, *Keeping Faith* (New York: Bantam Books, 1982), 27.

[44] See Robert E. Denton, Jr., *The Primetime Presidency of Ronald Reagan* (Westport, CT: Praeger, 1988).

[45] John Maltese, *Spin Control* (Chapel Hill: University of North Carolina Press, 1992), 2.

[46] Richard Perloff, *Political Communication* (Mahwah, NJ: Erlbaum, 1998), 61.

[47] Ibid., 62.

[48] Ibid., 63.

[49] Robert E. Denton, Jr. and Rachel L. Holloway, "Clinton and the Town Hall Meetings: Mediated Conversation and the Risk of Being 'In Touch,'" in *The Clinton Presidency: Images, Issues, and Communication Strategies*, ed. Robert E. Denton, Jr. and Rachel L. Holloway (Westport, CT: Praeger, 1996), 34.

[50] James Mueller, *Towel Snapping the Press* (Lanham, MD: Rowman & Littlefield, 2006), xv.

[51] Ibid., 68.

[52] Shirley Warshaw, *The Keys to Power* (New York: Longman, 2000), 320.

[53] Carolyn Smith, *Presidential Press Conferences* (Westport, CT: Praeger, 1990), 65.

[54] Ibid., 65.

[55] Ibid., 132–139.

[56] Warshaw, *The Keys to Power*, 318.

[57] Mueller, *Towel Snapping the Press*, 170.

[58] Smith, *Presidential Press Conferences*, 109.

[59] David Paletz, *The Media in American Politics*, 2nd. ed. (New York: Longman, 2002).

[60] Jan Leighley, *Mass Media and Politics* (Boston: Houghton Mifflin, 2004), 115.

[61] Graber, *Mass Media & American Politics*, 7th ed. (Washington, DC: Congressional Quarterly Press, 2006), 251–253.

[62] Timothy Cook, *Governing with the News* (Chicago: University of Chicago Press, 1998), 124–140.

[63] Paletz, *The Media in American Politics*, 267.

[64] Michael Grossman and Martha Kumar, *Portraying the President* (Baltimore: Johns Hopkins University Press, 1981), 273–298.

[65] Fredic Smoller, *The Six O'Clock Presidency* (New York: Praeger, 1990), 66–74.

[66] Ibid., 67.

[67] Perloff, *Political Communication*, 84–89.

[68] Robert Cathcart and Gary Gumpert, "Mediated Interpersonal Communication: Toward a New Typology," *Quarterly Journal of Speech* 69 (1983): 267–277.

[69] Kathleen Hall Jamieson, *Eloquence in the Electronic Age* (New York: Oxford University Press, 1988).

[70] See Cathcart and Gumpert, "Mediated Interpersonal Communication"; Michael Pfau, "A Channel Approach to Television Influence," *Journal of Broadcasting and Electronic Media* 34 (1990): 195–314.

[71] See Denton, *The Primetime Presidency of Ronald Reagan*.

[72] Jamieson, *Eloquence in the Electronic Age*, 166.

[73] Ibid., 166.

[74] See Denton and Holloway, "Clinton and the Town Hall Meetings."

[75] Roderick Hart, *Sounds of Leadership* (Chicago: University of Chicago Press, 1987).

[76] Ibid., 69.

[77] Roderick Hart, *Verbal Style and the American Presidency* (New York: Academic Press, 1984), 50.

[78] Perloff, *Political Communication*, 105.

[79] Ibid., 104.

[80] Cronin, *The State of the Presidency*, 137.

[81] Elmer Cronwell, *Presidential Leadership of Public Opinion* (Bloomington: Indiana University Press, 1965), 70.

[82] Michael Medved, *The Shadow Presidents* (New York: Times Books, 1979), 73.

[83] Graber, *Mass Media and American Politics*, 264.

[84] Perloff, *Political Communication*, 129–133.

Congress

Congress is a verbal culture.

—Harrison Fox and Susan Hammond

Members of Congress spend their time moving between the contexts of Washington and home—between governing and campaigning. Likewise, we tend to have two views of Congress. As an institution, we see it as a lawmaking body. While in Washington, we see legislators as members of the larger body who do legislative work, investigate, and work in committees. In a routine day a senator or representative may meet with ordinary constituents in the morning, lunch with a lobbyist at noontime, question expert witness in an afternoon meeting of a House or Senate committee, and receive an evening phone call from a cabinet official soliciting support on a close upcoming vote. In between these events, members may consult with a dozen colleagues, plan strategy on the introduction of a piece of legislation, tape a radio report to constituents back home, and review the schedule for a busy weekend of campaigning. In the meantime, staff members from the district will forward individual citizen requests for information, help, or advice to the Washington office for disposition. Members of Congress spend less than 40 percent of their time in Washington allotted to lawmaking duties.[1]

On the other hand, when we view them as individual members, they are representatives of our local concerns. We tend to judge our representatives by their service to the district, their communication with constituents, and the way they deal with district citizens or constituent service. Constituent service includes voicing concerns of the district, solving individual problems that citizens have with the government, and making sure that the district gets its share of federal money and assistance. Much of the constituent work is done by district staff members. Members spend a great deal of effort keeping in touch with constituents by mail, by personal appearances, and by print and electronic media.[2] The average member of Congress spends 120 days a year at home in the district (Senators average 80 days).[3] The frequent visits provide ways to be visible, raise funds, meet special interest groups, and explain votes and other legislative activities.

While congressional life is busy, it is primarily about talk. The primary job of a member of Congress is "talking" or communicating: with constituents by mail, media appearances, and public speeches; on the floor, in committees, during hearings; and with lobbyists at meetings, fund-raisers, and social gatherings. With regard to actual voting, there is not so much talking. Indeed, during the 2003–2004 session, for example, there were nearly 6,000 bills and joint resolutions introduced, but only 198 actual laws were enacted.[4] Thus, legislating is an endless round of exchanges in which information or support is sought from colleagues, the press, constituents, and interest groups. The currency of legislative life is communication with staff members, constituents, and peers.

This chapter examines some of the major relationships and communication processes that characterize the modern Congress. From a broad perspective, members of Congress must learn to work as one among many, conceding power in most settings, and sometimes winning it back by forming alliances, gaining important committee assignments, and getting the attention of the mass media on issues about which they feel strongly.

Legislative and Communication Functions

Legislatures have two primary functions: to provide oversight in the administration of the government and to pass laws. These two objectives are naturally related. The oversight of governmental operations—which today takes in nearly every facet of American life—includes the study of how agencies and commissions enforce laws or carry out administrative or court-mandated decisions. In the textbook model of such oversight, hearings and information from various committees and support units (for example, the Congressional Budget Office) produce the repeal or modification of existing laws. Such hearings also serve an "educational" function, providing the committee with the opportunity to orchestrate public opinion as a prerequisite to the introduction of legislation or as a counterweight to the president.

The legislative function is equally complex, although the basic procedures and traditions are well known. Bills are introduced by members, usually because they have a special interest in the subject, or because the legislation meets the needs of an important constituency. In what is usually a proposal's first test, it is routed to an appropriate committee according to what are sometimes unclear jurisdictional lines. The committee holds hearings, "marks up" the bill, votes it out to the floor, votes it down, or simply lets it die (as most do). A bill reported out of the committee is considered by the whole body, usually reshaped by key amendments, and voted on. It, or one similar to it, is considered by the other house and likewise voted on. Then differences between the two passed versions are worked out in a conference committee composed of a limited number of members from both the lower and upper houses. It then receives another vote in each house before it is forwarded to the president for signature or veto.

Few bills actually move through the Congress in such a straight sequence. Most are tabled, defeated, and amended in what is often a multi-year process. Final passage often comes only after repeated attempts over several sessions. When a bill is passed, it is usually far different from what its initial sponsors had in mind. Its adoption occurs only after a good deal of private bargaining and carefully negotiated compromises between party leaders and the president on key provisions. In all of this process a vigorous floor debate before well-attended sessions may never have occurred. But that is not to say that the legislative cycle does not involve a good deal of debate and discussion. The most widely reported summaries of the merits of bill are constructed by the news media out of the variegated fabric of press statements made by interested parties during hearings in committees and from presession publicity generated by lobbyists and others with financial or ideological stakes in the legislation.

Roger Davidson and Walter Oleszek argue that Congress is more than a collection of its members:

> It is a mature institution with a complex network of rules, structures, and traditions. These norms mark the boundaries of the legislative playing field and define the rules by which the game is played. Individual members generally must accept Congress on its own terms and conform to its established ways of doing things. Paradoxically, the institution at once both resists change and invites change.[5]

In the House, there are more formal channels of power and norms of behavior. Herbert Asher identifies seven norms of the House: relationships should be friendly, important work is done in committees, procedural rules are essential to be followed, members should not personally attack other members from the floor of the House, members should be prepared to trade votes, members should be specialists in at least one area, and freshmen members should serve "apprenticeships."[6]

Committees are an essential part of Congress. They serve two broad purposes: individually, members look for ways to benefit their constituents and institutionally committees become the centers of policy making, oversight of federal agencies, and public education through hearings. They provide forums for issue and policy debate.

Legislative Communication and Deliberation

As already noted, communication is not only the primary task of legislators but is also clearly at the core of congressional decision making. Members and their staffs work in a constant environment of competing messages from constituents, government officials, and other interested parties. However, the interaction between members of Congress and staff is equally important. David Whiteman who conducted a comprehensive study of communication between members and staff found a great deal of variation in the amount of interaction.[7] The amount of oral interaction is affected by the degree of hierarchy within the office. In addition, some members prefer communication in written form ranging from executive summaries of issues to full "markups" of potential legislation. As Whiteman observes, some members "are readers and some are listeners."[8]

He also found, not surprisingly, that most legislative assistants play an important role in member decision making. In terms of issues and public policy, most members of Congress maintain an "attentive but uninvolved stance, monitoring policy developments and responding as needed to legislative events."[9] It is the legislative staff who are the major communicators about policy information, who inform members of details and interpretations of pending legislation. Staff members play major roles during three stages of member decision making: when members are attentive to issues while staff monitor policy development and formulate responses; in shaping members legislative agenda by identifying key issues to address; and shaping specific responses and alternatives to legislation for member advocacy.[10]

On a daily-routine basis, congressional members receive three types of information from staff: policy information, political information, and procedural information.[11] Policy information includes understanding the causes and magnitude of a problem and the impact proposed legislation has on budgetary issues as well as on specific constituencies and society at large. Political information refers to the position of other members, the point of view of party leaders, and the views of constituents. Procedural information includes the tracking of legislation, the schedule of activity in committees and on the floor, as well as the rules that govern consideration and voting of measures.

Paul Quirk recognizes that the predominate attention, images, and impressions of Congress focus on lobbying efforts of special interest groups, various political and ideological coalitions, and raw political power of congressional leaders. However, he argues that there is a great deal of constructive deliberation that goes on in the halls of Congress that benefits the quality of legislation and public policy.

Deliberation in Congress is important in three ways. First, adequate and full discussion of issues makes resulting policies more legitimate. There are opportunities for all sides of an issue to be heard. Second, congressional debate educates the public on issues of concern through news reports highlighting key arguments and positions. Finally, hopefully good policy and intelligent legislation are the end products of issue deliberation.[12]

Quirk defines congressional deliberation as "the intellectual process of identifying alternatives, gathering and evaluating information, weighing considerations, and making judgments about the merits of public policies."[13] Such deliberation deals with both substantive considerations as well as political ones. According to Quirk, policy deliberations include several important elements: identifying and developing alternative policies, estimating the consequences of those policies, assessing the ethical or emotional significance of policies and consequences, and refining provisions of proposed legislation.[14]

Of course, the primary vehicle for congressional deliberation is debate. "Members listen, and may contribute, to a stream of discourse about policy choices. Other actors—such as the president, other executive branch officials, interest group representatives, and various experts—also contribute."[15] Legislative debate may be formal or informal. The primary formal settings include committee hearings, committee markups (drafting legislation), and floor debates. Informal avenues are the meetings with interest groups, White House staff, and others from the executive branch to argue for or against potential provisions of a bill.[16]

Quirk makes the point that the rules, structure, and procedures of Congress influence the quality of deliberation. Some of the more important elements include: the amount of time and attention Congress gives to a decision; the available resources and expertise to address an issue; the information available for consideration; the opportunities for broad discussion among members; and incentives for deliberative effort, such as rules for selecting committee members and chairs.[17]

Although most of congressional deliberation is done in the full committee and in subcommittees, the final stage is the floor debates. This stage gains the most media attention and hence receives the greatest public awareness. According to Quirk, "a useful debate will feature direct confrontation between opposing claims, with substantial presentation of reasoning, evidence, criticism, and rebuttal. Finally, it will go on for a reasonable period and then end with a decision."[18]

The Built-In Dilemmas of Legislative Communication

From a communication perspective, legislatures present their occupants with a series of troubling limitations. Except for a few select leaders in the House and Senate, the individual member is usually subordinate to the power of others. There are a number of reasons for this, including the size of the legislative body. Any topic of general public interest creates heavy competition for public attention. The press is more likely to seek out statements and opinions from "key" legislative leaders.

A second problem is that members must consistently change the focus of their attention, and often their votes as well. This makes them agents of negotiation as much as agents of ideas, something the press finds difficult to track. Legislative roles are so varied. Every new legislative and oversight demand subtly shifts the meaning of a member's actions. A political party that is abandoned on one vote may be embraced on another. Likewise, a bipartisan coalition urging a particular program in one session may be hopelessly split when the issue arises again in the next session.

A third limitation is that party discipline in modern Congresses is uneven and often unreliable. Part of what has changed from the "old" hierarchical Congress is that members see independence as both a necessity and an advantage. In the age of the well-banked congressional candidate, the professional political consultant, and the heavy dependency on television campaigning, there is decreasing dependency on party organization.

A fourth problem facing all legislatures is that their structure generally casts their members into reactive rather than proactive roles. In the popular aphorism, the president proposes and the Congress disposes. The president tends to have the upper hand in setting the national agenda, but there are times, like in the latter half of George W. Bush's second term, when the Democratic congressional leadership can take some of the legislative initiative away from the president. Perhaps the most interesting communication problem facing the legislator is that reactive and frequently critical communication often has the effect of casting its source as a pessimist, if not a villain. All things being equal, it is easier to take an affirmative position than to hold back and deny the affirmations of someone else.

Finally, it should be noted that some facets of legislative life are simply out of fashion today. So much of what goes on in legislative deliberation seems either troublesome to the average citizen or at odds with the needs of modern technology. Except for private constituency service, such as helping a citizen find a lost Social Security check, there appears to be little public admiration for legislative craftsmanship or coalition building. Legislative skill is unlikely to be seen as a special gift. The mediation that represents the essential work of lawmaking will never fire the ordinary imagination in the same way that a visionary executive can. A president dramatizes the affirmation of universal values and national goals; the Congress carries on the essential but far less attractive task of representing the divisive pluralism of our current two-party system.

External and Internal Audiences

Members of Congress learn to function in two very different communication settings. They must maintain visibility in their own states or districts. At the same time, they must also work to master the sometimes Byzantine complexities of dealing with the internal support system on Capitol Hill. That structure includes an inner ring of colleagues and friends, an ever-growing number of staffers, and an outer ring of contacts represented by employees in federal agencies, members of the press, and interest group representatives. Most legislators prefer to work primarily in one of these two arenas, either building support through external appeals or mastering the internal "insider game" of governing. Both must be considered, but neither can be totally ignored.

As with all elective politics, the home constituency provides the member's ticket to the capital. A member of the House can never really think of the District of Columbia as "home" in the way it is for other high-level governmental employees. The congressional district generates a large chunk of the member's workload, particularly in the first few terms of service when the skillful exploitation of incumbency can pave the way for easier reelection. Everything else a member undertakes depends on building and mending bridges to the local community. The methods for doing this involve the prime tools of electoral politics: speeches, letters, press interviews, questionnaires, and appearances at countless meetings. Combined with the use of at least one district office, these tools serve to nurture sufficient local support.

Internal Channels

Internal channels of communication include the interaction with the ever-growing bureaucracy including a member's own staff, staffs of legislative leaders, committees, and a member's own party. These government employees are well trained, and many are from the academic and legal professions. Congress employs thousands of individuals for its own research and support agencies such as The Congressional Research Service, The Congressional Budget Office, The Office of Technology Assessment, and The General Accounting Office. Given the scope and impact of most legislation, many facets necessarily involve background study and, frequently, recommendations from the staffers, policy analysts, and lawyers spread throughout Congress and its research agencies.

Given that it has thousands of employees, it comes as no surprise that Congress enjoys a good deal of internal reporting about its activities. There are four news organizations that cover Congress for its members and other Washington insiders: *The Hill* and *Roll Call* are published in newspaper format twice a week; in addition, *Congressional Quarterly* provides a range of online and magazine-style services, as does *The National Journal*. Combined, they feature key issues before Congress, track progress on initiatives, and provide analysis of pending legislation.

External Channels

Members of Congress enjoy numerous opportunities to influence public discussion on a range of issues, especially on subjects relevant to their committee work. They have free mailing privileges, access to radio and television studios paid for in large part by the taxpaying public, access to impressive policy and economic research services, a wealth of standing invitations to speak, and the opportunity to cross-examine the leaders of countless agencies, businesses, and institutions.

In addition, the press has a long and well-institutionalized presence in both houses. Each side has separate galleries for the daily press, the periodical press, and radio and television. Each member assigns at least several staffers to handle press relations, which range from producing press releases to feeding sound bites into a machine that serves them up to radio stations back in the district. Many offices do quarterly newsletters, weekly columns for small local newspapers, and radio commentaries distributed to area stations. Some of the activities draw a fine line between constituent outreach and political advertising.

Members of the Senate have a greater chance to stand out as a resource or partisan voice in various forums of the national news media. The reality, however, is that most members of Congress labor in relative obscurity in terms of coverage by the press—especially in comparison to the coverage of the president.

When Congress gets detailed coverage of its actions, the coverage is most often negative. Reports of infighting and ethical violations are common, as are reports of procedural moves that seem to thwart the will of the majority. However, at an individual level, coverage is somewhat more positive. Those in leadership positions receive the most coverage.

Groups of one kind or another have always exerted influence on the decision making of Congress, and lobbying today has become a profession utilizing a variety of tactics. Direct lobbying is the traditional approach when lobbyists present their case to congressional staff or to the actual member. Member-to-member lobbying is also routine since garnering support for pending legislation is essential to passing law. Social lobbying, where lobbyists gain access to members at social events and gatherings, is another trusted means of sharing information and gathering favor. This includes the occasional reception to more formal corporate-funded "informational" trips. Usually, any single issue will bring a coalition of interested groups and parties to the table. Sometimes rival lobbying interests will join forces to promote or defend shared goals. Coalition lobbying has the advantage of bringing more money, contacts, and resources to bear on an issue. Grassroots lobbying, where organizations mobilize citizens to pressure legislators, is one of the most effective techniques. Legislators feel obligated to respond to constituents. Electronic lobbying utilizes phones, faxes, and e-mail to inundate a member's office with messages favoring or disfavoring a piece of legislation.[19]

Public opinion influences Congress, but in an interesting, and some would argue, indirect way. In all honesty, voters differ in terms of issue knowledge and attentiveness to national politics. However, the few who are informed and make their wishes known carry great influence over the direction and decisions of Congress. Robert Erikson and his colleagues observe "only an attentive minority actively makes policy demands and reacts to the actions and nonactions of Congress with their votes. Thus, when public opinion changes in the aggregate, informed and attentive voters are the ones who generate the change."[20] Thus, public opinion matters because of the involvement of informed voters who are more influential than their numbers would suggest.

Erikson and his colleagues also argue that the "liberal–conservative continuum" of public opinion is a major influence on congressional policy. Congress responds to shifts in public opinion, "moving leftward when liberal demands increase and rightward when conservative demands increase."[21]

Party control is important, and although Democrats and Republicans have different policy concerns and perspectives, their priorities are moderated by public opinion in order to stay in office.[22]

The pendulum swings from left to right in terms of political ideology because of public opinion. If public opinion favors more conservative policies, over time, politicians adopt more conservative postures resulting in more conservative policies and legislation. However, as the public lowers demand for more conservatism because its demands have been largely met, the attitudes and opinions from the liberal components get expression and subsequent congressional response.[23] In short, "liberal policy breeds conservative mood and vice versa for the reason that popular liberal legislation lessens the perceived need for more liberal legislation and popular conservative legislation lessens the perceived need for more conservative legislation."[24] Thus,

> when the electorate is in a liberal mood, the median voter sees existing policy as too conservative and welcomes more liberal legislation. When the electorate is in a conservative mood, the median voter sees policy as too liberal and welcomes more conservatism.[25]

Communication in Congress can thus be seen as a web of information and influence networks that link members to each other and congressional support staffs, and to the public via the mass media. Members who hope to influence public opinion on legislative issues seek external contacts that reach into their states and districts and sometimes into the national news media.

Congress on Television

C-SPAN was created in 1979 by the cable television industry as a nonprofit, public service entity. C-SPAN provides coverage of a wide variety of public affairs events. It most notably provided live gavel-to-gavel proceedings of the U.S. House of Representatives and of the U.S. Senate since 1986. With its three networks, C-SPAN also provides live coverage of many Congressional hearings, committee meetings, and press conferences.

Cameras in the legislative chambers has had a variety of effects, some intended, some unintended. There are charges of members "grandstanding," making highly charged remarks in order to make the news or to gain support of constituents back home. There are also concerns that the cameras have caused legislative debate to be more personal and partisan. Many members have mastered the use of "special order" speeches given on any topic at the end of the legislative day to reach out beyond the usually empty House. This provides an opportunity for members to address issues and themes for special interests, to serve as the source for colorful video for the news media, or to attract and nurture a national following. For many observers, cameras in the legislature are a mixed blessing.

Summary

Members of Congress are caught between two worlds—the world of Washington with national issues and concerns and the world of the home district with local needs and concerns. The job, in both realms, is one primarily of communicating: with fellow members, with constituents, with special interests, with staff specialists, and with media representatives.

Congress as a setting for communication offers a number of paradoxes. On one hand, the House and Senate are rich in human resources, including researchers, staffers, press relations specialists, and the energy of its members. Yet it struggles as a body to have an identity—a friendly face—that it can offer to the general public. Media attention and our need for a single leader give the presidency the preferred spot for defining and clarifying national issues.

Congress has dealt with the increasing complexity of national issues by fragmenting its decision-making structure into committees and specialized research staff. Most of the real work in each body is done in committee or in party caucuses. These features have generally made its work even more inaccessible to Americans, who have little time and even less inclination to follow its work. Except for those who keep up with Congress via C-SPAN and a limited number of other outlets, the body makes news only when there is the immediate promise of a showdown between party leaders or with the executive branch.

The legislative process calls for patience on the part of its observers and practitioners and respect for the rules and procedures of coalition building and compromise. As we have noted, most members seek power by mastering its "internal" processes: the "inside game" of the institution. By learning how to work their way into its committee power structure and professional staff, members are able to influence legislation within the realm of their specializations. Those who seek "external" channels to the public via the mass media have a much harder time. Media facilities in Congress are extensive, but media attention to Congress is limited, and heavily weighted toward the leadership of the House and Senate.

Notes

[1] Roger Davidson and Walter Oleszek, *Congress and Its Members*, 10th ed. (Washington, DC: Congressional Quarterly Press, 2006), 5.

[2] Ibid., 125–126.

[3] Ibid., 5.

[4] Jennifer E. Manning, *CRS Report for Congress: Congressional Statistics: Bill Introduced and Laws Enacted, 1947–2003* (March 3, 2004).

[5] Davidson and Oleszek, *Congress and Its Members*, 4.

[6] Ibid., 124–125.

[7] David Whiteman, *Communication in Congress* (Lawrence: University Press of Kansas, 1995), 28.

[8] Ibid., 28.

[9] Ibid., 36.

10 Ibid., 38.
11 Ibid., 40.
12 Paul Quirk, "Deliberation and Decision Making," in *The Legislative Branch*, ed. Paul Quirk and Sarah Binder (New York: Oxford University Press, 2005), 314–315.
13 Ibid., 316.
14 Ibid., 316–317.
15 Ibid., 317.
16 Ibid., 317.
17 Ibid., 324–325.
18 Ibid., 335.
19 Davidson and Oleszek, *Congress and Its Members*, 398–406.
20 Robert Erikson, Michael MacKuen, and James Stimson, "Public Opinion and Congressional Policy: A Macro-Level Perspective," in *The Macropolitics of Congress*, ed. Scott Adler and John Lapinski (Princeton: Princeton University Press, 2006), 79–80.
21 Ibid., 80–81.
22 Ibid., 81.
23 Ibid., 86.
24 Ibid., 88.
25 Ibid., 88.

The Courts[1]

> *The judicial organization of the United States is the hardest thing there is for a foreigner to understand. He finds judicial authority invoked in almost every political context, and from that he naturally concludes that the judge is one of the most important political powers in the United States.*
>
> —Alexis de Tocqueville

At first glance the various local, state, and federal courts of the United States seem to exist largely outside of the political system. It was clearly the intent of the writers of the Constitution to give the courts the status of impartial arbiters and fact finders insulated from the influences of individual factions. Federal judges and many of their counterparts in the states are appointed for life, immune from the more obvious pressures of public opinion. Such permanent tenure, Alexander Hamilton noted in *The Federalist Papers*, is an "excellent barrier to the encroachments and oppressions" of Congress and the best way to assure "steady, upright, and impartial administration of laws."[2]

The idea of justice is synonymous with fairness and impartiality. In theory, at least, the courts are not agents for any one faction, but guarantors of justice and fairness for all parties involved. The obvious symbolism of the traditional courtroom communicates this ideal. The judge is the beneficiary of what Jerome Frank has called the "cult of the robe." Special black garments make a symbolic plea to view the men and women of the judiciary as a "priestly tribe" removed from the rest of government.[3] The seating arrangement within the courtroom gives the litigants equal distance and equal access to the judicial arbiter, who sits on an elevated dais. Juries are literally and figuratively held apart from the proceedings by a barrier that defines their status as close observers, but also suggests their separation from the maneuvers of defendants, prosecutors, and other agents of the court.

In actuality, however, most judicial business occurs in conference rooms designed to bypass the rituals of a trial. Bargaining in private for quicker resolution of cases is the norm in both civil and criminal cases. Nevertheless, our courts are the primary settings for narratives about the resolution of conflict, the establishment of guilt, and the allocation of justice.

Three Functions of the Courts

As agencies of the state, courts perform three general functions. The first and most obvious function is to settle disputes, including conflicts that arise between individuals, corporations, municipalities, and states. When cases involve single individuals, this spectrum can extend from family and divorce courts, where the fallout of domestic crises are resolved in relative privacy, to much more complex cases where courts are asked to determine if certain contracts are enforceable. Nearly all disputes in the business community follow a relatively predictable pattern: a settlement is either worked out prior to the start of a court trial or a trial takes place that results in a decision about whether one of the parties has satisfied the conditions of a contract.

A second important function of the courts is to determine whether individuals or groups have violated laws, and, if so, to define and impose appropriate punishments. This is the familiar territory of the criminal trial, the kind of judicial action that is for many Americans the essence of the legal system. In both fictional and news forms, the details of crime and punishment provide a continuing and vital form of public theater. The courtroom drama remains as much a staple of popular entertainment as an enduring form of journalism. Witness the long line of *Law & Order* shows or the trial coverage of celebrities like O. J. Simpson and Paris Hilton.

The third function of the justice system in the United States is a much a consequence as a formal goal: A whole range of high state and federal courts increasingly share the function of policy making and policy implementation with the legislative and executive branches. This rule-making process makes headlines when Senate hearings are held to confirm federal and Supreme Court justices. Conservative voices decry the "activist" judges who "legislate" social policy without accountability, while more liberal folks welcome court mandates that force state and federal agencies to provide protections or services. It is this third function that has become an issue in state and national elections.

Politics and the Courts

In some ways, the diffuse U.S. legal system provides fertile ground in which to nurture political debate. Because the trial process has the effect of personalizing the consequences of laws in ways that other political institutions (such as legislatures) might not, courts provide a ready source of social details from which to construct popular narratives of tension and change. Although these narratives are a by-product rather than a purpose of its structure, the trial elicits for the public record the uniquely private features of personal and social conflict. Other institutions (such as Congress) reduce issues to generic principles and abstract "what ifs"; in contrast, the courts deal in the personal details of ordinary lives. This focus is in part seen in the common law tradition of building judgmental principles based on the particulars of individual cases. The insanity defense, for example, is almost always discussed in the popular media in the context of a specific instance, rather than through the abstract discussions of psychiatrists and legal scholars who focus on the underlying legal principles. In the public mind there may be a vague sense in which "the law" is understood as a body of abstract codes, but for most Americans the legal system exists at any time in the dramatic events that have surfaced in the national or local news agenda.

In addition to becoming the arena of justice for segments of society and their representatives, the nation's courts are also overtly political in several other ways. Prior to the twentieth century, the predominant legal philosophy was "formalism." In formalism, the application of legal principles embodied in statutes or prior precedents was a "mechanical" process. The decision in most cases was straightforward, discerning the meaning of words and guided by historical precedent. More recently, "legal realism" has emerged as the dominant legal philosophy where "legal interpretation is not a neutral, mechanical process, but a subjective, human one in which the judge's beliefs, values and politics come into play."[4] Today, legal scholars "generally acknowledge that constitutional provisions, statutes, and precedents typically leave gaps that must be filled by judges, and that judges with different values and philosophies will fill those gaps differently."[5]

There is also the nomination and appointment processes that cause great political debate. All 740 members of the federal judiciary are appointed. It is Article II, Section 2 of the Constitution that sets forth the criteria for the appointment of federal judges. It simply states that the president "shall nominate, and by and with the Advice and Consent of the Senate, shall appoint Ambassadors, other public Ministers and Consuls, Judges of the Supreme Court, and all other Officers of the United States." There is an assumption that politics should not play a role in judicial appointments, at the federal level as well as on the Supreme Court. If the judiciary is to adjudicate disputes among citizens and between citizens and government in an evenhanded way, the process of selection and confirmation should rise above the concerns of partisan politics. However, Peter Russell argues that, "no matter how the process is constructed it always has a political dimension."[6] In fact, the process of selecting judges has always been political. "The politics of that process—presidential nomination and appointment with the 'advice and consent' of the Senate—is a raw kind of politics in which conflicting considerations of ideology and policy are ventilated in a public arena."[7]

In recent Democratic and Republican administrations, we have witnessed an increase in the use of recess appointments by presidents to advance nominations stalled in the Senate; we have also seen an increase in the Senate's use of "holds" (parliamentary tactics to avoid nominations reaching the Senate Judiciary Committee) and filibusters to delay approval of federal judgeships.[8] For example, during the Clinton administration, Republicans placed "holds" on over one hundred federal judgeship nominations. Likewise, Democrats did the same to George W. Bush during both terms. In 2004, in a rather bold move, President Bush appointed Charles Pickering to the Fifth Circuit Court of Appeals during the congressional recess. Twice the Senate had denied Pickering confirmation, once by party vote and second in a failed attempt to end a filibuster.[9]

Since 2000, the battle for the ideological heart of the Supreme Court has become part of every presidential campaign. Republicans tend to pledge appointment of "strict constructionists" (or those following a formalist philosophy) to the courts while Democrats tend to promise to appoint more activist judges (or those following a legal realist philosophy). In the twentieth century, politics was the primary motivation in presidential selection of court nominees and played a role in the confirmation process as well.

Brian Tamanaha thinks that the "U.S. legal system, to put it dramatically, is in danger of becoming less of a system of law" and more a system of arbitrary decisions because "focusing on ends [has become] the paramount goal of judges in their decisions" and judges increasingly are rendering decisions according "to their own political views or preferences."[10] He argues that "rather than function to maintain social order and resolve disputes, as Hobbes suggested was the role of law, combatants will fight to control and use the implements of the law as weapons in social, political, religious, and economic disputes."[11]

The politics of the nomination process today is a balancing act. The nominees must be careful not to fully disclose opinions or views on potential issues or cases they may have to review. However, they must reveal enough legal philosophy for senators to gauge their potential approach to social issues and cases. Most senators, at the very least, want to ensure that nominees will decide a case according to the law rather than based on some political agenda. However, the trend in nominations is highly partisan, with party-line votes being the norm; support for a nominee may be withheld "even in the absence of substantial allegations of misconduct or unfitness."[12] Benjamin Wittes observes that the modern confirmation process "thrives on unpleasantness and aspires constantly to pressure nominees to make promises concerning the substance of their coming jurisprudence."[13] As a result, "nominations to the high court today represent major political confrontations, grand mobilizations of the political bases of both parties, along with their affiliated interest groups and sympathetic academics."[14]

There are four explanations why there are such fights today over nominations, Wittes speculates. First, there are those that argue nothing is really new about the contentious nominations. Nominations have always been political and partisan throughout the history of our nation. The second explanation holds that the nomination process has changed because of the liberal influence of seeking policy results rather than straightforward adjudication, as discussed above. The third explanation blames conservatives and Republicans for attempting to "pack" the court with ideologues. For more than a decade, conservative groups and organizations have highlighted the need for the appointment of more "constructionist" judges. Finally, some view the change in the judicial nomination process as simply a part of the larger erosion of civility in U.S. politics and culture. In addition, the narrow margins of partisan control of Congress for a number of years contribute to the intensity of nominee examinations.[15]

It had been 11 years without a change in membership on the Supreme Court, a modern record, when Chief Justice John G. Roberts Jr. and Justice Samuel A. Alito Jr. took their seats during the 2005 term. The late Justice Byron R. White, who retired in 1993 after 31 years, noted that every time a new justice joined the Court, it became a different Court. Chief Justice Roberts was 50 years old when he took the oath of office in a courtroom ceremony on Oct. 3, 2005. His arrival marked a generational shift. He had once been a law clerk to his predecessor, Chief Justice William H. Rehnquist, who had died a month earlier at 80 after a year-long battle with thyroid cancer. Along with Justice Alito, the Court has made an obvious shift to the right, beginning with decisions during the 2007 session. Interestingly, one-third of the decisions from that session were decided by 5 to 4 margins. This Court represents the divided views and philosophies of the American people.

The Courts in the Times of National Emergencies

Eric Posner and Adrian Vermeule observe that "when national emergencies strike, the executive acts, Congress acquiesces, and courts defer. When emergencies decay, judges become bolder, and soul searching begins."[16] This is certainly the case related to the "War on Terror" and the invasion of Iraq by the United States. In the shadow of 9/11, the American people and vast bipartisan majorities in Congress supported President George W. Bush's actions immediately after the attack as well as the decision to confront Saddam Hussein. Not surprising, as the confrontation in Iraq continued, challenges to the actions and assumptions relating to the presence of U.S. troops there were voiced in greater numbers.

The passage of the Patriot Act in the aftermath of 9/11 is an example of executive and legislative action that was a "reaction" to a national emergency. For some, the act went too far in terms of investigative and surveillance authority. In addition, there were concerns about the treatment of terrorist "combatants" and interrogation techniques used by Americans. Allegations of intemperance increased across all legal arenas as the "War on Terror" continued. In 2007, the Supreme Court entered the fray by agreeing to review the legality of holding terrorist "combatants" without "due process" of civil hearings or court proceedings.

There are two primary views concerning the role of law during national emergencies. The first is called the "deferential view" where judicial review of governmental action should be relaxed or suspended during the time frame of the emergency. This means that some constitutional rights might be relaxed so the executive branch can properly deal with the threat. The second perspective is called the "civil libertarian view" that argues constitutional rules should not be relaxed during an emergency. To do so is simply counter to the values and foundations of our society. In truth, although there is a tension, American response historically has been somewhat between the two viewpoints, with some "reaction" with moderation and continued revision of legislation and actions, some through Congress and some through the courts.

Communication Skills and the Legal Profession

Oral and written communication skills are fundamental to the practice of law. Two of the top 10 skills necessary for attorneys identified by the American Bar Association involve communication. One skill set is oral and written communication and the other includes interpersonal and negotiation skills. Communication for attorneys is more than just conversation. They must be able to speak clearly and concisely in both written and oral form. Today, regardless the type of practice, attorneys spend the majority of their time drafting a wide array of legal documents. Attorneys are also expected to memorize and recall large quantities of legal material.

Language is an important tool of attorneys. In court, good public speaking skills can win cases often regardless of the alleged facts of a case. Presentation is as important as the structure and content of an argument. The ability to speak persuasively is critical. Thus, the basic skills of public speaking, debate, and formal presentation are important. Finally, listening skills are important if attorneys are able to understand clients and colleagues with whom they will interact on a daily basis.

The Publicity Functions of Litigation

Most local, state, and even national courts go about conducting their work without the attention of the mass media or the general public. However, fairly routinely a case will grab national attention, ranging from the divorce of a celebrity, to a murder trial, to one corporation suing another. The higher the visibility of the case, the greater the likelihood that its details will raise questions about process and public policy. Many of the cases that do gain national exposure usually touch on issues of class, race, access to power, or policy.

The Politics of Prosecution

The process of determining who will become a defendant in a criminal or civil trial is partly selective, as it is in every complex society. Justice in the United States is frequently pursued at the discretion of the police, prosecutors, judges, regulators, and victims. At various times all of these interested parties may function as gatekeepers in the application of justice. Using a wide variety of crime reports and general population surveys, for instance, criminal justice experts estimate that over half of all assaults and rapes go unreported by their victims; most burglaries go unsolved; and the vast majority of "victimless crimes," such as gambling and prostitution, remain concealed.

Local prosecutors have a great deal of power. In consultation with grand juries, they largely determine which cases to pursue, those to settle out of court, and those to drop. They seek to bring forth cases that will result in successful prosecution, those worth the time, effort, and utilization of limited resources. There are many elements of consideration: could pursuing the case become embarrassing? Does it involve a high-profile leader? Is the case strong enough for conviction?

As public servants, prosecutors may be viewed as "crime fighters," arbiters of justice, and protectors of community values. Often, the position of prosecutor or district attorney provides a path toward politics and public office. Many prosecutors become mayors, work in state and federal government, and then move to hold public office. High-profile cases generate media attention. For example, in March 2006, members of the Duke University lacrosse team held a party off campus. An invited stripper, Crystal Gall Mangum, who was African American, accused three members of the team of rape, assault, and sodomy. Amid the allegations, racial tensions increased, the team was suspended, and the coach fired. District Attorney Mike Nifong conducted over 50 media interviews and called the accused men various names, including "hooligans." All the while, Nifong was involved in a reelection race for his position as district attorney. As the case continued to unfold, media outlets and defense attorneys became critical of how the case was being handled.

Nifong delivered ongoing public commentary that maligned the character of the accused players and that exaggerated and intensified racial tensions across North Carolina, as well as throughout the nation. As the details of the scandal unfolded, it became clear that the players had been falsely accused and that District Attorney Nifong was guilty of gross prosecutorial misconduct. Subsequently, all charges against the players were dropped; Nifong later resigned from his position, was disbarred, and was found guilty of 27 out of 32 ethical violations. The three accused members of the team received a settlement from Duke University. At the very least, this was a story of a district attorney who enjoyed the instant fame, allowed ambition to supersede his official duties, and abused his public trust.

The Politics of Litigation

Another important way the courts function as extensions of the political process is in the way civil litigation can be used to generate favorable publicity. Many groups use legal action as a way to activate public opinion. Civil suits may manifestly seek financial damages, changes in the conduct of one of the parties, or a combination of both. But they also function to raise concerns or orchestrate general public opinion for the future.

Among the most specific rhetorical objectives of litigation is the chance to shape public opinion against a defendant, which is frequently a scenario that gives the upper hand to those who take on corporate giants. Litigation attracts attention and sometimes taps into considerable public sympathy for the victims portrayed in widely reported news stories. For example, the decision by an environmental group to seek damages on behalf of the residents who live near a corporation's factory can carry a certain level of credibility that simple charges of pollution do not. The filing of a suit binds the corporation to respond. In some cases, just the threat of a public trial satisfies the prime objective of the plaintiff, which may be to put the company on the hot seat and garner some type of settlement. Both parties to the conflict may find that the uncertainty of a verdict is less desirable than an out-of-court settlement that allows each side to save face.

Television and the Courts

The large majority of those who administer the courts in the United States view the publicity value of mass media coverage with skepticism and occasional hostility. Former Supreme Court Chief Justice Warren Burger's legendary contempt for television journalism became one of the most identifiable features of his tenure before he retired. He repeatedly cautioned clerks and staff in the Court to avoid talking to the press. It was not unusual for Burger to specify to a group that he would speak before them only if broadcasters were excluded.[17] His reactions were extreme, but they reflect what have been the feelings of many who control the judiciary—that publicity is not a constructive force in the administration of justice. In 2000, Chief Justice William Rehnquist denied requests for media to cover the Court's historic post-election deliberations without providing reasons. However, audiotape of the proceedings was made available quickly upon conclusion of the hearings. More recently, Chief Justice John Roberts expressed that the Supreme Court is still not interested in televising its hearings: "All of the justices view themselves as trustees of an extremely valuable institution. We're going to be very careful before we do anything that will have an adverse impact on that."[18]

Much of the wariness about media coverage of criminal cases concerns the effect it may have on potential jurors and witnesses. Widespread coverage of crime pits two important constitutional principles against each other:

freedom of speech and the right to a fair trial. On one hand, the First Amendment protects the rights of journalists to print or broadcast information about crimes, including photographs of crime scenes and interviews with victims and witnesses, but does this coverage infringe on a defendant's right to a fair and impartial trial, a right guaranteed by the Sixth Amendment?[19] Furthermore, extensive coverage of arrests and pretrial proceedings have sometimes made it difficult to find jurors who have not already formed opinions about a defendant's guilt based on what has been reported.

The issue may be further complicated when a trial actually begins; judges and journalists then must deal with very specific questions of privacy. For example, to what extent should the victims of crimes and their families have the protection of the courts to keep their names and faces from public view? Are witnesses to be given any protection if their testimony could place them in possible danger? It is easy for most people to accept a judge's decision to restrict the reporting of the names of children and other vulnerable victims. But members of the press are hostile to any court proceedings that give weight to "gag rules" issued from the bench and that restrict reporting. In general, court cases that have challenged the concept of the open courtroom have resulted in decisions that favor journalistic access. But for many jurists and observers there is a qualitative difference between access for the print media and access for cameras. The immediacy and sometimes intense visibility of video coverage is often questioned, primarily on the grounds that it may change the process and put unreasonable pressures on the participants.

The federal judiciary prohibits televised coverage for all proceedings. Some states, however, allow cameras into the courtroom primarily upon the decision of the judge. Other states allow coverage, but only if all trial participants agree. Still other states allow televised coverage only of appellate proceedings. Today, 43 states allow coverage at the trial level.[20]

There are several concerns about the effects of cameras in courtrooms in addition to the issue of a fair trial mentioned above. Some fear that the presence of a camera will have an effect on trial participants, such as create witness distraction, nervousness, and distortion of testimony, or make jurors less willing to serve. In addition, there are concerns that cameras may prolong trials with dramatic testimony and antics. Cameras may well encourage theatrics by the attorneys. Today, the standard example of negative consequences of cameras in the courtroom is the O. J. Simpson trial.

In contrast, there are those who argue that all court proceedings, ranging from state courts, to federal courts, and all the way to the Supreme Court, should be open to full media coverage, including the use of cameras. Supporters for coverage argue that advances in today's technology have made cameras less intrusive. Courtrooms could be wired for audio and video with small wall-mounted cameras. Digital video and photography continue to reduce the visual impact of cameras in the courtroom. In addition, media outlets could cooperate by sharing video, pooling reporters, and following strict behavioral guidelines.[21]

Camera coverage of state, federal, and Supreme Court proceedings does have some benefits. It could enhance public education about the legal system and even increase the public's confidence in our judicial process. As Al Tompkins argues:

> I always thought the single best public relations the judiciary could make would be to allow the people to see the system as it really is. It is neither as neat and tidy as Perry Mason nor as dramatic as Matlock. In the end, the banning of cameras from the courtroom serves only one purpose. It preserves the mystique and mystery of the court but does nothing to illuminate the citizens. That is antithetical to democracy.[22]

As with any tool, the presence of cameras in the courtroom is neither good nor bad. It is how the media portray the proceedings that influence the perceptions of the public. However, this has always been the case. At least, with cameras in all levels of the courts, the perceptions of the legal process are less likely to be distorted and there would be a permanent audio-visual record of important cases that mere reporting or verbal transcripts are unable to fully capture.

Summary

In this chapter we have argued that the courts are a major agent in the influence of public discourse about U.S. politics. The conventional view that the courts are apolitical because they exist outside the administrative and legislative institutions of government does not hold up under close scrutiny. In many ways the judiciary contributes to political debate and public discussion. Some judges and prosecutors are elected; others are appointed. Some courts issue decisions that make policy. Today, the intense battles over the confirmation of federal judges and Supreme Court justices represent the classic dispute over the role and function of judicial officers. Do they apply laws as written or make social policy?

Civil and criminal trials have a natural dramatic structure that can make them ideal settings for distilling larger cultural conflicts. They can focus attention on the effects of controversial policies. Trials personalize issues in ways that make it easy to attract media attention. They sometimes focus attention on tensions in the society that flow from group feelings of social alienation or rejection. Trials that include television coverage carry the special opportunity to emerge as major events, especially when celebrities or high-visibility crimes are involved. The televised trial can turn outrage and vindication into instant pleasures available to everyone, visceral responses that do not have to be confirmed by the disembodied facts of a secondhand narrative.

We have also argued that litigation frequently has a political effect—and sometimes a political purpose. Prosecutors may make calculations about the nature of public opinion and how it squares with the need to pursue or to ignore certain kinds of crimes. Organizations with public policy objectives may make the same calculations, knowing that the publicity value of a lawsuit against a key institution can energize supporters and focus public attention.

Finally, we have explored the debate over the use of cameras in the courtrooms. There are advantages and disadvantages. Although cameras could open the judicial process, it could also work to trivialize and sensationalize certain legal proceedings.

Notes

[1] Gary Woodward contributed to portions of this chapter.

[2] Alexander Hamilton et. al., *The Federalist Papers* (New York: Mentor, 1961), 465.

[3] Jerome Frank, *Courts on Trial* (Princeton, NJ: Princeton University Press, 1950), 256–257.

[4] Michael C. Dorf, *No Litmus Test* (Lanham, MD: Rowman & Littlefield, 2006), 10.

[5] Ibid., 10.

[6] Peter Russell, "Conclusion," in *Appointing Judges in an Age of Judicial Power*, ed. Kate Malleson and Peter Russell (Toronto: University of Toronto Press, 2006), 420.

[7] Ibid., 420.

[8] Michael Tolley, "Legal Controversies over Federal Judicial Selection in the United States: Breaking the Cycle of Obstruction and Retribution over Judicial Appointments," in *Appointing Judges in an Age of Judicial Power*, ed. Kate Malleson and Peter Russell (Toronto: University of Toronto Press, 2006), 81.

[9] Ibid., 83.

[10] Brian Tamanaha, *Law as a Means to an End* (Cambridge, England: Cambridge University Press, 2006), 2.

[11] Ibid., 2.

[12] Benjamin Wittes, *Confirmation Wars* (Lanham, MD: Rowman & Littlefield, 2006), 6.

[13] Ibid., 2.

[14] Ibid., 2.

[15] Ibid., 10.

[16] Eric Posner and Adrian Vermeule, *Terror in the Balance* (New York: Oxford University Press, 2007), 3.

[17] William Rivers, *The Other Government* (New York: Universe, 1982), 95–96.

[18] The Associated Press, "Chief Justice Says Court not Interested in Allowing Cameras," July 16, 2006.

[19] John Zelensny, *Communication Law*, 2nd ed. (Belmont, CA: Wadsworth, 1997), 231–233.

[20] Al Tompkins, "A Case for Cameras in the Courtroom," Poynteronline (November 28, 2000). Retrieved 13 September 2007 from http://www.poynter.org/content/content_view.asp?id=5132

[21] Ibid.

[22] Ibid.

15

Politics and Popular Culture[1]

> *What we are experiencing, then, is a fundamental change in political com-munication in America. . . . Politics is now clearly an integral part of enter-tainment programming."*
>
> —Jeffery P. Jones

Jeffery Jones argues that contemporary scholarship on media and poli-tics perpetuates three myths: news is the primary and proper source of polit-ical communication, the most important function of media is to transmit "information" for citizen education, and "political engagement" requires cit-izen action such as voting, going to rallies, or participating in marches. Jones himself, on the other hand, prefers to approach political communication from a cultural perspective that recognizes a more intimate role all media play in the daily lives of citizens. Today's "mediated citizenship" encom-passes the central role of media in all its forms, sources, and variations that contribute to the understanding that citizens have of the state and their rela-tion to it.[2] This mediated citizenship results from four assumptions:

That [we] employ a complex ensemble of media that have extensive reach into our lives as citizens and consumers; that media have differen-tial effects on the meanings that come to constitute political reality; that we must look beyond information acquisition as the primary reason for how and why citizens employ political media, and instead see the inte-grative aspect of media usage; and that we exist in a culture of mediated engagement with politics that structures our political lives in unprece-dented ways.[3]

Thus, from this perspective, we engage in politics every day and media are central to that engagement. Our political culture is a culture "in which every-day life and politics are now intimately intertwined because of media."[4]

Civic discourse has merged into the language and forums of public amusement. News is now marketed as entertainment and competes with other prime-time programming for ratings. With so many cable and satellite offerings, most programs aim for a specific audience and deal with themes of social and political life. Hollywood continues to generate films and documentaries with targeted social messages and political issues. And, occurring within just the past couple of decades, political talk dominates AM radio, and cable political shows rival network programming in prime time. In this chapter we briefly explore the communication of political themes in entertainment and popular culture. We conclude by examining two recurring themes in the analysis of popular entertainment.

The Culture of Division

Robert Collins conducted a "cultural" study of the politics of the 1980s, essentially, the Reagan Era. He finds several themes that still influence our political culture today. According to Collins, the 1980s

> were a time of fundamental realignment in American life. . . . American culture moved away from the bourgeois regime of values, mores, and institutions, which had held sway for most of the twentieth century, toward a new more secular, postmodern, multicultural, and therapeutic cultural order. In effect, and paradoxically, politics moved right just as culture moved left. The friction generated by these contemporaneous developments helped spark the so-called cultural war of the 1980s and 1990s, a brand of cultural conflict that has strong echoes (as in the debates over gay marriage) in the early years of the twenty-first century.[5]

According to Collins,

> Beginning in the 1980s and accelerating thereafter, political and cultural conflict began to overlap as the two political parties became increasingly polarized along cultural and religious lines. One result is the political and cultural intertwining that gives meaning to the popular concept of a Red State–Blue State division in American life.[6]

Since that time, U.S. culture has become coarser, more vulgar, and more fragmented.

In the aftermath of the 2004 election, pollsters found that an individual's level of religious commitment and activity was the primary indicator of voting behavior, certainly more so than education, gender, or income. Social issues such as embryonic stem cell research, gay marriage, regulation of abortion, immigration, and a general coarseness of culture provided a context for defining public life and moral values. The various social issues appealed to specific electoral constituencies and became the yardsticks to measure candidate values and personal faith, even in a time of war and international instability.

This relationship between religion and politics reached a new intensity in the 2004 presidential campaign.[7] The personal faith of both candidates and the potential impact on governing and decision making became issues throughout the campaigns. Candidates were forced to address issues of faith in speeches, interviews, and during two of the debates.

Leading up to the election were a series of "events" that raised "value" issues and concerns for many Americans. The movie *The Passion of Christ* was released to great fanfare on Ash Wednesday, February 25, 2004. For months it was the number-one movie in the United States. By Election Day, the film had generated $370 million in the United States alone.[8] Continuing throughout the year there emerged additional items of "value" concern. For example, there was the uproar over Janet Jackson's halftime "costume malfunction" during the Super Bowl; local battles over prayer in schools, posting of the Ten Commandments, challenges to the phrase "Under God" in the Pledge of Allegiance; and perhaps the greatest stimulus, the one vote majority ruling of the Massachusetts State Supreme Court in favor of homosexual marriage. Courts across the United States, from local up to the Supreme Court of the United States, ignited a renewed "culture war." Simultaneously, more conservative Christians began to feel targeted and humiliated by members of the news media, by folks in Hollywood, and by various social groups. From a religious perspective, there is a difference between what some refer to as "universalists" and "particularists." Universalists generally believe that all the great religions of the world are equally true and good. Public debate about social issues should be consensus-driven, less judgmental, and display much more tolerance. Particularists do not view all religions as equal. There is right and wrong, good and bad. While universalists say they rely on reason, education, and science to back their positions, particularists rely upon scripture and tradition. For example, universalists would view hot button issues such as abortion as religious but private and thus argue that they do not belong in the public arena. However, particularists view abortion as a moral issue of life. It is not a scientific debate about when life begins. It is a debate about the social issue of should human life be protected and thus belongs squarely in the public realm.[9]

Since the 1990s, however, universalists often intimidate, mock, and condescend to particularists. Indiana Republican Congressman Mark Souder best expresses the frustration of particularists:

> I hope I can clearly communicate that the consensus power structure is so blindly universalist that they aren't even aware of their behavior. Even the rise of FOX News baffles them. They can't understand that to millions of people, Tom Brokaw, Peter Jennings, and Dan Rather, as well as CNN and other cousins, all espouse a breathtaking uniform universalist view of the world. Conservative Christians, as individuals, do not separate their lives into a private and public sphere. To ask me to check my Christian beliefs at the door is to ask me to expel the Holy Spirit from my life when I serve as a congressman, and that I will not do. Either I am a Christian or I am not; either I reflect His glory or I do not.[10]

A Gallup poll in late October 2004, focusing on moral values and the role of government, found 71 percent of both Bush supporters and Kerry supporters rated the state of moral values in the United States as "only fair" or "poor." Although both Bush and Kerry voters agreed as to the moral climate in the United States, Bush voters were more than twice as likely to believe that government should promote traditional values than were Kerry voters.

Thus, today the cultural wars continue, in terms of political parties, social issues, and political ideology. Although we still govern from the middle, the extremes on both sides of the issues and political parties seem to dominate public debate.

Political Storytelling through Film

Portrayals of the nation's civil life have always been a feature of our public media. D. W. Griffith's spectacular silent epic in 1915, *Birth of a Nation*, is an early landmark in film history. Woodrow Wilson is alleged to have said that it was "like history written by lightning."[11] It not only refined many of the current conventions of narrative film, it also stirred controversy for its positive treatment of the Ku Klux Klan and its overt racism.[12] In World War I, government use of film as a persuasive tool was augmented by all forms of media, including hundreds of popular recordings glorifying American honor. These recordings and the Victrolas to play them were routinely issued to troops in the field. By the time World War II began, the popular media of most nations was awash with themes intended to enshrine the civic affairs of the state. There was even a Hollywood production unit responsible for instructional and propaganda films.

In some ways drama is the perfect vehicle for mass-oriented political discussion. It comes to the receiver in an attractive context (as entertainment) and in a perfect persuasive environment (e.g., a movie theater, or one's TV at home) when the viewer's defenses against persuasion are reduced. Dramatists routinely function as messengers to the society about its successes and failures. As Hugh Duncan observes, plays and novels have "historically something of the same importance as journalism has for our own day."[13] They allow us to see our counterparts respond to shifting situations, many of which are personal, but they also play out against the panorama of our times. Popular melodramas, comedies, and films are well suited to show the ironies and hypocrisies of government and modern life. Even forms of mass media with ostensibly nonpolitical objectives frequently contain at least an implicit political subtext or motivation. An exhibit, film, or television program that may have the manifest goal of simple entertainment can itself be the direct outcome of an intensely political agenda or a sustained power struggle—for instance, the apocalyptic *The Day After Tomorrow*, a film depicting catastrophic effects of global warming.

In considering films as forms of political communication, according to James Combs,

> We are given to understand that the movies are . . . forms of communication which can be used by the "author" or creator of that form to commu-

nicate a widespread message, and that message may be one that involves the representation of persuasion, and more specifically, propaganda.[29]

He thinks "movies are mentors and metaphors for all our lives and maybe even for our politics."[30] For Combs, "movies become a contributing source in the ongoing conduct of national social and political discourse."[31] When we expose ourselves to movies, we are "engaged in a learning process," whether we realize it or not.[32] Thus, "in the history of twentieth-century America, the movies are an important part of the 'flow of social discourse' that constitutes, and sustains, a political-culture-in-time."[33]

Dan Nimmo argues that

> movies of all genres—be they screwball comedies, musicals, westerns, science fiction, historical sagas, gangster, private eye, romance, war, religious, or what have you—touch directly or indirectly on matters that go to the heart of politics: conflict and consensus, power and authority, order and disorder, etc.[34]

For Nimmo, that there are degrees of propaganda to films. Of course, most documentaries address social issues and political topics. As a result, they are by definition propagandistic; that is they provide overt persuasion messages to influence beliefs, attitudes or behavior—for instance, the 1985 documentary by Ken Burns, *Huey Long*. Then there are films loosely based on an actual political figure or historical event. For instance, the 1989 *Blaze*, starring Paul Newman, or the 1995 *Kingfish: A Story of Huey P. Long* starring John Goodman. While presenting a message, they are also entertaining. However, although the majority of films are primarily for entertainment purposes, Nimmo argues that all films have the potential of propaganda because they portray a set of values and human nature and behaviors.[35] Again, we learn from watching films. They play a large role in our political socialization throughout our lives.

Political Talk

The decade of the 1990s brought in new programming types and cable channels that offered new forms of political talk on television. These new programs, according to Jones, "challenged the assumptions of what constitutes knowledge, who gets to speak, what issues can be addressed, as well as what types of political talk audiences will find both informative and pleasurable."[14] Of course, political talk programming has its roots in network journalism. First was NBC's *Meet the Press* in 1947 followed by CBS's *Face the Nation* in 1954. The journalistic roundtable started on Public Television in 1969 in various incarnations such as *Washington Week in Review* (PBS 1967), *The McLaughlin Group* (PBS 1982), and *Capital Gang* (CNN 1988). Today, not only are there are all types of political talk shows, but there are also dedicated news cable channels—FOX News, MSNBC, CNN, and CNBC.[15]

It was AM talk radio that transformed the nature of political talk and punditry. The enormous success of Rush Limbaugh ushered in a populist, common person and a commonsense approach to political discussions. Programming dominated primarily from a conservative perspective. Cable outlets soon followed suit providing programming aimed to mobilize populist emotions by incorporating citizen participation and commentary: "Political commentary and opinions from viewing audiences could become part of the programming via e-mail, faxes, voice mail, phone calls, chat rooms, video-conferencing, and bulletin board systems."[16] The more conservative radio talk shows, such as Rush Limbaugh's, empower audience members by bashing the "liberal media" and encouraging the "populist skepticism of elite authority."[17]

With the transformation of political talk shows also came changes in stylistic features. The host or participant is no longer an independent, objective participant. He or she tends to speak from a certain perspective or issue position. Second, many of these talking heads are celebrities in their own right. They are well known, demand large speaking fees, and often become the subject of stories themselves. Finally, in competition for ratings, the shows must have an edge—generate excitement, controversy, and confrontation resulting in "spectacle."[18]

Jones thinks FOX News had the greatest influence in changing the nature of political talk shows. He argues that FOX News blurred the boundaries between news/information and advocacy/opinion. For Jones, FOX News transformed television news as a genre, "elevating talk shows to the status of news and substituting interpretation for information, opinions for reporting."[19] He also argues that at FOX, style and substance are "one and the same." "FOX solicits viewers with a barrage of flamboyant graphics and video game-style sound effects that mark its distinctiveness and pronounce its extreme self-consciousness of style."[20]

Another interesting development was the innovation of "humorous" late-night political talk shows. Beyond simple jokes and celebrity banter of network late-night fare, cable options provided "aggressively iconoclastic, sharp-tongued, and sharp-witted comedian-hosts" who offered programming that "addresses the fakery in public life as manifest in news and late-night television talk."[21] *Politically Incorrect with Bill Maher, Dennis Miller Live,* and *The Daily Show with Jon Stewart* dealt with politics directly and aggressively through rants, parody, and sometimes, insult: "The humor, anger, amusement, dismay, and disagreement are all mixed in the narrative flow each show creates."[22] Jones vehemently argues that these shows do not trivialize politics; rather, "these shows demand a level of sophistication or knowledge about both politics *and* popular culture."[23]

Politically Incorrect was instrumental in the blurring the boundaries between entertainment and news talk programming. Jones claims it led the way for the subsequent shows of *Dennis Miller Live* (HBO, 1994–2002) and *The Daily Show* (Comedy Central, 1996–) that mixed the more traditional celebrity talk with more serious-minded political talk.[24] *The Daily Show* has become a phenomenon with audiences greater than network evening news shows. Even though *The Daily Show* is a fake news program,

> its faux journalistic style allows the show's writers and host to question, dispel, and critique the manipulative language and symbolizations coming from the presidential campaign while simultaneously opening up deeper truths about politics than offered by the "objective" reporting of mainstream journalism.[25]

In effect, for Jones the postmodern notion of *fake* is more real than the *real*.

Many social scientists and academics bemoan the fact that *The Daily Show* is not only the primary source of political information for today's young people, but for most, it is the *only* source of political information. How could this be a good thing? How can young people seriously engage in political campaigns and issue discussions based on the "fake" information and opinions on a comedy show? We find it of interest that during the 2004 presidential campaign, the University of Pennsylvania's National Annenberg Election Survey found that viewers of late-night comedy programs were more likely to know the issue positions and backgrounds of presidential candidates than those who did not watch late-night comedy. This was especially true for viewers of *The Daily Show* with Jon Stewart on Comedy Central.[26]

The 2004 presidential campaign was notable for the unprecedented amount of direct political action and activity that occurred within popular culture during the campaign cycle. As Jones notes:

> From documentary and feature films to nonfiction books and novels, television talk and comedy programming, radio shows, Internet humor and blogs, and music videos, concert tours, and CDs, popular culture was saturated with and consumed by popularly mediated political expressions.[27]

Michael Moore's *Fahrenheit 9/11* portrayed Bush as incompetent, lazy, and corrupt, wrongly leading our nation to war. Alan Peterson responded with *Fahrenhype 9/11*, written in part by former Clinton advisor Dick Morris. The anti-Kerry documentary *Stolen Honor* raised questions about Kerry's Vietnam service and his antiwar protests at home. Music artists such as Bruce Springsteen, John Mellencamp, Dave Matthews, James Taylor, and the Dixie Chicks participated in "Vote for Change" concerts in key states supporting Kerry. There were numerous celebrities supporting youth engagement and voting efforts.[28]

Two Recurring Themes in the Analysis of Popular Entertainment

Two frames of reference are often used in assessing the political side effects of a society awash in the products of popular entertainment. Each is very different but shares the same function of serving as a starting point for deeper excursions into the analysis of political messages in "nonpolitical" media. The first is the idea that the media extend experience to realms far beyond localized values and knowledge, thereby resituating us into less parochial and more global frames of reference. The second deals with those who hold the power to control media content.

Theory of Liberalizing Influence

Part of the conventional wisdom that comes with the study of the pluralistic mass media in Western nations is that together they create a "window on the world" that has unprecedented breadth. Mass media within the reach of nearly everyone provide a wealth of new experiences that expand horizons and widen perspectives. When measured against the limited experiences of any one individual, the opportunities made possible by television alone represent a vast increase in a person's range of cultural consciousness. Distance is no longer an impediment to gaining access to the diversity of human actions, attitudes, and tragedies. We can now extend ourselves into the lives of others in ways that were not possible just a generation ago. Thus, media exposure is *liberalizing* because it places us in frames of reference beyond our own provincial concerns. At the same time, it raises problems about the effects of extending the outward margins of our own experience. We are sometimes the reluctant beneficiaries of scenes and events created dramatically that illuminate features of racism, social custom, religious practice, cultural tradition, injustice, crime, or violence.

Even commercial television's strongest critics have found examples of entertainment programming that discuss issues that might never surface in the consciousness of some: for instance, the 1970s sitcom *Good Times*, the 1980s *Degrassi* series,[36] the 1990s *Roseanne*, or the various *Law & Order* series. In the contemporary media climate, it would be difficult to avoid exposure to the lives and values of other classes and groups in the United States. Even some of the most innocuous entertainment in the United States tends to be racially and ethnically inclusive, expansive rather than narrow in representations of class, tolerant of political and cultural differences, and optimistic about the young.

However, there is a problematic side to the liberalizing influence of pluralistic media. The very pluralism that defines the culture can also appear to undermine it. As some argue, it encourages the erosion of traditional U.S. values and principles. Those responsible for the content of popular culture have contributed to the coarseness and crassness of contemporary U.S. society by providing films of extreme violence—The *Rambo* series, *Saw* (2003), *The Hills Have Eyes* (2006); angry rap music by rappers such as 50 Cent, Snoop Dogg, Dr. Dre; pornography—*Behind the Green Door* (1972), *Insatiable* (1980), *Sex* (1995), *Fashionistas* (2003);[37] hostile portrayals of those in authority positions—*Cool Hand Luke* (1967), *The Wild Bunch* (1967), *Chinatown* (1974), *Syriana* (2005). Popular culture also embraces the funding of questionable "art" (the provocative works of Andres Serrano and Robert

Mapplethorpe), secular and revisionist views of the life of Christ (*The Da Vinci Code,* The Jesus Seminar, *The Last Temptation of Christ*), attacks on "traditional" gender roles (Betty Friedan's *The Second Stage,* Holly Devor's *Gender Blending,* Judith Butler's *Gender Trouble*), and the general espousing of relativistic values and ideas. For more conservative social critics, U.S. culture has abandoned its Judeo-Christian anchors while falling into the pit of moral relativism resulting in a collapse of moral authority.

Theory of Elite Control

Another important assessment applied to the most pervasive elements of entertainment and popular culture is that it reflects the values and economic interests of an elite power structure, notably a homogeneous alliance of media owners, advertisers, and taste-makers centered on the northern east and southern west coasts. In contrast to the traditionalist's fear that these owners have alien agendas, elite theorists hold that media content reflects the ideas of a mostly white, male, and affluent class driven by the search for profits. In effect, the control of media by large conglomerates not only influences content and but also reduces the pluralism of media voices. In addition to concerns about corporate size and power, arguments about elite control also note that corporate owners have an inherent bias against raising questions about larger issues or fundamental problems that persist in society. The content they inevitably produce is hegemonic, favoring fantasized remedies to problems rather than realistic political solutions.

This hegemony argument generally runs along the following lines: Most of the nation's media are in the business of selling *audiences to advertisers*. Media content is constructed as a way to obtain, or *hook*, the attention and interest of audiences. That hook needs to be sufficiently deep to keep restless consumers attentive long enough to see the advertising that is interlaced into media content. Two separate clients thus need to be satisfied. Audiences have to be entertained or informed in a nonthreatening way; advertisers need to be convinced that the media they are purchasing time or space within fit their corporate objectives.

Since politics involves controversy, and controversy intensifies anxieties, the most stable entertainment—especially on television—is that which is *apolitical*. But apolitical does not mean nonpolitical. Even though most popular entertainment avoids controversial issues and unpopular ideas, that process itself is a political option. The world of prime time generally opts for what amounts to a subtle deference to most of the segments of the established economic and social order. With some exceptions, this results in depictions of a world where individuals know their place, where order triumphs over disruption and dispute, and "the system" and its subsystems, such as the courts, the health-care system, schools, and businesses, generally work.

Harmless family and workplace sitcoms have dominated prime time in the past. Sitcoms depend on a durable formula of trivial plots and characters that have been depoliticized of everything except a veneer of political correctness. Films, novels, and occasional television dramas may present unpleasant images without the closure of a happy ending, but television programs that depend on a loyal audience week in and week out generally do not.

Elite theory thus flows out of an old view of how the powerful in a society seek to maintain their place within it. Those who have succeeded and been rewarded by the society are naturally going to see little need to change it. In this perspective, elite control of the mass media and their content depends on creating widespread public quiescence through programming that entertains and reassures. Harmless and politically neutral content guarantees return visitors to a medium. This same content also increases the likelihood that relatively contented audiences will be delivered to the advertising messages of corporate advertisers.

Summary

All elections since 2000 have been relatively close, intense, and highly partisan. On almost any social or political issue, advocates storm the airwaves with pronouncements of justice, allegations of hypocrisy on the other side, and predictions of doom if the opposition prevails. During this time, new forms of political talk appeared on radio, on television, and in films. There was a blending, especially on prime-time cable talk shows, between reporting and commentary. Documentaries were used to attack government policies, political candidates, and pending policy legislation. Late-night comedy programming came on the scene focusing on social and political issues as well as on government officials and politicians. Hard-hitting parody, sarcasm, and insult became the means of revealing deeper truths about the state of affairs and the polity than straightforward news reporting. They provided, especially among younger audience members, a way to address political and social issues in a way that actually enhanced critical thinking and involvement.

In today's popular culture, it is virtually impossible to separate the political from the nonpolitical. It is through the media that we engage and participate in politics much more so than *just* through the act of voting. Our civic discourse is part of the entertainment and popular culture. We follow issues, candidates, and campaigns through a wide variety of media programming: from talk radio, to prime-time comedies, to news talk shows, to reading blogs, to late-night comedies. Perhaps, more than any other time in our history, as citizens we are in a true 24/7 political environment as part of our popular culture.

Notes

[1] Gary Woodward contributed to portions of this chapter, originally found in Robert E. Denton, Jr. and Gary Woodward, *Political Communication in America*, 3rd ed. (Westport, CT: Praeger, 1998), 279–292.

2 Jeffrey P. Jones, "A Cultural Approach to the Study of Mediated Citizenship," *Social Semiotics* 16, no. 2 (June 2006): 365.

3 Ibid.

4 Ibid., 379.

5 Robert Collins, *Transforming America: Politics and Culture in the Reagan Years* (New York: Columbia University Press, 2007), 5.

6 Ibid., 254.

7 See Robert E. Denton, Jr., "Religion and the 2004 Presidential Campaign," *American Behavioral Scientist* 49, no. 1 (September 2005): 11–31; and Robert E. Denton, Jr., "Religion, Evangelicals, and Moral Issues in the 2004 Presidential Campaign," in *The 2004 Presidential Campaign: A Communication Perspective*, ed. Robert E. Denton, Jr. (Lanham, MD: Rowman & Littlefield, 2005), 255–282.

8 B. Kit, "Hot-button Movies Iced for Top Golden Globe," *The Toronto Star* (November 11, 2004), A27.

9 "One Electorate Under God? A Dialogue on Religion and American Politics." Pew Forum on Religion & Public Life (July 21, 2004). Retrieved 31 August 2004 from http://pewforum.org/events/print.php?EventID=59

10 Ibid.

11 Martin Williams, *Griffith: First Artist of the Movies* (New York: Oxford University Press, 1980), 74.

12 Robert Sklar, *Movie Made America* (New York: Vintage, 1975), 58–61.

13 Duncan, *Communication and Social Order* (New York: Oxford University Press, 1968), 79.

14 Jeffrey Jones, *Entertaining Politics* (Lantham, MD: Rowman & Littlefield, 2005), 36.

15 Ibid, 37.

16 Ibid, 48.

17 Jeffrey Jones, "Beyond Genre: Cable's Impact on the Talk Show," in *Thinking Outside the Box: A Contemporary Television Genre Reader*, ed. G. Edgerton and B. Rose (Lexington: University Press of Kentucky, 2005), 167.

18 Jones, *Entertaining Politics*, 38–39.

19 Jones, "Beyond Genre," 157.

20 Ibid., 163.

21 Jones, *Entertaining Politics*, 52.

22 Ibid., 58.

23 Ibid., 59.

24 Jones, "Beyond Genre," 157.

25 Jones, *Entertaining Politics*, 126.

26 Jeffery Jones, "'Fake' News versus 'Real' News as Sources of Political Information," in *Politicotainment: Television's Take on the Real*, ed. K. Riegert (New York: Peter Lang Publishers, In Press), 3.

27 Jeffery Jones, "The Shadow Campaign in Popular Culture," in *The 2004 Presidential Campaign: A Communication Perspective*, ed. Robert E. Denton, Jr. (Lanham, MD: Rowman & Littlefield, 2005), 196.

28 Ibid., 200, 202.

29 James Combs, "Part IV: Political Communication and the Movies," in *Movies and Politics*, ed. James Combs (New York: Garland Publishing, 1993), 236.

30 James Combs, "Introduction," in *Movies and Politics*, ed. James Combs (New York: Garland Publishing, 1993), 3.

31 Ibid., 4.

32 Ibid., 8.

33 Ibid., 20.

34 Dan Nimmo, "Political Propaganda in the Movies: A Typology," in *Movies and Politics*, ed. James Combs (New York: Garland Publishing, 1993), 279.

35 Ibid., 281–289.

[36] Seen on both Canadian Public Television and American Public Television. See http://
www.nostalgiacentral.com/tv/kids/degrassi.htm for additional information on this internationally recognized series that included *Kids of Degrassi Street*, *Degrassi Junior High*, and
Degrassi High.

[37] Hard-core pornographic films have skyrocketed in production. In 1988, 1,300 films were
made; in 2005, 13,588 were made.

Political Ethics
An Oxymoron?[1]

We will not survive the 21st century with the ethics of the 20th century.
> —Len Marrella

Do we have a crisis of leadership in the United States today? Are we truly electing the very best among us to public office? Are the best and most qualified even willing to run for office and serve the country? As a nation, have we lowered our standards for and expectations of those who run and their performance in office? In the aftermath of the presidential election of 2004, "moral values" was reported in exit polls as the primary issue of voter influence. Just prior to the election, some 71 percent of Americans, according to a Gallup poll, rated the state of "moral values" in the United States as "only fair" or "poor."[2] Political ethics includes both the expectations of Americans and the actual performance of our politicians.

Ethics and Our National Character

Since the beginning of time, humans have expressed a concern for ethics. Plato's *Republic* is essentially a work of political ethics, as is Aristotle's *Nicomachean Ethics*. For both Plato and Aristotle, the "good" person was a conscientious citizen contributing to the city-state. The notion of civic virtue implies a citizenry that is informed, active, selfless, enlightened, and above all, just. Ancient Rome was steeped in this view as well, with Cicero, and later Quintilian, also writing on civic virtue.

Much has changed in the intervening millennia. Life today is more individualistic; we are concerned with self-actualization, "success," comfort, convenience, acquisition of material goods, and the pursuit of happiness. For nearly two decades, there have been increasing numbers of studies, polls, and news articles lamenting the decline of ethical behavior in the United States. As early as 1987, the cover of *U.S. News & World Report* asked, "A Nation of Liars?" and *Time Magazine* asked, "What Ever Happened to Ethics?" *Atlantic Monthly* in 1992 and *Newsweek* Magazine in 1995 explored the absence of a "sense of shame" as a norm in our culture. Lying and cheating among adults and among our children have become commonplace. More recent surveys show that 80 percent of high school students admit to having cheated at least once, with half stating they did not believe cheating was necessarily wrong. In fact, many indicated that it is *necessary* to lie, cheat, or steal in order to succeed. Even 54 percent of middle school children admit they have cheated on an exam. Ninety-two percent of high school age children report that they regularly lie to their parents.[3]

The number of college students who cheat is equally as disappointing. Seventy-five percent of college students admit to cheating. By the summer of 2002, there were well over 300 Internet term paper sites offering essays on thousands of subjects. Today, there are thousands of people offering to write custom papers, some promising a 24-hour turn around for an exorbitant fee. The Web site "eCheat" brags of having "an archive of 60,000 professionally written papers available for purchase."[4] In 2004, a poll conducted by Zogby International revealed that 73 percent of college students agreed with the statement that "what is right and wrong depends on differences in individual values and cultural diversity" versus the 25 percent who believed that "there are clear and uniform standards of right and wrong by which everyone should be judged." Two percent were uncertain.[5] Sadly, the same general disregard for ethical behavior can be found among the general public. A national poll revealed that 30 percent of individuals admit to putting extra work experience or educational experience on their resume, 40 percent admit to telling someone that "the payment is in the mail" when actually it isn't; and 55 percent admit to lying about their age in order to get a special discount, to name just a few examples.[6]

According to Michael Josephson of the Josephson Institute of Ethics, "We have become desensitized to the enormous significance of lying. The effects are all destructive, generally lowering the level of trust in anything we read or hear."[7] The cumulative effect is to give everyone permission to lie because, most certainly, the powerful do so. In the summer of 2001, a Gallup poll found, for only the second time in 50 years, ethics and morality near the top of the list of most important problems facing this nation. Seventy-eight percent of respondents thought our moral values are "somewhat" or "very weak."[8] It seems that our nation is in an ethical slump.

Historically, there has always been great skepticism about the practice of politics and, above all, about politicians. In many public opinion polls, politicians rank below professional sellers of cars and lawyers as the most dishonest profession. Part of the problem is the continual string of "bad" actions of many politicians, which, some argue, began with Richard Nixon. Add to this mix the numerous allegations of sexual misconduct in office by congressmen and presidents, not to mention convictions of fraud, bribery, and solicitation, and one begins to see why politicians are such a loathed lot in general.

Some ethical dilemmas arise because of the difference between campaigning and governing. George H. Bush's reversal of his pledge not to raise taxes in 1992 ("Read my lips. No new taxes") was portrayed by his enemies and the mainstream press as an act of willful deception and outright lying, not as an act of leadership and conscience. Some scholars attribute his tax reversal as a major reason for his defeat in 1996. Bill Clinton campaigned with the promise to have the most ethical administration in the country's history. He left office with an administration that had the greatest number of convictions and guilty pleas by friends and associates, and the greatest number of cabinet officials to come under criminal investigation. As another example, some citizens question the veracity of George W. Bush's proclamation that Iraq had "weapons of mass destruction"—which then became justification for going to war against Saddam Hussein. A growing number of Americans think he and his administration simply lied about the possibility of biological, chemical, or nuclear weapons. In addition, during the 2000 presidential campaign, Bush had argued against nation building, saying in the second presidential debate, "I'm not so sure the role of the United State is to go around the world and say, 'This is the way it's got to be.'"[9] These words did not match his choice of actions in Iraq. Other concerns are raised about the actual process of getting elected. Many citizens assume that politicians will say or do almost anything to get elected. For many, the critical question becomes whether ethical politics is possible or whether the notion is simply an oxymoron.

Democracy, Leadership, and Ethics

The qualities of honesty, integrity, and trust between leaders and citizens are fundamental to a healthy democracy. Without undertaking a detailed philosophical discussion of democracy, one can identify several critical characteristics of a democratic form of government that are relevant to this discussion. The notion of *accountability* is essential to the notion of democracy. Because citizens delegate authority to those who hold office, politicians are accountable to the public for all actions and deeds. Elections are a means of regulating accountability; citizens elect/don't elect a candidate based on their perceptions of that candidate's accountability. In the United States, news journalism serves as a check on political power and authority; the watchdog function is a long-standing tradition of the American press. *Information* is critical for citizens to make informed judgments and evaluations of elected officials. Naturally, incomplete or inaccurate information can lead to bad public decisions. A *free marketplace of ideas* is vital to a thriving democracy. Diversity of thought and respect for dissent are hallmarks of the values of freedom and justice. When multiple viewpoints are heard and expressed, the common good prevails over private interests. Finally, democracy is a process of what Dennis Thompson calls *collective deliberation* on disputes of issues and fundamental values.[10] It is the national and public debate that determines the collective wisdom and will of the people. Thus, personal ethics are fundamental to democracy.

Bruce Miroff argues that moral codes that shape public expectations of leader conduct change over time.[11] Indeed, the standard of morality in the the twenty-first century is very different from when the presidency was established. To illustrate the differences, he compares what he calls republican character with democratic character. *Republican character* is composed of the classic qualities of courage, resolution, moderation, dedication, and control. Such characteristics are not psychological but constitute objective behavior subject to public judgment. Republican character was a lofty and cultural imperative. Miroff suggests this was the public's expectation of presidential leadership of the 1790s, for example. In contrast, the *democratic character* is one of the people. A president need not be *better* than us, but *similar* to us. The democratic standard allows a president to be personally flawed in the private sphere as long as it does not impact job performance: "The standard of democratic character upholds a president who is perceived as effective and successful in pursuing an economic and social agenda favored by a majority of Americans."[12]

There was a strong public expectation of moral public leadership in the eighteenth and nineteenth centuries. People were elected because of their past and often heroic behavior. Public service was viewed as a trust, an obligation, and an honor. By the twentieth century, *management skills took priority over character*. The rise of the professional politician replaced the genuine public servant. Elected office became a prize, not an opportunity. Personal power rather than genuine public service became the motive. Politics became a game, not a method or channel of service.

The Founding Fathers had a clear view of the type of person who should serve as president. Alexander Hamilton, in *Federalist Paper* number 76, suggested that any person elevated to the presidency should be "a man of abilities, at least respectable." The office requires men of "character," "wisdom," and "integrity." Indeed, the office requires "a livelier sense of duty and a more exact regard to reputation." This view was presented in opposition to members of Congress who, by the nature of that institution, would have those who bring local biases and "prepossessions."[13]

Hamilton thought the office would greatly influence the occupant:

> The sole and undivided responsibility of one man will naturally beget a livelier sense of duty and a more exact regard to reputation. He will, on this account, feel himself under stronger obligations, and more interested to investigate with care the qualities requisite to the stations to be filled, and to prefer with impartiality the persons who may have the fairest pretensions to them.[14]

However, cause for removal from office was very clear for Alexander Hamilton. In *Federalist Paper* number 65, removal is based upon "the abuse or violation of some public trust. They are of a nature which may with peculiar propriety be denominated *political*, as they relate chiefly to injuries done immediately to the society itself."[15]

James Madison wrote in *Federalist Paper* number 57,

> the aim of every political constitution is, or ought to be, first to obtain for rulers men who possess most wisdom to discern and most virtue to pursue the common good of the society; and in the next place, to take the most effectual precautions for keeping them virtuous whilst they continue to hold their public trust.[16]

Clearly the forefathers envisioned rather specific criteria for the occupant of the office. For them, character and integrity were integral requirements for the position of leadership. The notion of character in those times included the qualities of courage, resolution, moderation, dedication, and control.[17] Inherent in our democratic belief is the ability of the whole to select one capable of leading us through tough times or dangerous events, possess the wisdom to articulate a social agenda and legislative programs, and to serve as the ultimate model of citizenship. As Michael Genovese argues,

> presidents who lead in the democratic spirit create leaders, foster citizen responsibility, inspire and empower others to assume leadership responsibilities in their communities. Democratic leaders establish a moral vision: pursue egalitarian goals; question, challenge, engage, and educate citizens; and offer hope.[18]

Clearly our founders followed Aristotle, who recommended that a true student of politics must study "virtue above all things."[19] Moral virtues, such as those of "courage, moderation, and justice" dispose us toward good behavior. Moral virtue, for Aristotle, comes about as a result of habit. Thus, repeated "good" acts develop facilities for acting rightly in the future. From this classical perspective, the "good life" is the morally good life, and political authority is responsible for creating an environment for citizens, and hence the state, to develop themselves morally.[20] In some senses, our country was founded using a top-down model—virtuous president to virtuous officeholders to virtuous citizenry. Rabindra Kanungo and Manuel Mendonca categorize virtues into four groups. The *moral virtues* consist of honesty, truthfulness, decency, courage, and justice. *Intellectual virtues* are thoughtfulness, strength of mind, curiosity. *Communal virtues* include neighborliness, charity, self-support, helpfulness, cooperativeness, and respect for others. *Political virtues* are commitment to the common good, respect for law, and responsible participation.[21]

Moral leadership emerges from the fundamental needs, aspirations, and values of the followers. Presidential historian Robert Dallek expresses the challenge best:

Successful presidential leadership has always relied on moral authority: a president's conviction that he is battling for the national good and public perception that he is a credible chief committed to advancing the national well-being. Few things are more destructive to a president's influence than the belief that he is a deceitful manipulator more intent on serving his personal needs than those of the public.[22]

Robert Putnam has popularized the notion of "moral capital." As citizens, we make moral judgments about people, places, and institutions. When our judgments are positive, they inspire trust, belief and allegiance that politically may in turn produce willing acquiescence, obedience, loyalty, support, action, and even sacrifice. In this manner, then, it is important for politicians to be seen to serve and to stand for something apart from their own self-interests. In short, they must establish a moral grounding. according to Putnam,

> This they do by avowing their service to some set of fundamental values, principles and goals that find a resonant response in significant numbers of people. When such people judge the agent or institution to be both faithful and effective in serving those values and goals, they are likely to bestow some quantum of respect and approval that is of great political benefit to the receiver. This quantum is the agent's moral capital.[23]

Moral capital is different from mere popularity. Popularity may be based in part on moral judgment or appraisals but is more often based on other sources of attraction. Popularity may be bought, but moral capital cannot.

Leadership is essentially about relationships, and at the heart of any relationship is trust. For two decades, Kouzes and Posner have surveyed the general public to identify the characteristics of most admired leaders. Only four characteristics continuously receive over 50 percent of the votes: honest (89 percent), forward-looking (71 percent), competent (68 percent), and inspiring (69 percent).[24] Note that trust emerges as the single most important characteristic. People want to know their leaders are truthful, ethical, and principled.

Mutual trust is the foundation of democratic government, of self-rule. John Locke viewed the special relationship between citizens and the executive as a fiduciary trust: *the government as trustee incurs an obligation to act for the public good.*[25] In giving our support and trust to a leader, we the citizens bestow legitimacy upon the government and its leaders. In a sense, trust is given in exchange for a vote; elections determine the object of trust, but then that trust must be earned through deeds, words, legislative actions, and so on. In general, the public cedes power to make decisions based on implicit and explicit understandings. It is assumed that politicians will act in the public interest, not in self-interest. It is assumed that leaders will be honest with the American people, encourage debate, and provide the appropriate information to support their decisions and actions. Finally, it is assumed that elected officials will use the powers of the office in a reasonable, responsible, and competent manner.

The trustee relationship between leader and citizen implies higher standards of behavior. We all recognize there are differences among actions that are legal, ethical, and moral. Because elected officials act for others, they assume rights and obligations average citizens do not assume. In addition, as a trustee, standards of conduct are higher than those usually found in the marketplace. Thus, Dennis Thompson asserts that actions taken by private citizens that may be permissible may indeed be criminal if done by public officials.[26]

Studies have also shown that ethical conduct by leaders increases ethical conduct by followers.[27] Ethical behavior by leaders may excite admiration but also invite imitation. With ethical leadership, public cynicism decreases and public trust increases. However, Kouzes and Posner argue that over time, when we lose respect for our leaders, we lose respect for ourselves.[28] As Edmund Burke wrote, "great men are the landmarks and guideposts of the state."[29] When guideposts misdirect, citizens who follow their leaders begin to falter and become lost. Thus, trust is the bond that holds a democracy together: trust in government, in public institutions, in social and private relationships, among each other, and so forth.

For a president, the public's confidence and trust provide the context from which to initiate policy, respond to challenges, and govern. The more trust and confidence the public has in a president, the more latitude the president has to take action and to shape policy. Trust often translates into support, and Bruce Buchanan identifies five historically proven advantages of high public presidential support. First, public support increases the support of presidential programs and legislation in Congress. Second, public support influences a president's ability to conduct foreign policy. Third, public popularity ensures more favorable media coverage and treatment. Fourth, strong public support increases presidential credibility within the executive branch of government as well as in other segments of the government. This was how Reagan was able to foster the notion of smaller government, less regulation, and so on. Finally, the very strength and enthusiasm of public support generates more self-confidence and effectiveness of presidential performance.[30]

Thus, moral leadership is especially required in a democracy because of the unique relationship between the elected servant and the citizenry. There is a strong correlation between public trust and government and the moral authority or character of the presidency. "Moral authority comes from trust and with trust there can be great synergy. Do not underestimate the power and value of moral authority. It is essential; and it depends on trust."[31] Complementary to this line of thinking, James McGregor Burns calls for "transforming leadership" that seeks "sustained and planned social transformation," and "raises the level of human conduct and ethical aspiration of both leader and led."[32] Such leadership responds to "fundamental human needs and American values."[33]

Citizen trust is a critical element of democratic life. Much of today's rise in public alienation is fed by incessant scandal, and our mistrust has created political habits and institutions that now continue to produce more mistrust and cynicism. We continue to lose good people in public service. Take away public trust in the president, for example, and, as James Barber succinctly predicted

> we the people may turn him into an entertainer, who, however seriously he may take himself need not furrow our brows with real-world calculation.... Presidential campaigns become an extended political holiday—a trip to the nation's psychological beaches and mountains—a "suspension of disbelief" analogous to the restful anticipation one feels just as the lights go down and the curtain goes up in the theatre. The distinction fades between actors who play candidates or Presidents (Robert Redford, Henry Fonda) and Presidents struggling to act winningly in an essentially playful politics.[34]

Constitutional Authority and Public Morality

The notion of authority is a central concept in social and political thought. There are many forms of authority: bureaucratic, technical, professional, to name a few. But all forms of authority are based upon the structure of the social relationship between an individual and the state. Such a relationship may range from coercion based on ruthless force, to unreflecting obedience based on habit, to enlightened deference based on a sense of values. The role of authority in government not only upholds moral, ethical, and intellectual standards but also guarantees social and political freedom while concomitantly acting as a barrier to centralized, arbitrary, and despotic power. We use authority to protect our rights, to provide order and security, to manage conflict, and to distribute the benefits and burdens of society.

The authority of our government—its very structure, rules, and laws—originates from the Constitution. The *moral* authority of government originates from the collective beliefs, attitudes, and values of the citizens. Moral authority may be generally defined as the felt obligations and duties derived from shared community values, ideas, and ideals. From a democratic perspective, the very nature of authority as defined as the ability to evoke purely voluntary compliance must be moral in form and content. Otherwise, social violence, chaos, and coercion would be the norm. A social hierarchy is maintained by a willing acceptance of the social order, a unifying set of common values, and a worldview that enshrines and legitimizes the established order. Moral authority rests on voluntary consent. Thus, democracy cannot exist without core, shared values. And political values are the distillation of principles from a systematic order of public beliefs.

The primary characteristic of our society in the nineteenth and the early twentieth centuries is that of a social contract. We attempted to build a comfortable society based on a covenant, contract, or agreement for the mutual advantage of the members of society—the citizens—and the government. Essentially, free people govern by free agreement. The rise of contractual relationships result in the elimination of autocratic, repressive, and coercive governments replaced with governments contractually elected, limited in power, and contractually obligated to respect the rights and specified liberties of the citizens. By means of our Constitution, Bill of Rights, and common laws, the very values and prerogatives of society are promulgated and virtually guaranteed: freedom of religion, speech, press, and assembly, to name a few. Contractual government is democratic government, a "government of the people, by the people, and for the people."

Thus, at the heart of democracy is the notion of a contract; at the heart of any contract is notion of trust. There was a time in the United States when citizens understood the terms of their relationship or contract with government and with each other that was based upon trust. The concept is very simple: I won't kill you, if you won't kill me; I'll help protect your property if you help protect mine; I'll help build your barn if you will help build mine; I won't run the red light if you won't either; If something happens to me, I know that as a member of the larger community, my children and family will be protected and taken care of. Our contract with each other is based on mutual respect, honesty, and responsibility.

Our contract with government, as argued, is based on trust. As a government "of the people, by the people, and for the people," it means that the common good will prevail. Government, in all its actions, will be fair, just, and operate in the interests of all citizens. Today, it appears that we no longer trust government, corporations, or even each other. We are now a divided, as some say, a "50/50" nation, either of the "red" or "blue" states. For too many Americans, our "social contract" has become null and void. Ultimately we are all in a mental state of psychological egoism—all interest is self-interest.

A government is only as good, decent, and moral as its citizens. The conduct of civil affairs in the United States has always occurred under a cloud of considerable public distrust. This distrust is an important but largely negative backdrop that conveys meaning to every other part of the nation's life. James Madison, in *Federalist Paper* 51, recognized the tension between the needs of a centralized government and the needs of a free people. He wrote:

> The interest of the man must be connected with the constitutional rights of the place. It may be a reflection on human nature that such devices should be necessary to control the abuses of government. But what is government itself but the greatest of all reflections on human nature? If men were angels, no government would be necessary. If angels were to govern men, neither external nor internal controls on government would be necessary. In framing a government which is to be administered by men over men, the great difficulty lies in this: you must first enable the government to control the governed; and in the next place oblige it to control itself. A dependence on the people is, no doubt, the primary control on the government.[35]

Individual integrity, responsibility, and accountability are the best check on government abuse. An individual's moral judgments are dependent on the administration of moral dignity and action. This is one of the reasons we argue that no distinction be made between public and private acts for our elected officials. The collective social values of citizens become the conditions necessary for the existence of political authority. The government that encompasses and expresses our collective values ensures the respect and voluntary compliance of all citizens. Political authority rests on the assumption that it exists to promote the good of those who accept it, that the common good will prevail, not the self-interests of those in authority or by the exercise of force.

By its nature, politics encourages a wary skepticism; the traditions borne out of the nation's emergence honor the idea of freedom as a protection against governmental power that can easily be abused. Even so, today there has been an intensification of public distrust in many basic U.S. institutions; moreover, there seems to be an increasing disconnection between the nation and its civic life. Paradoxically, while we have never had more access to the processes and moments of the political process, we have never felt less a part of that process.

Political Communication and Ethics

The disciplines of rhetoric and communication studies have long been interested in the subject of ethics. There is universal agreement that human communication demands concern for ethics. Richard Johannesen argues that

> potential ethical issues are inherent in any instance of communication
> between humans to the degree that the communication can be judged on
> a right–wrong dimension, involves possible significant influence on other
> humans, and to the degree that the communicator consciously chooses
> specific ends sought and communicative means to achieve those ends.[36]

Because communication involves the process of creating and selecting symbols, some scholars argue that all intentional communication transactions inherently involve some degree of persuasion. We choose one symbol rather than another because it more accurately embodies our message—and/ or because we believe that symbol will resonate with the person with whom we are communicating. As discussed in chapter 2, language is the vehicle for social interaction, a practical tool for getting things done. Through language, we define social roles and rules for behavior. Interaction with others creates the reality within which we respond and act. It makes a difference if we convince someone that a glass is either half-full or half-empty. In the former, there is a sense of hope and optimism. The latter involves caution and perhaps even despair. Ethical choices about language are mandatory in a society that negotiates boundaries of conduct through communication.

Freedom of speech is a fundamental value of democracy. With that freedom comes responsibility—responsibility for the form and content of our communication behavior. Thus, at the heart of democracy, and certainly politics, is public communication. The quality of that public communication directly impacts the quality of our democracy and society at large. For instance, does the language used during a city council meeting encourage discussion or does it shut down discussion? Decent citizens can honestly disagree with political solutions to problems, but it is the nature of the language used to convey these differences that can enable or shut down further discussion or engender trust in the process.

In the past, religions were the primary source for ethical standards. In the United States, the political separation of church and state—the constitutional prohibition of the creation of a State Church—has created separation in other arenas as well. Steven Carter fears the trend in our political culture to treat religious beliefs as arbitrary and unimportant to social life. Those who espouse religious beliefs, attitudes, and values in public are often portrayed as ignorant, extreme, and even potentially harmful. Carter believes that religious beliefs and values should inform public policy: "Democracy is best served when the religions are able to act as independent moral voices interposed between the citizen and the state."[37]

Persuasion is an essential tool of communication and, hence, politics and campaigns. As a tool, the process of persuasion can be used by both good and bad individuals for equally good or bad purposes. No one persuasive strategy or tactic is good or bad. Strategies and tactics of persuasion are just that—strategies; it is how and why they are used that provide a context for a value judgment. Furthermore, the motives of persuaders determine if the use of specific strategies is good or bad; For example, most academics and politicians qualify overtly emotional appeals as being inferior to more rational or logical appeals. However, one could argue that using a strong emotional or fear appeal in a teenage anti-drunk driving ad may well be appropriate. On the other hand, most would say that using a fear appeal as a threat or as means of blackmail is highly inappropriate.

When we communicate with a persuasive intent, we are seeking change in others rather than in ourselves. We expect those we address to changes their attitudes or behaviors, which may in some ways be risky for them, even while we remain relatively comfortable with our own. Thus, the persuader gives up nothing while asking others to alter their lives. Under these circumstances, there is an understandable need to consider whether a communication transaction that places most of the risk on the receiver meets certain minimal standards of fairness and decency. The risks persuaders may ask others to accept may be financial ("A vote for me means lower taxes, higher wages, and an increase in social security payments"), psychological ("We'll secure our boarders and continue monitoring terrorists in order to prevent another 9/11"), social ("We have an obligation to help those who cannot help themselves"), or physical ("We need to reinstate the draft, at the very least, universal service for all citizens between the ages of 18 to 23").

The concern for communication ethics, and as we noted with politics, is about social relationships and trust. Sissela Bok argues that

> there must be a minimal degree of trust in communication for language
> and action to be more than stabs in the dark. This is why some level of

> truthfulness has always been seen as essential to human society, no mat-
> ter how deficient the observance of other moral principles."[38]

She concludes that "trust in some degree of veracity functions as *a foundation of* relations among human beings; when this trust shatters or wears
away, institutions collapse."[39]

St. Augustine put it simply and directly:

> it is evident that speech was given to man, not that man might therewith
> deceive one another, but that one man might make known his thoughts
> to another. To use speech, then for the purposes of deception, and not
> for its appointed end, is a sin.[40]

In fact, we can never know the full or the whole truth. But we have choices in
what we say and how we say it. The distinction for many scholars between
truth and lying is the *intent* to mislead or not disclose.

Summary

Traditionally, communication is viewed as the primary means through
which a nation forges a common identity, a common purpose, and a common resolve. Perhaps the most outspoken elected official lamenting the
decline of American morals and character, Arkansas Governor Mike Huckabee argues, "Over the past thirty years, a decline in moral character has
produced a decline in the character of our society."[41] The lack of moral leadership is demonstrated in the continuous uncovering of unethical behavior at
all levels of society, from denials of risks to public safety from corporations
to illicit acts in the halls within the White House. If indeed, the American
public has no concern about the character of our leaders, then it is a clear
reflection on the moral condition of us the citizens as well.

Of course, it would help to return to the citizen-legislator and the public
servant rather than maintain reliance on professional politicians who spend
their careers acquiring power, becoming rather superficial, photogenic, and
poll-driven. With citizen-legislators and leaders, we would get authentic
messages, not the rhetoric of saying what they think we want to hear; or even
worse, saying and doing anything to simply get elected.

Charles Goodsell argues that effective governmental leadership is fos-
tered by a concept of what he calls, "political professionalism." The concept
embodies a set of normative principles that include a competence for power,
a capacity for synthesis, an ability to exercise discretion within constraints,
and possession of a service ethos.[42] It is, of course, the "ability to exercise
discretion within constraints" that is useful to our consideration. Goodsell
argues that one of the characteristics of any profession is "a substantial
degree of collective self-governance through standard setting and regulation
of conduct by the profession itself."[43]

As a nation, our greatest threat is internal, not external. We must stem
the growing tide toward political cynicism and despair. First, we must find

common themes and values that transcend our ever-deepening cultural differences. The notorious "red states" versus "blue states" dichotomy may be exaggerated, but it is harmful nonetheless. We must all be able to identify, to articulate, and to appreciate the core values of the United States. We need to reaffirm ourselves to our national civic values—the principles embodied in the Declaration of Independence, the Constitution, and the Bill of Rights—that bring us together as a people. The ideals of freedom, equality, democracy, and justice provide the basis for building community and trust. How can we survive as a society if we deny commonality and praise autonomous individual behavior? We need some common acceptance of what is acceptable, what is fundamentally right and wrong, good and bad.

Second, civic responsibility, accountability, and initiative should once again become a keystone of social life. Moral discipline means using social norms, rules, customs, and laws to develop moral reasoning, self-control, and a generalized respect for others. Such an approach to social life will help citizens recognize the values behind the laws, have a better understanding of why laws are needed, and increase the feeling of moral obligation to respect government institutions. Democracy as government "of the people, by the people, and for the people," shapes the form and content of political action in the United States. Democracy makes government accessible and accountable to ordinary citizens.

Finally, of course, we desperately need moral leadership in the future, not defined by a specific set of standards or dogma, but clearly recognized by the public as possessing the moral authority of governing. In short, in order to elect better leaders, we must become better citizens, friends, and neighbors. As Governor Huckabee declares, "Character is the issue, and your character makes a difference every day—in the work you do, the candidates you vote for, the people who look to you for leadership."[44]

Notes

[1] Much of the information, arguments, and material in this chapter are based on "Constitutional Authority and Public Morality," by Robert E. Denton, Jr., in *The Moral Authority of Government*, ed. Moorhead Kennedy, R. Gordon Hoxie and Brenda Repland (New Brunswick, NJ: Transaction Publishers, 2000), 108–112; "Dangers of 'Teledemocracy': How the Medium of Television Undermines American Democracy," by Robert E. Denton, Jr., in *Political Communication Ethics: An Oxymoron?*, ed. Robert E. Denton, Jr. (Westport, CT: Praeger, 2000), 91–124; "Ethical Considerations of Persuasion," by Gary Woodward and Robert E. Denton, Jr., in *Persuasion and Influence in American Life*, 5th ed. (Long Grove, IL: Waveland Press, 2004), 337–368; and *Moral Leadership and the American Presidency* by Robert E. Denton, Jr. (Lanham, MD: Rowman & Littlefield, 2005).

[2] "Bush Voters Support Active Government Role in Values Arena," Gallup Poll News Service. (November 29, 2004). Retrieved 3 December 2004 from http://www.gallup.com/poll/content/print.aspx?ci=14158

[3] Glen Altschuler, "Battling the Cheats," *Education Life*, January 7, 2001.

[4] Retrieved 13 September 2007 from http://www.echeat.com

[5] http://www.zogby.com

[6] Carolyn Kleiner and Mary Lord, "The Cheating Game," *U.S. News & World Report*, November 12, 1999.

7 Josephson cited in Karen S. Peterson, "High-profile Fibs Feed Public Cynicism," *USA Today*, (July 5, 2001). Retrieved 13 September 2007 from http://www.usatoday.com/news/health/2001-07-05-lying.htm

8 Ibid.

9 "Bush's Top Ten Flip-Flops." (September 28, 2004). Retrieved 13 September 2007 from http://www.cbsnews.com/stories/2004/09/28/politics/main646142.shtml

10 Dennis Thompson, *Political Ethics and Public Office* (Cambridge, MA: Harvard University Press, 1987), 3.

11 Bruce Miroff, "The Contemporary Presidency: Moral Character in the White House: From Republican to Democratic," *Presidential Studies Quarterly* 29, (Fall 1999): 708.

12 Ibid., 711.

13 Rossiter, *The Federalist Papers* (New York: Mentor Books, 1961), 414.

14 Ibid., 455.

15 Ibid., 396.

16 Ibid., 350.

17 Rober Wiebe, *The Opening of American Society* (New York: Vintage, 1984), 12.

18 Michael Genovese, *The Presidential Dilemma* (New York: HarperCollins, 1995), 107.

19 Aristotle *Nicomachean Ethics*, ib. 1102–1103.

20 Richard Regan, *The Moral Dimensions of Politics* (New York: Oxford University Press, 1986), 14–18.

21 Rabindra Kanungo and Manuel Mendonca, *Ethical Dimensions of Leadership* (Thousand Oaks, CA: Sage, 1996).

22 Robert Dallek, "Can Clinton Still Govern?" *Washington Post National Weekly Edition*, October 5, 1998, 22.

23 Robert Putnam, *Making Democracy Work: Civic Traditions in Modern Italy* (Princeton, NJ: Princeton University Press, 1993), 10.

24 James Kouzes and Barry Posner, *Leadership Challenge*, 4th ed. (San Francisco, CA: Jossey-Bass, 2007), 31.

25 George Sabine and Thomas Thorson, *A History of Political Theory*, 4th ed. (Hinsdale, IL: Dryden Press, 1973), 484.

26 Dennis Thompson, *Political Ethics and Public Office* (Cambridge, MA: Harvard University Press, 1987), 83.

27 William Hitt, *Ethics and Leadership* (Columbus, OH: Battelle Press, 1990), 3–4.

28 Kouzes and Posner, *Leadership Challenge*, 33.

29 As cited in James Kouzes and Barry Posner, *Leadership Challenge*, 3rd ed. (San Francisco, CA: Jossey-Bass, 2002), 28.

30 Bruce Buchanan, *The Citizen's Presidency* (Washington, DC: Congressional Quarterly, 1987), 1–15.

31 Len Marrella, *In Search of Ethics* (Sanford, FL: DC Press, 2001), 182.

32 James McGregor Burns, *The Power to Lead* (New York: Simon and Schuster, 1984), 20.

33 Ibid., 16.

34 James David Barber, *The Presidential Character* (Englewood Cliffs, NJ: Prentice-Hall, 1972), v–vi.

35 Rossiter, *The Federalist Papers*, 352.

36 Richard Johannesen, *Ethics in Human Communication*, 5th ed. (Long Grove, IL: Waveland Press, 2002), 2.

37 Carter, *The Culture of Disbelief* (New York: Anchor Books, 1993), 16.

38 Sissela Bok, *Lying: Moral Choice in Public and Private Life* (New York: Vintage Books, 1989), 18.

39 Ibid., 18.

40 In Ibid., 18.

41 Mike Huckabee, *Character Is the Issue* (Nashville, TN: Broadman & Holman Publishers, 1997), 1.

42 Charles Goodsell, "Political Professionalism," in *Executive Leadership*, ed. Robert Denhardt and William Stewart (Tuscaloosa: University of Alabama Press, 1992), 7.

43 Ibid., 16.

44 Huckabee, *Character Is the Issue*, 3.

Index